Richard Harding Davis

Dallas Galbraith

Richard Harding Davis

Dallas Galbraith

ISBN/EAN: 9783743305717

Manufactured in Europe, USA, Canada, Australia, Japa

Cover: Foto ©ninafisch / pixelio.de

Manufactured and distributed by brebook publishing software (www.brebook.com)

Richard Harding Davis

Dallas Galbraith

BY
Mrs. R. HARDING DAVIS,
Author of "Waiting for the Verdict," "Margret Howth," etc.

PHILADELPHIA:
J. B. LIPPINCOTT AND CO.
1868.

Entered according to Act of Congress, in the year 1868, by
J. B. LIPPINCOTT & CO.,
In the Clerk's Office of the District Court of the United States, for the Eastern District of Pennsylvania.

LIPPINCOTT'S PRESS,
PHILADELPHIA.

To my friends at Manasquan, I inscribe this story, in which I have tried to outline their coast, and the curiously genuine, kindly human life upon it: in remembrance of the hearty good-will with which they have made my home among them pleasant for many years.

R. H. D.

MANASQUAN, July 26, 1868.

Dallas Galbraith.

CHAPTER I.

"TELL him that it was on this coast that the ship went down. Let him send me warranty, and I can find the treasure hidden among these rocks."

The two or three fishermen who were loading the schooner pricked up their ears: there was a secret undercurrent of meaning in the deliberately worded message, perceptible to every one of them; some obscure, mysterious significance which seemed suddenly to oddly set apart the words and the man that spoke them from themselves and their everyday work. They looked up from the barrels they were lifting, turning perplexed faces out to the great plane of the sea, or along the desolate coast, and then glanced shrewdly at each other: they joked about it when they went under the hatches, out of his hearing; but the jokes had but little relish in them, and fell dead; and the men went on with their work after that in silence, chewing the cud of the matter, as is their habit.

It was a colorless, threatening evening out at sea; a nipping gust driving the few white sails in sight, like shivering ghosts, across the horizon that barred the east like a leaden wall; the masses of water moving towards shore, slow, sombre, dumb. But this was only the sea: no one can tell in the quietest summer day, on land, what storm or disaster is hid in that womb of death yonder.

On shore, the mellow October sunset was shining pleasantly on the white beach, up to which the yellow, fishy little schooner was hauled close, and on the men in their red shirts: the raw wind was tempered to a bracing breeze, and the waves lapped the sand and the keel of the vessel, with a tamed, sleepy purr. The marshes, because of the heavy rains that year, still held their summer coloring, and unrolled from the strip of beach up to the pine woods a great boundary belt of that curious, clear emerald that belongs only to the sea and seashore growths. Beyond this belt, two or three comfortable brown cows were grazing at the edge of the forest, and, here and there, in the forest, a whiff of smoke wavering to the sky, or a good-bye red glimmer of the sun on a low window, told where the houses of the village were scattered.

If village it could be called. About a mile from the schooner, and the little buzz of life about her, rose one of the two great headlands well known to all mariners: they jut out into the sea as though they were grim, warning sentinels over this terrible coast of sunken breakers and whitening bones. A sharp ridge struck from this upper headland into the background of forest, and in the circling hollow which it formed lay the lonely collection of farmers' and fishers' houses then called Manasquan. A curiously old-time, forgotten village, to belong to the New World: shut in from any world by the ocean on one side, and the interminable pine forests at the other, through which at this time only the charcoal-burners had burrowed their way.

The man (a middle-aged Quaker) who had sent the message which had so puzzled the fishermen, was a stranger on this coast: its strange solitariness, the utter silence into which it fell when transient sounds had passed, oppressed and stifled him. He had paced up and down the hard beach all the afternoon, watching with his dull, light-blue eyes the Sutphens seining, and after that, the loading of the schooner. It seemed to him, of all corners of the world, the one totally forgotten and passed by in the race. He wondered if justice ever overtook crime here—if even death remembered to harvest his crop. Something of this he dropped in a half-intelligible way to old Doctor Noanes, who came limping up from his rickety house by the ridge to walk with him, wearing a patronizing air towards him before the fishermen, but secretly a little afraid of the sharper wits of the strange Friend. But he fired at the slur upon the village.

"We're of older build than New York," he said, "but we've kept clean of crime and c'ruption: we've held to the ancient landmarks: there's no families gone in and out from us since colony times. Them nags of mine, now, has no flash strains of blood, but their grandsire carried my grandsire, Peter Noanes, into the fight at Monmouth. I don't ask better than that."

The Friend, who had taken off his broad-brimmed hat, the better to catch the evening air, stroked the gray wisps of hair on either side of his ruddy face, fixing on the dried face of his companion his lack-lustre eyes.

"The men," Noanes said, "ord'narily followed the water;" and he began to sonorously roll out their names—Laddouns, Van Zeldts, Graahs, as though it were the calling of the great Jewish tribes or Scottish clans. His hearer was forced to remind himself that there were not twenty men, all told, among them. A belief was creeping on him that this community was a power in the land, if it did act only through ships' mates and the masters of coast schooners; leather-skinned, hairy-breasted men, who brought back from their voyages but little profit or knowledge beyond their wages, and fresh stories of storms at sea.

"Manasquan men be known as seamen throughout the civilized world," asserted the Doctor, shoving back his wig peremptorily. "Ther's Jim Laddoun; he was hired as mate in an English brig. He's been as far as the Barbary Coast. Them Britishers know a good thing when they see it, and snap it up, quick enough."

"True, true," deliberately—the attentive gaze never leaving the pupils of the Doctor's eyes. It was a queer trick the stranger had; with a slight crook to one side of his head, it gave him the look of a deaf man, or one absorbed in his companion's words. At any rate, it usually drew out from people a good many more words than they had intended to speak. The old Doctor found it gave a real gusto to their talks: he told his best stories to the stranger—stories that included the histories of the Van Zeldts, Graahs—all of them. (He had silenced his wife when she echoed the village wonder as to who the old, brown-coated fellow was, and what secret business he came to pry into.

"He's a well-bred person—the best bred I've met for years. What should you know of men of the world? Do you think there's nothing at Manasquan which educated people think it worth while to inquire into?")

"Laddoun? Laddoun?" replied the Friend, thoughtfully. "Thee belongs to that stock thyself, Doctor?"

Noanes gave a pleased sniff. "You have a keen memory for genealogies. Yes, my mother was one of them. But there's only two of the name now—the mate I told you of, and the young doctor at the village."

"George. A generous, genial fellow, eh? Hospitable, I should say."

"Oh, I'll warrant for him! He'll be having you to feed and liquor at the inn before now. He's a little too free with both his money and his gab—George. He keeps a dozen lazy beggars up, now. But he'll mend, likely. The Laddouns had always brains and pockets like sieves. They're slack,—leaky."

"He has seen the world, he tells me. On his brother's ship?"

"No; he went to lectures in York and Philadelphia. I can't say that it spoiled him much; he come back, thinking better of old Manasquan than ever, showing more sense than I looked for. There wasn't a child in the village that didn't take a holiday when he come. George is a main one for children, especially when they're big and hearty. My Bob used to count on him. No, I've nothing against George Laddoun," reflectively.

"There he is."

They had made a turn on the beach, and were coming toward the schooner with the leisurely pace befitting their age and gravity. Laddoun, coming down the ridge with a boyish whistle and leap, stopped, with a shamed blush and laugh, before his fellow-practitioner. "This bracing air makes a boy of me," apologetically, bowing to both of them. "But a famous leaper like you," to Noanes, "can forgive a fellow. I'd like to have tried you at the standing jump, twenty years ago."

"I'd have put you to your mettle, sir. A pleasant-spoken dog," complacently lighting his pipe as the young man went on, and measuring his broad back and low height critically. "A well-built fellow, say? strong joints, and sockets well oiled. D'ye see? his limbs move easily in his clothes and shoes. I'd like to have tried a leap with him well enough. But them days is over. The old lion's bones is stiff."

The Quaker had paid but slight attention to the short, athletic figure, or its loose-fitting suit of gray corduroy. If he had any fancy for compelling the secrets of other men into his own keeping, he apparently looked for them no farther than in the pupils of the eyes. George Laddoun had met him at first with his pleasant, bold glance, turning it, however, in a moment uneasily away. The young fellow, with all his stout muscle and hot blood, was easily abashed as a girl.

He came up to the fishermen with a cheery "Hillo!"

"Hillo, Laddoun!" It was young Jim Van Zeldt who answered him, with his hands in his pockets, shifting his cigar from one side of his mouth to the other. He was the owner of the vessel. The other men were too busy straining over a barrel which they lifted to speak.

"You've got a hefty load there," pulling off his coat, "Take out your cigar, Jim, and put your own shoulder to! Yo, ho!" as the barrel went in. He worked along with the fishermen until the loading was done, singing some students' song, he had learned when abroad, in a billowy, free, bass voice. Nobody thanked him when the work was finished, and he stood perspiring more than any of them, sopping his shining black hair and red, handsome face. But the men knew, of course, how much better stuff was in him than in that milk-faced Jim Van Zeldt, who paid them to the last penny for their work, but never lifted a finger to help, or cracked a joke. Jim was the only man on that beach who paid for work; with the others it was all "neighbor-help." Evening had come on before the last load was in: a gray, gusty evening, as we said—the strange silence and melancholy which belonged to this coast, as though the dead beneath the curdling breakers would not be forgotten, growing deeper as night approached. Doctor Noanes was gone, but Ledwith, the strange Friend, had come closer to the schooner, and was standing with his white, pursy hands rolled into each other, behind him, watching the men from under the shadow of his wide-brimmed hat, with the usual inexpressive, abstracted look on his fat face. The men resented his presence with that uneasy impatience which animals show when a strange creature not of their sort is near. This man was foreign to them. His dress, speech, habit of silence had never been known to them before; and under these was a stronger instinct of alienism from their salty, seafaring ways. It was noticeable that they stood aloof from him as much as might be, leaving his tall, square figure, in its outlandish garb, like a strange shadow, alone on the beach. It was just before the last cord of wood was taken in that he gave the message to Van Zeldt. It came out of a curious custom belonging to the beach. The mails were carried at long intervals, and even then were of most uncertain delivery. The schooners which carried the fish, game and lumber up to the New York markets, ran, too, at irregular times—only, in fact when it suited the convenience of their owners—but the means of transportation they offered were secure and rapid. It became, therefore, a habit with the masters of these vessels to make a sort of public notice of their time of departure and willingness to carry messages or parcels to the upper harbors. There were many of these little formal old customs hanging about the settlement.

When Jim Van Zeldt made his announcement, it was responded to by no one but the stranger, Ledwith, who apparently was prepared and waiting for it.

"We'll turn off for the night now," said Van Zeldt, when he had spoken, looking out to the gathering shadows.

"I have a message for thee." The clear, decided voice made Van Zeldt and the men turn: the words which followed were in a lower key, slow, measured, as though he weighed each by some hidden meaning known to himself alone.

"When thee reaches New York, a man will meet thee on the wharf, habited in a dress like mine, asking for tidings of the ship Terror."

"She does not ply on this coast," interrupted Laddoun, with the off-hand, peremptory tone habitual to him, which expressed a thorough knowledge of all matters, great and small.

The Quaker's dull blue eye did not turn on him for an instant: yet in the momentary stolid pause which he made, the young man had an uncomfortable sense of having been weighed and found wanting.

"He will inquire of thee," he resumed, in the same slow monotone, "of a vessel lost years ago—the Terror: tell him that it was on this coast that the ship went down. Let him send me warranty, and I can find the treasure hidden among these rocks."

"I will carry the message," said Van Zeldt, gravely, with no word of question or surprise. Laddoun checked the exclamation on his lips after a hasty glance at the dark, solid figure, and immovable face turned seaward. It sent a chill of doubt and fear over his healthy body, as if he had unconsciously touched the repellant pole of an electric battery.

"The ship Terror was lost on these rocks fifty years ago," he said in an undertone to Van Zeldt, as they walked up the beach together, leaving the stranger still watching the melancholy sea line—"an emigrant ship, with three hundred souls aboard."

"You're never at fault, Laddoun," admiringly.

"There are few matters into which I have not looked," smiling, and running his thick white fingers through his glossy hair. The little chord of vanity struck had brought him altogether in tune again. "But there was no treasure in her. That old fellow is after Kyd's doubloons, and he thinks to throw us off the scent by lugging in the name of this wreck. But he had need to be awake early to blind George Laddoun, eh? or you, Jim," with an encouraging tap on the back.

They walked in silence up the grassy break through the woods which one or two wagon-ruts marked as the road, and stopped where a path struck off to Van Zeldt's house. Laddoun lingered, breaking the bark off a dead cedar, with an unwonted softening and hesitation in his look and motions.

"You'll make a quick run of it, Jim?" he said. "You'll be back in time? For Thursday?"

"I know. I'll try, Laddoun. The more because Noanes tells me you're going to bring but a few of us in."

"Yes. A man's married but once, and he ought to have his own way about it. I'll treat the village afterwards; they sha'n't complain. But there's rough jokes made at our country weddings that I don't choose my wife to hear."

With the tender inflection in his tone, and quieting of his eye, there was a certain swelling defiance in his whole burly body, which to mild little Van Zeldt was thoroughly lordly. A man was in no mean sort a hero, who could put Manasquan at arm's length thus.

"You're the right sort, George," he said. "When you're settled and a householder, you'll bring matters up to the right standard hereabouts. They be to follow you like sheep the bell-wether—that they be."

"It won't be to their injury, then," frankly. "Things need cleaning and managing as they don't know. I'll do what I can for the place," loftily. "And for you, Van Zeldt," putting his hand on the smaller man's shoulder, as a prince might caress a favored courtier. "You'll not fail us on Thursday? I want none but true friends about me and Lizzy."

The pompous voice a little unsteady, and the florid face losing color. "I'm serious when I say that I mean to push your fortune, old boy," after a pause.

"There be'n't a day when you're not pushing some fellow along."

"So? You think that of me? Well, well! it's little I can do. But God help us! it sickens me to look down on any man below me in the mire; and it don't need money to give help, always. For you, I'll strengthen your trade up yonder. I'm not a man without mark in the great cities, Jim. The world's deep as well as wide, and one can dig secrets out of her in Manasquan, and make a name, as easily as where men crowd together. I like to think I'm here in the woods, dragging out of nature the means to fight death up yonder." The whole manner of the man altered; a generous glow flushed to his temples, his voice rang out earnestly.

"You mean them chemicals, Laddoun?" after a puzzled pause. "I thought that boy of yours did that work. He's put his soul into the herbs and black-drops he makes out of them. It's a pity, too. It's trifling work, and he be genooine," raising his voice, "Galbraith be; I've reason to know that. He be the kind of man to anchor to."

Laddoun combed his whiskers with a pleased smile.

"Yes, he's good stuff. I discovered him. I made him."

Van Zeldt turned quickly, but was prudently silent. Laddoun was unwarily touching on a matter which hitherto had been held secret.

"Made him as entirely as you cut those decoy-birds out of poplar yonder"—then stopped, with a gulp for breath, as if checked by some inward sting. "Well, he's useful, as you say, to collect and sort materials under me. But a hand—a hand. It is the head that is needed in my trade," touching his narrow, high forehead with the forefinger, on which shone a round purple stone. "Good-bye, Van Zeldt. You will be down at the shop to-night?"

"Yes." Van Zeldt stood leaning over the trunk of the fallen cedar, a generous twinkle of admiration through all of his insipid face, as the stout, broad figure disappeared in the shadows of the woods. Laddoun was moulded out of such different clay from his own! There were men to command and men to serve, just as there were king-fish and clams in the sea yonder.

Even the cool Quaker, who had taken the bearings of most men's minds with those lightless blue eyes of his, had felt, against his will, a sort of magnetism in the young village hero under all his coarse, thin varnish; something which warmed the air about him, put a hearty, genial look on the face of things. Van Zeldt, therefore, was not to blame, if Laddoun, with his mysterious talk of cities, and of secrets dragged out of nature, crowned, too, with his lucky love-making in a quarter where he had failed, became to him a sort of demi-god; and if he watched even the yellow cotton gloves, the high hat and boots, asserting themselves blackly beyond all other hats and boots, with a dumb envy and wonder. Nor was poor Laddoun, either, much to blame, if he accepted himself at the same valuation. The men about him had labeled him with the highest trade mark, even when they were all boys together.

He went tramping along, his heavy boots crunching on the needles of the pines, roaring out one of his everlasting songs. He was one of those men who constantly feel their blood, which happened in his case to be slightly thick and viscous; men with nervous lips, the balls of whose eyes habitually inflate and contract, and whose lids are often wet with tears. His nerves were all on edge now; the days were full of zest and triumph; full of thoughts of the medicines he had invented; of his wife, of the place he meant to hold in the village. Two or three generations back, one of his Milesian ancestors had rid himself of the family fortune in a few years of tempestuous jollity and hospitality; but his blood, eyes, and uncertain lips had stayed behind as heirlooms, and Laddoun had them now, with all that they implied.

While he was in the middle of the woods he met Galbraith, whom the village people called his shop-boy, but whom Laddoun, in his melodramatic way, had dubbed his familiar. To him, as he walked home with him, carrying his basket and tin cases of roots, he relieved his mind of his plans: how Van Zeldt was to be pushed up, and a school-house got under way, and a poor-contribution taken up before winter, and also a public subscription for a testimonial to old Doctor Noanes.

"They do such things in towns, Dallas, eh? And I'm ruining the old fellow's practice. Besides, it will bring the people together. We need unity, centralization," with a sweep of his eye over the hamlet, as though it covered a vast community, ending with a glance for approval at the tall, raw-boned lad beside him, who was watching his face eagerly with a bewildered look.

"I've no doubt you're right, Laddoun," he said, gently; "there are a good many words I don't know the meaning of yet," quietly shifting the tin cases to the other arm.

"So? Poor fellow! It will come in time," putting one hand on the bony shoulders, and looking kindly into the girlish face. "Say! Galbraith, these are a cursedly old cut—your trowsers. I must rig you out new for the wedding. It's a shame I let you wear a shirt like this," pulling out the ragged edge of clean flannel about his neck. "I'm a poor patron, they'll say."

Dallas looked down at his uncouth rig, and laughed: a hearty roar of a laugh. "But I'll only take what I earn," said he.

"Pshaw! there should be no such talk between you and me." They exchanged a swift, significant glance, which gave to the boy's face for the instant a curiously old, worn look.

"Why shouldn't I give to you? There's nobody in Manasquan to whom I don't mean to give a lift."

"Look what you're doing! Curse it, you lout! look there!" savagely dragging Laddoun off the path.

"What do you mean? Nothing but a lame quail? Bah!" stooping coolly over the mangled mass of bloody feathers which Dallas picked up and turned over, drawing quick, spasmodic breaths, which made Laddoun smile as he would at the rage of a child.

"Why, you young viper! you'll turn on the hand that feeds you?" good-naturedly. "Your muscles are steel, Dallas. You shook me as if I were a stick. Put that thing down; I did not see it."

The quivering of the bird on his palm seemed to madden the boy. "You did not see it? You see nothing, George Laddoun. You've nobody to speak the truth to you but me. It's well enough to keep your eyes on the sky, making plans, and let your feet and hands do what they will. But murder comes of it."

George Laddoun's face, against the background of the tree on which he leaned, grew suddenly of a deathly white; but he gave neither word nor motion, only to lean forward, and scan with half-shut eyes the boy's face as he turned the quail over gently in his hand, putting it to his cheek again and again, as a woman would be apt to do. If Galbraith had any thought beyond the bird, he held it out of sight with a skill which baffled Laddoun. Presently, he laid it down softly.

"It's dead now," stretching out his arms with a long breath. "I was rough with you, Laddoun," turning to him.

"Yes," with a loud, uncadenced laugh; "I should say you were cursedly rough. You forget who you are, and who I am, Dallas."

"I don't forget," quietly gathering his scattered roots into his basket. "But you have had an easy life. Now, when I see a thing put under foot like that, I think I feel the lash on my own back again."

"If you remember the lash, you oughtn't to forget who took it off," keeping the same intent scrutiny on every shade of meaning in the boy's face. "Whatever comes to me, there are reasons why you should be true to me, Galbraith."

There was nothing melodramatic in Dallas to answer this touch. "You've been a good friend to me, Mr. Laddoun," he said, simply, "but I mean to tell you the truth for all that;" and picking up his basket he jogged along in a grave silence. Laddoun followed him, making, with laborious efforts, indifferent remarks from time to time; but all the vivacity and spirit had died out of him. He tried to shut his eyes to the boy's past life, and look at him with a stranger's cool judgment. Was there no secret hid under this old-fashioned sincerity, this simple-hearted, credulous nature? There was not a child in the village who would not run after the queer, lank boy to make him head in the game of ball or marbles, nor an old woman who had not some time shared her cup of tea with him. Laddoun scanned, as a man on trial for his life would the faces of the jury, the unmarked features of the lad, pausing again and again on his eyes. They always had baffled him. The rest of the face held nothing; it was but a child's—indistinctive; worn perhaps by hunger or want, but the eyes were deep-set and sparkling, full of sweet temper and laughter.

Nothing more? Was there any power of reticence in them to hold back a fatal secret for life?

George Laddoun could not tell; they had baffled a keener inspection than his, and that not long ago; even while he watched him now they turned on him, steady and honest. One thing he knew, that they belonged to something stronger than himself.

Galbraith, boy like, forgot his trouble after a while; began to whistle shrilly, grubbing under the scrubby bushes for roots, after his usual fashion, stopping when they came to an open bit of sand to set down his basket and turn summersaults to the other end. Laddoun waited good-naturedly, leaning on the fence.

"Well done, Dallas!"

"I'm growing too fat—I'm not as limber as I was," looking down with a pleased laugh.

"I'm sorry that I worried you, Galbraith," placing his hand on his shoulder in a half-timid, deprecating way, very different from the patronizing tap on the back which was his ordinary greeting to the villagers. "I'd no mind to bring up old times to you. They're dead and gone now."

Galbraith nodded. One of those vague notions which children have crossed his mind—a wonder whether those old times were not dead and in hell; but the impression was but slight, and a moment afterwards, with a loud hillo! he was rooting under some leaves for a great bee-ant, like a lump of crimson velvet.

"I want you, sir, and some of your brothers! Yo, ho!" çaging it in a leaf.

"Poor Dall! There's nothing in his brain but childish folly," thought Laddoun as he strode on. "He throws all trouble of old times out of his mind, just as water on the boil gets rid of scum and dirt a-top;" and with a sudden feeling of relief, he began to throw snatches of bass into the lilt Galbraith was whistling. With the relief his own boyishness awakened and the habitual propensity to do something kind, he left Galbraith squatted on the ground with his ants, and hurried on to a little wooden shanty, which was set down, like all Manasquan houses, in the middle of the cedars.

"The little chap's been at work since dawn. I'll build his fire for him," pushing open the door and going in. In a few moments a pile of wood was crackling on the hearth, and George, rubbing his hands, came out, and waving his hat to Dallas, who came slowly up the path, turned off towards the far farm-houses. In a moment, however, the boy was panting after him.

"That was downright good in you, Mr. Laddoun. Come back and eat your supper with me. I've made a broiler for crabs, and it's famous; you ought to taste them these cold nights," pulling at his coat while he spoke.

"I can't, Dallas; I'll send some of the boys down, though."

"All right! Tell them I have the crabs."

Doctor Noanes, in his buggy, meanwhile had driven up and stopped. "Take a seat, Laddoun; I'll give you a lift. That's an honest-faced boy," when Galbraith was gone. "Yet there are queer stories afloat about him," with a side glance at his companion's face. It was imperturbable.

"What sort of stories?"

"That you picked him out of some den of corruption. That he has a tolerable black record, if one could see it."

"Any place outside of Manasquan is a den of corruption, according to the talk here," with a rage which struck the shrewd old doctor as too sudden to be real. "As for Dallas, you can see for yourself what he is. There's not many men could make a place for themselves, as he's done, in this village. And he's bare sixteen."

"He's got to be a necessary sort of fellow to everybody, that's true," warmly. "I don't know his equal for nursing, or coddling children. There be my Joe, now; when he was down with the scarlet fever, nobody would serve him but 'Dallas—Dallas.' So I sent for the fellow, and I'll say this, that under God he saved the boy. There be no woman about our house, you know, and he took the place of one. Still, I thought I'd mention the queer stories to you. You'd best contradict them."

"You are very kind."

But Noanes remembered afterwards that he did not contradict them to him, but remained gloomily silent during the remainder of the drive.

CHAPTER II.

GALBRAITH meanwhile went back to his house, and prepared to spend the evening. It was but a little, broken-down shanty, that had been used by one of the Sutphens as a cow-shed, until it was too far gone for that, when he had given it to Dallas for his help in harvesting. The half dozen boys of the village had collected and made a regular frolic of helping him patch it up, and it had been a sort of rendezvous for them ever since, as Dallas was their leader. He kept a watch for some of them now, while he put away his basket and cases in a damp out-shed, and pulled off his clog shoes, running to the door between-times to peep down the winding paths which now began to shine white in the night. Then he disappeared into the shed, and after a prodigious noise of splashing in a tub of water, came out with his toilette made. A queer enough looking figure when the best was done: no wonder Laddoun had laughed, for the clean flannel shirt had belonged to a much smaller man, and gaped open at the neck and ran up the arms, leaving bare the broad white throat and brawny wrists: the patched trousers, too, were cut off by the knee, and met by a long pair of women's gray stockings. But Dallas had some odd notions, picked up in that mysterious outside world from which he came, which puzzled the two or three Manasquan boys with whom he ran.

The nails on his big burned hands were always white and trimmed, his breath sweet, the miserable clothes clean. "Them be the little marks that belong to the gentlemen out there," he said. "I soon learned 'em. Just as you kin tell the best mackerel by the signs about the gills."

When he came in from the shed, he attentively surveyed himself in a broken bit of looking-glass, and then sat down before the fire to toast his half-frozen feet, whistling softly to himself and beating time on his knees. The boys were long in coming, and he would go hungry rather than eat the crabs alone. Perhaps, however, this heroic resolve re-awakened the inward gnawing, for he got up hastily with the words half spoken, and putting his famous broiler over the clear fire, in a few moments the green, spongy things were fizzing and sputtering out a savory odor on it. He stopped his whistle and began to pace about uneasily. He wished the boys would come. As for being alone in the woods, he did not heed it, though he could hear the cry of the panthers, he fancied, night after night. But Laddoun's gun hung on the wall, and there was no such marksman on the beach as Galbraith. It was the sea he feared: the rising sound of the surf thundering up the shore in the silence made his cheek pale and a cold damp come out over his forehead. His terror (if terror it was) had come long ago, with his first sight of it. Laddoun had quizzed him about it then, and tried to laugh it off.

"Most landsmen have that feeling to the sea at first," he said. "It'll soon wear off, Dallas, with a boy as courageous as you."

"I'm not afraid of *it*," he said, slowly. "It's the voices I kin hear in it, Laddoun."

Laddoun made no reply. He never heard voices in it, but he guessed shrewdly what the sickly boy meant, and never spoke to him of it again.

Galbraith was no longer sickly, but the dread had not worn away. When the latch clicked, and a face was thrust in the door, his heart jumped with relief. Any living voice would drown these far-off dead ones, if it were only little Tim Graah's. So he took his hand, and pulled him in, with a boisterous welcome, which sent the blood to Tim's face, for he was but a little fellow, and not used to notice from the big boys.

"I come to say there was nobody coming, Galbraith."

"Except yourself, little 'un. You're just in time."

"Kin I eat supper with you? Kin I set the table, Dallas?" eagerly; for the fact of a boy who lived alone, cooked for himself, and worked in roots and herbs and beetles, was to him what a fairy story would have been, if ever he had heard one.

Galbraith nodded, turning and salting the crabs, and Tim proceeded to spread a white cloth on the miniature table, and put thereon a loaf of bread, and butter, cocking his head to one side and glancing about him at the whitewashed walls, the clean boards of the floor, and the little neat bed in the corner, with a sense of half-ownership.

"Our house is cleaner than any in the village," he said at last. "You've got a lot of women's gear about you, Dallas. How did that come?"

"I was sick when Laddoun first fetched me here. I'd but little to do, that winter, but creep about from house to house, getting acquainted like, and the women they made much of me and cured me. So when I began to housekeep, they all brought me a sheet or a towel, or the like. I've got quite a stock now."

"My mother gave you that bed," chattered the child. "She cured the feathers herself. I hearn her say she saw purple scars of lashes on your back, and she was bound never to let you sleep hard another night. Be the scars there yet, Dallas?" in a half-frightened whisper.

But Galbraith did not answer; he had not heard him, Tim supposed, being busy over his cookery. He turned with the crabs on a dish in a moment, and set them down with a loud, forced laugh.

"Bring the chairs, Tim, and fall to," going from door to window, nervously closing them.

"Be you shutting out the sound of the sea?" laughed Tim. "You can't do it, Dallas. It'll foller and foller. I've tried it in the woods."

When they were once seated at the smoking supper, however, Dallas forgot the sound of the sea, or whatever had pursued him. He had a way of giving himself up so childishly to his fun, and a habit, too, when serious, of showing his great ignorance through incessant questions, that even Tim Graah felt himself his superior. While Dallas set openmouthed, listening intently to the story of Jane Graah's marriage, Tim regarded him as little better than a fool. One would think, from his questions, he never had lived where there were women before.

"Where will you live when you are married, Dallas?" the story being finished.

"Here." The answer was grave and prompt. "There's a place up on the river nobody knows but me. I'll build a house there."

"Thee has matured thy plans early," said a quiet voice behind him, and turning, the boys saw the Quaker Ledwith in the open door. "Thy supper smelled savory, Friend Galbraith. Thee must blame it for making me unlatch the door and come in uninvited."

Dallas colored with pleasure. "There's a crab or two left," looking in the dish, and then bustling off for a clean plate.

The Quaker seated himself, his thick arms crossed on the little table; his square, solid figure seemed to fill up the room, and Tim, from being an honored guest, felt himself dwindle suddenly down into the usual superfluous nuisance of a boy.

Ledwith remained a moment doubtful after the dish was placed before him; the delicious morsel tempted him. Then he pushed it from him. "I think I will not eat thy bread and salt, Dallas," he said. "Thee has a comfortable little house here; very comfortable. But a gun, eh? One would not think thee needed defence for thy house?"

Tim, whose wide-awake gaze never left the stranger's face, wondered here, more and more, how, without apparent motion, the stolid light-blue eyes took in and noted all that was in the room; but Dallas laughed unconcernedly, clearing away the dishes.

"The gun is Laddoun's."

"Laddoun's? But thou art a keen marksman, they tell me. Does thee not find thy skill wasted on this beach?"

A trace of significance crept into the last words. He checked himself suddenly, coughing behind his hand, and sat looking steadily in the fire, while Galbraith made some boyish efforts to entertain him, discussing the schools of mackerel that had run in last week, and the chance of a nor'easter before November.

"Thee has learned the lingo of the beach soon," looking up at last. "Thee has got quite a salty flavor into thyself. Here's thy workshop? So?" suddenly facing about to a little closet immediately behind him. Had the man eyes in the back of his head, then? Tim dragged behind them with a pale face, one hand gripping Galbraith's shirt sleeve. But Dallas hurried eagerly with a candle after the Quaker, who stood in the recess quite motionless for a moment; in that moment, however, he had absorbed every item about him, and classed and rated them.

"Shelf of old books—bought off of stalls—De Candolle, Bartram, Pursh—a botanist, eh? half-worn-out works on chemistry—how many? old treatises on geology. These cost a pretty penny!" while Galbraith passed his hand over them with an unconscious caress, brushing the dust from one or two. "Bottles full of ore and sand. Boxes of herbs and earths; a pick—shovels. What is in that cupboard?" sharply, tapping it with his cane.

Galbraith opened it with a proud flush; the Quaker gave a start of surprise. "A battery! Chemical apparatus—manufactured out of old vials and pipes. Thee has a wonderful cleverness, boy," turning over the queer substitutes for retorts and crucibles with a smile, and speaking in a quick, changed voice. "I had a fancy for the study when I was a boy, but I took to—to making analyses of a different sort." He turned on Galbraith as he said it, measuring him from his light hair to his patched shoes.

"Of a different sort, and I am not wanting in skill, they say."

Dallas was silent; for the first time, the sharp-eyed little Tim beside him noted that he began to share in his own uneasy scrutiny of the stranger. He drew back a step, and jealously locked the door of his closet, keeping a furtive glance on Ledwith, who smiled unpleasantly, stroking his fat chin with his white hand.

"I won't disturb thy little make-shifts, my lad. Come out. It's thee I have business with." But he waited patiently, with a real interest in his flabby features, while Dallas carefully replaced some bits of ore that had fallen on the floor.

"Now, some men in my trade would call thy hobby tomfoolery; but I had a leaning that way once myself, as I told thee," complacently. "I went through college. I can see thee is one of them men that was born for no other use than to dig into them matters. Unless—thee is stopped in the way," with a leer and a wink. He took the tallow candle from Dallas, and inspected him gravely as he put it slowly down on the table. "Knowing what I know of thee, Galbraith," he said, deliberately, "thee is as curious a specimen of a human being as ever I met. And my experience in them is not small."

The tall, raw-boned fellow stood in the middle of the floor, the yellow light full about him, looking into the Quaker's face with a demeanor as grave and moderate as his own. Even to Tim there was something at odds and incomprehensible in the scarecrow gear, in the childish face, with lank, light hair brushed behind the ears, and the sane, grave, dark-blue eyes, into which Ledwith stooped and peered, and stooped and peered again, his own eyes jeering one moment and sternly questioning the next, but without effect. Beyond a distressed surprise, there was no sign of flinching or inward consciousness in the lad.

"Well, well!" standing upright and rolling his hands one in the other with a discomfited impatience; "I've hunted many a rabbit in my day, and let 'em double as they would, I had 'em at last. So this is Laddoun's work-shop? It's here the brains are, eh? I thought as much. Some of these days the young whelp will make his fortune with a Laddoun's Balsam or Pill, and look for thee to grub on in the background? Hardly, I fancy; the brains will take their place in the end. I see thy cards, Dallas."

"You are talking of what I don't understand," said Dallas, bluntly, with a queer quaver in his voice; "nor you either, I suspect, Mr. Ledwith. Laddoun has apparatus at the shop. I know nothing about balsams or pills. I do my work because it is the only work I could ever understand. I'm counted uncommon dull at other things," simply.

"Thee has a won-derful cleverness," with an approving snap of the fingers and significant nod, as one actor might encourage another on the boards. "But this chemical business; did thee learn it thyself? Is thee self-taught?"

"No. I had a chance," shortly, turning away.

"Thee don't care to go into thy past life, eh? That's natural. Young people like better to look forward than back," with a shrewd smile. "I'll leave you, boys, now; good-night! Thee had better load thy weapon, Dallas; thee might need it for defence," with a chuckle.

Galbraith closed the door after him, and stood for a moment beside it, with his back towards Tim; when he turned and came to the fire again, the look with which he had met the Quaker was gone; here was nothing, Tim saw, but the boy who had played ball with him, and cooked the crabs with such jolly fun half an hour ago. But he moved as if he were tired and sick; pulled Tim up to his knees, holding his hands on his shoulders. When the boy looked up at him he saw that his eyes were fixed on the fire and were red and full of tears.

"Tim?" he said.

"Yes, Dallas," gently, putting his fingers upon the big hand on his shoulder.

"Tim, why be'n't I like other boys?"

Tim looked up bewildered, but the grave, anxious countenance was bent intently watching his own, and Dallas gave him no help with his answer.

"Like Manasquan boys?" sharpening his wits. "Why so you be, Dallas. Only for your house here, and your crockery and bottles; and," reflectively, "then you've got no mother or sisters belonging to you. All of us has them. That's a difference."

Dallas made no reply, but he suddenly turned his face away. He did not hide it, however, from the sharp eyes that were on him. Tim's face flushed as he saw it. "You're kinder than the other big boys, Galbraith," quickly. "There be'n't one in the village that has as many friends as you. You be the only one that won't lie or drink, the women says. *I* don't heed the stories they tell. Nobody heeds them. You kin look anybody in the face, Dallas."

"So they tell stories, do they?" with a sad, slow smile. After a long pause, he said, as if thinking aloud, "There never was such good men as here, Tim. I never was in a church till I came here. No. Laddoun took me in that first evening. I didn't understand old Father Kimball, but it was so quiet there, under the hill, with the trees outside. The hymn too—it was a tune that——; well, I'd heard that tune long ago. And coming out, the men was so friendly. When Laddoun told them my name, they nodded in their sober way and spoke very friendly to me, first one and then another, goin' through the woods. I'd often thought, when I was a little chap, if I could come across God, He'd be something like that. Quiet and friendly. Not asking where I'd been, or what I'd done, or about things I'd no share in bringing on myself." The words came out slow, unconscious, the reasonable, grave eyes still fixed on the fire. "It's been the same with Manasquan people ever since," after a short silence. "They've treated me as if I was one of themselves. There's not one of them has told me of the difference between us."

Tim's black eyes grew keener. "What be the difference, Dallas?"

The simple, credulous face turned, and the answer came quickly. He was talking to the child just as he would have reasoned with himself if he had been alone.

"Sometimes I think there be'n't any. You boys will grow up men just like them, and you say, Tim, I be like the other boys. But sometimes it seems as if I weren't allowed a chance like every man has. It weren't by my will that I was born—down there. It weren't my fault that—No matter," hastily rising. "I'm doing the best I can here. God knows I want to be a decent, God-fearing man like your father, or Father Kimball. I never knowed men like them. And if I'm dragged back now— It seems as if there was something agin me in the world. I doubt it's too strong for me," lifting his arms, and letting them fall.

"You look strong enough to fight anything, Galbraith," said Tim, encouragingly. "Who be you afraid of? The Quaker?"

Dallas walked to the window and glanced out. "It be time you were off, little 'un. It's after eight. Your folks 'll be in bed, and all Manasquan besides. I'll leave the light in the window. Now! Make a run for it." He stood in the door to watch the little chap cross the woods, giving him a cheer to keep his spirits up.

The cheer and the cold sea air brought himself up out of the slough, as a stroke on the face will make a man feel his strength all over his body. Whatever this something was which had been against him, ordering his birth and childhood in vice and poverty, it faded now out of sight.

"Strong enough to fight anything," Tim had said. Was that true? After all, what had he to complain of? He was a strong, athletic boy, standing in the door of the home he had made for himself. He looked over his shoulder at his bottles, picks, retorts, and laughed. Nothing makes a man feel his footing so sure in the world as to know his right work, and have it well gripped in his hands for life. And everybody was so friendly about him! From the day he began to try to pick off those old stained rags of his childhood, hands had been held out to help him; first Laddoun, and now all Manasquan, down to little Tim. What did it matter for this man Ledwith?

He and his mysterious hinted threats began to seem unreal as a nightmare to Dallas, as he looked out into the pleasant dusky shadows of the woods and the starry blue overhead. It was all clear enough! The world was just what a man chose to make it. There was nothing stronger than himself to drag him down. Nothing!

He drew long breaths of the delicious cold into his strong lungs, threw back his broad chest, feeling every muscle in his body stiffen. The boy's heart was big and tender just then. If they would suffer him, he would live among them in Manasquan until he died an old, white-headed man. They were all so dear to him!—so friendly! He wished suddenly for some one to tell all this to—this rush of strength and happiness that made his eyes wet and his cheek burn like fire. Tim was out of sight, but poor Dallas sent out suddenly into the night a stirring, boyish cheer. It came back loud and ringing from the woods, and again and again in low, cheerful echoes farther off. He looked up to the bright, smiling sky, wondering if God, of whom he had a dim notion, was there, and had heard him; wondering whether He was behind all this good luck that had come to him. He stood silent a moment, thinking.

He went in and closed the door, and after he had undressed, pulled the fire-logs carefully apart, so as to leave the room in shadow; then he stood hesitating by the bed, his face red and then pale, and kneeled down at last, hiding his head in his hands. But in a moment he got up, all trace of color gone from his face.

"I am afraid," he muttered. "I'm afraid," and stretching himself in bed, lay wakeful, staring out into the flickering shadows, saying nothing. But the prayer in the boy's dumb heart was audible to God as if it had been trumpet-tongued. To help him with his chance, to bring good luck to him—good luck. To make a man of him.

CHAPTER III.

A YELLOW Jersey wagon rolled up the road to the squat little porch of the tavern, where half a dozen leading Manasquan men sat smoking in the hazy, mellow warmth of the October afternoon. The leathern flap was put back, and old Father Kimball, who preached on this beach once a month, thrust out his lean, sagacious face, nodding to them:

"How is it with you, brethren?"

There was quite a stir and tumult; here was the first actual beginning of the wedding programme. Joe Nixon, the tavern-keeper, knocked on the wall to give the news to the women inside, and then went up to the wagon as spokesman for the party. "You'd better come in, sir, and take something hot. No? Brother Noanes' folks be expectin' you, I know; still—"

"You are going to have a lively week of it, heh, Nixon?"

"Jest so, Mr. Kimball. Van Zeldt's schooner is to be run in this afternoon. A heavy cargo, I hear. Jim's venturin' in pretty deep, lately. A matter of fifty dollars in silk goods, they tell me, alone. Considerin' his capital, that's risky. When them New York dealers get a man to speculatin', it's all up with him. They soon smelled out Jim's capital."

Kimball shook his head. "I'll talk to Van Zeldt. Is that all your news?"

Nixon came closer. "There's the weddin' to-morrow evenin'; you've hardly forgot that? Your pocket'll know the difference when it be over, or I'm mistaken," winking back at the men.

"That's so," said Graah, taking out his pipe. "There be nothing close-fisted about George Laddoun. He's got the pick of the village girls, too."

"You're right there, William;" and the other men nodded, and pushed down the tobacco reflectively in their pipes. "You're right."

"The day after the weddin' the infair's to be held at old Mrs. Laddoun's," continued Nixon, hastily gathering up the reins of the conversation again; "the whole village is bid, young and old. I hear Laddoun is having his con-fectionery down from New York. I don't know what truth there is in that."

"I heern, too," said a man who had not yet spoken, "that Van Zeldt is bringin' down fireworks as his weddin' present. I've read of them fireworks; blazin' temples, and armies in the sky. Such as we read of in the book of Revelations. Seems to me that be hardly the work for a church-member. It be mockin' the Scriptures."

"Both them reports," said Graah, severely, "came from Pete Van Zeldt. He's a onreliable boy. I'd take them reports with caution, Mr. Kimball, and not venture on repeatin' them, if I was you."

"Anyways, we're havin' stirrin' times," broke in Nixon, impatiently. "Stirrin' times! Manasquan's wakin' up. I count, too, confident on George Laddoun. He has the materials of a great man, Mr. Kimball, that young man; an' when he's settled down, I make no doubt he'll give this town a h'ist up such as it has never had. He's known in high quarters, George is, and he promises to put his shoulder to the wheel in the Legislature, and get that railroad down from New York. By next winter, gentlemen, we'll have the iron horse in Manasquan."

"I've bin listenin' for that horse's neigh a good many years," said Graah, satirically. But the laugh did not follow which he expected.

"We made no doubt of havin' that railroad in my father's time," said Nixon, gravely. "He had his wires all laid, as you might say, ready for pullin'. He'd hev give the land for a depot himself: half an acre there by the cedars. But he was took away suddently. Of pleurisy."

"Well, good-bye, brethren," said the preacher, who had no mind to enter on this interminable railroad-field of talk, every inch of which he knew by heart. "I'm afraid Sister Noanes' dinner will be cold."

"One minute, Mr. Kimball!" and Nixon put his hand on the wagon-door and began to whisper, glancing back, as if for approval, at the other men, who nodded and put the word from one to to the other. The old man listened with his brows knit, muttering "Umph" to himself, but with a pleased smile.

"A very good thing!" he said emphatically, aloud. "A pleasant little plan, and the lad deserves it, brethren. Well, good morning. Wedding weather, eh?" and the yellow wagon rolled leisurely away.

Back from the road, half hidden by Graah's cedar swamp, was the old Byrne place; nothing but a strip of pasturage and bit of pond, beside the house. Laddoun would come into possession of it tomorrow in right of his wife. Laddoun had added one hundred acres to another since he left college, until he was one of the largest landholders in the county.

"Chemicals, I suppose," said old Mr. Kimball, with a puzzled knot in his forehead. "It's a business I don't understand. But it pays him well." He had fallen into the habit of thinking aloud in his continual, long, solitary journeys. He leaned forward to see if the Byrne house was open, and saw a blue rift of smoke coming from the chimney, and at the same time Dallas Galbraith going into the woods through the stubble-field. "Hollo, Dallas! Here!" he shouted.

Father Kimball had an odd liking for the boy. He was more pleased to meet him than he would have been anybody in Manasquan. He had taken his part strongly years ago, when the men at Nixon's tavern began to hint at queer suspicions about the strange boy that Laddoun had brought among them.

"Don't I know a good tree when I see it?" he said, vehemently. "There's a hundred signs beside the Scripture one of fruit. Clean bark, stout limbs, the leaves with a healthy rustle in them. Jest so with human nature. The boy's a strong, manly fellow, sound to the core." He liked to watch the lad wrestle or swim, as he grew older, finding him different from the drowsy Jerseymen about him—full of vitality, zealous, terribly in earnest in work or fun: took pleasure in contrasting their nasal drawl with his free, sonorous voice. Galbraith's tones, by the way, were remarkable in their sweep and sweetness of intonation: one reason why Manasquan people were always thoroughly awake when near him, and, perhaps, why they were attracted to him. The old man went on calling to him as he crossed the field, chaffing him, and Dallas shouted back answers to his jokes; not very witty, perhaps, on either side, but enough to make them both laugh, being in the humor for it.

"What is the meaning of this holiday rig?" scanning Galbraith's suit of blue flannel, cut in a half-sailor fashion. "A present from Laddoun, eh?"

"No, I bought it with my own money; Elizabeth Byrne planned and made it," with a complacent glance downwards. "I rather like my looks in it. I am going to the house now. She's there."

"It is well for you that Laddoun's wife is what she is, Dallas. You'll be thrown into the machinery of that house a good deal, and George—is uncertain. But Lizzy—well, Lizzy's temper is like the honey off of buckwheat; it's a rough flavor, but it's sweet and warranted to keep. She's the surest friend you've got, Dallas. And you have more than you know, my lad," laughing significantly as he nodded and drove off.

"I know what Lizzy is," said Dallas to himself. He had a fancy that to-morrow would be the beginning of a new and the best chapter in his life. George *was* uncertain in temper, and he was necessarily a good deal in his power. But Lizzy— But she would be waiting in the door for him, and he was half an hour late; he started at a full run across the stubble-field to the woods which lay between him and the house.

Father Kimball had said it was wedding weather; and Elizabeth had the same fancy when she came to the door to look after Dallas, and felt as if she had stepped into a bath of warm, sweet-scented sunshine. She had been too busy all day to look out, but now her house was in order; she had bathed and put on her stiff, new white dress, and smoothed her brown hair till it was like shiny satin folded about her head. George Laddoun would pull it down, when he came, most likely. There was a certain quiet positivism in her round, solid little person, in the very bow of her ribbons, that irritated him through all of his passionate love. "It's a hint of backbone, that don't belong to your nature, Lizzy," he said. "What does a woman want with backbone?"

She was very anxious about this defect of hers, as Dallas found out; for he was the only one to whom she spoke of it. "It is the habit of teaching so long that has made me dogmatic," she said, and made constant humble efforts to cure herself of it, for George's pleasure.

She had been teaching in the woods school-house a good many years: sewing between times, boarding with one old farmer's wife and another. Meantime the little brown Byrne house and the land lay unoccupied, just as her father left them. But when she found she was going to marry George Laddoun (people said, at first, Jim Van Zeldt, but Lizzy knew better), she began to use the little store of money she had laid by to repair the old homestead, and make it fit for his home. If it had been a palace, she thought, it would better have suited that princely young fellow. Dallas had helped her tack carpets, put hinges on doors, weed the garden beds, hang the calico curtains. She forgot that he was not a woman, sometimes, and talked to him as if he had been. The consequence was, that Galbraith often wished that Laddoun knew the girl as well as he did, and so would be more just to her and tender.

She had an hour or two for him now, before George came. She had a bottle of wine to give her lover, but she and Dallas were going to have a cozy cup of tea together. She had a surprise for him. One room, and that the one with the widest outlook from the windows and the tightest-fitting window-frames (which means much on this windy coast), she had set apart for the lonely boy. "I'll not have him sleeping like a wild beast in the woods any longer," she told Laddoun. "Let him keep his hut for a work-shop. But Dallas shall live with me."

To which George assented eagerly. Elizabeth never pleased him so much as when she gave a little evidence of Irish extravagance or hospitality. The doors of his own house and heart were open as a market-place; the more that tramped through them, the better; but the key of Lizzy's was turned; and when anybody asked for a place at her table or in her friendship, she scanned them as cautiously from behind her bars as if it were a quiet convent into which they wanted to enter. So all the village heard of the reserved room for Galbraith with surprise, and said, with Father Kimball, that the boy had made his best friend now.

"Lizzy be a queer one; she be different from Laddoun. Her likings and dislikings come to be a part of herself, like snails on a rock," old Graah said.

Everybody knew of the room but Dallas himself; it had been the talk of the village that day that she was going to surprise him with it, and they all, for their own purposes, kept the secret. He fancied, however, as he went by the farmhouses on his way, that there was a peculiar twinkle in the women's faces as they called to him, an unusual fun and cheerfulness, and that their voices never had sounded so hearty and kind. The men at Nixon's, too, as he passed, joking about his clothes, did it with an undercurrent of meaning in their lazy talk that touched him, he did not know why. There was not one of them to whom he had not tried to be useful in his small way, in their thronged fishing-times, or in the sickness last year, when one or two were down in every house. So, when they wished him good luck, and threw an old shoe after him, he thought they had, perhaps, been talking of him, and found how much they all were his friends.

"And so they are," said Dallas, shying stones vehemently into the pond, with a choking in his throat. "There's not a man or woman in Manasquan that isn't my friend. I think some one must always have managed my luck for me," his face grave, but not daring to look up.

Now the truth of the matter was this: and it was, to make no mystery of the thing, the secret of Nixon's whisper to Father Kimball. Manasquan people might, as George Laddoun asserted, be over-boastful, and rate their village too highly, but they were clannish, swore by each other to the exclusion of the world, and were fond, too, in a simple, generous way, of humoring their favorites, of little fêtes, processions and the like. So when it was noised about that Lizzy had set apart a room for Galbraith, and meant to give a home to the lad, it was quite in keeping with their habits that there should be a general contribution in order to make the room comfortable and snug, and that they should make a little glorification of the matter by keeping it quiet until Lizzy should break it to him. So they all watched the tall, lank boy, in his holiday suit, making his way through the woods, with a genial, inward satisfaction. A deserving, good creature, whom the world had abused until Manasquan was shrewd enough to find out his merit.

The air was sun-lit and sweet-scented, as we said; the woods through which he walked were silent and motionless as though they had stood in it unmoved for centuries. It was the edge of a great and almost unbroken wilderness that he skirted, gigantic pines, with bare, hoary trunks, rising into a thick sheet of foliage above. There had been times (when the world turned a harsher face on Dallas than to-day) when he had thought this forest one of the places where Death himself hid, so monstrous were the elfish growths that matted every limb, of unnatural mosses, and lichens of diseased and feverish hues. The more dead the bough was, the more vivid and strong was the parasite that fed on it.

But to-day his unwholesome fancy was forgotten, and Galbraith suddenly stopped his crunching step over the crisp needles of the pines, and drew his breath with quick surprise and wonder at the infinite beauty over which the sunshine flickered through the green, arching dome overhead. The delicate Southern moss hung in trailing webs of palest grayish green from every bough and bit of rough bark; the dead trees were massed with a filagree covering of purple, scarlet, of silver fretted with black; the wax-like leaves of the pipsissiwa starred the path; on every side the crimson fruit of the cactus opened its heated heart to the late warmth. Dallas broke off a bough which was one wonderful flowering in violet and green, crimped and curled leaves folded one above the other, but it crumbled in his hand—a lump of slimy, rotten wood.

Who was it that had so carefully turned all this death into beauty? Even where a bunch of mushrooms thrust up their heads, the brown needles thatched them like a miniature roof, and a ray of sunlight, striking obliquely through their transparent stalks, glorified them into clear amber pillars for the fairy temple. Dallas walked on more slowly. A great quiet came into his mind, up through all its boyish jumble of ideas about fishing, and roots, and the work he wanted to do for Elizabeth. He— Whoever it was that had brought all this good out of rottenness and decay, was it He that had brought him out of that miserable old time into this village? Was it?

The lad's eyes grew curiously steady and clear. The wind hinted a low, mysterious music in the pines, the sea, with warm, violet waves, caressed the shore, but no voices from old, miserable years moaned in it.

Some of us need to be lashed with defeat before we find out the real strength of the man within us, but some of us, like Dallas to-day, have to feel friendly hands touch us, and the world's seldom-seen, real, just, beautiful face clear shining into our souls. Then we see what we were meant to do in this life, and resolve to begin at once to build with gold instead of stubble.

Lizzy, when she saw Dallas coming up the path, went down to meet him, and looked curiously at him. He had been at work with her all morning, in high good-humor, quizzing her about her locked Blue Beard's chamber, whistling, and lilting out sailors' songs up stairs and down. He was quiet and grave now, as if he had come up out of church.

"No one came up with you, Dallas?"

"No." He thought it neglectful that George was not with his bride this last evening, so affected not to understand her anxious question.

They sat down on the low steps of the porch, but she could keep quiet but a little while. "Dallas, where is Laddoun?"

"I do not know, Lizzy."

"That stranger, Ledwith, has been following him about all day. I am afraid of him," uneasily getting up. "He has a fish's eye, dead and cold. I wanted George. I have something to tell you, Dallas," blushing and smiling, "and he could have put it into better words than I. George is a good speaker, I think?" timidly.

"That he is," heartily. "It's a great thing to have talent, like Laddoun. If one wants to do anything in the world, I mean. It's just like a heavy man walking in the sand; no matter where he goes, the print is there, deep. Now I—"

"You? When it comes to drawing, Dallas, I think you have a true genius," eagerly; and she went into the room and stopped before a miserable picture of a man's head, purporting to be Laddoun's, wherein the outlines were all false and the features daubed with colors. Dallas looked at it complacently, his hands in his pockets.

"Yes. If I have any talent, it is for painting, I think."

"And your experiments—your plans?"

"Oh, that's my work," indifferently; "that all comes natural to me. If you'd shut me up in jail, I'd find the way to those jobs all the same. But my painting is a different thing."

She listened attentively. She wanted him to feel that he was cared for in every trifle to-night. She wanted him to feel no lack of mother and sister in at least this one hour of his life. She guessed the starved, solitary childhood he had led, and thought of the scars and lashes on the lean back underneath his new clothes—of the wounds which even now sometimes opened and bled; and her voice trembled a little when she told him to come with her and see what she had hid in the Blue Beard's chamber.

"It is something which will help you to paint better all your life," she said. She stopped at the hall-door to call to George's mother—a little, withered old body in a clean, brown calico dress, her gray hair knotted back without a cap—who was putting some chickens in the coop. She came up with a significant smile in her eyes.

"No, Lizzy, I'll not go in with you," whispering in her weak, pleasant little quaver of a voice. "The lad's more of a stranger to me than to you, and it might damp his pleasure. He's had hard roughing it in the world, I'm afraid, poor child!" and she stood nodding and smiling to them as they went over to the low, painted pine door, and after they had gone in, nodded and smiled to her chickens, talking about it to herself.

Now they were in the room, Lizzy had meant to make the matter very plain to Dallas, but she forgot all that she had thought to say. "We wanted our best friend to come and live with us," she stammered out, the tears coming to her eyes; "and that is you, Dallas. And the people in the village wished you to know who were your friends, and they sent you these tokens—for—for your home. Their names are on them."

When he turned, pale and astonished, she had slipped past him and closed the door behind her. She wanted him to be alone, to go over the little gifts with which the room was filled, from the rag-carpet, which only Mrs. Laddoun could weave, to the fire-irons from poor Becker, the smith. She wanted him to find that there was no name omitted, no man or woman in the village who did not count him as a friend. When she went in again, which she did not do for a long time, the lad was standing with his back to her, looking in the fire; and as she came up to him, she saw how colorless he was. He talked but little at any time, and when he was deeply moved was dumb, as now. Even Lizzy's sensible eyes grew dim when she looked at him.

"I did not think the trifles would matter so much to you, Dallas," touching his arm gently.

He did not answer her for a minute, and then said, "You don't know how different it was with me back yonder. I wasn't like other boys." She turned her head quickly away, fearing to pry into his secret.

"It was not I who thought of this," she said, with a little heat on her face, "nor Laddoun. It was Jim Van Zeldt. Last summer, after the sickness, he said the village owed you some sign of thanks. Jim's heart's in the right place," speaking with an effort. Lizzy was always eager to do justice to the man whose love she had put from her.

She saw that Galbraith would not talk of it, even to her. So she turned and went into the little dining-room, where the table was set for supper. He came out presently, and followed her about in a dog-like way, trying to help her, his face still and bright.

"He said hardly a word," old Mrs. Laddoun said afterwards, "but he looked as if a heart of stone had been taken from him, and a heart of flesh put in him that night."

The evening came on quickly. Lizzy closed the doors and lit the lamp, to shut out the twilight and the rising sound of the tide. Laddoun had not come. His mother, who had nobody else to care for, and was as nervous about the man as when he had been a tottering baby, put on her cloak and went in search of him. Lizzy laughed at her, tying her own woollen cap on her head; but after another hour had passed, she grew more silent and moved about uneasily, glancing out of the window, her face paler. Laddoun was not wont to neglect her, and this was the eve of their wedding.

An hour or two before they had heard loud voices down on the beach, and had seen two or three men lounging at intervals down through the marshes: they knew Van Zeldt's schooner was in.

"But even if George had gone to help unload her," she said anxiously to Galbraith, "they have stopped work now. The Graahs passed by half an hour ago back to the house; and there are two of the wreckers," as a couple of men came across the stubble-field. She noticed that they walked close to the fence, looking furtively at the house, talking eagerly to each other. After a while, Nixon and his son came up from the beach, directly toward her gate, stopped there, and debated for a moment, and then turned suddenly, and went off together. Lizzy stood at the door, watching the two dark figures disappear in the mist over the marsh: the wind was rising, and came with shrill, foreboding cries through the pines: the sea began to mutter and moan with dreary and uncertain meaning. Lizzy tried to laugh again at her vague dread of coming evil, but told Dallas of it, frankly.

"It is as if some one told me George Laddoun never would come to me again," she said. "Go and look for him, Dallas. I cannot help being foolish and weak to-night."

Galbraith put on his cap with a cheery laugh. She thought she never had seen a stronger, lighter-hearted look than that in the boy's eyes. "I'll send him to to you in five minutes," he said.

"Come back again, Dallas," detaining him. "This is your home now, remember."

"Yes, I know. Home!" turning to look back from the edge of the woods at the open door and his room beyond, which his friends had made ready for him.

An hour passed, and another: the supper was cold, and Lizzy had let the fire die out on the hearth. She had gone out, and stood leaning over the gate. It was some joke they meant to play her, she thought. It was impossible that misfortune could come to her on her wedding eve! But she scarcely knew that the night had fallen—a wide, starless, melancholy night—and that the chilly salt gusts of wind from the marshes had wet her face and clothes. The tide was coming up with a subdued roar now, and one storm-cloud after another was slowly sweeping across the sea-horizon.

Presently, at an hour long after the time when the village was ordinarily asleep, she heard a step close at hand, and Jim Van Zeldt came up and stood beside her. She tried to smile carelessly. She would not ask her old lover for news of George Laddoun.

But he did not give her time. He was looking past her into the cozy little house where the light was still burning.

"So that is your home?" he said. Jim had quiet, womanish ways, always. When they were children and "promised" to each other, he would have suffered her to put her foot on his neck any day. So, finding Laddoun more manly, she thought, she had flung Jim and his love off as she would a worn-out shoe.

"Yes, that is to be my home," in a controlled voice. "Will you come into it, Jim?"

He did not seem to hear her. In a minute he put his hand on hers where it lay on the gate. It was the first time for many years, and she noticed that his fingers were cold and clammy. "I came to bring you some bad news, Lizzy. But I never hurt you in my life, and, please God, I never will. I can't tell her, Mr. Kimball."

"What is it?" she said, with a hot mouth, to the old preacher, who had come up on the other side.

He went straight to the point, having no faith in the sham of breaking bad news: "There was a great crime committed years ago in New York, my child: some say forgery, and others murder; and they have traced the men who did it to this beach. The pretended Quaker, Ledwith, was a detective. His warrant to arrest them came in Van Zeldt's schooner to-night."

"Who are the men?"

"George Laddoun, Lizzy, and Dallas Galbraith."

PART II.

CHAPTER IV.

GALBRAITH made a short cut through the woods down to the beach, where he thought to find Laddoun. He went slinging along with nervous strides, making great leaps now and then, and shouting shrilly like a madman after them. He was but a boy, and the excitement and triumph of the night must find vent somehow. He wanted Laddoun. He would like to drag the old fellow up into his room, and watch his face redden and eyes shine over every little gift there. It was the very thing to touch George to the quick, and bring the tears to his eyes. He wanted the whole village to come and share in the happiness it had given him—to see how grateful he was. He felt as if he were full of hot words, as if he must break his silence and tell them his story, to force them to care for him as he did for them.

Yet when he saw two of the men who had been kindest to him coming through the woods, he hid behind a thicket, and let them pass. That old nightmare of bashfulness throttled him, as it is apt to do boys of the best blood, and his throat choked, his legs and arms grew self-conscious and heavy, and his tongue stiff.

He forgot his errand and George Laddoun, and walked more slowly. It was then, in this swell of his great joy and content, that the thought which had been tugging at his heart all day pressed up barely into words.

"If—if my mother could see my room!" he whispered, stopping quite still and looking down. As he went on after that, scrambling over the bay-bushes, and climbing fences, he said it to himself more than once—

"*Mother?*"

He seemed to be growing more fit to say it since the villagers had given him this credential. The truth was, this was the thought that had made him dumb and pale when Lizzy first showed him the room. In a moment he saw a little fresh-looking woman coming into it, with her gray, watchful eyes fixed approvingly on him. He could see even the dress she wore—the pale brown silk, the white lace, the pearl ring on her small hand; things which at other times set her far off from him, with an impassable gulf between them. But this room and its meaning would have made her approve him. He thought he had taken a great step nearer her to-night. No wonder even old Mrs. Laddoun perceived that he looked as if a heart of flesh had been given him instead of one of stone.

Galbraith was like all other boys, except in this: that the incentives which first hasten them on into manhood, and give them fibre and weight, were all centred for him in that quiet little woman whom he had left years ago. If he could shift—be done with his ragged clothes, his lank, awkward body and vulgar ways, if God or his own effort—anything— would make a gentleman of him, he could go back to her. Love, money, fame, were but words to him. She and the world in which she lived were realities.

He thought, to-night, he was beginning to go back to her.

Just as Dallas came out of the woods into the salt grass, two men passed him. The night was dark, and his steps were deadened in the sand: they did not see him, therefore.

"Cradock," said the smith, Becker, "has been lying in hiding in the Quaker's room since yesterday. It was thought he might be needed."

Now this brought Galbraith to a sudden standstill. Cradock was the sheriff of the county: he had visited Manasquan once, years ago, and since then had served as a bugbear to frighten children to sleep. His coming was the portent of some great calamity; and Dallas, who had shied many a stone at policemen in New York, had so fallen into Manasquan ways that he clapped his hands with a sudden terror when he heard of it.

"What did he hide for?" asked the other man, who proved to be Nixon.

"Laddoun would have had warning, you see."

"George Laddoun be no more guilty than I," said Nixon, doggedly. "I wonder at you, Becker. It be easy for strangers to send a dog down hill when his friends give him a kick."

"Where be he gone now, then?" triumphantly. "When Cradock came down with the New York man on the beach, as the schooner ran in, Laddoun was there. In his new rig, to go up to' Lizzy's. When he saw them together, he turned off up the marsh, they do say, pale as a corpse. I always misdoubted Laddoun. Where did he get the money to buy the cranberry bog yonder?"

The men passed on into the woods. Dallas did not stop them, asked no questions; whatever their news might portend to him—whether it brought some old crime of his own or danger for Laddoun out of that mysterious old time, it did not stun him as it had done George. He had slunk through this long grass an hour or two ago, as though his brain and limbs were palsied; but Dallas ran swift as a hound, and bent half double, on the same path as soon as the men were out of hearing. The boy had the soldier-quality in him which the man lacked, and sprang naturally to arms on the first hint of danger, alert and defiant. His guilt or innocence was a secondary matter.

There was no indecision in his course. He knew Laddoun's hiding-place. There is a river, or an arm of the sea, which breaks into this county for about six miles—a broad, deep backwater, rather than stream. Coming to its edge, Dallas ran groping along until he found a long, narrow-pointed tub (a sneak-boat, as the fishermen call them, used for duck-shooting), pushed it off the sand, shut himself up in it, and, with a vigorous thrust or two, headed rapidly upstream. The water, curdled with the rising tide, stretched up between the rolling dark hills on either side, a sheet of glittering, steely blue.

A short, steady pull brought him to the point where the white, sandy road to the post-office struck through the pines: one or two crab-cribs were anchored there, and on the beach a seine-reel thrust out its shadowy, empty arms. This was the out-point of the village travel: beyond was a region unknown to the Manasquan world. In all Galbraith's root-hunting explorations of the head-water country, he had never encountered a single inhabitant of the sleepy Jersey village. Ben, an old clam-digger—who had no name apparently but Ben—had once built himself a hut a mile or two above the road, but he was dead years ago: so the story went, as Dallas knew. The hills and defiles on either side of the broad water up which he floated were silent and untenanted as a shore in Hades. Almost as spectral and beautiful, also: the moon, a pale, thin bow, rising low in the sea horizon, threw timorous, dim lights up into this far-inland valley, where the tide crept and bosomed itself for a transient rest. Along the shore the knobs and peaks of hills grouped themselves in fantastic forms, bare, save for the cover of short, soft grass, sinking back into dusky, wooded slopes behind. Here and there one of these bald summits lifted a dead tree in relief against the sky, on whose topmost limb a fish-hawk sat flapping its wings and keeping a tireless watch over its nest. Higher up the stream, where the water was quiet and less bitter, the wooded hills crept closer to its edge, sheltering little comfortable hollows between them, which seemed to wait for cozy homes. Before one of these Dallas involuntarily lifted his oars, looking at it gravely. It was the place where he meant to build his own home some day. There was space for large buildings and a grand sweep of lawn. The boy's air-built castle was not a cottage: a fine, solid house instead, and its furniture planned to fit the silk and pearl ring which he had once seen his mother wear, and which held her far off from him. She should lose nothing when she came to him. Then, remembering Laddoun, he rowed on, shutting his teeth fast.

Galbraith's search lasted all night. At the head of the inlet, or where it breaks squarely against a hill (a thin, narrow creek being the only conduit reaching it from the interior), the water forms a shallow, umber-colored bed for numberless flat, marshy islands, covered with reedy, salt grass of every shade of brown and saffron. Between these flats Dallas poled his boat slowly, closely scanning the banks and slopes of the hills, afraid to call aloud lest he might wake the loud, resonant echoes which wait, ready and angry, along these shores, as though impatient of the continual heavy silence.

When the dawn came, however, filling the sky and even the brown water with pink flushes, and the air with cold, delicious odors from the pines, Galbraith sprang on shore, and hurried to a black figure which he saw lying under a knotted old cedar half-way up the sand. It was Laddoun, asleep, his usually florid face haggard and colorless, his shiny clothes and boots filthy from dragging through the mud of the marsh. He had dropped down so carelessly that the tide plashed about his ankles.

"Laddoun! Laddoun!" All the repressed excitement or terror of the night made the call vehement; but the young man turned over with a heavy snore. If Laddoun was on the brink of the grave, he would relish his cut of beef or his sleep, Dallas thought. He shook him savagely, remembering poor Lizzy just then, and how the wedding morning was dawning for her. "Mr. Laddoun! This is no time to sleep like a log," dragging him up by the heavy shoulders.

George looked about him, dazed for a minute, and then got up, and, turning to the water, wet his face and head.

"What have you to tell me, Dallas?" looking at him at last.

"What have you to tell me? I've followed you all night to know. What does Cradock want with you? What kin I do for you?" pressing close, his chin quivering and eyes on fire. "There's no time to lose. What kin I do?"

Laddoun looked at him steadily, and then sat down doggedly. "You don't ask me what I've done?"

Galbraith's face altered, and his tone curiously became that of an older and more reasonable man than his companion. "No, I don't ask. I thought it was some of the old troubles back there," jerking his thumb over his shoulder. "I be no judge of any man. I'll do what I kin. What is the quickest way of getting clear of the business? This is—" He stopped.

"It's my wedding morning, I know that," getting up and sitting down again with an oath. "It's my ill luck, hounding—hounding me, as usual;" scolding on, in a tone at which Dallas could hardly hide a smile, listening with a boy's keen sense of humor. Laddoun always faced trouble with pettish ill-temper, and, if nobody else could be found to bear the blame, had his Luck ready for a fag to be lashed for his sins.

Galbraith interrupted him. "Is it money that's wanted?"

Laddoun avoided his eye, jerking pebbles nervously into the water. "No. It's not a debt," dryly. "I knew that Quaker the minute I saw him with Cradock. I thought, before, that his cowardly phiz was familiar to me. He's Bunsen—on the detective force. You know?"

Galbraith nodded. He put his hands behind him presently, steadying himself against the cedar, and wet his lips once or twice before he spoke. Laddoun watched him shrewdly.

"You've no reason to want to come in his way, either?" sharply. "You've been in hiding this many a year, Master Galbraith."

"I don't want to come in his way," gravely. "But I've not been guilty. I'll let no man say that. I've not been guilty."

Laddoun shifted his position uneasily. It was curious that in this moment of his own apparent peril his thoughts seemed to be concerned exclusively with the boy, on guard with him, as it were, watching him with a mingled pity and alarm.

"I'd like to know the truth about you, Dallas Galbraith," he broke out. "Since the day I helped dig you out, along with the others, from that coal-pit in Scranton, three years ago, nigh dead with the chokedamp, you've been a puzzle to me. Do you remember that day?"

"Yes, I remember it."

"A queer black beetle you were! Do you mind, when I'd brought you to, how you begged me to hide you, to let you be counted as dead or missing, to get you out of Scranton? For the love of God to get you out? Well, did I do it? Did I share what I had with you after that? Though how could I tell what sort of criminal I had in hiding?"

"Yes, you did. But you did not think me a criminal, Mr. Laddoun?" passing both hands over his head with a slow, patient gesture.

"How could I tell? Appearances were against you," hotly, lashing himself into a rage. "I think I played the part of a good friend to you, Galbraith. I was but a poor devil of a student, but I never treated you as a servant. I went share-and-share with you. What I saw of life, you saw."

"Yes, I saw it," under his breath; and poor Dallas wondered when it was that he had grown into the knowing man he was now. It was such a little while, before he was dragged out of that pit at Scranton, that he had been a child sitting lazily beside his mother while she pored anxiously over his books, both of them sitting down on the carpet to play marbles with real relish and fun when the lesson was learned. Such a little while ago!

When he heard what Laddoun was saying again, he found he was talking of some of the sprees he had gone through in New York.

"Well," rubbing his chin with gusto, "we saw life, Dallas, if we have to pay for it now. But you were always a puzzle to me."

"This is no time to talk of that. Cradock is on your trail."

"Yes, it *is* the time," vehemently. "For, if you were not the knowing little rough I thought you, I'd rather have lost my right hand than have served you the trick that I've done."

Dallas looked at him, bewildered, a moment. "Trick? I don't understand. We can settle that afterwards. Is it one of the old gambling matters, that Bunsen has tracked?"

"No," turning away.

Dallas stood deliberating. Boy as he was, he had helped Laddoun out of many of the drunken scrapes into which he was perpetually plunging with his two or three chums. It was the worst set among the medical students into which he had fallen; and Laddoun was generous, ready to fight or pay for them to the end. When he was in the mire, however, he was quite as ready to howl his complaints out loudly: his silence now, therefore, puzzled and alarmed Galbraith.

"You've land enough to clear you from any debt," he said, in a perplexed tone, "and debt was always the worst of your troubles. And I'll say this: that the least part of the money was spent on yourself. That be true of you, Laddoun."

"I know it. But I don't begrudge the help I give the fellows! I don't begrudge it. While a man lives, let him live!" the dark red mounting to his handsome face and his eye sparkling. "But this matter—now I'll make a clean breast of it, Dallas!" flinging out his hand to him. "But for God's sake be merciful to a man! I was hard pushed. You know the old man we lodged with, in Lispenard street? Just we two?"

"Adamson? Yes."

"Well"—mumbling the words rapidly, and sopping the sweat from his forehead—"I was hard pushed. It was either the money or ruin, and he was a hard old file: he had not a drop of anybody's blood in his veins. Now, Dallas, you know he was a hard file—an old beast? More than any man I ever knew."

"Go on," drawing his breath shorter. "What do you mean?"

"You ought to know what I mean," angrily. "You must have every word spelled to you now-a-days before you'll understand it. You remember a cheque which you drew for me, at the Metropolitan Bank? I paid my endorsement for Pancott with it, and you settled some other scores, just before we came here."

"I know. It was Adamson's cheque. He owed it to you."

"So I told you," in a low voice, turning his back on him and going down to the beach.

"Didn't he owe it to you? He never gave away a rag," with a laugh. "And it certainly had the old man's name on it."

"He did not sign it, Dallas."

Galbraith had leaned forward to catch the half-whispered words: for a moment he did not comprehend them.

Then he stood erect, the color gone from his face.

"You mean that you—you— No, that can't be! You're not a thief, Laddoun."

"No, I'm not a thief," facing him, and putting one hand on his shoulder. "Be quiet. I signed the cheque, and I suppose in law they'd call it forgery. But I meant to pay it back to him. Now you know I meant to pay it back, Dallas? Nobody that knows the sums I give away, and how I spend money like water, would suspect George Laddoun of robbing the man of his wretched shinplasters. It was to help Pancott I took it. The old miser had thousands hid away, and I thought I could make it good to him some time. Do you understand?"

"Yes, I understand." But the lad spoke stupidly, and looked at him, Laddoun saw angrily, with a sort of dumb dismay.

"Never couple the name of Laddoun with thief again, then," haughtily. "It was a miserable business. I never did replace the money. I never had it, you see. And then, when we left the house, I recommended a man named Parker to the old fellow as a boarder, and I found afterwards that Parker was a bad lot. I wasn't to blame there, either. I hardly knew the man. But it ended badly."

"We saw in the papers that Adamson was robbed and murdered. Do you mean that—?"

"No. I don't say who did it. But it never was discovered, and I know now that Parker was a bad lot. It was I that brought him to the old man. I wish to God my hands were clear of that!" gloomily. "It's my luck."

"It never was discovered," Dallas repeated mechanically, trying to steady himself, pulling the cuffs down over his shaking wrists.

"No." Laddoun looked at him steadily, squaring himself before him. He was ashamed that the words he had to say made him quail before this insignificant, lank boy: he made what strength and courage he could for himself out of his own portly, handsome presence. "No. The detectives have had it in hand for months. They had a notion that the party who did the forgery—finished the job. But they've no proof of that—not an atom," hastily passing his hand over his mouth. "It's only the suspicion. But that is enough to damn a man's whole life."

The first shock over, the reasonable look began to come up into the lad's eyes. He put his hand affectionately on Laddoun's arm.

"You need have no fear," with an unsteady smile. "You're not the sort of man, Mr. Laddoun, to be suspected of murder, let them prove the forgery or not. A man's character counts for something in law, I reckon."

"They've no proof of the forgery against *me*, Dallas." It cost George Laddoun a harder wrench to speak the words than he had thought: his mouth fell weakly open when he had done, and he watched the boy as a convicted felon might his judge.

But Dallas only answered quietly, "I'm glad of that; mostly for Lizzy's sake. What does Cradock want, then?"

His stupidity provoked Laddoun; it was easier to go on. "They've no proof against me. I wasn't even in New York when the money was drawn. You had taken other cheques, which Adamson had given me, to the bank," watching Galbraith's bewildered face furtively as he spoke.

"Then it's all right," relieved. "Nobody would suspect a dull boy like me of it."

"You're not counted a dull boy here, and you weren't there. Old Bunsen, or Ledwith, or whatever he calls himself, has spread the notion through the village that the head-work of the shop is done by you; and back there in Philadelphia, there was none of the fellows that didn't wonder at your odd knowledge of chemistry and the hand you wrote. You'd better use of your pen than I had. It was cursedly queer in a coal-digger's boy. I'll say that. Old Adamson used to say, 'There's a heap of brains under that boy's yaller hair.' No, you'd not be counted too dull to do it."

Dallas stood still one breathless moment: then he came slowly towards Laddoun, a fiery heat rising to his cheeks and eyes.

"You thought of that? You made a tool of me? You brought this on me?"

He had put his hand on Laddoun's collar as he spoke, and when he had done he flung him from him fiercely, as though he had been a dog; he did not even look to see where he fell into the muddy tide, but, turning away, walked up the beach.

Laddoun gathered himself up without either scowl or oath. He liked the boy better for the blow. He stood looking at him where he had seated himself on the sand, his hands clasped about his knees, staring down the river, up which the morning ripples glistened redly.

"Galbraith!" venturing toward him at last.

The boy was deaf and dumb as a stone.

"Galbraith, you don't think I meant harm should come to you? As God sees me, I meant to replace the money and make it all square with the old man. Besides," hesitating, "I didn't think you'd scruple to do it, even if you knew."

Still no answer.

"You know there was a queer suspicion about you, Dallas. Now, you know there was," in a whining voice. "You didn't seem to belong to your station. Why would you want to be counted for dead if you'd done nothing amiss? Why did you wince just now at the thought of the detectives? Why did you keep so dark about them times before I dug you out at Scranton? 'S long as I've knowed you, there's never a word dropped from your lips about them times."

A change came into the lad's face— an almost imperceptible change—but it brought a sharp qualm to Laddoun. "If I wronged you," he continued, impetuously, "I'd give my right hand not to have done you this turn. I've spent my life serving others, and it seems infernally selfish to see you in this scrape and know that I can get off scot-free. But I never meant harm to come of it. It's my luck."

Dallas staggered to his feet. "I don't know what's luck," he said, dully. "There's something that's kept its hold on me and dragged me down, down, since the beginning. I'm tired of fighting agen it. I reckon it's God. But for you, Laddoun," turning on him fiercely, "if you think you'll get off scot-free, you're mistaken. You wrote me a letter from Albany, where you'd gone on a spree, saying that Adamson had given you the cheque, and telling me where in your bureau to find it. I've got that letter now. It was uncommon kind, and I kept it—like a fool! I never threw away a kind word."

"You've got that letter?"

"Yes." Laddoun walked up to the boy, looking straight into his eyes: the man, like any animal driven to bay, was not without a certain courage.

"It will not help you, Dallas, to bring me in with you. They would take that letter for a plot between us."

"You worked for your punishment, and you shall have it. If the lifting of my hand would clear you, I wouldn't do it."

"The lifting of your hand would clear me. There's no proof against me but that letter."

If he had hoped by this to move the boy to any sympathy, he was mistaken. Dallas gave a short, savage laugh, and turned off—did not look back even when the sound of oars broke the stillness, and Laddoun, with an oath, cried out that the men were on them. "There is no use in running. Cradock is armed," he said.

Dallas made no reply, but stood quietly, watching the boat pushing its way slowly through the narrow black currents between the marshy islands.

"When I saw Cradock with the Quaker last night," said Laddoun, in a thick, rapid tone, "I thought they'd scented you out, Dallas. They had no proof against me. I couldn't stay to see you taken and know I'd brought it on you. That's what I'm here for. They have no warrant against me. There's no proof but that letter against me."

But Galbraith was silent. The men had brought the boat up to the shore at last, and one after another sprang ashore. There were Graah and two fishermen, beside Cradock and the pseudo Quaker. They all watched the two figures anxiously as they came nearer. Laddoun put on his hat and threw back his chest, bowing with a faint imitation of his old pompous politeness.

"Aha! they don't mean to make fight," said Bunsen, in an undertone. But the sheriff was looking intently at Galbraith. The wind blew the boy's thin, fair hair back, and there was something in the childish face and reasonable, woman's eyes that had its effect on the old man.

"That be'n't the face of a bad one," he said, doubtfully. "You've made no mistake in the lad?"

"I've made no mistake. That fellow's got more wit than you or I, in some ways, innocent as he looks. Graah can tell you that."

"I've got no ill word to say agin the boy," said Graah, stopping short for emphasis, his solid voice going up and down with the swing of a pendulum. "I know nothin' but good of him. An' George Laddoun's my neighbor. I come here to see fair play, an' so I tell you; an' if them men say they're innocent, I'm on their side, constable or no constable."

Bunsen glanced at the ponderous village authority with a slight smile, and passed him. Cradock touched the handle of a pistol in his breast-pocket. "Better keep clear of this matter, Mr. Graah," he said.

"As if I be afeerd of his pistols!" muttered the old man, aloud. But he winced before the officer's indifferent good-humor: it symbolized the law. He and the two men stood apart, watching, while the others went up to Laddoun and the boy. They held their breath to listen; and no wonder. It was ten years ago since Cradock had made an arrest in Manasquan, and it had become a date in the fireside stories; and these were the village favorites. It was as if a pestilence had broken out with an hour's warning in their midst.

"When he took hold of the boy," old Graah said to his wife afterwards, "I tell you I felt an in'ard tug an' choke, just as when our Joe was nigh drowned in the under-tow. I couldn't but think of the sickness last summer, an' how the lad went about from house to house, nor how the little 'uns made much of him. I count them judges—little 'uns." But in the village gossip over the matter, Graah went no farther than, "I say nothin'—law's law."

Laddoun met the officer with another bow. "One too many for an innocent man," Cradock muttered.

"You had business with me, gentlemen?"

Bunsen nodded. "Not pleasant business, Doctor Laddoun. But no doubt you will be able to adjust the matter satisfactorily. We men of the world see these things in a different light from our friends here," beckoning back to the villagers.

Laddoun combed his whiskers, smiling with a ghastly counterfeit of ease. "I have no idea of the nature of the difficulty," he stammered, not having yet determined on his course of defence. "Appearances may be against me, but I can set it right—I can set it right."

"Until you know the proof against you, it is better to commit yourself as little as possible," said Bunsen, dryly.

Laddoun's countenance steadied at this. He drew from it that the proof was slight, and thought the warning friendly in Bunsen. He noted shrewdly, too, that the detective, while he talked to him, kept his eyes on Dallas with a sort of critical admiration.

"They give the boy credit for the brains of the concern," he thought, with an odd mixture of relief and annoyance.

Then Bunsen went over to Galbraith. "I have a warrant for you," he said, putting his hand on his shoulder and raising his voice. The others stood listening.

Dallas took the man's hand off quietly, but his grip was like iron. "I'll go without force," he said, in a shrill, loud voice, speaking, not to the officer, but to Graah and the fishermen. "I took the cheque to the bank. But I'm innocent. I'm no thief."

He went alone before them all, and took his seat in the boat. When they were all in, and had begun to row down stream, he put out his hand to Graah's knee. "Mr. Graah?—" he said, in a low voice.

But the law was beginning to have its effect on the old man: his jaws worked nervously as he chewed his plug of tobacco; he kept his eyes turned down from the lad's face, and moved his fat knees with a little shuffle of relief when he took his hand away. This was the last appeal that Dallas made—then or afterwards. He was dumb, unless when spoken to, during the time that elapsed before he was removed for trial to New York. Watchful, too; his eyes turning to one face after another with a look which brought the tears to many of the women's eyes. If they had spoken out boldly the faith they had in him, God knows how differently it might have gone with the boy. But the shadow of authority was a power in Manasquan: a man once in the clutches of the law was guilty till proved to be innocent.

Going down the river, the sun shone out brightly. Laddoun talked to the detective and Cradock, with the old affectation of ease, about the unimproved condition of the land, the chances of marl in a field back of the beach; even pointing out, with a shaking forefinger, the swarms of red and black-winged lady-bugs on the marsh-grass. Bunsen answered him pleasantly, but his attempt at indifference told badly on Graah and the fishermen. They scowled at him doubtfully, askance. A Manasquan man in Cradock's terrible grip had no need to chatter of marl or bugs.

When they came to the landing-place, there was a strange silence noticeable on shore, by which one might know the great calamity that had fallen on the village. The seines were still wound on the reels, the mackerel-boats empty and at anchor: for the first time in many years, old Calcroft, the clam-digger, was gone from his post. Laddoun, glancing feverishly from side to side, saw that the front shutters of most of the wooden houses were closed as they passed up the long, sandy road. There was the usual caucus of men on Nixon's porch, but they sat in gloomy silence, staring into vacancy, as the prisoners went by.

There was not one of them who did not hold the boy, at least, to be innocent; not one of them who, if he were going down in the treacherous sea yonder, would not have gone out to save him. But what fault have we to find with the cautious Jersey villagers? Which of us has not seen some soul going down in deep waters and kept a discreet, conventional silence, when a cheerful call and a hand held out would have brought them to the shore?

There was not one of their faces which Dallas did not read with his slow, unappealing eyes; but Bunsen alone suspected what was hid beneath the lad's unnatural composure: nothing escaped him, from the slow settling of the blood under his nostrils to the faint breath drawn at long intervals. He guessed that this matter had nigh pushed the boy to some strange extremity. "But he must have some friend to fall back on: there'll be a rope held out to him, surely, at the last."

Cradock whispered to him that Dallas seemed too dull and childish for such work as forgery, and Bunsen contented himself by pointing out his firm step, different from Laddoun, who cringed along beside him. "The boy's of another strain of blood from any of these people hereabout; there's breeding and strength in him," and he recounted the story of the chemical apparatus; for Bunsen was but like less shrewd men, and was awed by any knowledge which he could not possess.

He would have rated Dallas as dull enough if he could have seen how utterly he had given up all hope of acquittal. The letter would be proof of Laddoun's guilt, but not of his own innocence, he believed, because Laddoun had told him so. When Cradock spoke to him, he only repeated the same words mechanically: "I took the cheque to the bank; but I'm not a thief."

They had but one place, two rooms in the back of a vacant house, in which to confine the prisoners until evening, when Squire Boles, who was absent at a woods' meeting, could give them a hearing. Bunsen ushered them into a narrow hall, smelling of fresh pine, on either side of which was a square apartment.

"You'd better take one room, Laddoun, and the lad the other. Mr. Cradock will smoke a pipe with me, here. Send me up some tobacco, Graah. When will I leave Manasquan?" repeating the old man's whisper aloud. "Well, if matters go against our friends here, as soon as I can get a requisition. I've had a pleasant sojourn in Manasquan," patronizingly. "And by the way, Graah, if any of Laddoun's or the lad's friends would like a word with them, they can come up. I want all things to be friendly among us."

Laddoun and the boy, standing in the opposite doors of the hall, heard him. Dallas came forward. "I have friends," he said, in a strained, distinct voice. "They showed that to me last night. Tell them I'm no thief."

Graah listened with his head down on his breast, but made no answer. Then Dallas went into the room allotted to him, and sat down on a pile of boards which had been left on the floor. Laddoun came inside of the door, glancing back, lest he had been seen. "Galbraith!" in a shrill, desperate whisper, beckoning with his hand. "For God's sake! There's no proof against me but the letter. Think of Lizzy!"

"Tut, tut! my man. This won't do," and Bunsen shoved him good-naturedly out of the door. But Dallas had listened to him with an unmoved face, sitting with his hands clasped about his knees on the planks, the sunlight falling about him.

Laddoun, locked up in the little eight-by-ten room, paced to and fro like a caged bloodhound. He had a real affection for Galbraith, and between that, and a consciousness which he would hardly acknowledge to himself that he had not "played the fair card by him," the boy filled his mind more than Lizzy or his own danger or shame. He swore to himself half a dozen times that he would call in Cradock and Bunsen and make a clean breast of it—let the boy off.

That would be the generous thing to do; and while the heroic spasm lasted Laddoun was quite capable of doing it. He had his hand on the door-knob to call Bunsen, when it was pushed open, and the officer came in.

"I came to have a pipe and chat with you, Laddoun."

The young fellow drew himself up on guard. "I don't smoke, here. It stupefies me, and I'll keep my wits awake to-day, Bunsen."

"A talk, then," seating himself leisurely on the chair which he had carried in, his opaque eyes on Laddoun's flushed face. "I'll be frank with you. It's the best plan with shrewd fellows like yourself."

Laddoun laughed coarsely. "Too shrewd to be humbugged," he said; but he began to comb his oily whiskers with renewed complacence.

"No. I show you my hand. I tell you fairly that I think that boy has used you. He's a deep one, and I'd like to trace him back to the beginning. Tell me what you know of him: it won't go harder with you if you do," meaningly.

Laddoun made one or two turns, his brows contracted, a half word escaping him now and then. Whatever was his struggle, the dead gray eyes above the pipe appeared to take no cognizance of it.

"I can't tell you Galbraith's antecedents," he broke out. "I helped drag him out of a coal-pit in Scranton, where there were a dozen diggers killed with the choke-damp. It was when I was in Philadelphia, and I and a lot of fellows were up in the coal country on a spree. Being doctors, they called on us. It was at night, and I had this boy in a shed by one of the heaps of coal-dust when I brought him to life. He begged me to hide him and let him pass for dead, and I did it. I've kept him since. I think I've been a friend to Dallas Galbraith," doggedly.

"I should say you had," soothingly. "Pass for dead, eh? That hints at a bad record. I judge Master Galbraith had made acquaintance with men of my trade before."

"It don't follow that he had, by any means," sullenly. "The boy's back was purple with wales and scars when I got him. The men in the pits had used him brutally. That's the whole secret of it."

Bunsen smoked in silence a while, then he took up another trail. "So it was with you he learned the rudiments of his trade—chemistry, botany, and the like? He told me he had had a chance."

"He had no chance with me. It was an old thing with him: I never knew where he learned it. He was cursedly close-mouthed. And I don't think I deserved it. He'd had the training of a gentleman's son, Dallas had, though he'd learned the talk of the Scranton pits since. But when you get below the coal-soot on him, and the coal-ways, there's a boy that I don't pretend to understand."

"I must say that he has treated you ungratefully," suggested the detective, with affectionate earnestness. "So he kept his own counsel, did he?"

"He's showing his gratitude to-day," with a bitter laugh, remembering the letter. "As for his secrets, I never tried to worm them from him. There were places and people he was afraid of, as a child would be of ghosts in the dark. He's nothing but a child in most ways, after all," in a relenting tone. "But he can keep his mind to himself, as I never could do."

"Did you know that he applied for entrance as student in one or two laboratories while he was with you?"

"No. But it's likely. He had a natural hankering for that sort of work. The fellows helped him to books. So did I."

"But it needed an entrance-fee, which he could not pay," he continued, his eyes still on Laddoun. "He applied in one place the very day before the forgery. He needed money for the fee and his board, if he left you. That is a proof against him: it looks badly."

"Yes, it looks badly," rubbing his hands nervously one over the other.

Cradock called to Bunsen just then, and he rose, picking up his chair. Laddoun's imbecile hand went shaking up to his collar and his mouth, hinting at his secret.

"Do you want to say anything more to me, Doctor?" suggested Bunsen, staring at the opposite wall.

"I? No. What should I have to say?"

"Good morning, then."

"I might probably think of something to mention. Will you be outside if I should?"

"Outside, just within call. You don't think of it now?"

"No." But the detective still held the door open and waited a moment, and in that moment Laddoun held his own chance of manhood and Galbraith's fate in the breath of his nostrils.

"No," he said, and the door was shut.

CHAPTER V.

LADDOUN ate a hearty dinner that day. Nixon sent up the best mutton-chops his kitchen could furnish to the prisoners, and by the time they came the young doctor was sure of acquittal. He had sent in his mother to talk to the boy, and he had no doubt he would destroy the letter. Dallas could not withstand a woman's tears.

She found him still sitting on the pile of planks, his hands about his knees, as he had been since morning, only that the untasted meal was spread out cold on its tray on the floor, and the sunshine had crept farther from him to the opposite wall. The old woman said but little, and shed no tears. A great age seemed to have fallen on her chirrupy little figure and face since morning. She stood looking at the floor at her feet, her gray hair not so wan or old as the features it framed.

Dallas rose when she came in.

"George tells me that you can clear him by a word?"

He made no answer: she would not have heard him if he had.

"I can't beg it of you," steadying herself by one groping hand on the wall. "I'm not strong. I've buried seven children in my time, but there's no blow been like this."

She waited a few moments, unconscious, he saw, that he was there. When she turned to the door, he took her by the elbow and helped her gently. She was muttering about "George," but had altogether forgotten what she came to ask of him. When Bunsen opened the door, she made her formal, old-fashioned little courtesy to them, and went away without saying a word. But an hour or two afterwards Galbraith saw her sitting on a log outside of the window of Laddoun's room. There she sat all day, motionless. If she had gone down on her knees to him, it would not have made the boy's heart so sore as the sight of her sitting there.

Father Kimball came up in the afternoon and talked to him, but Dallas made dull, irrelevant answers. He could not understand the old man's words; they sounded like water falling far off, they had so little meaning in this matter—this pain of his. He broke into a text of Scripture which the good old preacher quoted, with—

"If I could prove that I was used as a tool—what then?"

Father Kimball's eye gathered its quick shrewdness. "By Laddoun? I'll tell you candidly, my boy, the evidence is strongest against you: there is only the suspicion of collusion with George. The cheque was drawn by you, the money was paid out by you, and there is abundance of testimony as to your remarkable skill with your pen. Even if you bring proof that Laddoun was a confederate, you cannot clear yourself."

"I cannot clear myself." He went on repeating these words so long to himself that, with his haggard, colorless face, the old man feared he was becoming insane. "You'd better eat something, Dallas," he said. "And be patient. If you are innocent—and I believe you are innocent," quickly catching the boy's unsteady eye—"be patient and trust in the Lord. He will deliver you if you are one of his children."

"If I am found guilty," abruptly, "what is the punishment?"

Father Kimball coughed once or twice before he found courage to say, "Surely you know, Dallas. You will be sent to prison."

Dallas got up as if his joints were stiffened, looking out into the sunlight: his lips moved as if by machinery. "I did the best I could," he said, "and it's come to this."

The old man's eyes were full of tears. "You can't make your own lot," he said, taking Galbraith's cold hand in his. "The Lord has it in care. That is, if you are one of His children. Every hair of your head is numbered. But if you've never been converted, your good intentions and works are but as filthy rags, in His sight."

Dallas turned his pale face on him, bewildered. Father Kimball saw that he was using an unknown tongue, and he suddenly turned to worldly matters.

"Have you no friends, Dallas? No father or kinsfolk? I've often suspected you were of better birth than Laddoun knew. If it is so, tell me, my child. Let me apply to them. If they have influence, your whole future may depend on it."

"It's all done with to-day," Dallas said, as though talking to himself. "If I can't clear myself, there's no future for me. Do you think I'd go back a jail-bird to my mother?"

He sat down again, and after that seemed to hear nothing that the old man said to him. When he was gone, Tim Graah climbed up to the outside of the window, and after Dallas had whispered a few words to him, disappeared into the woods, running like a hare. Now, there had not been a word spoken by either of the prisoners, all day, which had not reached the thick ears of the leaden-faced man sitting on a chair tilted back in the hall, just outside of their doors. He had his own reasons for sifting their secrets.

But Tim had caught sight of him. He did not try, therefore, to scale the window again. Instead, a bit of bark, with one or two papers wrapped about it, was thrown in a half hour later, and fell noiselessly at Galbraith's feet. One was the old letter from Laddoun: the other a brown paper wrapping, on which was printed in big text: "All us boys is frends to you, Dallas. Timothy Graah."

Dallas laughed, and colored, when he read it, folded it up and hid it in his shirt: then took it out to read over, laughing again, but with the tears coming slowly down his cheeks. The other paper he kept in his pocket. He did not read it over again.

Just before dusk he heard a noise in the hall, Bunsen and Cradock moving from their chairs, and a woman's voice. They opened Laddoun's door.

"No. I will see Dallas," she said.

It was Lizzy. The sight of her roused him as nothing else had done: there she was, with her yesterday's face, quiet and steady. If the terrible blow had touched her, it had left no traces. While he looked at her smooth hair, the knitting stuck in her black silk apron, the well-blacked shoes, the whole matter seemed like a dream, and his old self came back to him.

"I'm glad you came, Lizzy," holding out his hand.

But after taking it she did not speak for a moment or two. Then she said, cheerfully, "I came to see that you were doing all that you could for yourself. First, eat," opening a covered basket which she carried. Dallas obeyed her, at first from his usual submission, and then, like a boy, ravenously. When he had done, he pushed away the basket and sat looking at her. The good taste of the food, the hearty warmth of her presence, made his fate loom up colder and more terrible. It was so natural to just be a boy, to eat and drink, to live a careless, jolly life, like the rest of them.

"Now," nodding slowly, one finger laid in her palm. "What proof have you of your innocence? I mean to put it into shape for you."

"I have no proof. There's been something agin me from the first, Lizzy. I can't fight it."

"That is childish," sharply. "I believe in your innocence as much as—as I do in Laddoun's," hurriedly. "If I were a man, I'd force justice from the law. I'd never whimper."

"As you believe in Laddoun's?" he repeated, in a slow, thoughtful undertone.

She did not answer him for a minute, and he noticed that she put down the basket which she was adjusting, and rested her hand on the wall. "I did not come here to talk of Laddoun. There is no proof against him. If I did not believe him to be innocent, what would become of me, Dallas?"

"I know, Lizzy."

"But it is you who are in danger. What can I do for you?"

Dallas was standing before her, a compassionate smile on his face, as he noted how her firm, hard voice clung and lingered to Laddoun's name. But when she spoke of himself, he grew grave and quiet. "We will not talk of the chance for me," he said. "There is none. It has not been my fault. I wish you would tell them all I am no thief. That is all I can say."

Elizabeth looked at him long and searchingly. "If I did not think George Laddoun innocent, what would become of me?" she said, her very lips growing pale.

Galbraith drew a long breath: then he smiled cheerfully, and took her hand. "There will be no proof against Laddoun, Lizzy," he said.

When she went out, she saw him standing in the middle of the room still smiling cheerfully after her.

She did not go in to see Laddoun.

Squire Boles came up to the vacant house when he reached home after dark, and it was there that the prisoners had their hearing. The witness had been at Nixon's all day; a bank clerk; a quiet, bald-headed gentleman, in a shining suit of broadcloth, who walked about among the barefooted fishermen, watching them with the askance, deferential courtesy of a hare let loose among a gang of mastiffs on their parole. He noted their grim reticence with surprise: not even the landlady asked him a question. They knew that Laddoun and the boy's future depended on his tongue. It was not their habit to gossip when deeply moved.

People went up to the vacant house after dark, and crowded into the hall, silent as if they came to a funeral. When the door was opened, they could catch glimpses of the room in which Squire Boles sat behind a high desk, carried up for the occasion, his book, ink and spectacles spread out under the light of two tallow candles.

Cradock stood beside him, stern and unsmiling, and, behind, the solid gray face of the detective was dimly seen in the darkness, no unfitting figure, it seemed to the fishermen, to decide on this matter of life and death.

"They say," they whispered to each other, "that Boles' verdict be as good as final. Bunsen's hinted one of them be sure to get off, but it's a dead certainty agin the other. Which, I don't know."

When Laddoun and the boy were led in through a side door, the crowd without stood on their tip-toes, trying to discern from their faces which was the guilty one. The boy stood near the open fireplace, in which a log or two had been kindled, and bent forward, his hands behind him, so that the light flickered over his fair hair and pale, quiet features: Laddoun was in shadow, but they could discern his ruddy, careless face and portly swagger; now and then, too, he nodded and smiled to some one without.

"Whichever be the guilty one," said Nixon, sententiously, "he be as good as dead to us. No jail-bird need show his face in Manasquan agin."

His voice was loud. He saw Dallas raise his hand to his collar, and as suddenly let it fall. Old Mrs. Laddoun pressed her way among them into the room, dropping a courtesy as she went.

"My son George be in trouble, gentlemen," she said, slowly; "my son George be in trouble," with a feeble little smile. They all stood aside to let her pass, and many of them muttered a "God help her!"

There was another woman who sat outside on a bench in the corner, with her face turned from the door. They whispered among each other that it was Lizzy. Poor little Jim Van Zeldt hung about near her. He was confident that Laddoun was innocent, but there was no telling how the verdict would go, and he wanted to be near her if she needed any help.

Then the door was shut. There was a profound silence outside : they could hear a low, monotonous voice within, and knew it was the bank clerk giving his evidence. Old Father Kimball came into the hall out of the woods.

"I thought you did not mean to come up, brother?" one of the men whispered.

"I could not refrain," the old man said. "I could not stay away while the souls of two of our brethren, as we may say, are on trial." Then he walked to the far window and stood with his gray hair uncovered, looking out into the night. They knew he was praying.

The door opened presently and Graah came out. The evidence was over.

"How goes it, Graah ? how goes it ?" crowding about him with pale, anxious faces.

But the old man choked when he tried to answer, and shaking his head hurried out.

"It be the boy. He wur main fond of the boy," they said.

They could see Dallas standing forward alone, his head held up, his face resolved and pale. The old justice peered over the papers, his head shaking. These prisoners were his friends and neighbors : he had prayed to God that he might deal justly with them. In his agitation he mixed all the forms of his law-book together in his talk : there was a cool smile on Bunsen's face listening to him.

Laddoun's black, bold eyes, yet in the shadow, glanced warily around. "You cannot commit me on such grounds. There is not warrant for even suspicion," he said defiantly, wiping his mouth again and again.

"Young man, we know the law," and the justice shuffled his rusty wig to and fro uneasily. "Is there no farther evidence against Doctor Laddoun? I cannot commit him on the mere ground of being this lad's employer and most kind friend. He was your friend ?"

Dallas looked up. "He helped me when I needed help," he said, slowly.

"There is no evidence against me—none," Laddoun cried, vehemently. The boy turned his quiet eyes on him. There was a silence for a moment : those who were nearest to Dallas saw a change come on his face, as though he heard a cry which they could not hear. Then there was a sudden flash among the wood embers, and a paper which had fallen among them burned to ashes.

"Stop!" said Bunsen. "One word with this boy. Have *you* no proof against Laddoun, Galbraith?"

There was a pause, broken only by the crisp crackle of the fire. The crowd in the hall pressed nearer, and held their breaths to hear, as Dallas spoke.

"No. I have no proof."

"Then you are discharged, Doctor Laddoun," said the justice. "For you, Galbraith" (the boy turned and faced him), "you are remanded to the custody of this officer, to await a requisition for trial in your own State." The old man got up, pushing back his spectacles with a shaking hand, and then leaned forward with both hands on the table. "From the evidence before me, I have little doubt how that trial will end. You have had a chance among us to— We treated you as one of our own sons. But you have lost your chance among men now—and—" He broke down here altogether. "May God have pity on you, Dallas!"

There was a sudden confusion, and then as sudden silence, as Laddoun turned to go out among them, a free man. Bunsen nodded and congratulated him. Laddoun gave a loud, uncadenced laugh, which broke off abruptly. He almost staggered as he walked, his face purple, fumbling at his cravat. They all put out their hands and pulled him out into their midst ; but he said nothing, glancing back uneasily at Dallas. Jim Van Zeldt saw Lizzy stand up as Laddoun came out and was welcomed back among them ; she looked at him steadily a moment, and then turned and went out into the night alone.

Dallas Galbraith, with the detective's hand on his shoulder, stood looking at the door where their faces were massed, turned again towards him for the last time.

He had had his chance among them, and it was gone for ever.

"I did the best I could," he said, putting out his hand before him like a drowning man. Then Bunsen led him out through the dark side-door, and they saw him no more. That was the only stroke he made against the tide which was washing him out—out.

CHAPTER VI.

"How far to the Stone-post Farm now, driver?"

"Madam Galbraith owns land all along the road, but the Stone-post Farm is in the next county."

"She was a Dour by birth?"

The driver nodded shortly.

"And is fond, I surmise, of gathering her own kin about her?"

"I reckon she is. She has the country hereabouts swarming with 'em. Wimmen like her, without chick or child, are full of their whims."

"My own name is Dour," ventured the young man, buttoning his worn kid gloves nervously and coloring a little.

The driver, a short, pursy man, shot a keen glance over his shoulder at the lad's pale, hatchet face, long black hair pushed behind his ears, and well-kept clothes. "You don't favor the old Madam's stock, anyhow," indifferently; and, flicking his leader's right ear, he began to whistle.

Paul Dour, who was pluming himself inwardly on the keenness of his guess about the old lady, lapsed into silence. He felt himself vaguely to be snubbed. These people of the West (as he called the Ohio valley in which he was traveling) disappointed him. It was his first journey out of New England into the raw, uncultured regions which form the members of the body of which it is the brain. He had intended to be charitable in his judgment of them—to insult no one by his criticism—making that allowance for all short-comings, social or otherwise, which became a just, clear-sighted philosopher of the transcendental school. Now, Paul's modicum of Concord philosophy had dribbled down to him diluted through a dozen conduits. Consequently it proved a very mild haschish indeed: his visions were few, though his mental contortions many. However, he had none the less faith in it. Here was the leaven which was to impregnate the mass of the American people. As clay ready for the hands of the potter, so the swarms of thriftless, inadequate slaveholders, and the brute physical and moneyed force of the Middle States, waited for the informing New England mind. Paul, like most of the lads and young women who go out from New England, anticipated a great deal of quiet amusement, though but little additional knowledge, from his venture.

But it was dull work so far. The Pennsylvania Dutch he had found curiously indifferent to the informing element which was to vivify them. Could this stolidity, he thought, with alarm, extend farther? His self-complacency was unusually thin-skinned: every pin-prick caused a painful contraction. The very farm-houses which he was passing now, with their solid foothold of unhewn stone, their wide acres, their giant oaks pre-empting the earth, as it were, and all the material good that therein is, annoyed him. They would better have befitted his own section, the old homestead of the country, than did its flimsy white wooden tenements. He missed the dissatisfied, tentative disquiet to which he was used, in this warm, mellow air, and in the composed faces of the people. He was curiously let alone. Nobody seemed to need his history or his thought. The people were decent, decorous, minded their own business. But as for the conversation, what seed of progress lay in that? Facts—facts—facts—he heard nothing else, from the New York auction clerk who had crossed the Jersey ferry with him, to this coach-load of passengers with whom he traveled through the West Virginia hills. What did he know of the duty on iron, or the rates of grain in Chicago? Yet, he was uneasy. After all, could such things as these affect the daily lives, and therefore the souls, of the great commonplace masses of men, more than the subtle refinements of a pure philosophy? These Western people had a strong common-sense code, to which test they brought all religion, politics, the life of a man, or the food of a horse. It stunned and baffled him.

"I fear," he said, to a fellow-passenger who was mounted on top of the coach beside him, "we generalize too much with regard to the Western people in New England. We mass them in our hypotheses and conclusions. No doubt there are curious inflections of character in different States, owing to climatic influences and the like."

"There are only two influences at work on men, sir—God and the devil," sharply, jerking the flaps of his black coat together.

"Oh!" said Paul. He scanned the small, loose-moulded face of his companion with new interest. A white neckcloth and intolerant gray eye were the salient points about him.

"I have been a laborer in this vineyard a great many years, and I find nothing so pernicious as this cant of influences. God has but his few messengers of the preachéd word (of whom I am one of the humblest), but Satan lies in wait at every corner. You must forgive me, sir," more gently; "but I understood from you that you were going into one of his pitfalls unawares, and it is my duty to warn you. You are young and ingenuous: pardon me."

"I am going to a friend's—Madam Galbraith's," said Dour, with a little vanity, at naming a power in the land.

The clergyman shook his head, and momentarily closed his eyes. "She is a relative of yours?"

"That I cannot tell. The truth is, I have never seen her, and would be glad of any information you could give me. My visit has altogether the flavor of an adventure."

The clergyman opened his eyes curiously. Bob Penly, the driver, turned half-way round, whip in hand.

"I graduated in a college in Massachusetts two weeks ago," proceeded Paul. "There was a classmate of mine from this neighborhood, and through him I heard of her as a probable relative. I wrote to inquire, and for reply I received an odd epistle. I have it here." He drew from his pocket a large sheet of thick paper, on which these words were scrawled in a masculine hand: "Sir: John Bligh, whom I know to be a truthful lad, and moderate in his statements, apprises me that you are a Dour, and also a poor young man, and deserving. It occurs to me that you are a grandson of Peter Dour's. He emigrated from this county to Vermont in my father's time, for what purpose God, and his own cracked brain, only knew. Whether you are or not, I will be pleased if you will come to the Stone-post Farm. You are invited to remain during a fortnight. We can in that time determine whether a longer stay would be agreeable to you or me. As you come for my whim, you will permit me to pay for it.

[*Signed*]

"HANNAH DOUR GALBRAITH."

"John Bligh was my classmate," explained the lad. "He said she was an eccentric old woman and wealthy, and it might be the making of me. Besides, I had never seen the West; so I came. Some men might have been offended at her bluntness. But I liked it."

"She is a wealthy woman," said the preacher, beating his knee with the letter; "very wealthy. She has said to her soul, 'Soul, take thine ease: eat, drink, and be merry.'"

"She has said it to a lot beside her soul," said Penly, pulling his reins energetically. "There's as many poor as rich fed at her table."

"She paid my expenses," resumed Paul, hastily. "I'm poor, as Bligh said," with a frank laugh. "As for the deserving, I hope the old lady may find me so."

"She is not chary of her money," resumed the clergyman, in a tone of patient mildness. "She sends it where her whim blows. like the wind scattering the leaves yonder. Yet it is the Lord's: she is but a steward, Robert Penly," severely. "And with it she lures young men like this over her threshold, where there is card-playing and dancing continually. It is not for me to judge," turning again to Paul, "but I never pass the boundary of her land, and look at the house perched on the mountains, that I do not think of that other Woman of old, clothed in scarlet, who sat upon the seven hills, drunken with the blood of the saints."

Bob made an angry cut at the off horse. It was a rigid Presbyterian community, and Bob himself carried about the bag on Sunday in a country church, so that he felt his mouth in a measure gagged.

"I've heerd she seldom goes to church, and never gives a red to missions or the like," at last he said, compromisingly.

The preacher bowed assentingly.

But Bob could not forget a loan that had been made to him the winter that he was down with the rheumatism, when the twins were born—how the queer old Madam had paid his rent, and sent in pork enough to last until spring. "Take that filthy plug out of your mouth, Robert Penly," she said, "and keep it out until you have paid me." Bob burst into a chuckle.

"Well, she's a law to herself, I reckon," he said, "and to other folks too. Captain Galbraith, we call her. My wife, now, thinks there's salt enough in her big body to savor the whole county. Doctors differ, you see, parson."

The clergyman rebuked the familiarity only by silence. "I would be sorry," he said, mildly, turning to Paul, "that you would suppose me a common gossip, used to malign my neighbors. But the house to which you are going is the only one in the neighborhood where the amusements and corruptions of the world find entrance, and Madam Galbraith's position and generosity make her example weighty, as you see. Besides, the power of her tongue—" he added, in a lower voice. "Her words burn like scalding drops, at times," and his pale face grew a shade paler; from some bitter remembrance, Paul fancied.

They fell into an awkward silence after that, only broken by Bob's persistent whistle. The road wound circuitously up and down steep hills, passing by lonely farms, clusters of two-storied brick houses huddled on the edge of every water-course, each shouldering the name of a city, then out again through the great sweep of forest, in which Paul was doubtful whether he might confidently look to find wigwams or not.

The early November frosts had browned and rotted the crimson and yellow leaves of the mountain foliage, and left but the shape and grouping of the trees, stripped of their cover of color, sharply defined against the sky: an infinite study of form alone. Mile after mile this rare limning edged the mountain horizon, an endless variety of simple, noble shapes outlined in black upon an amber, crystal-clear background. For the Indian summer still lent the red and golden tints of August to the sky and to the haze which hung half-way up the hills, escaping from the chilled, muddy creeks below.

At one of the farm-houses the clergyman alighted, carpet-bag in hand: he held up his hand to Paul, who shook it heartily.

"You will not take my warning amiss? You are on the Galbraith lands now."

Dour glanced hurriedly at the wide creek on one side, and the shelving mountain-sides, blood-red with iron, on the other, with a quicker beat of his pulses. What if the terrible old woman made his fortune, after all? For if his inner eye kept a fixed regard on the pure Central Truths, his outer gray ones had as shrewd respect for next year's income.

"No fear," loftily. "The old lady shall not prove my Mephistopheles. But we will get on admirably, I dare say. I can accept all natures, provided they have the human element. Bligh had an essay of mine—Psychical Axioms; and I think she has seen it, and hence my invitation," blushing ingenuously in spite of himself.

The preacher shook his head. "No.

You're a Dour, that's all. She has never been able to find kinsfolk of her own name. Psychical Axioms, eh?" and with an amused laugh he nodded, and, jumping the worm fence, turned into a stubble-field.

"Considerin' the season, he might have wished you a jolly Thanksgivin'," said Bob, dryly, as the red coach lumbered off again up the hillside.

"They keep Thanksgiving to-morrow at the Stone-post Farm?"

"I reckon," with a nod that was as emphatic as an oath. "Don't you be misled by him," with a contemptuous nod backwards to the spare black figure in the field. "Parsons is good in their way, but they're narrer. That's it. They're narrer. They don't see without glasses. Now Madam, she makes the whole country-side keep Christmas and Thanksgive along with her. I'd not like to count the bar'ls of flour and turkeys that left her place yesterday."

"No children, you say?"

Bob shook his head. Paul was young. What if this respectable old ogress found him her nearest kinsman—and heir?

"A widow?"

"No. Old Mr. Galbraith, he's there. It's he that says where the flour and turkeys is most needed."

"I remember a Galbraith once," said Paul, half aloud, reflectively. "A boy of about my own age. He was tried in New York when I was there in the Christmas holidays. My uncle defended him. But that was years ago."

"It was, now?" Bob dearly loved a story, but he scorned to betray too ready an interest, the speaker being but a lad. "And *his* name was Galbraith? Like enough. They're plenty as huckleberries. But they're decentish folks, ord'narily. And your uncle got him off, hey?"

"No; he did not. It was a clear case of forgery. But my uncle was curiously interested in the boy, I remember." Dour was silent, recalling with an effort the particulars of the old, painful story, but he gratified Bob with no more of it; and Penly, after filling up the time with a critical squint at the scenery, stroking the dust from the brown terry waistcoat that covered his fat little paunch, and glancing at his pinchbeck watch, began again:

"We're a bit behind time. That near horse, he's off his feed now. Well, the old couple—the Madam and her husband—had a son once. I didn't tell you. But he was like a good many of your high-bred colts—he wasn't worth nothing. They raised him too much, likely. He was fed and slept accordin' to rule. When he was a baby, she never hired a nurse, I've heerd say: no woman should touch him but herself. So he slipped the tether and made off. He married a silly girl of this neighborhood and took her along. It was an awful muddle."

Paul's curiosity, always alert, was roused. "How did it end?" he said.

"I knowed young Tom Galbraith well," said Bob, breaking into a comfortable trot of talk, that kept time with his horses' tramp. "There wasn't a man about the drinking-shops and stables in the county that didn't know him. So I never looked to hear any good of him. He took his wife acrost the mountains, East, and there they scuffed along from hand to mouth, I've heerd since, till he died. There was a good deal of outcome in his wife. She was a Jennings—an orphan girl. So she fought along bravely, sewin' and the like, for her and the boy. She never wrote to the Madam, even when the child was born."

"There is a boy, then?" said Paul, coloring as his boyish visions of heirship suddenly vanished.

"Yes, there was a boy. But he's dead. There's somethin' cur'ous about that boy's death, a mystery like, that nobody knows the bottom of but the old Madam. They say his mother put him to dig in the coal-pits at Scranton, and that the choke-damp killed him. But it's a dark story through and through."

He was silent for a while, and then began again in a louder voice. "Tom Galbraith's boy would have been welcome here by high and low. He might have drunk and flung out his money like water, as his father did before him, but he'd have come to nothing worse, coal-pits or not. 'Tain't in the blood. It was the want of brains as ailed Tom, but he was as honest as his mother; and she—well, it's likely she is an old heathen, as the parson says. But I've experienced the world this fifty years, and she's as clean a card as I've known in the pack, take her altogether."

"And Tom Galbraith's widow?" bringing him back to the road.

"Well, she's back now—Mary Jennings. She's changed her name again. She married a Captain Duffield, East there, some do say, to save her and her boy from starving, but some say it was after the boy's death. I don't know. I think it's likely she wanted somebody to trim off her pink face and curls, as poor Tom never could do. She was mighty fond of her pretty face, Mary Jennings was. But the story goes that Duffield used her like a devil. However, *he's* dead. Only a month or two ago. And hearin' that, the old Madam sent for her. My wife says she'll be there this Thanksgiving."

"To-morrow?"

"Yes, to-morrow. She's of a different stock from the Galbraiths, you see. Well," hesitating, "she's a sort of far-off kin of my own. But that don't matter. The old Madam would take her out of the coal-pits themselves, purvided she was honest. But she's a terrible judge when a man makes a slip," shaking his head. "There's things I could tell you— I hope God 'ill be slacker in judgment than them that's like her here."

They were entering the crooked streets of a little village on the side of the hill, and Bob blew his horn shrilly.

"Now I've got a load to take up here," he said confidentially to Paul; "the Rattlins. Well, they are a lot! They're going to spend Thanksgiving at the Farm. Along with you. They go once a year, and it lasts two weeks. There's eight of them. He's a preacher, Rattlin is," jerking out the sentences between the jarring of the wheels. "And eight of them to feed. There's a tough fight for you! I hope you'll be kind to the little man, sir," slacking the pace of his horses to a walk as they went up the hill. "This is his year's one holiday, I take it. He has three p'ints for preaching, lyin' within fifteen miles, an' he gets a bare five hundred from 'em, and that but half paid in; and preachers can't turn an honest penny at odd jobs, like the rest of us. Consekently, they're half clothed, them Rattlins, and whole starved. Lord, here he is! Like a little cricket, as usual. Good morning, sir," touching his cloth cap respectfully, and drawing rein.

A little man, hardly as high as the wheel, stood suddenly beside it, rubbing his hands, his thin cheeks red and wet with perspiration.

"You did not forget us, Robert?" panting for breath. "We've been on the watch for two hours. I really thought you had forgotten this was the day we were to go. Though that's hardly likely. We've been up since sunrise, so as to be quite ready. We'll not detain you, Robert. The baggage is on the steps."

"We're behind time, sir. As I was saying just now, this here horse is off his feed."

"Off his feed, eh?" anxiously. "Let me examine him," applying his ear to the horse's chest. "He is hoarse, Robert. He ought not to be out in this chilly air. I'd recommend covering his breast immediately. I have a blanket that I'll lend you for the purpose. I'll make a short cut across the fields for it."

"If they have one, it's about as much as they do have," said Bob, looking gravely after the retreating figure, with the thin black summer coat fluttering about it. "My wife says they all slept under newspapers last winter. Not bad kivers," as Paul laughed. "But the world owes that little man a decent keep. Why, I'll bet you it's months since he's tasted meat; and as for debt—Lord, sir, they owes for their bread for months back. Skinner hasn't the heart to press 'em. Everybody likes them Rattlins."

The coach had rumbled through a narrow lane, and drew near to a little box of a house, with the usual patch of a lot beside it filled with tomatoes, beets, and a row of parsley. The house was just closed, and Mrs. Rattlin brandished a key which was nearly as big as itself. The tide of Rattlins ebbed and flowed about the great hair trunk that was set down directly in the middle of the road. When the coach came in sight they hallooed and swarmed over it, over the fence, the two babies scaling their mother's plump little sides until she was forced to sit down and relieve her own turmoil of mind by slapping and kissing them.

"Did you ever see such a lot?" said Bob, whipping up the horses. "Did you ever see such a little woman? 'Pon my soul, she's good enough to eat! They're all as round and fat and jolly as ripe mush-millions, and how they get jolliness or fat out of the skimped life they lead is more than I can tell. Jest as mush-millions get juice out of sandy sile, likely. Well, here you are, young 'uns! Jest hold the reins a minute," throwing them to Paul. "I'll load this wagon myself," scrambling down among them, and beginning to strap the hair-enormity on behind, and to throw in various odd bundles of shoes and frocks tied up in gingham handkerchiefs, over which Mrs. Rattlin anxiously presided, while the preacher himself, with one of the boys, strapped the white worn blanket over the horse's chest. Then he felt its ribs, and went about among the other horses, his head knowingly on one side, looking into their mouths, feeling their flanks and backs, followed by an admiring regiment of boys.

"You've some fine stock here, Robert, fine stock! I used to be a judge of a nice animal: well, to tell the truth, I owned a good mare once, myself—a very good mare."

"That's the bay, Jenny, at Whitcrosses," said Bob, in the deferential tone which he always used to the little man. "I heern she was yourn once, sir."

"True, true. I often go down to Whitcrosses, and she knows me yet, I really believe. Yes, I was as fond of Jenny as of one of these little chaps. But it wasn't convenient for us to keep her," with a momentary gravity. "But I think, Penly," energetically, "there's few men can live to my age with eight children, and say they have lost nothing but a horse," the thin little face reddening with a sudden brightness, which made even Paul, up on the box, nod and smile down to him, and feel a sudden warmth about the air.

He had a New Englander's quick eye, and he was used to petty scrapings and makeshifts of economy. He could see the colored shirt peeping out under Rattlin's old-fashioned linen collar: see the seams where his trowsers had been turned wrongside before for the two bigger boys (worn terribly thin under the knees): he knew at a glance that the pink ribbons were dyed at home which fluttered over Rosy and Gerty's pretty, shy faces, yonder by the fence. All of their clothes were for summer wear: they had no business to be wearing them now: they had no business to be laughing and poking fun at each other, at all; but they did it, and that in a fashion which showed Paul that it was a practice to which they were born, and not a weakness of the moment. The world, Bob said, "didn't give them a decent keep," yet they made much of the old monster every day, took it by the ears, and warmed their hearts over it, as if it had been Kriss-Kingle himself, with arms and back loaded with goodies for them.

It was contagious, somehow. Before he knew what he was about, Paul had the reins tied and was down among them, joking with Rattlin, packing in baby after baby among the straw which filled the bottom of the coach, scrambling over the boys, and quite aware that this expedition to the Stone-post Farm was such a holiday as came but once or twice in a lifetime. They were all in at last, even to the blushing Rosy and Gerty (Paul blessed their untimely gingham frocks, for how else would he have a glimpse of the plump, pink arms and shoulders?) Then he shut the door, and climbed up to the top again, where Mr. Rattlin and Bob were seated, and away they bowled, confident that there was as much fun and good-humor and chubbiness and rosy cheeks and ribbons boxed up below, as any five feet square of an earthly coach could hold.

The afternoon sky clouded over, and the whole temper of the day became gray and gusty, but Bob told his raciest stories, and the horses tramped along as if they had drunk spiced cordial instead of water at the inn; even Paul broke out into some hearty college song; and everybody, Penly and the Rattlins, girls and boys, caught the chorus in time, and roared it out together until the hickory woods, on each side, rung. Then they came to the half-way-house, where the horses were changed. Presently, a great cracked gong sounded, and Bob went in to his dinner. Dour was half-famished with his long fast, but he shook his head when the landlady called to him. He could not go in and leave the wistful little man and his party outside nibbling from their paper of stale crackers on the porch. He went in to the grocery and bought some cheese, however, and they made a regular picnic of it.

"*I* never take dinner at a tavern," said one of the boys, coming back with his hands in his pockets from gravely inspecting the happy eating people within.

"Traveling is very expensive, Mr. Dour," said Mrs. Rattlin.

To which Paul replied that it was, and that he generally was provided with crackers, and not obliged to depend on the inns; and then they all got into the coach again, Paul crowding in between Miss Rosy and the youngest boy.

However, at the next village where they stopped, a man came out of the post-office and put a bank-note in Mr. Rattlin's hands. Openly, before them all. He made a little speech, too, saying that it was a small Thanksgiving testimonial from some of his flock, and that they wished him many happy returns of the day; at which Mr. Rattlin grew red and choked, and was as full of eager gratitude as though they did not owe him two quarters' salary.

"It will pay Skinner, Gerty!" Paul heard Mrs. Rattlin whisper, with her little joyous chirrup of a laugh.

But it did not pay Skinner; for at the very next inn Rattlin got down with a good deal of excitement in his manner, and presently they were all brought in to a stew of canned oysters, such as seldom was eaten before: Penly and Dour, the inn-keeper and all; Mr. Rattlin himself going out with a soup-plateful to the old ostler who was watering the horses. Mrs. Rattlin, after the first wince of chagrin in her blue eyes, was the very life of the party. This carnal dissipation gave a sort of wicked flavor to the day, which was very relishing: they mounted into the coach, noisier and more reckless than ever, to finish the journey, the men going on top again.

Evening was closing in before they entered the Stone-post Farm.

"You're on the old de-main now," said Bob, pointing with his whip to the low fences made of stone blocks, with rails between, which gave a name to the homestead. "You've been crossing bits of the Dour land all day, spread out like a spider's claws, but you're in the heart of it now. The Dours were among the first settlers in this West Virginia country, you see: all big, strong-jinted men, I've heerd: they had to hold their ground agin the wild beasts and Indians. Yon's the fort they built in the old times for safety, when there was a rising among the savages," nodding to a low, mud-plastered range of buildings on the slope to the left. "The Madam, she's the last of them: she's got the land, and she's got the pluck and the grit of all the old Dours in one. Yon's the house," pulling up to give effect to the first view.

Paul looked slightingly at this type of an old Western homestead, that had grown up in the hollow of the mountain as slowly as the gigantic oaks that stood sentinel about it, and, apparently, with no better defined idea of architecture than they. It belonged, too, as much to the ground on which it stood: the great blocks of gray stone came from the mountain, and the brick, turned a dull brown through long rain and sun, from the soil under their feet. It stretched, with its barns and out-buildings, over the space of a small hamlet. The landscape, with its broad fields, frequent watercourses, and sharp mountain ranges, differed from the miniature farms of New England: to Paul's eye it lacked refinement; the house finished and gave expression to it all, as a face to a body. It was liberal, large, hospitable; and it was content to be nothing better than it was for ages to come.

Coming nearer, Mr. Rattlin nodded with keen admiration. "That is what I call a picture," he said, and Dour could not contradict him. The great valley below lay in shadow, but the evening light rested on the mountain summit and on the old house at its base. Its gray and ruddy brown walls harmonized so cheerfully with the natural tints of the ground and rocks, that Nature, Paul fancied, had thrust out welcoming hands to draw it into closer companionship. The warped black shingles of the roof were crusted and edged with moss, and the wild ivy had climbed with its persistent three-fingered leaves over its sides until they were covered with masses of clear crimson. The windows, deep set in the stone, began to glow red from within in the chilly evening, and rifts and trails of bituminous smoke poured from the wide stacks of chimneys, yellow and black, across the pale sky.

"There she is herself!" cried Bob, pointing to a short, largely-built woman crossing a field, ploughed for wheat, with slow, steady pace, a stick in her hand, with which she seemed to be testing the depth of the furrow. "She goes about her farms like an officer on guard—the Lord help Joe Driver if them furrows ain't straight! She'll keep going till old Death taps her on the back, I reckon, some day, in her walk." But he stopped joking, and put on a grave face when Madam Galbraith, perceiving the coach, waved her stick for it to stop, and came down the hillside towards them.

Paul had time to look at her curiously: old as she was, her step was firm and free as an Indian's: her dress was of coarse gray cloth, the upper part cut like a man's coat, her head covered with a flannel hood: she halted at a wide opening in the road, and beckoned them to come closer. Bob drove up slowly.

"Who have you here, Robert Penly?" in a loud, clear voice. "Tut, tut!" tapping on the side of the coach; a pair of keen eyes, under shaggy white brows, inspecting the passengers inside and out rapidly. Paul kept silence, not deeming it fit that his introduction should be given in this informal manner.

"Mr. Rattlin, eh?" as the little man jumped down and stood in front of her. "You are welcome, sir. I think good comes under my roof with you." She bowed as she said it, with a curious stately grace in her cumbersome body. She passed over Dour without notice, and thrust her head inside with a strange anxiety, he fancied, in her face, shutting her wide mouth grimly. The high-featured, large-boned woman, standing in the rough road and twilight, had seemed repellant and coarse to Dour; but when she pushed back the flannel hood, exposing the swarthy clean skin, broad forehead and deep-set eyes before which he quailed, he thought it, reluctantly, a grand head, and framed aptly in the reverend mass of silvery gray hair.

"Ha—women folks? women folks?" as a babble of greeting welcomed her from inside. "And that's all? Well, I'm glad to see you all, youngsters. You'll always seem like a girl to me, Mrs. Rattlin, in spite of your brood. Go on. Up to the house. It ought to be like home to you by this time. If you think of anything which would make you give thanks more heartily, let me know it;" and patting the head of the nearest boy, she turned away from them.

"Stop, Penly! What does your company mean by driving such miserable hacks as these?" touching the horses with her stick. "They are a disgrace to the country. Stock that ought to have been out to grass years ago! Tell them it must be stopped, or I'll give them winter fodder for their cattle, and"—lowering her voice—"see that they miss their mail contracts next year!" with a cynical laugh. "Drive on, now. No, Mr. Rattlin; I beg that you will go back to your seat. I'll walk alone—walk alone, and lifting her stick by way of farewell, she struck across the field again.

Young Dour smiled superciliously.

"She has been used to the charge of a large tenantry," said Rattlin, jealously. "It has roughened the husk a little. But she is discomposed to-day. Usually, it is like coming to a Christmas fire to be near her. A great, genial, tender heart she has, that woman."

"She's disapp'inted," Bob broke out, "in not seeing Mary Jennings. She sets such store by the memory of that boy of hers that even the woman who forgot him is dear to her because she was once his wife."

Madam Galbraith was joined at the end of the field by a gentleman, who held the turnstile for her to pass through, and then walked silently beside her towards the house, his hands clasped behind him: a tall, spare man, carefully dressed, with a few thin white hairs straggling from under his hat. He watched her nervous strides and passionate, long-drawn breaths gravely, but without a word. Finally she stopped.

"James!"

"Yes, Hannah."

"The woman has not come. She'll not come. It is in keeping with all of her life. A pink-faced, frivolous trifler: she lured Tom from me; she hung about his neck like a millstone; she hid the birth of his boy from me; and now—" She stopped, her nostrils distended and white. It was her only sign of passion. The little gate on which her hand rested shook violently.

He put his own on it. "Hannah?" he said, "Hannah?" gently.

Her whole burly frame seemed to cower, ashamed. "I forget myself, James. Let me go in a while alone."

"Tell me first what is your disappointment? Why do you bring the woman here? Tom is dead, and his boy— We had better bury them out of sight, Hannah." The quiet gentleman passed his hand over his pale face as he spoke; it was a common gesture with him, and, like all his motions, had in it something mild and reticent; but his wife was struck by it as never before. She looked at him keenly. Was it possible that her husband had held their dead son closer to him than she, in all her loud agony of grief? But James Galbraith's secret thoughts were not to be uncovered, even by his wife.

"I want her near me," she said. "I want to touch her face because he kissed it at the last: to hear her voice, because it was dear to him. I am a fool, perhaps, and a dotard. But the nearer I come to the grave, the more I hunger for something of my own. I'm an old, branchless trunk. I had but my boy. There's not a dog now that wouldn't be nearer to me than all the world of men and women if he had loved it."

He held his quiet eyes on her, calming her. "I understand," he said.

They entered the gate and passed into a wide hall. A great coal-fire threw alternate yellow light and shadows through it. She stopped him by the arm in front of it. "James," in a low, hurried whisper, "don't laugh at me. I told you long ago I did not believe that Tom's boy was dead. I lie awake at nights thinking, What if God would give him to me, a pure child as he is, to atone for the mistake I made with his father? I never believed he was dead. If the woman comes, I will force the truth from her!"

"Yes, Hannah," mildly.

Madam Galbraith went to her own room and locked herself in. It was her habit when deeply disturbed.

But her husband sat quietly before the fire, his delicate fingers pointed together, looking into the sudden flames and shadows. He had no need to turn a lock upon his grief.

If the simple-hearted gentleman kept the boy he had lost near to him in his every daily walk and thought, no man knew it. His odd, fastidious, kindly ways and quizzical humor apparently filled up his little rôle in life. Even his wife would have said there was in it nothing more than these.

PART III.

CHAPTER VII.

"DONG-DONG!" The slaked housefires thrust out angry jets of flame to explore the darkness; cattle stamped in the stables; cocks crowed back their indignation through the unbroken night at being wakened too early. "Dong-dong!" Floors began to creak under unwilling footsteps; dull candles to sputter and wink; sleepy maids to creep stumbling down from their garret roosts; the Rattlin brood chirped under their quilts; the little preacher turned uneasily on his pillow; but still the sullen clamor went on. It was only the great housebell of the Stone-post Farm which usually stood on the hall table. It was a weight for a man, and had a clank like a blacksmith's anvil; but a young woman, who thrust her colorless face out into one of the dark upper entries to listen, fancied it had a human voice. "To work! to work!" it said. "Give thanks. Begin anew. Amend your mistakes. Your life is in your own hands." The woman closed her door behind her, and came out into the darkness fully dressed.

Perhaps that was what it said. Madam Galbraith rang the bell herself, striding up and down the chilly, pitch-black hall, clearing her throat like a man. At every anniversary she refreshed her soul by penitence and a new code of good resolutions, and dragged the household out of bed a half hour earlier the next morning.

Her night had been sleepless: that thought of her dead scape-grace son dwindled her life down before her into a paltry failure. Well, there was a fragment left: in that there should be no mistakes. If she had been a man, she would have worked off the rank, nervous vitality of her brawny body and brain in some struggle for freedom—Cretan or Fenian: as it was, she haled the petty world under her from beneath the blankets to face their work in the middle of the night. Nobody paid such wages in all the country-side; but when in these moods the woman was a terrible slave-driver: the stolid Dutch hands who worked for her might as well stem her will as a log run counter to the sea under-tow. She called herself a catholic, liberal thinker; but her real creed in her own world was, God is God; and Hannah Galbraith is his Prophet.

Still, it hurt her that the crowd of house and farm hands were sullen as they gathered into one of the outer kitchens and waited for her. Why could they not see what was best for them?

Was not work and thanksgiving better than sloth? She went up the stairs and struck with her stick two or three times on a door.

"Honora!" she cried. "Don't delay, Honora!" She was sure of the little girl's good temper if she drove her all night. Then she went down to the kitchen and took her position behind a table, the oil lamp lighting up her hawk-eyes and the shaggy white hair above them. She had her farm-book and bag of specie before her, and began counting out their wages.

"I pay you now because a man can give thanks better with a full stomach and pocket. I want but a quarter day's work done. I'll see that all of you have something extra to thank God for. Except you, John Hawley and James Lane. You'll spend the day in bringing up your husking. You were drunk yesterday. The Lord wants no prayers or hymns from a man who shirks his daily work."

She marshaled them as a general his men; some to the pantry, the field, the mill, the kitchen: omitting no minutiæ; her voice grew loud and unctuous. The petty authority gave her, evidently, a great pleasure. God had put power in her hands, she thought: there were hundreds to whom her will gave comfort or poverty: she did her duty well. Suddenly she hesitated, glanced uneasily about her; the glance always passing with marked indifference over a quiet woman in clothes of a dull chocolate color, who stood in the shadow. There was nothing peculiar in her appearance beyond the unusual want of color in the solid features, but Madam Galbraith faltered before the steady eyes, as though she and her power had been but a sham—a house of sand built on sand. She shut her book and got up.

"I did not look to find you here," with a manner of forced politeness. "My people are used to the hardships of early rising."

"It is no hardship to me," said the woman, quietly.

"Open the shutters, women," in a loud voice, turning away, "and go to work; go to work!"

But they hesitated—a sudden brightening on their faces: it might have been from the clear dawn that filled the room through the open windows, or from Honora, coming in with and seeming a part of it. She said good-morning as she passed among them: there were none of them whom her childish smile and nod did not reach. They were all fond of Honora. People always thought the little girl's voice was different from any they had heard before, and, when they had been with her a little while, felt as if they had a share in her, and were in some sort related to her. Madam Galbraith nodded to her to follow, and, when they were out in the hall, led her by the hand. Honora never would be other to her than the little two-year-old whom she had taken from her dead mother's side. They went to her own especial room, where a fire was burning: piles of clothes of all sizes and materials lay around. Madam Galbraith loaded herself and Honora, chuckling and talking over them like a great boy on a frolic: then she covered all over with shawls, and out they went into the hall again, walking stealthily. She had no mind that even her husband should know that the poor Rattlins owed their clothes to her. Only Honora: secrets like that suited her.

They softly laid a great bundle inside of Mrs. Rattlin's door, and then hurried up a dark passage toward a room where Rosy and Gerty and some of the little ones were chattering by candlelight like a nest of pigeons. But Madam Galbraith stopped short with an angry scowl: there was a swinging lamp over the door, and beneath it stood the little woman in the dull-colored dress, her cool eyes curiously fixed on them. Madam Galbraith thrust all her parcels on Honora, feeling into her very marrow like an overgrown school-girl playing at Santa Claus with his pack; but she lingered, trimming the lamp, to hear the outburst of girlish cries and rejoicing inside. She could see, though the door was shut, how Honora was already on her knees, hard at work in the midst of the floor, helping to dress the little ones in their bright little dresses, kissing the chubby white arms and feet, and how the Rattlin girls, as usual, shied off, half afraid of her, because she was delicately dressed, and knew no more of their talk or of beaux than a baby. She wanted to play out her own part of Santa Claus. She would have relished every bit of Honora's fun, to the tying of the last baby's shoe. While she stood gravely screwing on the lamp chimney, the comely, quiet little woman beside her, in her stuff dress, became an intolerable weight and irritation. Only the day before she had spoken to her husband of it:

"I am under the surveillance of my housekeeper as thoroughly as though we both were Jesuits, and she had all the secret power of her Order to back her," she said, with a nervous laugh. "She looks as though she had some mean nastiness of my life in reserve in her hands, ready to lash me with it some day. Laugh as you like," annoyed, "but I have something more to tell you. The other day she heard Honora named as my heir, and since then she has regarded the child with a positive malevolence. Credit me, James, that woman has power to injure us. My instincts never deceived me yet."

"She seems to me an altogether harmless and commonplace person, Hannah." But his quiet eyes followed the housekeeper whenever she came in that day. He was jealous of anything that concerned his niece, Honora.

Madam Galbraith, having hung the lamp carefully, turned its full light on the staid figure before it, inspecting her with her air of cool domination. She had a habit of meeting with absolute silence enemies with whom it was not worth while to wrestle: it insured their defeat. Even women whom she caressed were dwarfed by her coarse strength, recognized themselves as pretty, dollish, incapable, liked to get away from under her eyes. But the little housekeeper met her with her usual undisturbed, practical air.

"Do you want me?" knocking her ash-stick on the floor. "Why do you follow me about?"

"Only for orders, madam," promptly. "Do you expect other guests to day?"

"I expect my—my late son's wife."

"I know that. I have kept a fire in the west chamber for her for two days."

Madam Galbraith waited for a moment, and then would have passed her, nodding slightly, but the woman put out her steady hand, detaining her. There was a moment's pause before she spoke:

"I heard—a rumor perhaps—that her son was alive and coming with her. Your grandson. Shall I prepare for him?"

She looked up and quailed momentarily before the stern regard fixed on her.

"It may have been gossip. It came from some words you dropped, madam. You believed him to be alive."

"There is doubtless much gossip and cackling among my people over words which I let fall," calmly. "But few of them would venture to carry them back to me again. Why do you do it?"

The woman's face was bent thoughtfully on the floor, but there was no reply.

"What is your motive? You have a motive."

"Yes. I have one," boldly.

"Come, that's better! Be candid, child. What do you want from me?" good-humored with the first hint of a chance to give.

"I? Nothing."

"Do you play the spy from sheer love of the part, then?" with a sneer.

"I—a spy!" the pale, thick nostrils dilating suddenly. "And yet," slowly, and considering, "I deserve it, perhaps. But I am a poor dissembler. Better I had faced you at the first and told you my errand. I did my work badly."

"You did it badly," with her seldom-used manner of a great lady towards her serf. "Never burrow or mole with me, woman. I cannot be hurt by it. I've crushed many a snake in the road yonder under my sole," glancing down at the large, coarsely-shod foot.

"I never meant to hurt you," absently.

"You meddled from curiosity, then? Like your sex." Madam Galbraith had risen into her favorite strident, lecturing voice, and rolled the words like sweet morsels under her tongue. "I boasted of you as the first woman I knew who did your work for your work's sake. Like a man. 'When women learn to work like men, they'll be paid like men,' I said. And I paid you, while you were thrusting your hands from sheer idleness into the lives of other people. From a silly hankering after romance."

The solid, brown little figure had remained immovable during this harangue; but at the last words she looked up, anxiety and pain, that would not be controlled, breaking through her apathetic face. Madam Galbraith fancied that they had been so controlled beneath it for years. But her voice was, as usual, quiet and moderate. "Did I thrust my hands into anybody's life?" looking at them as she raised them. "I think sometimes there is a stain on them heavier than murder. But it was not my fault. Could I have kept them out? One cannot live alone. People are so tangled and knitted together—together," touching her breast lightly. "You are at ease, thinking only of yourself, and you waken some morning to find a great wrong piled up against your soul in which you had no part. But then you give up your whole life to undo it. That is no romance. It is a common, practical matter."

Madam Galbraith scanned her keenly a moment. "American women delight in giving up their lives," she began to dogmatize, "for one whimsey or another. They throw themselves, with half-grown bodies and brains, at the feet of the first fellow who makes them a pretty speech, and make a god of him; and then they nurse and drudge with their children until at middle age they are but hysteric, sickly pests of society. And single, middle-aged women, like you, undertake a reform, to amend some wrong, as I judge you mean to do by your incoherent talk. That is the maddest of all," raising her voice when the other would have spoken. "Let criminals alone. When the taint's in the blood, it will break out. I never knew a vicious man cured. I know—I know— The Lord's grace. Well, that will ensure them safe passage over the river yonder. But He never really cleans them till they come to the other side. That's my experience. What do you see in my face?" stopping short before the searching eyes bent on her.

The woman turned away with a long breath. "No matter. I have undertaken no reform." She continued, after a slight pause, "It matters much to me that you should not think my work romantic or foolish. It is practical—a mere act of justice. But I have given up something for it. I am a middle-aged woman now, as you said."

"What had I to do with it? Why did you spy upon me?"

"You had much to do with it," with energy, looking her straight in the eyes, without blenching. "I traced you out and came here to find what manner of woman you were—genuine and sound at the core, or a monstrous sham, a thing of straw. I came to see what your noted generosity was worth. I find it a ready charity when the stomachs of men are ailing, but—"

"Go on," quietly. "What do I lack?"

"There are worse pangs than those of hunger. To-day will test you. But I believe this of you, Madam Galbraith: that, in a case more pitiful than that which Christ wept over, you will be as merciless and cruel as the grave, ignorant and faulty as you are. I am rude. But I have worked for so many years to this end, and my disappointment is bitter."

"To-day will test me, eh? Then we will wait until to-day is over to pass judgment," gravely. "I think you wrong me, good woman;" and, turning from her without farther question, she went with her heavy steps down the hall.

The other looked after her earnestly. "There is something greater in the woman than I thought," she said, seeing how calm her temper was.

Then she went into her own housekeeper's room, full of her prim, comfortable belongings. It was not likely that she would be suffered to occupy it after what had passed, and it was, after all, her only home. For two years she had been here, first coming as seamstress, then growing into a necessity in the household as Madam Galbraith's almoner, Honora's teacher in embroidery, and the like. Working constantly towards some end which to-day would foil. One would have looked for some womanish tears of disappointment, now that she was alone; but she only sat down, with her hands folded over her black silk apron, and looked steadily in the fire, presently pouring herself out a cup of tea from a kettle on the hob, and sipping it slowly. Then she went to the mirror and carefully brushed her shining black hair, winding it in smooth folds about her round head; pinning on a clean collar; knotting the bow at the throat above the chocolate dress. Not a twinkle of vanity in the steady eyes; yet these little pinnings and brushings and tea-drinkings had given her constant comfort during the years just gone—years whose strain of anxiety and loss had not worn a wrinkle in the smooth, pleasant face, but only blanched it slowly, slowly, leaving it every day more chalky and bloodless.

CHAPTER VIII.

"Now, no wood-fire can equal this, in my notion. All it needs is its poet," said Mr. Rattlin.

Paul Dour looked down compassionately both at the fire and the little man, who, in his shining black suit, new from crown to toe, looked more than ever like a cricket. They were on the rug before the great parlor-fire, waiting for breakfast. The fire lacked the poetic element belonging to the wood, Paul thought, but it at least was warm. The jetty, glossy masses of coal were built up on a glowing crimson bed, and out of their hearts burst scarlet, yellow, violet heats, little Ariel flashes of emerald and blue, lightening and vanishing before one could wish them to stay; sturdier flames of a lusty saffron hue climbing tipsily up to the great background which walled in the mass of color—a mysterious cavern heavily hung with black, plumy wreaths of long-ago dead smoke. Caliban-like faces were looking at him out of the depths of white heat, and fairy leaves and grottoes rose in endless fretting of gray moss over the fieriest spaces.

"There's the poetry and welcome of a hundred forests gone down into that fire," persisted Mr. Rattlin, blushing at his bit of fancy. "What's your green log, sputtering lonely and black, and sending up sometimes a shower of hasty sparks, to that?"

Dour smiled superciliously. The fire — the whole ménage — was Western: comfortable and wasteful. He weighed the country and its people in his palm, as it were, as though he had been here for a month. He could give the essence of the whole in a two-page magazine article: he would like to sketch in his coarse-grained hostess by one or two Hogarthian lines; for the usually good-tempered youth was nettled. Madam Galbraith had given him a tremendous grip of her broad, warm hand, in sign of welcome, the evening before, and was altogether cordial and gracious. But when he spoke of his name, she stood on guard.

"Dour? No, lad, you're none of our kin. The letters spell the name, maybe, but not a bone in your body or blink of your eyes," tapping his narrow chest, and her probing eyes scanning him as though he had been a head of cattle that she meant to buy. "Eat, boy. Eat heartily for a fortnight, and I can tell better what you're worth. That slop-diet down East takes the healthy stamina out of men's brains. Your creeds and theories are as airy and bloodless as ghosts, for every-day use, till they have Western strength put into them."

"If the old Western women were such coarse beasts, what were the young ones?"

Pleasanter to look at, certainly: there was quite a crowd of them between him and the window which framed the frost-touched autumnal landscape without. Mrs. Rattlin smiled, delighted, over to him from where she sat, regarding with wonder her own crossed, idle hands:

there were half-a-dozen thinly-built matrons, in dyed second-best silks and fly-away caps on their black "fronts," who never had heard of transcendental philosophy, and knew New England only as a great factory of teachers and clocks, yet whose faces wore that late, wise, patient beauty which comes to the ugliest good woman in middle age. There were Rosy and Gerty, brimming over with smiles and blushes and dimples, in a group of girls. The poor little souls had said their thankful prayers that morning with energy. The soft, warm-colored merino dresses fitted so perfectly, and were just short enough to show the dainty boots beneath; and the dear children were so snug and well fed; and there was the charming young man of the coach to meet; and after whispering half the night about him, they were sure he was not engaged. O love! love! And to be married, and to have a house of one's own!

Dour, however, looked loftily down on them as on playful kittens. His wife must be an intellectual helpmeet. All the girls were gathered about one who attracted him curiously. She wore a delicate, lavender-colored dress, which might, he thought, have been born into the world ready made, to suit a fresh, innocent young girl in the morning. This one looked singularly fresh and unhackneyed, even beside those rosebuds, Rosy and Gertrude. But she was painfully ill at ease, had lost her color, glanced about in an evident appalled perplexity to know what next to say to them. With them, conversation was brisk enough: it turned incessantly upon "he," "he"—went, came and ended there. The "he" meant half the young clerks and farmers in the county. The talk sounded very sweet and maidenly to the men in the room, Paul included, and pleasant as the chirping of young birds in spring.

Madam Galbraith nodded good-humoredly as she came in and heard them. "Come to me, Honora. Chatter away, girls. Only don't let the hare chase the hounds. Come to me at once, Honora," sweeping on towards the open breakfast-room. But the young lady slid away from both her and the girls, Paul saw, and in the confusion of placing the guests contrived to ensconce herself snugly by her uncle; and they two made a long, comfortable meal, and were merry and sharp-witted together at their leisure. The little girl had no style at all, but Dour determined to test what sort of metal was in her for an intellectual helpmeet, hearing that she was Miss Dundas, the declared heir of the Galbraiths.

Eat? How they ate! Smoking venison, juicy beef, game, corn and wheat biscuit in yellow and snowy flakes, coffee, whose very vapor was invigorating, rising in a thin smoke from the old-fashioned, ball-like cups. But the damask was white and satiny, the silver heavy and glistening, the air fresh, the circling faces happy. Dour found the new atmosphere, after all, fill his lungs satisfactorily, and ate until every one else had finished. Madam Galbraith, too, formed a fitting head to the great table. If her guests had been marshaled by the thousands, the genial hospitality in her face would have met all their needs. Now, as hostess, she was her real self: her acrimony, her anger against her housekeeper, her fierce, nervous watch for Tom's wife, were gone, and one could compare her to nothing but a generous, great fire, to which all her world was free to come and be warmed. Her dress transformed her, too: the glistening white hair was rolled into a sort of natural crown, and the royal purple color which she wore draped her broad, athletic frame as aptly as long ago the brawny limbs of bluff King Hal.

After breakfast was over, Paul dexterously made his way through the talking groups to the window where Honora stood by her uncle, cutting the leaves of a new book for him. Mrs. Rattlin had confided to him that the young lady had been given the education of a man. "Latin and Greek, sir—Greek!" Besides, it was a pleasant picture in the morning sunshine—the slender, bending figure, in its clear lavender drapery, and the gray-headed old man leaning back in his arm-chair, watching her through his half-shut, kindly blue eyes. Miss Dundas, too, had an unusual air that attracted him, as though she were something that had been kept clean and set apart—the bell of a wild columbine with the dew yet upon it. But a stupid woman was a flower without fragrance. She stiffened awkwardly erect, and blushed unbecomingly as he came up. Her lucid eyes grew vacant.

"The very sunlight gives thanks today, Miss Dundas."

"The sunshine? It is good for the late wheat."

Paul picked up her book.

"A Review? What a comfortable age it is that we live in, when all philosophy and science comes served to us in such dainty *plats!*"

"The book was for her uncle. It was too heavy reading for her."

"Oh, of course, of course. Her shelves now," patiently, "were no doubt filled with poetry? It was the highest utterance of truth, after all, and most native to a woman."

"No. She read no poetry. There were a few old verses she learned long ago, all that she cared for—"

"In modern poetry, yes. He understood that. Because her mind had been attuned to the grand Greek measures—Sophocles, Æschylus—"

"Greek prose or poetry had been but so many wearisome verbs and nouns to her," with a contraction of her forehead as if the very memory of them ached there. "She cared for no books."

"What! Honora here?" cried Madam Galbraith, coming between Paul and her niece. "My little girl will entertain you poorly, Mr. Dour," tapping on the girl's head critically, as though she were a puppet which she was rather proud of having made. "She has had no companions but her uncle and myself, and never has learned to make talk. Go, Honora, bring me a nosegay—chrysanthemums, anything. The ground's tabooed, young sir. I'm always frank with young men," with a shrewd smile after Honora as she went out. "I've had the whim of rearing one woman who will go to her husband, when I find him, ignorant of flirtation or Platonic friendship. The French know how to bring up girls. Young people strike out nothing but ill by friction together."

Paul colored and laughed. "It is a fair warning," he said. But the forbidden apples became suddenly very tempting to him.

"But is my little Nora altogether an idiot?" demanded Mr. Galbraith when she came back, and, throwing down the flowers, took up the paper-knife again. "No books at all?"

"None, unless when I can do no better," with a decisive little nod, speaking quick and quietly, now that she was alone with him, and with a clear, fine intonation. "They're so dead—to me. But then *I* can do no better. Yet it is something to read travels: you put a window in the house and Egypt or the Alps outside. But I think books are but a poor sort of life."

"What is better, Nora? You love nature, eh? your flowers, the old river here?"

"Not much. I like to see the crops come up well. But the sunsets you watch, uncle, and the storms and moonlight—now, they're all very much alike to me."

"What do you care for, then, child?" leaning forward and watching her attentively.

"People," laying down her book and knife and looking at him gravely. "They're the only things worth anything in the world to me. I'd rather," a curious intentness coming into her brown eyes, "hear Rosy and Gerty tell of their lovers, or their father talk of his chance of a better salary, than read any poem that ever was written."

"How is that, Nora?"

"I don't know," slowly, as one who was totally unused to put her secret thoughts into words. "Books tire me as much to-day as when you used to call me dumb Nonny. But to hear people talk brings all the good and bad in me up, uncle. I think, sometimes, I can see God and the devil through them, and Christ walking the earth. I can see in that way how all of us need

Him. I think, sometimes, it is in me to give some great help. I seem to come so near to everybody," growing slightly paler, her face more intent. "But no one knows I am near to them. Nobody but you, uncle. If there's any words here," touching her breast with a fine smile, "they'll never be spoken. I'm afraid I will be a very dumb woman. Stupid Nonny to the end."

"I'm afraid you will, Honora. Of all women or children I ever knew, you are the most reticent. Why, in all your life, dear, this is the first time you have spoken in this way to me. And the words now come almost against your will."

She did not reply, the awkward dumb spell being on her again, apparently, but brought a chair and sat down beside him, as usual. They were such constant and gay companions that people saw in Honora's face, when talking to him, a most winning and potent charm, and found her motions free and graceful—a noiseless music. But apart from him the poor girl stiffened again.

The old gentleman, with his new clue to his darling's heart, found a fresh zest in her old habit of incessant questionings about the outdoor world, her keen, silly interest in even the children about her, her awestruck faith in the learning of Mr. Dour and the beauty of Rose and Gerty.

"I think he is *épris* with one of them," in an eager whisper. "They have so many lovers! And their manners are so finished, uncle! Pray notice."

"Quite finished, my dear. They never will alter."

"I suppose not," wistfully. "But that sort of thing comes by nature. One need not try to gain it?" anxiously.

"No. It's too late, poor Nora," laughing quizzically. "You've moulded yourself on your old uncle too long. It's a hopeless case, Pet."

There was a sound just then of wheels crushing over the pebbly drive, and within a hush and stir and significant glance from one to the other as Bob Penly's coach bore in sight, approaching the hall-door.

The four-horses drew up with a flourish, and Bob, jumping down, opened the door and rattled down the steps for a small woman, in a gray traveling dress, to descend.

"Mary Jennings." But the words were spoken aloud by no one.

"Tom's wife," to Madam Galbraith. The woman who had stolen her son from her, hidden his child, and forgotten them both in the arms of another man. The watching crowd about her hardened her heart. Seneca should have said, "One is never less a woman than when with women." Had she been alone, she might have put her arms about the stranger's neck and given her a kiss in which her dead son had part. As it was, she remained standing, surrounded, as it were, by her court, to awe and abash the poor wretch.

"Where is my husband?" she asked. "He should be here to receive Mrs. — Duffield. And Honora?" She had a mind that Mary Jennings should see her accredited heir at once, and realize her own lost chances. Honora stooped behind the curtain, and opened the low window, nodding significantly.

Mr. Galbraith got up. "Yes, my dear, yes. I'll go. Let the women settle it. Thank you. You are always considerate, Honora," his voice shaken a great deal. When he was outside, he went slowly down the garden-path, forgetting to put on his hat, muttering, under his breath, "Well! well. To bring their quarrel over his grave!" He went out into the open fields on one of his long tramps, and did not return until near nightfall.

Honora, behind the curtain, looked after him, hesitating how to follow him unseen, when her aunt summoned her:

"Miss Dundas, you will come to me." At the moment the door opened and Dallas Galbraith's mother stood in the entrance. She cast a startled glance up the wide room, which seemed to be lined with strange faces, paused, and then advanced directly to the farther end, where the stately, lion-faced old woman waited for her. But the way was long, and Madam Galbraith's inflexible eyes, on which her own were fixed, took the strength from her.

She stopped, made a step or two, and faltered again. There was an instant's pause—too short to bring in Madam Galbraith guilty of rudeness, but long enough for a woman's petty cruelty—when Honora Dundas went quickly forward to her in the face of them all, very pale, but composed,

"You are welcome home," she said, gently, putting her arm around her. "My eyes are quicker than yours, Madam Galbraith," playfully, but looking in the old lady's eyes steadily. "It is your daughter Mary."

It was not the first time the old lady had found this pure little lump of clay, which she was moulding into a proper woman, turn into a bit of iron in her hand. Tableau and punishment were brought to the shabbiest of conclusions; but she put a good face on it, strode up with her hand out, blotting the little Dundas girl quite out of the matter, talking inwardly to herself with more vehemence than even her energetic greeting expressed:

"You are very welcome." (So! so! Tom *had* some excuse!) "I did not send for you unless I chose you to come" (fresh as a rose, after all that she has lived through!)—"unless I wished you to feel at home here. Take off your wrappings, child, and veil." (There's a deal of outcome in that face. Tom never had the upper-hand here.) The quick, intelligent glance with which Mrs. Duffield took in her new surroundings piqued her; also, that lady's society-bred lack of emotion. "Now we can see your face, my dear," with a courteous smile. "We've all heard it was well worth the seeing, eh? And it is rather late in the day for me to make acquaintance with it—which is hardly my fault." (I stung her there, I hope!)

Mrs. Duffield untied the inside rose-colored strings of her gray bonnet, and lifted it off with an obliging smile, as one would uncover a picture. "My beauty was never of the brilliant type. 'Winning,' rather, both my husbands thought. But it is altogether gone, as you see," pausing, as if for inspection. "Only my mouth and chin remain unimpaired, I believe. May I go to my own room?" after a moment's pleasant waiting. "I've reached that age when one needs a little repairing before meeting criticism," touching, with her light, fluttering fingers, the flossy puffs of brown hair that framed her sweet, oval face. "This dear young lady will lead me there, I'm sure," patting Honora on the cheek. "And a cup of tea and morsel of bread, if you please? I'm quite famished in your mountain air," with a pretty imploring motion. Then, laying her hand on Honora's arm, the little lady swept out of the room as naturally as if it had been always her home, with a half smile in her eyes for everybody they fell upon, that prophesied friendship as soon as they should know each other. Madam Galbraith stood in the middle of the room looking after her, with her gray eyes nearly closed, drawing a long breath, that sounded like a whistle.

"*Our* mountain air!" gasped one of the matrons to whom Mary Jennings had brought milk for many a day.

"My daughter-in-law no doubt assumed a new face and new manners to suit the world in which she lived," tartly, scowling on the speaker. "But '*Turpis Romano Belgicus ore color*,'" she added in a lower tone. She had been a bit of a Latin scholar, and kept some odd fragments yet with which to appall weaker woman.

But inwardly she only said, over and over, to herself, "Tom's wife? Tom's wife?" Her big bones and her homeliness never had oppressed her as now, in the presence of the daintiness of the woman for whom Tom had left her; but the heart beneath them never was so sore, or willing to be tender.

Honora followed up the stairs in a new flutter of admiration. Mrs. Duffield tripped before her into the room, threw her cloak on the bed, spread out her fingers before the fire: as usual, her every pose and motion was confident, complete: she took possession of the scene, as it were, by each, and made herself first actress in it. If she had been in the Sahara desert, she would have done the same thing. Nora brought her her satchel, uncorked the perfume-bottles for her, forgetting to be shy and awkward in her eager, dumb attention; standing by her as she loosened the waves of chestnut hair, and pushed it back from her peachy cheeks. This was a higher type of beauty than even Rose and Gerty's; and this manner! Honora secretly determined to copy it diligently.

There had been a great deal of work upon the details of that chamber. Even the servants had caught the idea of old Madam Galbraith when she superintended its arrangement. The lowest among them knew that Tom's wife was coming back forgiven to long-offended authority, and did their best to express that forgiveness in every pleasant little detail of comfort, and to give her the idea of a home. But incurious, winning little Mrs. Duffield was apparently blind to offence, forgiveness, or offered welcome. Her gray eyes swept over the room, and speedily the easiest chair was drawn to the warmest corner. She changed her dress for a flowing wrapper, and then ensconced herself in it.

"Now, my dear girl, a footstool. Ah-h! this is comfort. I wonder, madam, are they bringing my tea? Pray, do not ring! I was just born to be a trouble!" with a blush and laugh of deprecation to the person she addressed, a small woman, in a dress of dull chocolate-color, with a pale, sensible-looking face, who had been standing by the fire when they entered. She rang for the tea, as it was her place to do, being the housekeeper, but she forgot her place afterward, standing in the background, watching every movement of the stranger with a curious, breathless interest.

The scrutiny did not at all disturb Mrs. Duffield. Mentally, perhaps, she shrugged her shoulders, comparing the Western servants with those of the East, but she said nothing. When an overloaded tray was brought in, too, although she merely pecked bits of the various dishes, like a bird, she passed none by untasted nor unpraised. While she was eating—

"Now, my dear," to Honora, "could you not ask that delightful, curious old lady down stairs—your aunt, I believe—to come up and take a cup of this delicious tea? I should so enjoy a cozy chat with her! She would find it much easier to become acquainted with me thus, *en déshabillé*. What are you laughing at, child?"

Honora checked her laugh, but stopped, with a puzzled face, to stir the fire and lower the curtains before she went to execute her venturous errand. She found Madam Galbraith surrounded by a group of men, discussing the chances of coal in a new mine she had just opened. Her opinion was counted as heavier than that of most men in the county, usually, being weighted both by money and a broad, far-seeing business insight. She had made herself, too, what none of them were—a practical geologist. She was talking vehemently when Honora came in:

"Our young men go scampering off to raise cattle in Texas, or lay out agueland along the Wabash, and turn their backs on our own soil without once looking into it. It's the richest land in the Union, sir! I know it. Why, even the water of my creek yonder burns with fatness. Well, Honora, what is it?" as she pulled her sleeve. "Wants to see me, eh? In her own room?" a pleased softening coming over her whole face. "I see, poor child! She wants to make sure of my forgiveness," under her breath. "Pray, excuse me, gentlemen."

Honora ran quickly before her. She met the housekeeper coming out of Mrs. Duffield's room, and found that lady sipping her tea in an agitated manner, her cheek a trifle less deep in its peach-bloom.

"That is a most extraordinary woman, Miss Dundas. I think she is a little deranged. She watched me in so peculiar a manner that I asked her if she had business with me, and she replied that she had hoped for my help, but that she feared she had trusted to a broken reed. She is a lunatic, evidently. I will speak to Madam Galbraith about her immediately."

"I hope you will not, Mrs. Duffield,"

eagerly. "She's entirely sane. Why, she's one of the few people I know who, I think, have something to do in the world. I'm very fond of her."

"Oh!" looking at Nora with an amused, palliating smile. "But you are so young, my dear! I assure you that she is deranged. People who think they have a mission, that way, get one idea in their brains and go butting their heads against everybody with it. You meet plenty of such people in the East. You may safely set down anybody who is very much in earnest as being unsound in their intellect. But here is your aunt," rising and putting out her white hand with a winning smile.

"Yes, I'm here. You may go down, Honora. Just ring for this tray to be taken away. So you wanted to see the old mother, child?" putting her big arm over the other woman's shoulder and looking gently in her face.

"Yes; I thought it would be nice to have you here. Do take a cup of tea. I'm very fond of tea," chirruped Mrs. Duffield.

"Are you, my dear? It always seemed a faddling kind of drink to me. I drink water. Sometimes home-brewed ale. Sit down, sit down." She placed Tom's wife back among the dainty frills of the blue chintz chair and looked down at her a minute, as she might at a pretty picture; then sat down herself in front of the fire, a hand on each knee, waiting for the servant to leave the room, her eyes bent thoughtfully on the floor, her face growing corrugated and stern.

The door closed at last. She gave herself a mastiff-like shake, turning to the sweet-looking little woman, who lay back stirring the tea in the cup which she had retained, admiring its amber tint in the firelight.

"You had something to tell me, my dear?"

"No," nodding brightly. "Nothing in especial. I thought we would talk of old times or friends in the neighborhood, perhaps. I have been a long time away."

Mary Jennings? The old lady gave one haughty sniff, then checked herself. "You have suffered a great deal since then, they tell me," with great gentleness in her masculine tones—"a great deal of poverty and want which never should have been the lot of my son's wife. I'm glad that you chose to talk to me about it. I was afraid you might have some fear of the old dragon, even now."

The fresh-tinted face looked at her steadily over the cup until she had quite finished. "My dear Madam Galbraith," Mrs. Duffield then said, calmly, "you have never suffered poverty or want, or you would know how silly it is to go back to rake up their ashes. *I* never do it," and she lifted the spoon to her lips again with a firm hand.

"You are very wise," after a moment's pause. "You'll think me a brute to drag it up again. I was unkind and unfeeling."

"No, no!"

"Yes, I was," dogmatically. "You wished to talk to me of Tom?"

Mrs. Duffield was silent a moment: then she drank all there was in the cup hastily, as if to check some words that would have risen to her lips. "No. I did not wish to speak of Tom," slowly. "He was a dear, good fellow, and I was very fond of him. But we'll not talk of him, if you please."

His mother looked at her long and shrewdly. "I believe you. I believe, whatever were your faults, that you were fond of him and tried to do your duty to him. I heard that you supported him during the last years by sewing—that no wife could be more faithful or forbearing."

"By sewing, or sometimes by washing," in a matter-of-fact tone. "There was no merit about it. He was not able to work, and I was; and we had to live. What a fine view of the mountain gap there is from that window!"

"Not able to work? Whose fault was that?" in the identical bitter key with which she used to rate her drunken boy. "He gave up father and mother, and manhood itself, for liquor. And at the last to hang on to Mary Jennings' hands for his food!"

"Mary Jennings has never complained of him. I told you I would not talk of Tom, least of all malign him when he is dead. He was a good, generous fellow. He would have clothed me in velvets if he could."

"He left it for another husband to do that," savagely.

"Yes. Captain Duffield always dressed me well. He had ample means, you know. But it was a matter of pride with him. I do not think, indeed, that my second husband was what you would call a generous man."

"Will you answer me some questions, freely and fully?"

"With pleasure," smiling pleasantly.

"About your past life. It was partly for that reason I sent for you here."

The white forehead knit itself impatiently for a moment, but only for a moment. She rose and placed her empty cup on the mantel-shelf, and then settled herself comfortably back. "I will tell you anything you wish to know. But let us be brief, please. I never go back to find trouble, and it is so wonderfully pleasant here!" with a little shrug of enjoyment through her graceful little body.

"Is it, my dear? I hope you'll find it like home to you. I wish you to be happy here. I think you were fond of Tom."

"Oh, I am at home anywhere!" cheerily.

"It was of your second marriage that I wished to speak," for she had not courage to utter the real question aloud: now that the time had come, her heart seemed to choke and halt in the ponderous, steady beat which it had kept up for sixty years. She began far off from it.

"My second marriage? You have heard some unkind stories of Captain Duffield, I suppose?" flushing a little. "There has been a great deal of gossip carried back here about him, and his abuse of me, but I will not discuss it. He is dead now, and these very clothes that I wear are paid for with his money. I don't spare it in that way. I know he would be better satisfied to have it so. He had very good taste in dress."

"Yes. The gossip says that that will account for your marrying him."

"That is unjust," after a pause.

"There is another cause given, which, perhaps, is nearer the truth: that you and your boy were starving, and you did it for his sake."

There was no answer. Mrs. Duffield had her face turned from her.

"I do not ask you this to pain you, God knows! But I have a right to know something of my grandson."

"Dallas is dead." The voice sounded like that of another woman.

"I do not believe that he is dead. I never believed it. I am a strong woman. I have great property. I can give to him more love and power in the world than a hundred weak women do to their sons. I never believed God would leave me an old, dry, barren stock. I wish to know from you what manner of boy my grandson is, and how you lost him, as plainly and directly as you can tell me."

But Mrs. Duffield, instead of replying, got up and walked to the window from whence the mountain view opened, and stood there, her face resting on her hand, regardless of the heavy steps of Madam Galbraith walking impatiently to and fro. After a while she turned. The old woman could see no change in her face, and broke out again:

"I believe you cannot understand the craving I have for that boy. He is the last chance for me that my flesh and blood shall live in the world. I'm a lonesome old woman at times. What you can understand is, that I need an heir. Honora is but a chit of a girl. I grudge the place to her. If my boy had lived, I could have given him a position stronger than any man in the West."

Mrs. Duffield seated herself again, stretching out both her hands over the fire, as if she were chilly, When she spoke, it was with her ordinary courteous quiet. Something was lost from the quality of her voice, but Madam Galbraith's ear was too coarse or careless to discern it.

"The place you could give him does not import anything now," she said. "That was but a small matter."

"You have not answered my question," sternly. "I have a right to know something of the boy."

His mother hesitated before answering. "Yes, you are Tom's mother," she said, at last, in a low tone. "Well, there is not much to tell. When I married Captain Duffield, he promised that Dallas should be reared as his own son."

"Out with the whole truth! You married him to keep the boy from want. Why did you not apply to me?"

"No, I would not do that. I was determined that Mary Jennings' child never should come to you for alms. I had some spirit, some pride then, before my little boy died. Now—well, I think the world owes me some comfort and a living," with a laugh which was not pleasant.

"Go on. Dallas—?"

"Captain Duffield did not keep his promise," hurriedly. "He petted and fondled me at first, but he always hated the boy. He was a devil! Then, when the abuse began to extend to me, Dallas fancied that it was on his account—that if he were gone, his mother would be taken into favor again. And then—"

"What? Why do you stop?"

"He left me. He ran away," standing up and turning her face to her. Madam Galbraith drew back, startled, when she looked at it, and then put out her hand soothingly.

"Is that all you want to know? I never have named my boy since he died until this day."

"One moment. He died?"

"I traced him to the coal-mines at Scranton. I thought I saw him the morning I came there, among the diggers, but that very night there was an explosion in the pits, and he was in them."

Madam Galbraith did not renew her offered sympathy. She went stalking up and down, her arms folded, muttering at intervals in answer to her own thoughts. Mrs. Duffield looked up at her at last. "I must ask you to let me have rest, Madam Galbraith. I must be alone."

"Certainly. I will leave you alone, my dear. But tell me first, did you ever find that boy's body?"

"No."

"Well, then—but no matter what I think. It's all clear to *me*, however."

Mrs. Duffield waited until the door was closed behind her: then she locked and bolted it, and, throwing herself on the bed, cried long and bitterly. But silently, without either moan or sob: it dully seemed to her as if, with her dead boy, something in herself had died, for which she ought to make moan as much as for Dallas. She fell asleep after a while, tired out; but when, some hours afterwards, the great bell sounded for dinner, she arose refreshed, and began to dress carefully. It was a favorite dress that she wore that evening—a pale brown silk, with lace on the bosom and at the wrists, and at her throat a pearl clasp, to match a ring on her hand.

CHAPTER IX.

THERE was a foot-bridge which crossed a mountain-stream within sight of the house; and that evening, when the innumerable lights began to twinkle from the windows just before dusk, a man was pacing to and fro on it, with slow, grave and somewhat uncertain steps. The athletic build of the man—his features, cut in a few bold and fine lines, as if by a master's hand, who intended the face to express a great thought, should, to be in keeping, have carried with them a certain elasticity, vim, buoyancy. But his voice, when he bade "Good-day" to some passers-by, was marked by the same slow gravity and uncertainty as his motions, and his look had a curious, hesitating quality in it, as of a man set down in an unknown world, who held his own force in reserve, and tested the worth of the place or people who came beneath his eye. Now and then, however, he stretched his arms and drew vigorous breaths of the nipping air, suddenly looking up to the mountain as if air and mountains were new to him: keen pleasure flashing into his face; but it was observable that he neither sang nor whistled at these times, as a young man would be apt to do, gayly; that he kept the fur cap which he wore closely drawn over his forehead, not removing it to the passers-by, in the country fashion; even clasping his bare hands behind him, when they came up, nervously, as if his flesh were in some sort disgraced, and he concealed it even from himself. As the dusk came on, he stopped from time to time, shading his eyes and looking intently up the road that led to the long, lighted front of the Galbraith homestead; but it was not until the moon began to whiten the edges of the distant mountains, and throw their melancholy shadows over the sloping farms and glistening creeks below, that he saw a small, cloaked figure crossing a stubble-field toward him, the only moving object in the lonely twilight.

He was in the shadow when he first saw her, and came hurriedly out into the moonlight to meet her. It had become a fault of the man, perhaps, to dislike concealment—to drag everything into too open a light. The woman was short and solidly built, dressed in some dull brown color, as he perceived when she pulled off her cloak, which she did when she saw him, hastily, as if stifled and feverish from repressed excitement. When she came up to him, however, she put out her hands without any show of haste.

"Lizzy?"

"Yes, Dallas." But in spite of her quiet, her eyes passed over his face with the hunger with which they might look at one given back to her from the grave.

After that first greeting, they walked, side by side, silently down the road to the pier of the little bridge. He stopped there.

"Take off your hood, Lizzy."

She obeyed him, going out where the white light fell full on her prim figure and face. Something like his old quizzical smile came up on his face as he looked over the smooth hair, the black silk apron, the knitting stuck in its sheath. For five years Elizabeth Byrne had been planning and looking forward, in her sensible, practical way, to this night, when the boy should be free again: now it had come she could have cried and sobbed over him like any other hysterical woman. But she only took his hand up suddenly.

"It's just the old Lizzy, Dallas," and then let it fall again.

He nodded gravely. Presently he put out his hand, unseen by her, and felt with his finger and thumb the little shawl which she wore, one of Manasquan weaving, with the same slow, amused smile.

"I knew I would find you as you are," he said. "After the first letter you sent to me, in the worst days I thought of you as the one thing unaltered in the world to me."

She listened eagerly, her head bent down, noting every slowly-pronounced word or inflection of tone, as if by it she sought to read something that was hid beneath.

"I meant to tell you, Lizzy, to-night, all that I owed to you."

"No, Dallas, no."

"No. Only this: that twice, when all my own courage and strength were gone, and I had the means in my hand to rid myself of the hell I was in, I lived on, only that I might not disappoint you."

"That is over. You will make the best of your life now, for my sake?"

"For my own—for my own, Lizzy," with a manly heartiness in his voice that warmed the blood in her heart. "I'm but a young man. It came to me suddenly one day, when I had been there but a year, how young I was, the strength and health that was in me, the long life that was before me to fight down whatever it was that had dragged me back."

"The devil, Dallas," nodding sententiously. "It is Satan who brings fortune as unjust as yours was on any man."

"Whatever it is, is strongest in the world, Lizzy—call it God, or devil, as you will. If a man succeeds, it is by virtue of his own skill or honesty or virtue; though, in spite of these, he can't keep out disease or death at the last. I've had some time to think it over. But I did not come here to argue theology with you. I determined that day to make the best of my life, and I've not lost an hour since in whining or in idleness."

Whenever he spoke, she fell into the same observant, watchful attitude. He noted it anxiously. "Why do you listen to me?" hastily. "Have I caught the prison-accent? I used some unusual or vulgar word without knowing it?"

"It was not your accent I thought of. But there is a great change in it. You speak English: correctly, as far as I know. But with effort—as a foreigner would."

He gave a pleased, boyish laugh. "I tell you, Lizzy, I've had myself in training since that day. Night and day, in the vilest ward of the Albany prison. There has not been a look or a word or a thought with which I have not tried to work up out of that slough, to make a man of myself. What to avoid was plain enough: it was the very air I breathed. The chaplain was very kind. He got me off hours from work, gave me books besides those which you sent to me—books on my old drudgery, chemistry, and the like. Drudgery, but somehow I could not live without it."

"The five years have not been altogether a gap in your life, then?"

"No. But after to-night we'll speak of them no more." He was silent. Presently, a hickory bough, on which he had been leaning, snapped, as if it were a straw in his hand. He threw it down, turning to her again: "So much of my life was given up to—let us say justice. I will not begrudge any sacrifice I made. But it is done with now. To-morrow I will begin again, a new man. I am not so far behind my fellows."

Still the same eager watchfulness when he spoke, a silent scrutiny of something apart from and below the meaning of what he said. He was conscious of it, uneasily.

"You find me altered, Lizzy?"

"I have scarcely yet seen your face," evasively.

He put up his hand to remove the cap, but let it fall again. "Some other time," he said, hurriedly—"some other time."

"Why did you never admit me to see you, Galbraith? I came with a permit three times, and was turned away by your wish, they said?"

"Did you think I would be seen by you—there? You do not understand men, Lizzy," with a bitter laugh, and then was silent.

He fell into this grave silence at the end of every sentence, as though a difficult, useless task was over, of which he was glad to be free. The poor Manasquan girl began to think she did not understand men. Five years ago, a wrong, which seemed to her more cruel than death, had been done to this boy, of whom she was fond; and because she was fond of him, or for some deeper reason, it had been plain to her that the wrong must be atoned for. What she had done to this end, what given up, she only knew. She had looked, to-day, to receive the boy, the wreck of what he was, in body and mind; diseased, revengeful, vicious, perhaps. She was prepared for that. It was in her to care for him during the rest of her life with a mother's tenderness. It seemed to her but just that she, of all other people living, should do this thing.

But it was a man that was before her; strong, heady, reticent; swayed, she saw, by some dominant purpose, which she could not discern; with all his old outward frankness, yet holding his own and her secret thoughts in check. He, "passing through the valley of misery," had found in it a well from which he drank stronger waters than any she had known; whether good or ill, she had no means to know. His tone, his manner, his look were unanswering to her.

"Women like me can hardly understand a man," she broke out impetuously; "but I have instinct, like a dog, Dallas; and though you should not say a word of it to me, I know that I have made a mistake. I can serve you but little. You're no longer the same clay that I am: you've grown beyond and outside of me. My plans may do you harm, if they touch you at all."

"Is it so, Lizzy? Then it is I who am in fault," with a good-tempered, soothing smile. "What plans have you made? Had I a share in them? How is it that you are here?" his tone abruptly changing. "I thought of you always as at—the old place. Married, perhaps," with studied composure.

"No; I am not married. Nothing has happened to me of which I could make a story for you. You know why I wrote for you to come here? You will trust me that I did the best I knew, however it may end?"

"I trusted you, or I would not have come. All the money I have made there barely sufficed to buy these cheap clothes and bring me here. I've learned to count the cents, yonder, you see."

She hesitated. "You did not receive a package from me, then?"

"Yes," gravely. "But I can take nothing from you but advice, Lizzy. I am a man, now."

"I hope you will not let your pride hinder my plans, Dallas," timidly. "Do you know where you are?"

"Yes," quietly. "I learned it to-day. This is the Galbraith land, that should have been my father's, and, some day, mine. That is his mother's house yonder?"

"Yes."

"You wrote that there was an opening here for me. Did you bring me to ask alms of her?"

"Not alms. Hear reason, Dallas," catching his arm. "You brought your pictures with you? You believe still in the talent you have?"

"I've had nothing to shake my faith in it," his voice growing pleased and confident. "Genius or not, no prison was able to bar it out from me. The pictures were called wonders in their way. I," hesitating, "had difficulty in their making."

"Madam Galbraith is a lavish patron, Dallas. She is no mean judge of art, they tell me. Her money rusts in her hands; and she uses it at times to educate poor young men. Since I have known her she has sent a painter and musician both to study in Rome."

He listened silently as she stammered through. "And, as I supposed, you wish me to share in her bounty?"

"I wish you to share in what is your own," energetically. "You are the heir. You have a right to the very sums which she is squandering."

"In a word, I am the last of the Galbraiths. I heard to-day that she has chosen as her heir an innocent young girl. Look at this." He drew off his cap and let the light fall on the close shaven head and on a brass ticket which he wore inside of his coat, on which was engraven a number. "*I* am a convict. Number seventy-nine. For five years I have had no name nor place in the world other than that label and the crime attached to it. Am I in a fit case to claim my inheritance?" The grave reasonableness in his voice alarmed and dismayed her, being beyond her comprehension. She made a woman's answer by pulling at the ticket with tears in her eyes, as though the years of which it was the sign could be destroyed with it. It made his prison-life real to her for the first time.

He put her back gently. "No; I wish to wear it still. I have a reason."

Lizzy sat down on a heap of stones and said nothing. It did not matter whether she ever spoke again, she thought. Her plan had been that she would bring Madam Galbraith and her heir together by means of his skill as an artist, and that, when occasion came, the discovery would be made and he would be lifted at once into the purple and sunshine; marry Honora, perhaps, and end all like a fortunate fairy-tale. The plan had seemed to her commonplace and practical: now it stood in its true light—a womanish, weak, fanciful vagary. She looked up when he began to speak again slow and deliberately:

"I have a reason for keeping that prison-life before me, and for making what hasty strides I can towards fortune. I can push my way in the drug business. I know what the books can teach me, and there's a place where I can get a foothold. But that will be slow, and hard work. Now these—" he touched a small roll which he carried with a sudden lightening in his face. "If I have any power, it is as an artist. If she were to buy them at a liberal price, it would enable me to follow my art for life. It would help me sooner to my other purpose."

"You will conquer both fortune and fame, Dallas. Some day you will marry—" But she had put the fancy about Honora aside. The man moved and talked laboriously, painfully moulding himself into some fancied likeness of a gentleman.

"I have not thought of marriage since I was a boy. There is a woman, if she be not dead, whom I would like to see before I die—when I make myself a man of whom she would not be ashamed."

Lizzy's heart suffered a sudden qualm as she thought of his mother yonder at the house, and of what she was. What if she had searched out these kinsfolk of his, and dragged him here to face them, only to work ill?

But she would risk it. "Are those the pictures? Come with them, then, to Madam Galbraith;" and drawing her cloak about her, she went on before, hastily, without giving him time to answer. Dallas followed, in his usual slow, hesitating gait, covering his pictures with his coat to protect them from the dampness as tenderly as a mother would her baby.

She saw him several times, as they went, stoop and dig out some root with his fingers, as if the old habit were too strong for him; tasting them, and smelling the mould on his fingers with a long breath: once, when he saw that she detected him, he got up hastily with a nervous laugh, saying, "I beg your pardon. I begin to understand that I am a free man."

CHAPTER X.

THEY entered the house by a side-door. The long Thanksgiving dinner was over: through the basement-windows they caught glimpses of loaded tables spread for the farm and house servants, for it was the old lady's whim that all her friends and laborers on these high holidays should eat under her roof, and of the same food: the best she could give them.

Coming in from the solitude and darkness without, they plunged at once into an excess of light and warmth almost offensive. Lizzy hurried through the narrow, darkest halls to her own room, Dallas following her slowly. Each open door he passed framed a glowing picture: the deserted dining-room, gaudy with china, broken fruit and dripping wax-lights; the dim, quiet library; some young girls dancing in the great hall; sad pictures, strange and unfamiliar to him. How strange, or burdened with what significance of his loss, Lizzy, in her haste, did not consider, until, with her hand on the lock of her own door, she turned and looked at the pale face of the tall man who waited behind her with his bundle under his arm. She drew him in, and tried in her tactless way to show how awful was the pity in her heart for him.

"I should not have brought you here. I did not think how you had lost all these things."

"No matter. It will come right."

But she persisted: "I did not think what it would cost you to find your father's house what it is, and you a convict. You have had hard luck, Dallas."

"There is no such thing as luck. It is something that fights against us. Let me sell my pictures now and go."

She looked at the homely, powerful face, at the coarse, ill-fitting clothes, the brass ticket on his coat, and her heart failed her. How could she take this man down to them, and say, "Here is your son." Let him first have the chance to make the man of himself he purposed.

"Give me the pictures," she said. "Wait for me here."

In a few moments she opened the door again. "You must go down, Dallas. Madam Galbraith will see you herself." He went before her now, grave and silent. It seemed to her, as she followed him with trembling, cowardly steps, that the factitious, gentlemanly air which he had sought to acquire disappeared from him. She caught a glimpse of the wide, firm mouth, the sane, dark-blue eyes: this was more like the old Dallas she knew, who used to go slinging through the woods, his basket strapped upon his back.

"Where am I to go?" pausing in the great hall. She pointed to the open door of the library, where Madam Galbraith stood in front of a low, clear fire, and then followed him, far behind.

Dallas went in alone. He stopped where the shadows of the great bookcases fell heavily. She was leaning forward, her knuckles resting on the gaudily-colored canvas that was spread out on the table before her, while she inspected it contemptuously. So this was the test to which her charity was to be brought before night—a case of unappreciated genius! Some needy kinsman of her housekeeper's, doubtless: she had not forgotten her insolence of the morning.

She looked up at the tall figure in the shadow, contracting her eyes to see him better. But it did not matter what he was: she had nothing for him.

"You are the person who was mentioned to me as in need of assistance?"

There was no answer for a moment.

"No. I asked for no alms."

A thin, quiet-looking gentleman, reading by a lamp in the corner, laid down his paper suddenly as Dallas spoke, looking nervously toward him; but, after a moment's doubtful pause, adjusted his spectacles again and went back to his Times.

"No alms, eh?" with a satirical smile, passing her forefinger over the picture. "Your wings are stronger than those of most young geniuses. I find them usually quite willing to accept a gratuity—for the sake of art."

"I brought you my pictures to sell. I wish to take nothing from you unless I give you your money's worth."

Her manner instantly changed. She took up the canvas, scanning it for a few minutes attentively and not unkindly. "Then our business is speedily closed. I will not buy the pictures. That is all?"

"That is all." Dallas did not move to reclaim them, but stood absently looking at his father's mother, forgetting almost to breathe in his intentness. A curious instinct of kinship took possession of him, looking at her: in his large-boned, muscular body, which he inherited from her; in the bluntness, the fierce temper, the quick, generous blood. All shame was gone from him for the moment, and out of his old Manasquan life simple-hearted Galbraith, struggling to be a man, felt himself her son, and altogether worthy of her.

"You hope to maintain yourself by your art?"

"Yes," as if waking from a stupor, "I mean to do it."

"Then I will be plain with you, young man. Your fate may depend on it, and some day you will thank me for my candor." She paused abruptly, as the sound of some one singing came from an adjoining room. The voice was a singularly clear and natural one, the song mere snatches of some old ditty, chanted carelessly, but there was a strange flavor of heat and pathos in it. Madam Galbraith held up her hand attentively. When it ceased, she said to her husband:

"It is a wonderful gift, James. It startles me, sometimes, coming from so dull a child. Though Honora is affectionate—affectionate," waiting with a pleased smile for the approaching footsteps. Dallas and his fate, which she meant to control, had dropped altogether out of her mind. They heeded him no more than if he had been a stock standing there.

The trifling neglect woke him with a shock to his real self. His place for life was fixed. What was he, with the prison-brand on him and through him, the meagre education which he had acquired out of odd books in the hulks, to these people? He would turn his back on them and go down where he belonged. The struggle was hopeless: one-third of his life was gone in it already.

The door opposite to him opened and the singer came in, and, with a surprised look at finding the library occupied, went over and stood by her uncle. Only a simple, embarrassed young girl; but it seemed fitting to Dallas that she should have sent music before her to announce her coming.

Remember, he was just clear from the gangs of the Albany penitentiary, made up from the vilest slums of New York: for five years he had not looked on a young, pure woman. She came to him, too, at a moment when his brain was quickened unnaturally with repressed thoughts and passions. The effect was strange and lasting. Whatever famished, vague longing had been in him for that part of God's world which was pure and tender and holy, woke at the sight of her into an instant, inexorable pain; cried out within him, as the spirit which possessed the man whose dwelling was among the tombs, with a hunger for which he had no words. It was not woman or love which she alone suggested to him. She seemed to be the very type of that life from which he felt himself this moment to be shut out by his wrong for ever. There was no trifle which he did not note, the dim-lighted, scholastic room that framed her, the delicate, fleecy dress, the face, wonderful in its truth and childlike content with life. By some subtle instinct he understood at a glance the full relation between her and the old man on whose shoulder she rested. He too was fit to be their friend—one of a company from which all the world might be shut out.

With that thought he turned his back on them suddenly. Madam Galbraith resumed her interrupted lecture, clearing her throat:

"I think it but right to warn you of your defeat, young man. There is not a single evidence of power in these pictures. They are weak and turgid in design, and faulty in execution. You have not the first idea of the art. Give up the palette and go to breaking stones on the turnpike, and it will serve you better in the end."

"Hannah!" remonstrated a mild voice behind her.

She placed the picture before him by way of reply. Mr. Galbraith held it to the light a moment, and then shook his head gravely.

"I fear that there is but little promise here," gently. "Stay. What coloring is this which you have used, sir?"

Dallas hesitated. "I worked under difficulties. The colors were extracted from bits of woolen cloth, earths and vegetables which fell in my way."

Honora stooped over her uncle's shoulder eagerly. Madam Galbraith took one canvas again with a muttered "Tut! tut!" of surprise, inspected it for a moment, and then turned towards him, rapping on the table. "That pleases me!" vigorously. "There's no genius there, but there's wonderful persistence. I think well of you, sir! There is something better than genius in a man who tries to work out his worldly salvation through slow patience like that. How long were you in making those poor daubs?"

He was so long silent that they all looked at him curiously. Madam Galbraith repeated the question more gently than before.

"How long?" dully, bringing his thoughts back a long way. "I think it was but five years that I worked at them. But I was a boy when I began them in Manasquan—I had many friends there. Now— I think much of my life has gone down into those poor daubs, madam; and I fear it never will come to me again."

"And you worked, thinking that they were well done—that you had genius—all the time?"

"Hannah!"

"I mean to do something for the boy, James. But this interests me. What plans had you, if you succeeded? What did you aim at, eh?"

Now, Dallas, standing among them, ill-clothed, the jail-bird consciousness heavy on every limb and thought, afraid to speak lest some vulgar word should mark him, was conscious that his secret aim had been good and high. It was weak and worldly to assert it—to force himself up by it for a moment to their level. But it was natural; and he did it, watching eagerly Madam Galbraith's eyes for approval:

"I have had great difficulties, in making my pictures—in making myself anything I would be. I have had difficulties all my life. When I painted those pictures there were people about me whose chances had been worse than mine. I could not get away from the sight of them. They were before me night and day. I could not speak to them nor help them."

As his voice grew steadier and changed in tone, Mr. Galbraith laid down his paper and watched him keenly; but Dallas still stood in the shadow. He went on slowly, choosing his words:

"One thinks many thoughts in five years of silence. It is like going down into the grave and looking back on one's life. I hoped to succeed in painting. My pictures were called wonderful. I still think there is something in them."

"Humph! Go on."

"I never expect to marry or to love, as other men do. There are reasons. But one must have a plan; and mine was, when I had succeeded, to save as many as I could from the difficulties which I had known. I thought of taking little children out of the slough where I was, and doing what I could for them."

But he was rewarded by no kindling in the old woman's eye. She was intolerant of anybody's charity but her own.

"Little children, eh? And you a hearty young fellow! Whining about the sores on society! Go to work; marry a healthy girl in your own class, and make your own children what they should be. There's no better work for any man or woman. Now, I'll tell you what I'll do. You must have some knowledge of chemistry to have worked out this trumpery," pointing to the pictures. "Go to my woolen mills. They are ten miles down the river. I'll give you a line to the overseer. They can make use of you in the dyeing department. A low place at first, probably. But the point is here: Mr. Galbraith and I employ a great many people, directly, and in concerns in which we are stockholders—mechanics, sheep and cattle-raisers in the West, and professional men. My rule is—for he leaves the business to me—that capacity only shall command place. I will keep my eye on you, and I am much mistaken in you if you do not rise rapidly. You can go now. Honora, have you done studying those pictures? Elizabeth!"

Lizzy came from the door.

"You can take the letter to the young man. I will write to Mr. Vogt to-morrow."

"It does not need," said Dallas, quietly, yet speaking directly to the woman whom he knew to be his father's mother, and stopping now to choose no words. "It would be better for me and for you if you touched my fate no farther. I will be made and unmade no more as a puppet. I have been thrown to and fro like a football in the world by one chance and another since I was born. Surely it is time that what strength and purpose I have should count for something in my life."

Madam Galbraith made no reply. Something in the low, passionate tones seemed to stun her with a sudden remembrance. She put out her hand to silence him, looked at her husband as for protection, not against Dallas, but some ghost which his words had raised. He went on in the same repressed voice:

"For you, some day, knowing what I am, you may wish you had dealt with me differently. It does not matter now. You were unjust to me—unjust to my talent. You jeered at the one good purpose I had. You think you know men. Yet you would have given a place of trust and security to a felon."

Mr. Galbraith rose, and, putting his wife quietly aside, went into the shadow where Dallas stood, looking at him steadily before he spoke. He did a strange thing, too—took the man's hand in his delicate fingers, and held it a moment, as though he tested something by that means.

"You were a convict?"

"Yes."

"For what crime?"

"Forgery."

Mr. Galbraith was silent a moment before the next question: "Were you guilty?"

"No."

"Why do you suffer the man to palter with you, James?" demanded Madam

Galbraith, sternly. "A criminal never before has crossed my threshold with my consent. There is no hope for a man who has once sinned, in my judgment. Go to your room, Honora. This is no place for you."

Dallas did not glance at the girl. "I was not guilty," he reiterated, looking directly into the eyes of the old man.

At that, Honora stopped, near to the door, with a dreadful pity in her face, close to the indistinct figure in the corner, that was to her, so far, little more than a voice and great trouble, such as she never had met with in the world before.

"You are blind!" cried Lizzy, passionately, going up to Madam Galbraith. "You are blind and cruel. You play with the soul of this boy, and think it is sport. But it is your own heart that will suffer in the end."

Galbraith laid his steady hand on her arm to quiet her.

"Blind I assuredly was," said Madam Galbraith, calmly looking down at the pale little woman before her, "not to guess at the character of the man from his whining philanthropy. Why, too, would an honest man stand back in the dark and hide his face in that manner? We have had enough of this. What does the man matter to us?" But still she hesitated; for when once her hands had meddled in the control of any man's life, for good or ill, it chagrined her to let it go. Mr. Galbraith walked slowly to and fro, near to his grandson, his hands clasped behind him, his head sunk on his breast. He halted when Dallas spoke to him, silent and watchful.

"You are right in your judgment," he said, still looking steadfastly in the old man's face, which seemed strangely worn and gray. "Luck, as the world has it, has gone against me, so far as to bring me in guilty as a thief. So that I matter nothing to you." For the first time his eyes went wistfully about the room, and rested on Honora. "I matter nothing to you or yours?"

Something in the man's voice held them all silent: it was as if he pleaded for his life with a Judge invisible to them—beyond and above them.

He turned to the door at last. "Let it be so. The prison was not death, as I thought it would be when I went into it. There are other lives, thank God. than this which you live. But I wish that one among you had believed in me and thought me an honest man."

Honora, standing near the door, came up to him with the picture in her hand. "I believe in you," she said.

"Honora!"

But Mr. Galbraith put out his arm before his wife. "Let the girl alone," he said, sternly.

She did not hear them: she trembled very much, though not with fear, and stood silent before Dallas, who drew back from her.

"I never knew there was anything like—like this in the world before," stretching out her hands toward him. "I can do nothing. I cannot help you. Only, I believe that every word you have said is true, if you care to know that."

Dallas stood erect. He thought he had answered her, but, instead, his eyes only devoured her face with a meaning which neither he nor she understood. She laid down the picture, and then, as she was turning away, offered him her hand—a rare sign of equality for Honora to make to man or woman. He hesitated a moment. "I think I am fit to take your hand," he said, gravely, holding the pure, warm little palm firmly in his own.

The door closed behind her. "It is time this matter was ended," said Madam Galbraith, savagely. "There is nothing more to be said."

"Nothing more." He took up the pictures which lay rolled on a chair, and was turning away, when a curtain at the opposite end of the room was pushed aside, and a clear voice cried: "The Colonel tells me you have been enacting a bit of a tragedy. You talk loudly. Had you really a dreadful convict here?" A lady, in a soft brown silk, with lace edging it, and a pearl ring on her hand, came in smiling, and, still hidden by the sombre shadows of the fire-lighted room, Dallas Galbraith faced his mother.

PART IV.

CHAPTER XI.

MR. GALBRAITH came before his daughter-in-law hastily. "The —the man is still here my dear," mildly, motioning her back, "and his guilt is far from certain—to my mind."

He turned to brighten the flickering lamp, but succeeded in extinguishing it instead, his fingers being, as usual, nervous and incapable.

But before his warning, Mrs. Duffield's quick, comprehensive glance had detected the dark figure in the background, and she stopped, hesitating and shocked. To find that she had been, unconsciously, at once both rude and cruel, demeaned her, and wrung her heart with a real pain. She had seen the man draw back at her words and lean for support on the door-jamb. Poor wretch! Angry tears at herself rushed into her eyes. She made no word of apology to him, however, but turned with quick tact to Mr. Galbraith.

"I have no doubt that he is not guilty, sir. You would know an innocent man by instinct. While I—"

Madam Galbraith turned on her. "What ought my son's wife to know of crime or criminals? Young women chatter of vices now-a-days with which, in my time, they would have been counted besmirched had they but known the names. Even Honora—bah!"

Her son's wife lifted her sweet face and bright eyes gently toward her, her hands folded with a most nun-like simplicity: she paused a full moment before replying, taking counsel with herself, how, while she made amends to the poor outcast in the corner, she could send a decisive lance against the old griffin who was bent on riding her down.

Now Lizzy had no thought for any of them but Dallas. In this pause she tried to draw him out and away. That first sight of his mother, before the light grew dim, had shaken the slow, affectionate fellow in a manner which it had frightened her to see. She comprehended now what secret had lain hidden in the boy's breast during the years in which he had been a vagabond for this woman's sake: she began to see, looking into his pale face, turned toward Mrs. Duffield, what pith and strength there was in him beyond other men. In another moment the hungry cry, repressed for a life-time, would break forth, and he would throw himself at the feet of this shallow, selfish fool. Lizzy caught his wrist with a grip as strong as iron —or common sense.

"Dallas! come away from them," she whispered.

He shook her off gently. "It is my mother!" his lips hardly moving: standing still, listening breathlessly as the sweet, decided voice of the little woman was heard again, an expression of infinite pathos and tenderness softening the stern features, as if the childhood and boyhood lost for her sake had returned to the uncouth, hardly-used man at her first familiar tone. With the stupidity of a man he saw no under-meaning in her words.

"What do I know of criminals?" she said. "Why, I have felt what the temptations are—down there. Where you never have gone, dear Madam Galbraith. And I have very little faith in the law's justice, either. Prove a man to be poor and tempted, and half the jurors in any court count him guilty. I have been poor myself, you know. I am familiar with the landmarks of that country," with a piquant little nod and triumphant flash of the gray eyes as the indignant blood rushed into the old lady's face.

"It was my fault that my son's wife should have such knowledge to boast of," in a humiliated voice.

"Oh, indeed, no! You are generosity itself. But a little hard on ill-doers—ah? as a just woman should be. And we were sadly in the wrong—*mea culpa!*" beating her soft bosom with a smile. "But I learned in that way to sympathize with this poor fellow here."

There was an embarrassed silence. The graceful little lady standing on the hearth-rug was left master of the field. The very fire-light seemed cognizant of her prettiness, of the completeness of her dress and delicacy and Christian compassion: touched the flush on her cheek and the thoughtful bent head with bright admiring gleams. What with the tears in her innocent eyes, her well-fitting gown, and the integrity of her position, Madam Galbraith and Lizzy appeared old and dour and misplaced beside her, even in the eyes of the fastidious old gentleman pacing nervously to and fro. As for her son, the poor convict in the corner, the very lightest breath she drew, or motion of her white hand, seemed, in the fervor of his admiration, a thing distinct and new, and touching him as no miracle would.

Presently she turned her eyes on him, full of womanish tears; for in truth she was sore to think of what she had done, and would have gladly made amends. When their eyes met he began to tremble, let fall the roll of canvas which he held, and took an uncertain step toward her. He put up both hands to tear off the cap which covered his shaven head.

"Mother. It is I—Dallas!" he would have cried, but the words died in his parched mouth.

She watched him with alarm, the tears suddenly drying up in her eyes. "Does your friend wish to speak to me?" she asked of Elizabeth, with a certain sharpness in her tone.

Lizzy came in front of Dallas, putting him back. "He does wish to speak to you, Mrs. Duffield, but not now. Not before strangers. He fancied, from your kind words, that you would understand and feel for him. But it will be better you should see him alone."

"Oh, assuredly! Take him away, I beg of you. Another time, pray! Another time! Take him away."

Dallas stood irresolute a moment, looking at her: then, bowing awkwardly, he turned and went into the hall.

"I think you were right," stopping and holding Lizzy by the arm. "I could not speak to her there before strangers, you know. And I meant to be something which she would be proud to own when I came— Not that it would matter to her."

Lizzy did not answer: she only held him by the sleeve quiet a moment. The door was open, and Mrs. Duffield's musical voice came out energetically. "I was so shocked at what I had done! It makes me feel like a coward to strike anything beneath me. One might as well be harsh to a servant, or crush a poor toad under one's feet in the garden—things that cannot retaliate, you know, Madam Galbraith."

"You are a good little soul, I do believe, my dear," good-humoredly.

"No, I don't think I am," coloring. "That poor wretch was going to make a scene. I detest scenes. That is the difficulty with that sort of people: they never understand the gulf between us, and at the least encouragement they press on you with their disgusting ailments of body and mind. It is so dreadfully morbid, that sort of thing. I'm not at all morbid."

"Do you hear her, Dallas? Do you hear her?"

But he was carefully rolling up his canvas with the same quiet, wistful smile. "She does not know I am her son, you see, Lizzy. I have no doubt that what she says is very true, too. She had great penetration—my mother," as they went down the hall together. "I never knew a woman with so clear a judgment and such tender sympathies. Her very voice and smile are full of mercy. Did you observe?"

Lizzy only replied quietly that a sweet voice and smile had great weight with most men, thinking that Dallas was but like the others: a few pink and white tinges in the face and a trick of ready tears would outweigh the service of a homely woman's whole lifetime. Lizzy sighed, and choked the sigh.

They passed through the halls again, she following a long way behind. What were they to do? What were they to do? Her plans and sacrifices, her prayers for him for years, had ended now in nothing. This big, clumsy fellow walking before her, who had grown so dear to her through her pity for his wrong, had been left by God to be thrust out into the world to-night, to make what he chose therein of his undisciplined body and ill-taught brain, bringing nothing out of his past life but the cheap clothes, the convict's badge and the rejected pictures which he carried under his arm. She thought of Ishmael, thrust out from his inheritance into the desert. Dallas was as helpless, as ill able to fight his way.

Had God never heard her, then? Did he make souls to suffer them thus to drift about and rot on every changing tide like bits of unclean weed? Was this the way in which Christ kept watch over the wronged and weak?

Her face grew more colorless. As she followed him, the more immediate trouble seized her: What could she do with him now? What road were they to take together? Dallas solved the riddle, passing quietly out of the side-door and turning to the mountain-path, with the air of a man the reins of whose life were always well held in his own hand. He stopped at the little gate.

"Good-bye, Lizzy."

"I will walk with you to the stile, Dallas." She took the roll of canvas from him as they went side by side, and held it. She would like to have torn it strip by strip and thrown it in the muddy stream: she could have vented on the inanimate thing all the bitterness of her disappointment in men and God, who were alike blind. She had counted so long on these pictures, and the gift of which they were the sign. They were to have been the magic key which would have restored him to family and fortune—assured him splendid triumphs over his enemies. But they had been worth nothing. God had not been just enough to give even genius to Dallas Galbraith.

But she carried the roll quietly for a few moments, and then gave it back to him without a word. The stile at which they stopped opened out into the fields on the valley side: behind them the house rose against the mountain background, an irregular, imposing mass of shadow in the pale November moonlight, its numberless deep-set, red-burning windows giving a human life to the night. Occasional echoes of laughter or broken snatches of music came out to them where they stood.

Mountains and homestead and music all symbolized in some way, and made more real to her, the power and life of ease and culture which he had lost.

"Why need you stop and look at it?" she said, with repressed vehemence. "It's too late now. You might have been master here if you had kept silence and not dragged out your past life before them all. If you had but luck, Dallas! If there were any way yet for you to become famous, to make a fortune and triumph over them! My God, if you could triumph over them!" She turned her pale, irritable face toward him, stopping astonished to see the quiet cheerfulness with which he scrutinized the old building.

"A fortune? Fame? I had not thought of that," slowly.

"That is because you know nothing of life," with impatient acrimony. "*I* know it! What can you do without them? Luck's against you, Dallas! As for me, I put my shoulder to the wheel to no purpose. You threw your fortune away to-night, and you're here, a full-grown man, with neither skill nor money. It seems to me, because of your honesty, your life is to count for nothing—no more than the thousands of dull, worthless ones that crowd the world. And that is God's justice!"

He looked at her attentively, not replying for a moment or two: "No doubt you are right. I scarcely know what pushes men up. But money or notoriety seemed very far outside of the course I planned for myself. It may have been the five years of enforced silence that makes me see the world according to my own scheme, and leave out matters so essential."

But Lizzy had time while he said this to fall into a passion of remorse: "At any rate, you were honest. I had no right to taunt you with the injustice of the world to you. If you have no chance for success, it was hardly my place to tell you of it. I am as brutal as the others in there," nodding toward the house.

"You never could be unfriendly, whatever you said, Lizzy," he said, kindly. But he made no answer about his chance in the world.

"I am not myself to-night. It was a bitter disappointment. I never looked at yon house," facing the long line of building, "that I did not fancy you as the master of it. I thought there was One who would see that justice should be done—that you should have your fortune and place."

He watched her, as she spoke, closely and gravely: it had become a habit of the man, possibly because, after so many years of compelled silence, he could not follow the differing voices readily. He nodded, comprehending her, with a slow, half-amused smile.

"I've had little else to think of than the recompense coming to you. I thought you would marry Honora—" She checked herself abruptly, with an alarmed glance at his face, but he had turned to look down the road, buttoning his coat for departure, and, though she waited for him to speak, he said nothing.

There was a silence for a moment or two. She broke it at last: "You say neither money nor fame is the end of your schemes, Dallas. What is the end? What are you going to make of your life?" adding, when he did not reply, in a hesitating, apologetic voice, "I am more practical than you. I thought I could advise you."

"'Practical,' Lizzy?" the dark-blue eyes beginning to sparkle, and giving a quick, real old Dallas laugh. "Why you give me fortunes like a fairy godmother. Practical!"

But, with a woman's keen instinct, she felt that her question had been evaded, and that the steady, kind regard which, after he spoke, he held fixed on her face, was the sign of an impalpable barrier which shut her out from him.

"First, I am going somewhere to sleep and eat. I feel the need of it. There is a little tavern back in the gap yonder, which I saw yesterday: I will stay there for the present. The Indian Queen, they call it. I can find work among the farmers."

After? But she did not dare to ask. His very candor with regard to his present work and lodging drew the barring line about him. As to the use he would try to make of this life which had been so bungled and misplaced, it was a matter, she saw, in which God alone could meddle with him in future.

"I think it is more to the purpose," he continued, "to decide upon your course, Lizzy. It will not be right for you to remain here: my crime and disgrace will be visited on you."

"It does not matter. My work is done here. I have saved some money. It does not matter to me now where I go."

He did not seem to notice the dreary voice or face.

"Who is Honora?" abruptly.

"You saw her: she is Madam Galbraith's heir. She offered her hand to you. She is a charitable little soul. They have kept her in that house yonder as ignorant of the sin of the outside world as a babe in its cradle. She and her uncle will always remember that hand-shake, as if she had been an angel who stooped down from heaven with water to cool Dives' parched tongue."

Dallas was silent a moment. "The difference between us is great," he said, quietly.

"Yes; my plan for you there is at an end."

He did not reply. They had been standing on the same side of the stile until now: he put his hand on it to pass through, but stopped with a startled glance about him.

"What is it, Galbraith?"

"A man's steps, I fancied."

"It is probable: the workmen are closing the stables about this time, and passing in every direction home through the fields."

But he still held his head bent anxiously, with his hand behind his ear to listen, and it was not until some moments after that he looked up with a sudden breath of relief.

"My hearing plays me strange tricks sometimes. When will I see you again, Lizzy?"

"I will come to-morrow to that house where you are going. I know the woman well: I can board there for a little while before I leave this part of the country: that is," hesitating, "if you would like to have me near you, Dallas?"

"I have no friend but you. You are going back to—the old place?"

"No."

He looked at her downcast face keenly, wonder and doubt and a new light coming slowly into his own, as for the first time a suspicion of the truth came to him—that the girl, out of sheer sense of justice, had given up all she had for him, and left herself bankrupt.

It was like a wide window opened into a dark, unwholesome house, this sudden sight of the woman's loyalty to him, unflinching through his low, wretched luck. He realized even in that moment that the world would be different and sweeter to him for it every day of his life thereafter. But he only said, simply, "You've been a good friend to me, Lizzy," holding her hand a moment afterward.

Downright, outwardly stupid men like Galbraith have so little of that small coin of affection or gratitude, those words and looks, for which even women as sensible as Lizzy are willing to sacrifice their lives and think themselves well paid. As it was, she was wonderfully comforted by even this touch of appreciation.

"I began to think him insensible as this log," she thought, as she watched him going down the mountain-path. "I thought he was too dull to care for what he had lost—or—or anything else. But I wronged the poor boy. Dear old Dallas!" It was so good to have something come into her lonely life, to be cared for and watched over.

The stile on which she leaned was distant one or two fields from the house. The infrequent noises had died away, and the stubbled, saffron-colored slopes, with their dark, crossing lines of hedges, stretched in drowsy quiet to the sluggish creek, glittering blackly in the moonlight on one side, and on the other to the far, dun-blue boundary of mountains. Only an occasional whoop of an owl or the trampling of horses in the stables broke the silence of the night to her ear; but she saw Dallas stop suddenly in the alarmed, watchful attitude of a moment ago. He stood motionless, stooping close to the ground—a trick, when listening, which he had learned in his old woodcraft. Lizzy strained her ears, but she heard nothing. After a moment's waiting, Galbraith stood erect, glanced keenly at the low patches of brushwood on either side, and then, turning, came swiftly back toward her.

"What do you hear, Galbraith?"

"Nothing, it is most likely. Come, I will take you back to the house. It would seem but the shadow of a sound to you, perhaps, but I fancied danger in it."

She went with him, slowly at first, but with his strong hand on her elbow he hurried her along. "Your nerves deceive you, Dallas. I often hear strange sounds and see impossible things after I have been worried and in trouble."

"Why, I thought your nerves were steel, little woman?" laughing.

"Or it might have been the throb of the creek-mill," she argued, perplexed and out of breath. "I have heard it up here on a clear night. What kind of sound was it?"

"It might have been the mill," quickening his step.

"What danger did you apprehend?" anxiously.

"None which could not be met. I am a man now," under his breath. "Here you are at home again," opening the side-door. "Do not come to me until I send for you. Good-night, Lizzy."

His grasp of her hand was heartier: there was a prompt energy in his laugh and the ring of his voice, a decision in every movement, which she had not seen since his return. It needs danger to bring a man wholly into life, after all, just as pain does a woman. Lizzy, who had drawn much shrewdness, knowledge of men and of business, and capability into herself out of these years of dull endurance, which had nigh smothered out the light in Dallas Galbraith, crept up to her room, shivering in a cold perspiration at this hint of outward danger; got down on her knees by the window, watching the tall figure going quietly down the path again, the vast, dusky landscape that yawned about him, the mountains which suddenly grew spectral and threatening to her, uncertain from which quarter the sudden peril would come, and leaving him to face it alone. She saw him halt on the foot-bridge where she had met him that evening, and pace to and fro with slow and grave composure, as though it were a friend, and not an enemy, he waited to meet; with this difference, however, that he untied his cap and took it off, showing boldly to his foe the face which he would have hid from her.

The manner of the boy convinced her that there was an absolute, tangible danger at hand: she sheltered her keen eyes, scanning the fields and crooked roads leading to the house; but not a living object appeared on the wide, solitary space. Once she fancied she saw a shadow pass and repass behind a high-set Osage-orange hedge below the bridge, stealthy and watchful as a panther; but the next moment it so blended and was lost with the flickering shadows of the trees about it that she knew she had been mistaken. Which mischance of poor Dallas' past life or ill luck of the future had taken shape now to harm him? Why could he not be left to plod along like all the rest of the commonplace world? thought Lizzy, impatiently, forgetting that about the meanest of us the panther-like dangers wait in the very trees and houses, in the souls of passers-by, only that God's arm and sunshine are between us; and we chatter as we go of sunshine and houses, and nod to the passers-by, and see nothing of God or the death behind. So Dallas, waiting until late in the night for this crisis of his life which he fancied was upon him, began to think, at last, the valley held nothing more dangerous for him than the shadows of the trees, and the throb, perhaps, of the mill-engine.

He went off at a steady pace toward the gap where the little Indian Queen Inn lay, to get his supper and a bed. Any man meeting the sturdy young fellow would have found something in his look and bearing, stamped there during the last five years, which said that he was, more than other men, master of himself—that wherever his future road might lead, it would be one of his own choosing.

But behind the hedge a pompous, well-dressed man sat, stroking his red cheeks and black beard, waiting for him to go; and in the library a quiet old man was carefully writing letters; and, in her chamber, Honora sat up in bed, shivering in her night-gown, reading Jay's Evening Prayers to put some rebellious thoughts out of her head; and they all had his future life in their hands, moulding, moulding, moulding it, and knowing no more what they did than the *ebauchoir* in the hands of the sculptor, shaping a thing which will curse or bless the world.

There was a holly-tree which Dallas had once planted by his old shanty in Manasquan, and which was putting out its slow, prickly leaves, sturdily "determined to live," people said, passing by. Yet, after all, the sunshine came from beyond the boundary of the world to warm it, and the nor'easters from beyond the sea tugged to tear it from the roots, and the worms crept to its heart, and the slow juices of the soil, distilling there since the world was first made, entered into its sap, and it lay in the work of one and all of them to make it a heap of rotten-wood manure or a tree.

Yet, when the end came, it would be seen that they had but done as they were bidden.

CHAPTER XII.

WITH quick walking Dallas could have reached the Indian Queen before midnight. But he ached in every joint. He had gone directly from the Albany prison to the cars, and it seemed to him as if the weight of all his years of confinement were still upon his limbs, dragging him down. He lagged more and more, until he came to a great wood of oaks and nut-trees. There was no more walking that night for Dallas Galbraith. He was at home now. He slid his feet along through the dry leaves until they were up to his knees. It was so long since he had heard that confidential, crisp crackle! He took off his cap to feel the wind on his forehead, sniffed the air slowly, recognizing one familiar wood-scent and then another: then the cap was thrown on the ground and the canvas roll thrust into the hole of a hollow tree, and he began to go about, his eyes brightening, his ears set, from tree to tree, from the muddy bank of the creek into the brushwood, to and fro, peering, smelling, tasting. Just as a man would come back after long absence to the house where he was born, and hurry nervously back and forth to find the old landmarks again, and the changes which had of late crept in. Here in this oak was a woodpecker's nest burrowed through the fungus: he detected it yards off by the faint, vile smell, and, though the moonlight was clouded, he found two mole-keeps under paw-paw bushes, and about an ash bough, like a ring, the varnished nest of the orange-and-purple moth. The half-dried leaves hang late on the trees of this wood, as it lies low in a cove of the mountains. Galbraith went from one old forest monarch to the other, his hands clasped over his head in his old, boyish habit, putting his ear to their trunks to discover if he could now, as he once did, name the tree by the rustle of its leaves, smiling quietly when he found he had not yet forgotten their language. It seemed to him more natural than any other.

After a while, as its naturalness grew on him and its voices became more and more those which he used to know, he leaned against a gray old oak, quite still, the large-featured, pale face pressed against the rough bark. A Pagan might have so leaned in those long-ago first days of the world, entreating, from the unseen oracle within, counsel on the riddle of his life—the love or the hate that vexed his soul nigh to death; but I doubt if to this poor fellow, as he stood, came one thought of Dallas Galbraith, his petty wrongs or hopes. Yet I doubt also if he was conscious that any voice called to him from depths far underlying his own mean life, though the mother Nature beneath him, from whose womb we all came, and whose hold we thrust from us unthankfully, tried to win back this boy with an especial pathetic tenderness—a tenderness akin to that other unknown Parent who had given him life through her. Only a great quiet came presently to him through the inarticulate murmur of the forest, as it did when he was a boy; and after a while he heaped some dried leaves together, as he used so often to do, and, buttoning his coat about him, lay down and slept until morning.

A cold wind, fresh from the frosty chambers of the east, that forced his eyelids open, and made him stand up and run to and fro to warm his chilled blood, his face heating, his eyes kindling ; he, free to go where he would. Free ; the woods, the valley full of homes, the terrible mountains open to him, and, beyond, the great, untried world. No low plaster ceiling between him and the morning of the new day slowly unfolding in heaven from dazzling wet depths of pearl and rose : nothing to hinder him if he chose to stand idle and watch the shining flakes of mist hanging over some of the far-off mountain lakes, as though the spirit of the water, escaping from its frozen body below, suffered the glitter of its plumes to be seen by the sudden day. Free—altogether free.

Here went a squirrel's scratching feet through the leaves ; there was the Indian Creek curdling over its lead-colored slate bed ; underfoot, red, trumpet and purple mosses were blackening : over all, the white hoar-frost. One had need to waken every morning for five years in one of man's reformatory schools—a slimy stone cell, with a solitary seat in one corner and a cess-pool in the other—to understand what God-meant by these things.

Galbraith's body was as healthy as that of a savage : consequently, he had sprung up from his bed on the ground with a new lightness and freedom from ache, and went down to the creek to bathe, whistling some of the old Manasquan songs. He threw himself into the water, drank it, wrestled with it, shouting breathlessly to himself, wishing he had some hearty, good fellow to keep him company. How alive it was ! how it flashed, and held him down, and closed over him ! He came out glowing, clean without as within : the slimy cell, the Galbraith house, the Something that was always against him, all sunken into miserable dyspeptic dreams.

As he dressed, he heard far-off voices calling—a traveler on the road which he had deserted hailing some laborer as he passed. Galbraith listened without change of countenance, though the voice and the steps he had heard the evening before both belonged to that nameless ill-luck that had dogged and mastered him. It was upon his trail again : he had known that last night, with the first echo of the coming footsteps. But what with his freedom and the old wood-life come back to him, the pompous, tempting voice, and the vice and misery of which it was the sign, seemed as trivial and far-off a matter as the song of the bird from yonder maple, and to call as little on him for revenge.

The Spirit of Life may wait in a sleep under the bare November trees, or a plunge in the wood-creek, as ready as in the water of the font to wash away sin.

Galbraith took down his precious roll and buttoned it up again under his coat. "Now for breakfast !" striking out for the road again.

He was as famished as a hound after a day's run : after he had leaped the low fence into the road, therefore, he did not stop to look back. The traveler, who had caught sight of him when he first left the woods, followed him unseen. There was nothing stealthy in the man's walk : it was slow, weighty, grandiloquent —quite in keeping with his handsome, portly figure and the superfine black clothes that he wore. A magnificent jetty beard rolled down over his wide shirt front ; big carbuncles shone in his breast and wristbands ; a topaz on his thick, white finger. There was nothing furtive in the dead black eye with which he scanned boldly the trees and mountains, as he would have done any earthly potentate, weighing their value in his own private, native-American scales. Most men would have gone to him for charity, if they needed it, and never have been turned away empty. But no woman would have asked it from him. He had grown fat and scant o' breath in late years, and puffed hard with the exertion of keeping the lithe young fellow before him in sight. He did it, however, dropping hastily behind a friendly tree whenever Dallas turned his head to one side or the other. He stopped, at last : Galbraith had gone into a low stone house built under the shelter of the hill.

"There, eh? Now, as I've run him to earth, I may as well go back to town for my breakfast. I'll know where to find him. An infernal run I've had, from Albany to this backwoods! I wish the poor devil had a bottle from my champagne basket. It's poor grub he'll find yonder. Never travel without your own provision—that's George Laddoun's advice." Which was the current of his thought as he swelled and strode and panted back to town. Nobody but idiots think aloud, and George Laddoun had learned by this time to keep his secret opinions to himself, even about his drink and "grub."

The Indian Queen was just waking up. It was a queer little hiding-place, built of triangular wedges of stone, mortared with what appeared to be yellow clay, and had a solid, composed look at all times, ready to drop off asleep in the very middle of the day. As usual with country houses, the trees were cut away from about it, and the sombre shadow of the mountain fell back from it, leaving it to put on its brightest good-morning face for Galbraith. Any house that was a home would have seemed heartsome to him just then, so strong and zealous was he to begin his life over again; but, as it was, never was such a welcome as that of the homely little wood-snuggery. There was a broad, short porch, holding out a hospitable greeting, with two hickory-woven rocking-chairs on it, ready and waiting night and day: there was an open door, and a wide kitchen within. Was ever a fire like that great ruddy coal monster? Was there ever a chubbier, tidier woman than the brisk little landlady turning the buckwheat cakes? Never, when Galbraith was out in the world, did they cram such small spaces with such promise of good cheer: the very walls inside were draped in hams and links of sausage, and the porch was a tangled web overhead of dried peaches and onions. There was a mossy pump and trough standing with one or two cows beside it—a peculiar breed of cows, surely, wonderfully fat and comfortable; and a boy in a red shirt stood pumping, and hitching up his trowsers with the other hand—a singularly honest-faced boy!

Dallas came up with his heart throbbing thick and hot. It had cost him little to avow himself a convict to his kinsfolk last night; but now, if these laborers had looked suspicious or askance at him, it would have been like a savage blow in the face.

Washington, the cow-boy, however, nodded patronizingly, giving his suspenders an additional tug of courtesy. The stranger was of another quality from the wagoners who made the Indian Queen their half-way house to the village. "You're just in time," he said, nodding to the steaming cakes inside.

Peggy Beck came herself to the door. "You're for breakfast, sir?" She thought the pale, leisurely man in black clothes coming up the steps was an itinerant preacher.

It marked a turning-point in his life, that this clean, honest-eyed woman should courtesy to him and say, "Sir." He colored high. "Yes, I will go in," he said. She ushered him into a square little parlor, with striped carpet on the floor, puffed muslin curtains, and a table in the centre, with Lalla Rookh and a year-old fashion-magazine on it: she pulled out another hickory rocking-chair, padded with Turkey-red cushions, for him, and put a match to the wood and coal in the shining grate, chattering about the weather, and the road, and the markets down below. Dallas sat looking in the fire, rubbing his hands.

When the breakfast was spread before him, she brought in pen and ink, and a child's copy-book with a page or two of scrawled names in front. She begged his pardon, but "Beck, He was used to being in large hotels before He was married, and He had a fancy to kerry on the house on the same plan. He'd got up a register, as the gentleman would see, for folks as stays over night. If he (Dallas) would just enter his name there?" pointing to a blank where she had calculated there was ample space for the Rev.

"My name?—my name?" said Dallas, slowly, looking at the book.

Peggy nodded and smiled, and swept the plate of cold cakes from the table. When she peeped in, after a while, Galbraith still sat looking at the copy-book, the unused pen in his fingers. All that these years had brought to him in which he had been nameless and placeless in the world came up before him. Once or twice in that time he remembered he had written notes to the prison warden, asking for books and the like, and had signed them "Seventy-nine." There was no other identity for any man in that living grave than the number of his tomb.

Now— He looked up at the free air, the blue sky outside. The tears came into his eyes as though he had been a woman. Then he pulled the little book toward him, and, dipping the pen in the ink, wrote, slowly and carefully, *Dallas Galbraith*, looking at it a long time after it was done.

Peggy carried it without a glance into the kitchen, and then hurried to satisfy her curiosity. The hand was uncertain and shaky for so young a man, she thought; while there was passing through Dallas' brain inside some confused, half-understood words of a baptismal service he had once seen: "A death unto sin and a new birth unto righteousness."

Every trifle about him conspired to add to his content. When the heart of the earth is warm, one can find flowers in the poorest soil. Peggy had laid the little table with her choice china cups and a white napkin—things which belonged only to that long-ago part of Dallas' life with his mother; for, through all their want, she had held to these little outward shows. The old innocent time was coming back then. Presently, too, he heard Peggy's voice calling to Wash to build a fire in Mr. Galbraith's room. Now, Dallas had been a boy when taken from Manasquan; after that, a convict. This name belonged to a man, respected among men. The title which every ruffian bears among us thrilled the poor lad's blood. It put him, somehow, on a solid foothold, from which the future lay within his grasp. It "hailed him thane, that should be king hereafter."

Then a little four-year old fellow, in a blue blouse (on which Peggy had just pinned a white collar), came shyly in and stood wistfully inspecting first Galbraith and then the breakfast-table.

"My name's Matt," he volunteered.

"Will you shake hands with me, Matt?" said Dallas, gravely. But he did not hold out his hand until the boy had put his own red little fingers on it.

"You had no honey for breakfast, Matt?"

He shook his head solemnly.

"Nor meat? Then here's a chair. Don't take him away, madam. I'll have him here, if you please. It's a long time since I've had a guest, and I'd like the child to be the first. Another clean plate. And a napkin. Now, Matt! You're not half so hungry as I am, I'll venture."

"Lord, sir, you'll ruin the boy!" cried Peggy, chuckling with delight. "He's allus too forard, Matt is."

"I used to be very fond of children," said Dallas. "We will be good friends in a little time."

Peggy went out to meet her husband, making haste to cram all her news, with the final "peartness of Matt," into his progress from the hay-mow to the house. When Galbraith had finished eating and went out, holding the boy by the hand on the porch, he found Beck waiting for him—a sandy-haired, stocky fellow, with his trowsers thrust into his boots.

"Morning, sir!" nodding shortly.

Dallas took off his cap and faced him as he replied. If discovery or insult was to come, the sooner he met it the better. But the close-cut hair conveyed no other meaning to the man's mind than a new whim of the townsfolk.

"You've come from the country below, I reckon, Mr. Galbraith. It's full of your kin down thar. They do say, ther's been as many as thirty Galbraiths voted on election. But I don't fad myself with such things. I grind my own grist, *I* do."

"A safe plan, I think."

"You're goin' out for a walk, sir? Kind of colporture, now?"

"No. I thought I detected a species of marl in your soil yesterday—"

"Hey? What say?"

"Marl," in an explanatory tone. "And I'd like to look into it. Your little boy can go with me?"

"Matt? Well, now, what for would you be bothered with Matt? Lord, Peggy, what's the odds for the child's new hat? She's like a cluckin' hen, Peg is! And you're going to look for marl? Toh be sure—*toh* be sure!" watching him go down the hill with a perplexed shake of the head.

It was near dusk before Dallas returned. Beck and his wife were keeping watch for him on the porch, while a compact, business-like looking man, in a working suit of gray cassimere, stood impatiently switching his boot with his whip on the lower step. His horse was waiting by the post.

"Yon's he, Mr. Evans," said Peggy, as Galbraith came up the hill with Matt riding pick-a-back on his shoulders, the two talking earnestly, as though they were both men grown.

"He answers the description." The stranger inspected Dallas keenly as he came up and, sliding Matt off, bowed in his usual grave manner to the group on the porch.

"Matt and I are ready for supper, Mrs. Beck," he said; and then, without farther notice of any of them, sat down on the steps, and began to unload, out of his hat, his pockets and bundles secured in his shirt-bosom, bits of rock, earths and roots.

"It's the man," whispered Evans, nodding confidently to Beck and his wife. "Been pros-pecting the country around, sir? Sile's poor 's high as this. Needs manure."

"You have it ready for use," without looking up from his work. "I find calcareous matter through all the shale, which is nothing else than marl. Impure, but you would find it serve. I am surprised that it is not used."

"Calcarous, eh?" doubtfully, rubbing his chin. "Like as not. I'm not up in them things. What I am up in," briskly, "is work to be done and money to pay for it. I give good wages."

Beck and Peggy had retreated to the kitchen for form's sake, but left the door open to listen. In this sparsely-settled mountain district, where every man, ordinarily, drudged on at the same work from boyhood until old age, the offer which Evans had come to make appeared to them a something out of the rules of nature. But Dallas, with his brows knit, was sorting his stones, having forgotten, apparently, there was anything in the world outside of them.

"Look hyah, sir!" said Evans, raising his voice; "I'm on business, d'ye see? I have a stone-quarry some miles from hyah, and I'm on the look-out for men to work it—strong, able-bodied fellars. Seems to me you're of that make."

"What's the color of your stone?" looking up eagerly. "Olive and buff? How high does it lie over the coal-beds?"

"High enough for the beasts to have a devil of a pull up. As for the color, you'd best come look for yourself."

"I will. Rogers suggests, I remember, that, in the high micaceous sandstone of this range, there is a probability of finding Permian fossils. I'd be sorry to neglect such a chance."

"That's as you choose. But I came on business," sharply. "If you want steady work till winter sets in, I'll give it to you. I was directed to—that is, I'll make you a fair offer."

"Work? In the stone-quarry?"

"Yes."

While Evans waited impatiently for his answer, Dallas turned over his bits of coal critically, but with his wide mouth shut firmly. He was going back to the seaboard cities to begin life afresh, but he must see Lizzy again. And his mother? He had carried the glimpse he had of her last night all day in his heart—beautiful, richly clothed, gay—under all his plodding meditations on coal and earths. There was something in the picture which gave a sore pain to his simple, affectionate nature. He was glad she was clothed in purple and fine linen every day, but the remembrance of the purple and linen made him feel more than ever like Lazarus, who lay in rags and sores outside of the palace gates. She should not be ashamed of him. She should not see or know him until he was worthy of her. He would hurry to the East, find his fitting work and make himself a man. But, before he went, he meant to steal one last look at the sweet old familiar face. He must take care of Lizzy, too, and— There was a shadow of danger which he would not fly from. But he had no money to pay these good people for his board beyond to-night.

He put down his coal and turned to Evans. "I'll work for you six hours a day, at current prices, for two weeks, perhaps longer."

"And dictate your own terms? That's not the custom with my hands. But so be it; you're a pecoolar case. I'm not the owner of the quarry. You'll come to work to-morrow. Only six hours, eh?"

"I will not work full time," gathering up his specimens composedly. "There are matters that I must attend to. And I want to look into the structure of this bituminous trough of the Alleghenies. It is new to me."

"Well, good-day. I've done my part. The fellow's in a groove now, I reckon, that'll take him into luck if he's the right grit in him," he said, in a mysterious undertone, to Beck, when he came down to untie his horse, and then, tapping his old felt hat, he rode off.

When he reached the brow of the next hill he met a horseman coming into the road from a by-path, but riding so leisurely, and turning so promptly in the same direction as himself, that it occurred to Evans, afterward, he had been lying there in wait for him. He was careful to bow as they exchanged good-day: he flattered himself that he knew the gentleman when he saw him; and there was no mistaking the polish of this man. It asserted itself from his fine open face to his fashionably-made boots. There was no blinding Evans in matters of this sort. They fell into talk as they jogged along. Such a flow of language as the stranger had! Such knowledge of the resources of West Virginia, though he confessed he had been here but two days! How the mysteries of "two-thirds representation," "black basis" and the like rattled from his tongue!

Presently, in a break of the discussion, he said, carelessly: "You came up from the Indian Queen? There's a stranger there—a young fellow that I used to know—how is this they call him?"

"Galbraith?"

"True, true! His own name, eh?" with an astonishment which he tried in vain to hide.

"Why, what other should he have?"

"None other. Only some men," with a loud laugh, "use their names as they do their cloaks—put them off and on to suit the weather. Not that Galbraith is one of that sort. He's an old chum of mine—a clever, honest fellow. By-the-bye, he has some kinsfolk in this part of the State?"

"Very far-off kin of them old country people, I judge. They're well-to-do. I've just hired him as hand in my stone-quarry."

"You have?" The news seemed to affect the man curiously, considering its trivial importance, Evans thought; he rode on in silence, a gloomy depression growing visible on his face, and when he spoke, did it with a nervous effort at gayety. At the first cross-road he turned, touching his hat courteously.

"Glad to have met you," said Evans. "Call at my house if you're long in this part of the country. Introduce you to my wife and daughters."

"You tempt me, sir. Woman, fair woman!" pressing his fat, white hand to his breast. "That's the toast I drink! But I will not stay. I came here on business that brought me from California, and I see it's likely to be a miserable flash in the pan, after all."

Having left Evans, he put his horse into a gallop to ride off some secret irritation, and apparently succeeded, for when he reached the village tavern he got off in his usual glow of good humor, joking in a lofty way with the loafers in the bar-room as he passed through.

Going to his own room, he dashed off a letter, part of which ran as follows:

"I trust you will not blame me for my failure, McGill. No man could have more influence than I to push the matter in New York. George Laddoun's name, I will say, carries weight there. But it was no go. The market's overstocked by bogus California companies: the solid men laugh at the very mention of ranches or mines, and the solid men were what we wanted. I'm afraid it is all up with us on that count. There was another matter which brought me home at this particular season, which I did not mention to you. An old friend of mine had been in trouble, and I thought the time had come when I could give him a helping hand. Before God, Mac, I'd rather have hoisted that poor wretch on to good ground again than have cleared half a million by our plan. But having tracked him out here, I find that there is a chance of his falling heir to a good estate. If that's the case, as soon as he is placed we are sure of efficient help from him. I think I deserve it from him. I took the fellow out of the gutter, though I don't like to boast of such matters. If he don't do it willingly, I've a way to leech him. I can draw on him for what cash I please. He has a bad record, has Dall, and I fancy it would surprise his family here to see it opened up. But the business must necessarily be slow. I should not wonder if I came out to you in the spring, and let it lay over until it is ripe. Meanwhile—" etc., etc.

The letter was mailed that night, directed, in Laddoun's bold, clerkly hand, to J. T. McGill, San Francisco.

Meanwhile, Dallas sat eating his supper, with Matt beside him, until that small comrade's ambition gave out and he fell asleep in his high chair. Beck and his wife, with one excuse after another, came in afterward and talked until bed-time, finding Galbraith, as Peggy reported, "the quietest man she knowed, but with a laugh that was heartenin' when it broke out. And as curous to hear our talk of how people lived hyah as if he'd been blind and deaf all his days."

Galbraith, going up to his room, found white walls, a white bed and a crackling fire. He put away his treasures of ore and coals on the mantel-shelf with a proud sense of possession, and sat looking into the fire a long time. It seemed to him as if in this pure little closet, among these honest people, he was launched, and had sailed a long way on his new life, leaving the miserable shore far behind. It was a new world in which he found himself—one to which Peggy might well guess he had long been deaf and blind. Decent, simple, kindly. The old Manasquan air was about him again. Then the hobby of his life rose uppermost in the man's mind: the faces of two or three children he had seen during his confinement came before him, as they always did now when he was alone, but this time only to make the blood quicken and his eye flash.

"I'll give the little ones a chance," he muttered. "It is not so hard as I thought to clear myself and them of that filth of hell."

It did not seem hard to him, as he undressed and lay down to sleep, to make anything he pleased of them and of himself. Galbraith's narrow brain would hardly give birth to any impersonal scheme of philanthropy. It was not love of humanity that made him a reformer, but a simple love of children, and a resolve, born long ago in the extremity of his pain, to keep back from them the wolf that had so sorely torn his own flesh. He did not leave himself out of the question either: he meant to be cultured, efficient—whatever the best man was, up in that better world in which he meant to take his part. There were some dumb words, some vague hunger within him, which he had tried to express in the poor daubs of pictures which lay under his pillow. He touched them tenderly. He believed that even yet he should find language through them.

Most of all, he thought he would like to go back to Manasquan some day, and that the people there should know him to be innocent, and be friendly with him, as they once were. But that could never be. Never. There was no way on earth of clearing himself of that stain.

All of Galbraith's ambitions and plans were as yet bloodless and colorless compared to those of ordinary young men. Of money, because of the peculiar circumstances of his life, he did not know the power. Of women, since he was a boy he had seen only those who were harder and coarser than men.

CHAPTER XIII.

PAUL DOUR, going out for a stroll in the bright Indian summer morning, saw Miss Dundas' horse and her uncle's brought up to the gate for them to mount. It generally chanced that he was near when it was time for Miss Dundas to mount. Little, plump Gerty Rattlin was going through the garden-walks cutting crimson seed-vessels from the roses, and wild cotton-pods for a berry-pot. She generally was gathering berries for that pot when Paul went out for a stroll.

He saw her bewitching face peeping at him through the bare grape vines, a cherry-colored web of chenille tied over her dark curls; so he called to her "Red Riding Hood," and bade her take care lest she meet the wolf in the way; and then sauntered on more rapidly to the gate, with a very unnecessary heat in his cheeks, while the heart began to throb under Gerty's tight-laced jacket, as she snipped at the stems with her scissors. What did he mean by that? He must mean something by that. Perhaps the wolf was—Love. He had such an unusual, poetic way of putting things! The little woman was quite willing to meet that wolf in the garden. For two weeks she had been waiting for his coming, her stupid heart in an agony of hope and fear. She was calmer this morning. Last night Paul had held her little, fat hand in his, and offered to tell her fortune, "if there were a solitary wrinkle in the soft, rosy thing." That meant everything, of course! She did not go to her mother or Rose with the story, as she had when John Stokes, in the village, so nearly proposed: she laid awake all night hugging the words in her heart, pressing all the sweetness out of them.

She went up the hill for some brown pine-cones (you could see the gate from the pines). On the path she saw a bit of paper in which Dour had wrapped some cigars, and picked it up with a frightened glance around; the twist was in it fresh from his fingers, the odor was the same which hung about his clothes. She held it to her cheek, and then, her forehead all red and damp, hid it in her bosom. The smell of Killikinick was sweeter to her to-day than attar of roses. Some day, instead of a poor bit of paper, it would be himself that would belong to her!

Then rose the spectre of a Gerty Rattlin, lean and soured and shabby. That old-maid spectre has a malignant power over girls of Gerty's stamp. She turned from it and followed Dour direct to the garden-gate. She found Honora mounted when she came up, and Dour leaning on the gate watching her. She wondered, with a quick pang, if he noticed the satiny cloth in Miss Dundas' green habit, or knew the cost of the velvet hat daintily set on her brown hair. As for Honora, inside of the habit, she was nothing to the other girl but a silly child. Paul knew, by the tingling of his blood, that Gerty and her berry-pot were at hand; but he could not afford to let his blood counsel him in this matter. This moment of mounting was almost his only daily chance of approaching Honora: old Mr. Galbraith's quiet, amused glances had few terrors to him, compared to the fierce old duenna's sarcasms yonder in the house. And Gerty, he thought, as he cut the final notches in a willow whip he was fashioning for Honora—Gerty was but a beautiful domestic animal. It was an intellectual helpmeet a man of his calibre needed. Besides— Madam Galbraith, he saw had no mind to make a protégé of him; so if fate put a fortune in his way, he would be a fool not to pick it up. And to marry Love and a troop of semi-paupers like the Rattlins! He was no Issachar to make an ass of himself for life between two such burdens.

All this as he shaped the pretty little whip. He held it up. "See, Miss Dundas. It is a wand which one of the dryads has sent you."

The "silly child" looked solemn as an owl down at him from her deep-set, brilliant eyes. "I am very much obliged to you, Mr. Dour—the dryad, I mean. We are late, uncle!" nervously pulling her rein and cantering off. "You see I was terribly in the way," mysteriously, when Mr. Galbraith reached her side. "Gerty and he were out walking. It is very pleasant to watch people in love," with a little breath of a sigh.

"It must be very pleasant to be in love such fine weather as this," said her uncle, gravely, with a quizzical side glance at her.

"Yes, I think so," soberly. She drew off her glove, but when she took the whip in her bare hand, it was yet warm from contact with Dour's fingers. She threw it down with a shrug of her shoulders, at which her uncle smiled. He always suspected the personal instincts of the cool-mannered little body to be more vehement and strong than a man's. Yet, after all, Honora's antipathy to Dour was natural. No man is an indifferent object to a woman who never has loved. Until the needle finds the pole, it sways to and fro, attracted and repulsed, with many a pang.

They made a pretty picture riding through the woods in alternate light and shadow. Paul Dour looked after them. It was, after all, a great relief when his efforts at gallantry with Miss Dundas were safely over for the day. His jokes, his elaborated wit, his delicate allusions, full of college lore, seemed to fall on her brain like Puck's fairy shafts on muddy clay. There was no response. But wisdom counseled him to persevere. An heiress who did not know her value in the market was a something not to be found twice in life. He put on an armor of severe reserve when he turned to Gerty. Before he spoke, nature, however, had the dull country girl ready armed with her best weapons. She held up her berries, modestly blushing: there was an uneasy smile on her inexpressive, baby-face terribly pathetic to Dour, and the wind, or something more bitter, had forced tears into her eyes. It would be brutal not to praise her berries. He would even walk with the lonely little thing back to the house.

It was one of those days when the departing summer turns back to give to the earth a farewell embrace, full of the passion and pathos of remembrance. The dead leaves crisped drearily beneath their feet, the shadows of the branches flickered on her drooping head, the soft curls, the wet pink cheeks. He did not walk with her to the house. There was a quiet lane over which the arching trees met, shading the path even where the leaves were gone. Dour touched her arm and led her into it. Some power stronger than wisdom was at work with him, putting the heiress in her true light as a wearisome prig, converting the world into a triumphal throne, on which he, Paul Dour, sat regnant in this rare, dreamful day alone, with one worshiper at his feet. Then some nobler impulse rose and slowly mastered him. What could God give him on this golden morning so good as this loving woman? He leaned over her, his eyes upon her face. The woody scent of the berries came up to Gerty; the lane was long: she could almost feel his breath on her cheek. Through all the years that went before or came after, that hour on the Indian summer morning stood out alone for ever in Gerty's shallow life.

They came to a little gate over which a woodbine had climbed. It hung from the trellis now in a black, tangled web, framing the girl like a luscious bit of coloring, shutting her out from the world. Now, Gerty was one of those pulpy, dumpling, pink-tinted girls whom even women like to kiss and fondle, as they do babies. It was not the philosopher Paul Dour that stooped over her breathless and took her hand. It was a better man, perhaps, inside of that educated personage: the philosopher knew the cost of marriage, now-a-days, to the price of a pound of butter: all his pockets were buttoned against it.

"You look now as you did the day I

first saw you, with your hair blown about your face. I thought Love himself must have just such an arch, coaxing smile. Whom did you love then, Gerty?"

"Father and mother and Tony and Rosy." Gerty called off the roll of the Rattlins with an unsteady whisper, John Stokes suggesting himself secretly to her, but being rejected with scorn.

"And now, Gerty—now?" shutting his lips hard as he waited for her answer.

She turned her big, deer-like eyes to him, expectant, wistful. "Who should I love?" she said, faintly. Her crimson, dewy lips were near his own; the wind blew a tress of her shining hair over his face. There was a moment of silence, during which Paul Dour's thin features grew very pale. Then he gently put down the curl, and, taking out his handkerchief, brushed some dust from the knees of his best black trowsers.

"It must be near lunch-time," he said. "Rosy will laugh at us if we stand here starving all morning."

When he had escorted her to the door he strolled off, mentally clapping himself on the shoulder. "You're an honorable man, Paul Dour!" he said. "Most men would have kissed that girl's lips," thinking in his secret soul that he would give ten years of his life for the right to kiss them. Gerty ran up to her room, all flushed and breathless, and, not finding Rosy there, threw herself on the bed and sobbed a while, getting up twice to peep in the glass, to see how she had looked through it all. It was so kind in Honora to give her that lovely cherry-colored hood! Then she went into her mother's room, and, finding her all askew and besieged by the children, began to straighten her dress and comb her gray hair, stooping to kiss it now and then. Some day she would be rich and able to dress the dear little mother in silks as rich as Mrs. Duffield's! And the children should never know the hard times which she and Rosy had felt. Never! Paul was the good angel who would carry them all through.

Honora, meanwhile, had dragged her uncle about to half the farms in the neighborhood, as she did whenever he was tractable; sitting in the house, silently listening to the women discussing the last meeting of the Female Mite Society, while he gravely inspected pig-pens and orchards. He rebelled, finally, when Squire Pool's gate closed behind them.

"I'm going up to the mountains now," solemnly. "My brain has been submerged in gossip long enough, Honora, for sound health. I think the very fountains of it must have been broken up at the last sewing-circle. You have an insatiable thirst for that thing, Pet. You sit dumb, drinking it in as a sponge would water. Never a drop oozes back again, though. It comforts me to see that," with a half-anxious scrutiny of her face. Honora was a study of which he never grew weary.

She laughed, blushing uneasily. "Where will we ride, uncle?"

"Up the mountain, if you will. To the stone-quarry. Evans has employed some new men, whom I should like to see."

"I'll race with you to the creek, yonder?"

"Very well." Honora came in first, delighted as a child, scarcely noticing that the anxious look had not left her companion's face when he rode up. She went before, after that, singing to herself, stopping to gather ferns from the overhanging rocks, calling back to him now and then. They were deep in the mountains, and the day was far beyond noon, when a sullen thunder, echoing through the peaks, warned them that the quarry was at hand.

"I did not know that they were blasting rock to-day. Ride slowly, Honora, until I prevent them from lighting another fuse."

She nodded gayly and fell back, patting her pony's neck. Mr. Galbraith drew his rein as he passed her, and scanned her quickly from head to foot. It was a speculative, critical look, as if he were about to bring her before some tribunal, and wished to judge of the effect which she would produce. But Honora saw nothing of it. He rode away slowly, going round a bend of the mountain and out of sight. She grew tired, after a while, of pacing her pony to and fro on the little plateau where he had left her, and began to inspect a dusky, half-worn path leading into the forest of gloomy oaks. What woman can resist a mysterious, unknown road?

"Maybe it is a path which the ghosts of the dead Cherokees have made at night in their old hunting-grounds while the pale-faces are asleep among the hills," thought Honora. "Or I might find Giant Despair in there, or Doubting Castle;" and, smiling to herself, yet with her heart beating a little faster, she dismounted, and, tying her horse to a tree, threw her skirt over her arm and pushed aside the prickly bushes which had guarded the entrance to the path. The forest which she entered extended over the most desolate and solitary recesses of the mountains. The path but skirted its edge: the dead leaves of many years were heaped on each side in rotten, yellow masses against the rocks. She made her way through the gray-bearded trunks of the gigantic oaks and white-ash that frowned and nodded above, holding solemn converse together up in the sunlight, as they had done for centuries. Her human voice or human steps made no more bruit in their slow, incomprehensible life than the worm sliding across their roots. Honora was always strangely oppressed by the meanings of the dumb world about her. She hurried now out from the vast solitude and twilight to find the open day. The very sunlight seemed to have lost its every-day cheerfulness, and to belong to a world wherein the earth and the sea and the sky held council together as the ages passed. The little girl shrank within herself in the silence. She was dwarfed into something miserably small and shallow: she thought suddenly, she knew not why, of her crochet, of her whole paltry, dawdling life. Coming out from the path, for she dared not follow it farther, she stood suddenly on a ledge of the precipice. There was a silence that might be felt. Was it here that these eternal hills held hid their secret? Down at her feet a wide chasm opened out to the distant horizon, a sluggish, chocolate-colored stream dragging through it, shining with a dull lustre in the sun. On either side the sky rested on the round, clayey mountain-tops, while a strong wind drove the rack of torn, dun-colored clouds perpetually to the west. The mountain-sides had been lately drained by tempests; near her, masses of forest trees had been wrenched out and fallen together, leaving great, dripping wounds in the leaden shale; farther off rose the ledges of the Old Red sandstone, streaked as with veins of blood, and uncovered to the day but for the black creepers that draped and waved over the whole mountain's side. Beyond was the limestone rock—a white, wan, implacable rampart, lost in the far distance, barring out the outer world.

Honora turned her back on it all. "Day unto day uttereth speech," she thought, humbly, "but not for such as I."

The sun shone pleasantly on the deep grass under her feet. The ledge was wide and sheltered, and there, curled up by the rock, sat a boy watching her—a queer, quick-eyed little fellow, his clothes cut like a man's. Honora went up to him quickly and took his hand. If she too had been a child, one would have suspected that she was afraid.

"I am very glad to see you," she said, with a nervous laugh. "I'm very glad. It is Matt, isn't it, from the Indian Queen? How did you come here, Matt?"

"Pick-a-back. I comes every day. I don't know you, though."

"Well, that doesn't matter. You'd like me if you did. What have you under your hat there?"

She sat down on a boulder beside him as she spoke, glancing uneasily into the woods. She was sure her uncle would follow, and, to tell the truth, she had not courage to go back into the ghostly wilderness. "What have you hid there, Matt?"

Matt gravely took up his little hat, and a six-inch handkerchief spread out carefully beneath it, and revealed a heap of bits of yellow ivory, shells and flakes of shale. Honora gathered up a handful eagerly.

"What are they, child? Did you gather them? You are an uncanny little body to find such things in the mountains. There's writing on them!" holding the shale close to her eyes.

"He'll read it for you," said Matt, composedly.

"Who'll read it? It was the dead Indians who left this letter, I think."

"Did they?" said Matt, to some one behind her, and Honora, turning, saw a tall, powerfully-built man standing on the edge of the wilderness from which she had just escaped.

"No; I do not think the dead Indians wrote it," he said, quietly to her, as if continuing some conversation dropped an hour before. "It is the print of a fern-leaf that grew a great many centuries before there were either men or living animals on this continent. Will you let me look at it?"

As he turned it over in his palm, Honora ventured to take a breathless survey of him. He was clothed in a workman's gray trowsers and blouse, his brawny arms and throat bare; a hammer stuck in his belt; his motions slow and powerful; his looks and words slow, thoughtful, as one unused to talk with men. Since she was a child Honora had been reading the countenances of men and women with the hungry, unfailing instinct of a hound. It was her one knowledge. But this man's face called to her to halt, to show her own countersign. Yet he did not look at or seem to regard her: she had ample time to find what secret meaning she could in the heavy forehead, the simple, steady eyes, the benignant mouth, while he stood silent holding the fossil to the light.

While he stood silent, the man, Dallas, was waiting for her to read him. The moment he came out from the woods, though her back was toward him, he remembered her. While he was answering her, in his cool, lethargic tone, he remembered how she had put her hand once in his, and said, "I believe in you." In *his* hand. He was a convict then. Now he had begun his new life: he had gone up on the level where she stood. He had spoken to her, and then waited to find if she would remember his voice. What was she to him? Why need he, as he turned over the poor bit of shale, grow sick at heart as never before lest she should recognize him? He had seen a puzzled glimmer of recollection on her face when he first spoke, but it was gone when he looked up keenly at her, having waited long enough for her to identify him.

"I can show you a letter which the Indians did leave for you to read, if you care to see it," he said then, stooping to turn over Matt's heap of treasures. While he was searching he heard steps approaching, and a gray-headed old gentleman, his overcoat tightly buttoned over his spare chest, came out from the forest, his thin face flushed and anxious. "You frightened me greatly, Nora," he said, gently, not heeding the man.

Dallas stood up, and, bowing, looked him directly in the face. His grandfather's eyes would doubtless be more vigilant and suspicious than this young girl's. If he was to be dragged back again into that old slough of disgrace, so be it! He had thought over his whole life coolly in the last two weeks: there was no way while he lived of proving his innocence of that crime of Laddoun's for which he had suffered the penalty, and he had come to regard it as he might a leprous taint which chance had left on him, and which no virtue or effort of his own would affect. It was the unrighteous, damned spot that would not out.

It would be but natural and right if the old man would bid him begone from the girl's presence. Again he waited in silence.

But Mr. Galbraith returned his bow courteously, giving him only the indifferent, civil scrutiny which he would bestow on any stranger. When Dallas spoke, too, there was no interest beyond kindly attention in his manner of listening.

"I thank you for your care of Miss Dundas," he said, with his formal, old-school air.

At that Dallas came a step closer to them. An iron band seemed lifted from his heart for ever at that moment. His dark blue eyes resting on their faces without constraint, filled with a cordial light new to them. He was coming to his own slowly, but when the time came they would not reject him.

When he spoke, however, it was in his usual quiet tone. "I was going to show this stone to Miss Dundas. I helped to open a mound by the head-waters of the creek yonder yesterday, and I found it on the altar in the middle."

He handed Honora the stone, on which were cut two or three hieroglyphics: her uncle bent curiously over her shoulder.

"I am ashamed to say how ignorant I am in such matters. You think this was deposited there by the Cherokees? Their hunting-grounds extended so far north, I believe. Or there was an earlier tribe—the Mannahoacs: am I right?"

Dallas hesitated. "I believe," he said, modestly, "it is supposed that the race who erected the river mounds were extinct before any known tribes of Indians hunted here. I found bits of ivory with the stone, which do not belong to this country."

"What nation were they, then?"

"I never heard the name. I do not know what people would have been likely to cross the sea so early. I know nothing of history," with a humiliated look.

"It is less shameful to be ignorant of the histories of old nations than of the wonders which lie under our feet, to which I plead guilty," said Mr. Galbraith. "Now, you, I presume, have made Indian antiquities a study?"

"No; only as they came in my way. I have been grubbing and rooting always," with a light-hearted laugh. "I have lived among plants and earths; I mean, when I could choose my life," a sudden shadow crossing his face. "As for study, when I found a line in a book that helped me I never forgot it, of course. But I had very few books."

If he spoke from any morbid fear that they would overrate him and think him an educated man, it was unnoticed by Mr. Galbraith, who was intent upon the stone. "I have been told that in the heart of those mounds was generally deposited, about one skeleton, a liver-colored dust—the ashes of burned bodies sacrificed at the chief's death. Did you find it there?"

Galbraith nodded, with a quick glance at Honora.

"You did not tell me that?" she said.

"I could not speak of death to you. I do not know why," he answered, gravely.

"Will you allow me to look at your fossils?" asked her uncle, going over to Matt and sitting down beside him, leaving them standing alone together.

Honora had laid down the lettered stone, and stood looking at the light fern-stamp on the shale. It seemed to belong to that awful world of dumb trees and mountains and the eternal silent motions in the sky: it was a message from long-ago ages coming to her direct, into her commonplace, every-day life. Nothing like this had ever touched her before, neither from books nor men. She looked up at Dallas, whose eyes were fixed intently on her face.

"Where did you find this?"

"On the other side of the mountain. The coal is written over with them."

"I have seen it burned all my life and knew nothing of it. I have ridden over these Indian mounds every day. *I* did not know that there were messages from nations, whose very names are forgotten, in them. They were only so much clay and grass to me."

Galbraith smiled. But there was no smile on Honora's awed face.

"And this little leaf grew before God made man?" touching it reverently with her finger. "And you can read the history of the Creation written on the rocks as I would in the Bible?"

"It is written more plainly here than elsewhere," said Dallas, with more than his usual effort. "There is a coal basin beginning here and ending in Alabama, and down its sides there are marks of the last drainage of that great deep which covered the earth before the light was. I had read of it before. I am trying to spell it out for myself now. Sometimes it is as plain, even to me, as the ebbings of the sea on shore when the tide is out."

"You are trying to spell it out—*you?*" She looked up at him steadily a moment, then her eyes fell. Her mind was filled with vague thoughts of the rarely-remembered time when "the evening and the morning were the first day," and the earth came forth for ever out of darkness, written over with the records of its past life. And this poor stone-cutter had taught himself to spell those records out! Now, Honora had tried to read books on Geology, and dozed over them many a time. But the heart and secresy of the mountains was different from a printed page. And this man, who seemed to her strangely akin to Nature, and offered himself to her as its interpreter, took a sudden place in her heated fancy apart from all other men.

All women are alike: Rosy Rattlin, making a Melancthon to herself out of the first divinity student who is civil to her, or ignorant Honora, her clear, thoughtful face and luminous eyes downcast before Dallas, with his gray shirt and few odd bits of knowledge. This workman, she thought, full of simple gravity and unconscious power, was fit to live on the hills and read the testimony of the rocks. Something in this fashion must have looked and spoken, when the world was young, those "mighty men that were of old—men of renown."

She looked up and found again his eyes intent on her own. The blood rushed to her face as though he had read her thoughts.

Her uncle rose suddenly. "You have been very successful. How do you find time to make your researches? You have been working for the last two weeks with Evans, I think?"

"During part of the day only. That is for money," smiling. "This is my true work."

"That is true. Come, Miss Dundas, it grows late. We have to thank you for much pleasure, sir," bowing formally and turning toward the forest. Honora hesitated. Was that all? Was she to mount her horse and ride home to supper just as on other days? As if this man were a common laborer—as if the mountains were not suddenly inscribed for her with mysterious meanings, which only he could read? Why would her uncle hurry back to the shallow, vulgar life at the house? Why could she not sit on the rocks for ever and hear this wonderful, dreadful story of lost races and lost ages? She stood slowly tying her hat while Mr. Galbraith waited for her. All that he thought of this man was that he "worked for Evans." *She* understood human nature. She never had looked into eyes so strong and pure: it was clear to her they never had known any secrets but those of Nature. When she had tied and re-tied her hat, and yet neither of the men spoke a word which would lead to delay, she held out the bit of shale to Dallas.

"It is very wonderful," she said, "and you were kind to explain it to me. I know so little." She still looked at the fern, as if her curiosity were not satisfied, cunningly hoping he would leave it with her. There was a little drawer of keepsakes, of which no one knew but herself, where she would bestow it.

But downright Dallas took it from her, as he supposed she meant him to do. "I am glad I could give you any pleasure," he said, and turned away toward Matt. But only to straighten that drowsy urchin's head: then he followed Mr. Galbraith and Honora into the woods. She could hear his steady step coming through the crisp leaves behind her and up to her side at last, just as though he did not know that he wore the workmen's gray flannel, and that there was a great social gulf between them. It proved how different he was from other men.

He made no motion to speak to her, however, but walked silently beside her until they reached the open plateau where her pony was fastened: stood, too, gravely on one side while her uncle assisted her to mount, and bade him good-bye. Dallas bowed to them both without a word, and watched them go down the steep path, Mr. Galbraith cautiously leading the pony. When they were going round the spur of the mountain which would shut him out of sight, Honora gave a quick glance backward, and saw the gray, powerful figure still motionless on the ledge, his face turned toward her. As she rode on she puzzled herself in vain. What was the meaning of the strange look he gave her at parting, different from any which had ever fallen on her? There was nothing in it which could bring a blush to her cheek, yet her blood was stirred as by some uncontrollable instinct. *What could this man ask of her?* It was a wistful, questioning look which an exile might give when the light of his home began to shine upon him far off. It was as if he claimed his own.

Mr. Galbraith, meanwhile, had mounted, and they cantered briskly down toward the valley. The sun was near its setting, and a ride of two or three hours was yet before them. But Honora's usual chatter was silenced; her uncle's efforts at conversation meeting the hopelessly unanswering face and monosyllables which generally baffled those of Mr. Dour. Mr. Galbraith looked at her attentively.

"We will be late to-night," he said: "Colonel Pervis will have reached his last rubber, and Mr. Dour have talked your aunt to sleep."

Honora pushed back her hair impatiently. "Such trifling wearies one with the world!" she broke out. "To think of men—*men*, spending whole days tossing bits of painted card about, or chopping logic about words!"

"Why, what should they do, Nora?"

"Do? If I were not a woman, I would know first what the world is which we live in. It should not be so much sand and coal to me, worth so many dollars an acre. Why I used to think the Indian chiefs were heroes, uncle, who hunted and fished over these forests, compared to our traders and shopkeepers. But suppose a man held in his hand the key to the great earth itself, to its mines of gold and silver, and could read the countless rocks, with the messages from all the past centuries written on them; suppose he knew the secrets of all the herbs and trees, and could draw health or death from them. That is a life for a man, I think."

"I did not know you had so complete a theory of life made out," dryly.

"That seems to me a great work fo. a great man."

"Honora! Of whom are you thinking?"

She started and colored, but did not look at him. "Of Colonel Pervis and Mr. Dour," she said, innocently, after a moment's pause, "and of the way in which they waste their lives. It is very uncharitable, but you suggested it, uncle, did you not?"

* * * * * *

Dallas Galbraith, standing on the ledge of the mountain, watched them until they were out of sight. He did not move even then, looking with his cool, steady gaze into the darkening valley below. It seemed to him a great chamber of peace lighted by the cheerful crimson sunset, the moon hanging pure and far, a mere ghost of light, in the blue distance. The vast, tranquil change of day into night, the silence, the brooding calm, might have made some time his every-day life, so simple and native to him was it all. It was all homelike: the melancholy sough of the wind through the far ravines, the rustle of an occasional insect in the leaves underfoot, the gurgle of some mountain spring. He could see the workmen from the quarry going down a path which wound round a far hill-side—so far that they looked like lonely gray shadows. One or two of them saw him, and waved their caps to him good-night. He was a favorite already with them all. Dallas waved energetically until they were quite out of sight. No one knew what friends were worth until they had lived without them!

But it was not the sough of the wind or the good-night of the men that he was waiting for. Hark! The wind was against him, but surely that was the echo of a horse's hoofs on the valley road! Again: and then all was silent, and she was actually gone. The sound had brought the cordial strength into his eyes again. It was noticeable that the dress and wealth which had risen up as a barrier between Dallas and his mother never suggested themselves to him in connection with Honora. Even to Dour's far-off, trained, critical eye, there was a singular native freshness in the girl which brought to his mind the bell of a wild flower. To Dallas the wild flower was near and real: its perfume came home to him as did the silence and calm of the mountains—a part of himself.

What more the casual meeting with her had been to him, Dallas was beginning, perhaps, now that he was left alone, to spell out to himself. He sat down, leaning against the rock, his hands clasped over his head in his old fashion, and was quiet a long time. Then he got up with a composed, resolute face, like a man who saw his way at last through a tangled wood. Some sudden fancy seemed to strike him, for, with a half smile, he went to the face of the gray rock, and taking his hatchet and chisel from his belt, cut the date—the day of the month and year, adding neither name nor initials. Then putting the tools away he went back to Matt, who was stretched on the ground asleep.

"Come, old fellow," said Dallas, lifting him, "the day's late, and we have a great deal of work to do—a great deal of work."

CHAPTER XIV.

THE afternoon service was over, and the sunny little country church-yard was filled with groups of the neighbors, stopping under the cedars, according to custom, to exchange bulletins of health before they took their way across the lonely fields or mounted into the clumsy old wagons and carriages that walled in the fence. Honora, who had stopped to talk to the sexton while he locked the door of the little stone church, hurried down to her uncle, who waited for her by the gate. They were both bigoted Episcopalians; fasted rigorously, went to church through rain or snow, to the great spiritual satisfaction of Madam Galbraith, who, poor old heathen! had not been there but once in two years, and then had scandalized the congregation by lecturing the rector, on the porch, about his drowsy sermon, until both she and he were in a passion.

"The sun is so warm, my dear, that I thought you would prefer to walk," Mr. Galbraith said, as she came up. "I told John to drive on."

"I'm glad of it. Mrs. Duffield rode, of course? I believe she thinks it is coarse for a young girl to tramp and live out of doors, as I do," anxiously.

"Does she? Yes; she is gone; Miss Gerty, too. Mr. Dour watched for you, but changed his mind."

"And went with Gerty?" with a knowing nod. "That was right."

They stopped now and then to speak to some of the groups of stolid-looking men, asserting the day in long-tailed coats and broad expanse of shirt-front, and gayly-dressed women, with their books in their hands—a bit of mint put in to mark the place. Then, turning from the main road, they took their way down the hillside, the cool afternoon wind fresh in their faces. Mr. Galbraith fell into his usual leisurely gait in these mountain walks, his hands clasped behind him; a youthful, keen enjoyment of life coming out on the thin, sensitive face, despite its sober framing of gray hair and moustache—an expression which belonged alone to his out-door life, as Honora knew. Nothing escaped his slow blue eye. The warm light and chasing veils of shadow on the bright bronzed hill-slopes: the dreamy brown vapor of smoke hanging over the distant village, glowing into ruby where the sun touched it: the two or three cows standing about a quiet little pool in a shaded mountain bight. He did not point anything out to Honora: she did not see the shadows or smoke with his eyes.

After a while, however, he broke the long silence. "Honora," he said, suddenly, "there is a man who has a great work, according to your theory, coming toward us—Pritchard. He is a geologist by profession."

Miss Dundas ran her eye slightly over the lean, bewhiskered little man, and remarked, coolly, that some people made prose out of anything.

"He is a very practical, useful fellow—Doctor Pritchard," continued the old gentleman. "His summer vacation is over, and he goes away next week to New Mexico."

"Yes, sir. I don't know what to make of this plant," pulling a weed to pieces, impatiently. "I've been trying to study botany lately, and I never can tell the stamens from the pistils."

"No, I suppose not. Pritchard is attached to an exploration party sent out by government. Something about a railroad, I believe. But he will report on the geology and flora of the country. Here he is."

Miss Dundas, after a shy bow, went back to her weed, while Doctor Pritchard shook and reshook her uncle's hand. He had the *empressement* of a French dancing-master; besides, he meant to go home with them to dine. Mr. Galbraith's wines were famous.

"Would you, would you, my dear sir," in a fervent whisper, "allow me to present a friend to Miss Dundas and yourself? The gentleman walking with Squire Poole, yonder; handsome, stout—yes. He is most anxious to form your acquaintance: one might as well not be presented at court abroad, you know, as— Colonel Laddoun, it is. One of those clever, generous fellows whom everybody knows—yes. Met him in California—lucky dog there; quite a favorite in San Francisco, Miss Dundas; devoted to the ladies. You've no objections?"

In a few moments they came up to Laddoun, and he was presented. He was unusually silent, however, to the disappointment of his friend; his oily fluency of words and manner seemed chilled and stiffened after the first hasty glance at the old gentleman's quiet face.

"He has Dallas' eyes. Which I never could understand—curse him!" was his secret thought, as he stepped back by Honora, and made one or two heavy efforts to fall into an easy conversation with her. He grew silent in a moment, however, catching the drift of the Doctor's chatter.

"I go this week—yes. My stay here has been delightful, socially. And your country is rich in minerals—unlimited wealth under your feet, sir! An Ali Baba's cave, if you but knew the magic words to unlock it. By the way, I am taking a young man from here with me as assistant. One of your neighbors. A fellow that I met up in the mountains, in the stone-quarry—yes."

Honora dropped her plant, and, being tired, apparently, came a step forward and put her hand in her uncle's arm.

"Evans mentioned the man to me," pursued the little man, jerkily adjusting his spectacles, "and I fell in afterward with him at the opening of a mound up on Indian Creek. A remarkable case of a one-idea'd man, sir. The only people who amount to anything, by-the-bye. This fellow is a born naturalist."

"My niece and I met him near the quarry, I think. I doubt not that it is the same person. You remember, Honora?"

"I think I do."

"Do you take him with you as a laborer?" questioned Mr. Galbraith, politely continuing the subject which so keenly interested his companion.

"No—as an assistant. In an inferior position, of course. But he will rise. He will be of more assistance to me than a dozen purblind college-bred fellows, who have their opinions cut and dried for them. This young man has had but few opportunities, I judge; only studied the A, B, C of science, as I may say. But he has the eye of a hawk and a marvelous memory. Evans suggested to me to take him. I was surprised that the fellow had so much discernment; surprised—yes."

"It will be of advantage to him?" asked Mr. Galbraith.

"It will be an education such as rarely offers itself to any man!" emphatically. "I will extend my researches through South America, in all probability. We may be gone one, two, three years—"

"So long?" said the old man, with a quick breath. "I thought the expedition would return in the spring?"

"I spoke of my own plans, sir," loftily. "I was about to say that, if this young man answers my expectation, I will induce him to accompany me after I separate from the government survey. There is something in the boy which has curiously interested me."

"It's an old trick of his!" growled Laddoun, under his breath, adding, awkwardly, when he saw them look at him, "I used to know the man you speak of. Strangers usually fancied him."

"Yes, there is something very genial and attractive in him," rejoined the Doctor.

"I thought you were a stranger in this part of the country, Colonel Laddoun?" said Mr. Galbraith, looking steadily at him.

Laddoun's portly body moved uncomfortably under the scrutiny of the strange, yet familiar eyes. He began to toy with the heavy chain hanging across his waistcoat. "I am a stranger here. But I knew Galbraith when he was a boy."

The old gentleman's quiet gaze rested on him for a moment after he had finished speaking, but he made him no other reply.

"Galbraith? 'Pon my word," broke in Doctor Pritchard, "I forgot to mention that the young man's name was the same as yours. It is so common, hereabouts, that it did not attract my attention."

"It is common," said Mr. Galbraith. "All branches from the same family tree."

They had reached a stile where the path struck aside to the village. Doctor Pritchard stopped and hesitated.

"Well, Colonel Laddoun, here is our road. We must bid our friends good-evening, I presume."

"Good-evening, gentlemen," said Mr. Galbraith, promptly, Pritchard's visions of roast turkey and the Dour wines vanishing into air. "Come to us to-morrow, Doctor. Madam Galbraith especially desires to see you."

After they were alone he walked more slowly, to accommodate his pace to Honora, whose step was flagging: it seemed to have lost suddenly its accustomed elastic vigor. He fancied, too, when he glanced anxiously down at her, that her dark eyes were more unintelligible than usual. He did not disturb her, however, and it was not until they had nearly reached the house that she spoke, stopping at the very stile where Galbraith and Lizzy had stood.

"New Mexico is a long way from Virginia?"

"Yes, Nora."

"I suppose Doctor Pritchard and his party will never return?"

"Doctor Pritchard has no tie here, you know. He was making an examination of the Kanawha Salines, and came from there up to the mountains."

"Yes, I know." She drew a long breath after a while. "It is a good thing to be able to go out in the world to find work and knowledge—to find people who would be friends to you if you knew them better. It is tiresome—tiresome to be a woman, uncle!"

He put his hand gently on her brown hair and stroked it for his only answer. The bent head was so dear to him, and, do what he would, his hand so weak to guard it!

Laddoun swaggered smoking alongside of the little professor in silence. It needed a walk of a quarter of a mile and two or three cigars to restore his usual complacent tone. Then the bitter froth ran off. "I don't fancy your Galbraiths, sir! They're ill-bred—ill-bred! It is always the case with your petty country aristocracy! What the devil did the old fellow mean by looking at me as if I was a thief? Does he never meet a gentleman, that he must scan him from head to foot as he would a bullock?"

"You're too sensitive, Colonel," laughed Pritchard. "That hot, Southern blood of yours is always too ready to take fire. You are a Southerner, aren't you?"

"I—I am pro-slavery. To the backbone. But as for your Galbraiths, they had better take care how they insult George Laddoun. I have a fact or two in reserve for them that would make them wince to the marrow."

"You mean old James Galbraith here? A fact in reserve?" with an astonished peer over his spectacles.

"Ay: this old fellow. But let the matter drop: I'll keep my own counsel. So you're going to make the fortune of that boy up at the quarry?"

"No, not precisely. But I may put him in the way to make his own."

"So?" caressing his moustache thoughtfully. "Well, good-evening, Doctor," with a sudden start; "I have an engagement which I had nearly forgotten."

"I wish you had remembered it ten minutes sooner," thought Pritchard, as he strode off; "I would not have lost my invitation to dinner. Well! well! Now I thought Laddoun and the Galbraiths were people just suited to each other!"

Laddoun, while his companion went on slowly cogitating to the village, had stopped at a little farm-house by the way. "Lend me your fast trotter, Billy," he said to a young fellow who lounged out—one of his bar-room chums. "I want to reach the Indian Queen before night-fall: can she make it?"

"Yes. You need not ride her hard, either, to do it. Don't spoil her paces, Colonel."

"Oh, Lord bless you, no! It's not this nag's paces that I mean to spoil," as he mounted and patted the mare's black neck. He rode steadily through the mountain roads until the afternoon had changed into dusk and night began slowly to fall. When he caught sight at last of the little stone inn, its windows twinkling cheerfully far ahead of him, he pressed his horse fiercely, as if, through long brooding over his disappointment, his blood was fairly up.

Dallas Galbraith, walking up and down in front of the little porch in the twilight, listening occasionally to the Sunday evening gossip of Peggy and the boy, caught the first sound of the horse's hoofs echoing down the mountain side, and pointed out to Matt the fiery sparks struck out on the darkness, as any one whose heart is full and happy will notice and be amused by a trifle.

But when the black horse and his rider came nearer, Dallas stopped his slow saunter and looked at them in silence. Then he went up to the porch.

"I am going up the road," he said quietly to Peggy: "I do not know when I will be back. Good-night," taking Matt's hand, thrust through the railing. "God bless you, little fellow!" For he knew that the Luck which had been against him all his life was upon him at last in visible shape, and went to meet it face to face.

PART V.

CHAPTER XV.

COLONEL LADDOUN, seeing the figure coming toward him from the inn, pulled up the mare, and sat stiffly erect in the saddle. This fellow should stand, like the beggar that he was, at his stirrup. This fellow—whom he had taken from the dunghill, and to whom family and rank and an estate like a principality came and waited until he should choose to claim them. Luck might be on his side, but he should see that Laddoun was still master.

He swelled, he puffed, he played with Bill Thorp's riding-whip as though it had been a sceptre, his red lips growing redder, and his black eyes arrogant and defiant under the thick lids, as he watched Dallas coming nearer.

The twilight was distinct enough for him to see him clearly. By George! how pale the fellow was! Five years of living on prison-broth and stewed cocoa-shells. And Dallas used to dearly love a good square meal, and would share it with even a nigger! The boy had hard lines to pull, after all! Laddoun burst into a good-humored laugh, his face softening as he glanced downward over the baggily-clothed figure. Poor Dall! Where had he picked up that coat? Nobody with gentlemanly instincts could be tricked into making such a guy of himself; but Galbraith was always ready to be duped like a child; and as for dress— but, poor devil, it was not his fault if he had no fine perceptions.

He grew uneasy after that as he waited. Not with remorse that he himself had laid down the hard lines for the boy's life, nor with gratitude because the lad had put out his hand to save him from the gulf into which he had fallen. But he did remember, with a sudden spasm of the heart under his velvet waistcoat, how Dall used to admire his fashionable clothes, his bow, his princely manner—what a slave the fellow had been to him from sheer affection. "He loved me like a dog—Dallas. And he never made me ridiculous trying to copy me, either, like that idiot, McGill!"

He was within half-a-dozen yards of him now. It was the same old Dall! The steady, loping gait: mouth and nose still too big for the man's face as they had been for the boy's: the same inscrutable expression. A thousand remembrances swarmed up unbidden at the sight of him—of the journeys, the fun, the scrapes they had shared in the long, every-day life together: of Lizzy, who had been fond of the boy. Laddoun's face kindled into that affectionate, generous glow which his admirers so well knew. He got down with a certain hesitation from his horse, holding one hand out while the other rested on the saddle, as Galbraith came swiftly toward him. He stopped short, and they stood for a moment silent in the twilight, intently regarding each other.

Laddoun broke into a loud, uncertain laugh: "Why, Dallas, old fellow! I—I'm devilish glad to see you! 'Pon my soul I am. It makes me feel like a woman. Shake hands?"

Galbraith glanced from the florid, excited face down to the fat, outstretched hand, but made no other reply.

"You don't mean to bluff me off? As you please: George Laddoun never offers his hand twice," drawing back haughtily. He could not comprehend the silence of the other man, nor the tense compression about his nostrils and jaws. Was he afraid? Or did he mean mischief?

"Now, Dallas, you're keeping malice," he broke out, frankly. "There's nothing of that in me. I've got no account of old grudges. I came here to do you a kindness. I came clear from California to be on hand when you got free, and give you a helping hand. I followed you out here for that. George Laddoun's not the sort to forget old friends. I'd have walked the streets of Albany with you in your prison-clothes, and knocked down any man who insulted you."

"Yes, I understand."

"Then you need not stand off, weighing and measuring me. You'll find me the same jolly brick—old Laddoun. More heart than head about me, as every body knows. 'Pon my soul, the sight of you brought up things I've not thought of for years! There was Lizzy—now. Well," after a moment's pause, "my taste in women has changed, of course. But there's nothing like love's young dream. ''Twas odor fled, As soon as shed.' But you never cared for the sex." He felt, as he rattled over this uneasily, that his hold had slipped from the lad, never to be regained: his old dupe stood farther outside and apart from him than any other man, and the knowledge cost Laddoun, who was everybody's friend, a sentimental, unaffected pang. He hesitated, then cried impetuously:

"Come, Galbraith, there's my hand. Friend or enemy, as you choose. You know me."

"Yes, I know you, George Laddoun. But keep back. Don't touch me," drawing back as the other approached, his hands clasped tightly behind him.

Laddoun was startled out of his perpetual applause and patting of himself: he took a quick, keen survey of Galbraith. There was a sudden qualm of fear in his soggy, dull heart—something in the face before him reminded him that the man had had five years of solitude in which "to think it over."

The road was narrow and ran along the edge of a precipice. Galbraith was the more athletic and better built of the two. He had not spoken a word of the wrong done to him; and that looked dangerous.

"If I thrust my friendship on him, it will let loose the devil that he's trying to hold down," the Colonel judged shrewdly in the paralyzed instant that followed. Then he put his foot in the stirrup and slowly swung himself heavily up, keeping a guarded watch on Dallas. There was an aggrieved sense of injury in his manner. He was quite conscious that all the good feeling which had brought him from California had been thrown back in his face: he was not so conscious, to do him justice, of his disappointment in his plans of leeching the heir of the Galbraiths, though the disappointment was there.

Up on the mare's back, he looked about at the darkening twilight and down at the pale, controlled face of the man leaning back against the rocks, as from a vantage-ground of safety. It was but a boy's credulous face after all—never would be anything else: there was not a line of shrewdness or self-confidence in it.

Laddoun pressed his horse closer toward him. "Keep back from you, eh? It's on the cards," half closing his eyes, speculatively, "whether I leave you or not to shift for yourself, Galbraith. I can make or unmake you as I please," measuring his words deliberately. "I can bring you in heir of this very land you stand on, or I can speak a word that would cause your own mother to cast you off. You've marked out a straight road for yourself? Very well! Do you think Pritchard would take *you* as his companion if I choose to tell him what you are? Do you think that stupid Beck and his wife would keep you under their roof—let their boy go wandering about with a jail-bird? You cannot wash yourself clear of that."

He waited for an answer, but Galbraith was motionless. At the mention of the child he had only clasped his hands more closely behind him, the fingers strained until they were bloodless, and, turning from Laddoun, fixed his eyes steadily on the ground.

The fellow was insensate as a stone!

"I hold you and your fate there, sir—there!" cried Laddoun, loudly, holding out his soft, open hand and patting it with his forefinger. "You may scheme and work to build yourself up as you please. But if you throw off George Laddoun like a pauper and scoff at his friendship, it will cost me no more than the closing of my palm to crush you like a worm."

Galbraith made a sudden step forward. Standing in front of the horse's breast, he grasped the bridle. Whatever control he had held over himself was gone: his face was set and his eyes shone like those of a wild beast. But his voice was curiously quiet:

"I never mean to punish you for what you did to me. I let that go. But I am going to lead a new life. It is in my own hands, and I warn you that it will be safer not to stand in my way."

"I'd have been your friend, if you had chosen," sullenly. "You're the first man that ever chose George Laddoun as an enemy. You never can shake me off now. I'll show you to-morrow what your new life is worth."

Galbraith pressed closer on him. "Then I'll be free of you!" he said, slowly. "I am a better man than you. I count it no more crime to put you out of my way than a snake that bit me. Look out, Laddoun!"

His sudden onslaught wrenched a half whine, half cry from the Colonel: he grew deadly pale as he wheeled his horse about, throwing Galbraith on the ground. "The boy is mad," urging the powerful beast full on him. "I could ride you down like a dog. And I am armed. Stand back! Stand back, I say!" He brought down the revolver, covering Galbraith's breast.

Dallas stood one instant, watchful as a panther. "If you've a pistol, you are even with me," he muttered, and made the spring. Catching the bridle close by the horse's nostrils, he dragged her by sheer strength across the road to the edge of the precipice and held her there. The brute's terrible cry and Laddoun's yell rose together: her pawing hind-hoofs struck the pebbles down into the chasm. In that moment Laddoun, leaning forward, uncocked his pistol and threw it on the ground.

"I'd not kill *you*, Dallas!" he gasped.

Galbraith glanced at the pistol lying at his feet, and up at the mare and her rider, the insanity going out of his eyes, like a man from whom a physical spasm is passing. He pulled the horse up on level ground again with difficulty, for the strength given by his fury was gone, and held it steady until the Colonel, trembling and sopping the sweat from his face, had slowly alighted and crept across the road to where the pistol lay. Galbraith did not heed him: he stood mechanically stroking down the shivering, terrified animal.

"I am the worse devil of the two. There's not been a day for years when I would not have been glad to see him dead. And he—spared my life—spared my life."

Laddoun picked up the pistol and brushed it on his sleeve with an odd chuckle.

"Say, Dallas, come to yourself, hey? Now, I meant you nothing but good, as you might have known. I'll hold no grudge against you for this bout, boy. Nobody can say George Laddoun keeps malice;" and he held out his hand to the man who had tried a moment ago to murder him, with a frank smile.

But Dallas shook his head. "I'm no hypocrite. You're no friend of mine, Laddoun. No. You never shall be."

The Colonel took off his hat and pushed his hair back, doubtfully. The boy, like most half-witted people, was obstinate as a mule—hard to manage. Was the game worth the chase? He had a half mind to mount, and, washing his hands of the whole matter, start back to California in the morning. But then he glanced up at the mountains, rich in minerals, down at the broad river, through the grazing valley. It was the estate of a prince: some day to settle down as perpetual prime minister to the ruler of it would be no ill ending to his vagabondage. It was worth another trial, at any rate.

"Let us talk the matter over quietly, Dallas," he said, earnestly. "Look at it coolly. You are beginning your career: circumstances have so chanced that you have singularly little knowledge of the world, while few men have had my opportunity for mastering its ways to success. I offer you my help out of sheer regard for old friendship, and it seems to me you are but a headstrong, hot-headed fool to put it from you. That's how I look at the thing. You may have another view of the subject." He took out a cigar, and, striking a match across his boot, lighted it.

Galbraith, who had patted and soothed the mare into quiet, handed the bridle back to him. "I have no confidences to make to you. I am going with Doctor Pritchard, as you know, no doubt. It would be wiser in you not to interfere with me. I acted like a beast to-night, and I may do it again. I haven't the control of myself that you have—that any man has, I suppose." He turned away abruptly to go down the hill, with no word of leave-taking.

There had been a bitter, humiliated tone in his voice, which, Laddoun felt, came from some depth in the man's nature which he could not sound. He watched him as he went slowly down the hill with the amused admiration which he might give to a bull-headed, courageous dog.

"Now, that fellow," he thought, as he critically bit the end of his cigar, "knows that I did the job for which he was punished, yet he never blew on me, nor even taunted me with it to-night. He's too cursedly proud. Turns his broad back on me now, not caring to think what a target it is if I chose to put a bullet through it! I'll have another tug with him. I think I know how to fetch him down. Hi! Galbraith!" Finding that he did not turn, he sprang on the horse and cantered after him; but slowly, in order to allow Dallas to almost reach the Indian Queen before he joined him.

Galbraith paid no attention to the horse's tramp behind him: an utter, overwhelming sense of defeat seemed to shut him out from the world. Not an hour ago, walking up and down in the twilight, he had been picturing to himself the place which an educated gentleman, strong and kindly, could take in life—a follower of One whom Dallas, with the reverence of a child or a savage, never named aloud: thinking of this ideal hero, vaguely and in strange connections: with miserable, vicious little children, and with a pure young girl: wondering what chance there would be for him in this expedition with Pritchard to train himself into the likeness of such an one. This was but an hour ago; now, his hands would be stained with murder but for the manliness of George Laddoun: no brute could have wallowed in more besotted depth of blind passion than he had done to-night. He had gone to find the something that had always been against him in Laddoun yonder, and the stronger, viler foe in his own breast had risen and dragged him down. When the Colonel rode up beside him again he glanced at him indifferently, as if he and his malice were almost forgotten.

"I—I have had a long ride, Galbraith," said Laddoun, with well-acted hesitation, "and—well, to be honest, I'm hungry. I suppose your landlady can give me a bite of supper?"

Dallas' color rose, and he quickened his steps without looking up. "You'll be my guest, Laddoun?" he said, civilly, with an effort which the other took care not to notice.

"With pleasure, my boy!" heartily. "You were always a hospitable fellow. The old times have come back, eh?"

Dallas made no answer: but presently as he walked he loosened his cravat as though straitened for breath. They went down the road in silence, Laddoun tranquilly puffing at his cigar, a twinkle of amusement in his black eyes.

"Say, Galbraith! 'Pon my soul it's too good a joke to keep!" he broke out at last. "I sold you, out and out, up on the hill yonder. I know you so well, you see. When I threw down the pistol at your feet, it wa'n't loaded! Lord!" with a hearty laugh, "I'd have made another use of it if it had been. Though I'd be sorry to hurt a hair of your head, Dall. But you didn't suspect me, eh?"

"No, I did not suspect you," calmly, and with no sign of surprise or irritation.

"Well, your skull was always thick, boy. But it was a neat hit to make in the very jaws of death, as one might say," caressing his jetty beard for a long time afterward, and smiling to himself. The matter, on the contrary, seemed to pass out of Galbraith's mind at once. It mattered nothing to him what tricks Laddoun played on him: it was some ghastly power tugging at his heart within with which he wrestled in silence.

"Hallo! here we are," called the Colonel, pulling up before the porch and alighting. "And this is Mrs. Beck, eh?" taking his hat quite off as he went up the steps. "My friend Mr. Galbraith has promised me that you will give me a morsel of supper, madam. Pie, bread and cheese, anything you have. A slice of Sunday's roast goose, say."

"We *had* a goose for dinner," said Peggy, getting up in quite a flutter. "How could you guess that now, Mr.—?"

"Laddoun. Colonel Laddoun. This is your boy?" drawing Matt up to his knee, for he had entered the little living-room, and already seemed to pre-empt and fill it. But Matt pulled away, and went out whining to Dallas, who, after a few words to Mrs. Beck, paced slowly up and down the porch. The child took his hand, and looked up in his face, but Dallas avoided his eye.

It needed only a few moments for Peggy to spread an appetizing cold supper before the Colonel from the shelves of her clean little pantry, chattering, as she went in and out, of Dallas and the victuals alternately, while Laddoun listened, with a smile on his red lips under the moustache; but there was no smile in the keen, black eyes fixed on Galbraith, who, as yet, had made no motion to join him at the table. He knew Dallas had an Arab sense of hospitality: if he broke bread with him, he had ceased to count him as an enemy. But Laddoun made no effort to bring him in: it was a good test to show how they stood toward each other.

When the supper was ready, therefore, he ate of it alone, though every mouthful choked him, feeling like a dog to whom a bone had been thrown in charity. Dallas came to the door as he pushed his chair back and stood up.

"Try some of this old Monongahela, Galbraith?" eagerly—"to our better understanding of each other. Come."

"I will not drink with you, Laddoun. You are no friend to me."

Laddoun put down the untasted glass with a heat on his face which Galbraith's attempt at murder had not roused in him.

"As you will. You're implacable in a way that I cannot understand. It's not in my nature, thank God!" He closed the door and came up to Dallas, who stood leaning on the mantel-shelf. Laddoun hesitated and stammered before the steady, blue eyes, doubtful how to begin his last attack.

"I thought we could patch up our old break over a meal together," he said at last. "You used to be the prince of good fellows, Dallas. I came here to-night with the best intentions toward you, as I said. I have discovered a certain matter about you, of which I think you are not aware." He paused, but Dallas stood silent.

The Colonel paced slowly up and down; Mrs. Beck, outside, listening to the ponderous tread that shook the little house, with the respect due to affability when found encased in such superfine clothes and chains of Californian gold.

"It don't matter whether we are friends or foes," his sonorous bass voice rising into a sort of frank, heroic rhythm. "I'll do what I can for you, and then, if you say the word, I'll leave you to enjoy your good fortune alone. I have discovered who you are, Galbraith," with a melodramatic wave of the hand.

Dallas nodded, indifferently.

"You see those hills filled with mineral wealth, the arable slopes, the water-power in those creeks?" pointing out of the window, and rolling the words like a sweet morsel under his tongue. "You are the heir of this estate, Dallas Galbraith," with an unction as though he had declared the triumph his own. "You are the heir!"

"I know it," quietly.

Laddoun stopped short with amazement. "You know it? And you are going with Pritchard without putting in your claim? Do you mean never to take your rightful place?"

"I do not say that," said Dallas, hesitating. "I may come back to them when I am fit for that place. Not until then."

"When you've washed off the Albany smell, eh?" with a loud laugh. "A whiff of that would be damnation to your cause down in the Galbraith house, I fancy. The old fellow and his niece are narrow, religious bigots, and the old madam would cut off her own right hand if it had touched that of a felon's. I know the whole party well," his voice swelling perceptibly. "Pritchard and old James Galbraith and I are chums, in fact. He's got a capital run of sherry, your grandfather; but I forgot: you don't know much about wines," with a smothered laugh. "As for the little Dundas girl," putting on the leer with which he was used to fascinate women, "she's a nice little creature." He stopped short, seeing a great and uncontrollable change in Galbraith's face, and then continued, more deliberately:

"In my younger days I might have been tempted, perhaps. But George Laddoun's too old a bird to catch now."

He waited in vain for any reply.

"How long will you be gone with Pritchard?"

"I do not know. One or four years."

"The devil!" He could not conceal his chagrin and anger; bit his under lip, and then whistled, as he walked rapidly up and down, to keep himself silent. Even one year to a man who crowded his life as he did, meant an utter change of his base and relations. What was his secret hold on Galbraith worth if it was to be half a lifetime before he could bring his lever to bear?

"Tut, boy! What folly is this? I— you may be six foot under ground in as many months. Why should a young, hearty fellow like you thrust off your Luck even for a day when it comes to force good fortune on you? A year! You will come back in a year to find your grandfather dead, most likely, and the estate given over to that sober little Honora. And she," watching him shrewdly, "the property of some clever chap who knows how to pick up a good thing when he sees it."

Dallas raised himself up from the lounging attitude in which he had listened. "We have gone far enough," he said. "My mind was made up to go with Doctor Pritchard. You are wasting time with me. I shall not alter it."

Laddoun listened attentively, remaining thoughtful and silent a moment after Dallas had done speaking, slowly looping the tassel-buttons of his overcoat. His face suddenly cleared.

"Well, I throw the matter up. You will not take even fortune and a bride, if it be my hand that points the way to them. I'll bid you good-bye, Galbraith, and hope you may have another friend as willing and ready when you need him. As for me, I will not cross your path again."

"You have not pointed the way to fortune nor kept me back from it, Laddoun," said Dallas, with a half smile. "Your coming to-night has not altered my plans or position a whit. The time is over for you to affect my fortune in any way. I see that. If there are any enemies for me to fight, they must come nearer and be more akin to me than you are to do me harm."

The Colonel measured the cool, undemonstrative face and figure before him speculatively for a moment: then he relaxed into his usual good-humored nonchalance. "You will neither suffer me to be foe nor friend," he said, with a laugh. "So be it. Good-night. And good luck, Dallas!" and swinging on his glossy beaver with a half-cordial, half-mocking bow, he sallied out of the room, and in a moment had brought Peggy, Beck and Wash about him, eager and garrulous.

Dallas listened to his loud, musical, hearty voice answering, flinging back some parting jest to them after he had mounted, and his horse's hoofs began to ring down the rocky path. It sounded to Galbraith like a hateful, unmeaning refrain to which the words of his early life had been set. To-night he found that it had lost all power over him—had died utterly out of his life; and listening to it, a light-hearted sense of boyish freedom altogether new to him began to brighten the world. This bugbear of his youth proved, when fairly met, to be but a paltry sham; and then a broad, easy road to the best manhood had opened itself before him. As for the foe within, Dallas did just as we all do, and put it comfortably out of sight. Original sin, or taint of the prison, or whatever it was, there was a long life before him in which to subdue it. That was an easy matter!

What were those words of Laddoun's? "Fortune and a bride?"

The usually grave, composed young fellow took Matt nervously up on his knee, and sat glowering into the red cinders late into the night, deaf to that small man's efforts at conversation, until the fire burned out, and Matt, in despair, fell asleep and snored like a trumpeter. If Doctor Pritchard started during the next week, Galbraith must find some means to see his mother again, himself unseen. It was this visit which he thought he was planning now, fancying a casual meeting with her on the road. She would not be alone—it was not likely she would be alone. Well, and then? Lizzy would have thought her favorite an idiot if she had known his wild, incredible fancies that night: the years—the long, beautiful, healthy life from youth to far-off death—which he built out of that *then:* the chance that she would not be alone.

Laddoun, meanwhile, rode briskly back on the road by which he came. He wanted to sleep somewhere near the Stone-post Farm, that he could be there bright and early in the morning. If Galbraith chose to put off his chances for years, he (Laddoun) would put up with no such folly. He meant to take the fellow and his fortune in hand at once, and work them as puppets to what end he chose. He would begin the job to-morrow: he had no time to lose. There was a pig-headed stupidity in Dallas and these Western kinsfolk of his which would bring the boy's affairs into a hopeless muddle unless some man of ability would take them up and make what profit he could out of them for Galbraith and himself.

He was in high spirits when he reached Thorp's and called Bill out to take the mare. "Not a hair turned, Billy, though I put her to her mettle."

"You've got urgent business on hand, it seems, Colonel?"

"I have that!" emphatically. "I'm going to put a young fellow through in a way that'll astonish the folks in these parts. Going to see that he gets his rights, or I'll take the wind out of the sails of a certain party that I know. I hate oppression, Bill."

"A young fellow in these parts, eh? You couldn't give names, I reckon?" rubbing down the mare reflectively.

"Well, no, Billy, I couldn't. But you wait. When George Laddoun's about, justice 'll be done. That's my way. When any of the boys want a lift down in San Francisco, Colonel's the man. I don't say it boastfully. It's my nature, and I can't help it. Better for me if I could." He went off soon after, Thorp looking after him almost as much kindled with admiration for his generosity as Laddoun was for it himself.

CHAPTER XVI.

There was a bunch of flowers, in a little vase, on Madam Galbraith's breakfast-table next morning—a crimson camellia, with a snowy edging of violets. Gerty saw it the instant she came in. Mr. Dour had been down at the village last night, and there was a hot-house in the truck-garden there, and the bouquet was beside Honora's plate. Hers was on the opposite side of the table. A lump rose in her throat, choking her, and the dry tears began to burn in her eyes. Walking home from church yesterday, Paul had been barely civil to her, and was it any wonder? She had but two dresses in which to make herself look decent—the blue poplin and red merino—while Honora had a costume for every fresh humor and whim. Yet Mr. Dour thought that she was his own soul's true mate: he had said as much one day, and quoted Plato about it. She did not know much about Plato, but she did know that she would be glad to be his servant, to black his shoes if need were; and if he would make her his wife they could live nicely on—well, just next to nothing: she was a different sort of housekeeper from Miss Dundas. The poor fellow would never have to go about then with unhemmed cravats and ragged shirt-cuffs. But there was no hope of that! She believed Madam Galbraith had brought him there expressly to marry Honora, and they had him in their toils now; and as for her, she was growing old and shabby. There was quite a wrinkle between her eyes lately; and how miserable the ruffle of cotton lace looked about her neck beside Honora's lovely worked linen chemisettes!

She could not eat her muffin or chop at all, but merely sipped wretchedly at her coffee. Mr. Dour sat near her, but she would not turn so much as a glance toward him. She hoped she knew her duty as a woman. Miss Dundas came in late, just as her pony-chaise was driven in front of the windows. She wore a gray dress, edged with fur, and carried her little fur cap and gloves in her hand—all delicate and picturesque and winning, oddly suiting the dewy, clear eyes and fresh, emphatic little face: how could one ever make anything out of a stiff poplin look like that? Honora looked soberly at the flowers a moment.

"Jane," she said—"Jane, there is a mistake here. These flowers cannot be intended for me;" and began to chip her egg in severe silence. Mr. Dour scowled at her, but said nothing, old Madam Galbraith's eyes being on him; and the vase was carried by Jane ignominiously to the mantel-shelf, where the camellia began to wilt, and finally fell in the ashes.

"You are going to drive, Honora?" asked Mrs. Duffield, who was looking lazily over the last week's paper.

"Yes, down to the village."

"Alone? Your ponies look mettlesome, child."

"I am going alone." Miss Dundas' tones were without doubt cross: the flowers had made her heart beat more than she chose to perceive. She could not shut her eyes any longer to Mr. Dour's proceedings. Poor Gerty! It was a shame! a shame! And yet what must it be to be loved—to love?

Whatever might be the ogre or angel who made pictures before the young woman's brain just then, they kept her sitting at the table alone after every one else was gone—eating dry toast mechanically, quite unconscious of her pawing ponies, and of even Mr. Dour, who had held his eyes upon her during the whole course of the meal. She passed him, when she did rise from her breakfast, with such an indifferent nod, that he turned straight to the well-known blue dress in an arm-chair by the fire. But little Gerty did not even nod to him: indeed, her big eyes, patient and sorrowful as a cow's, were so intent on her tatting that she did not seem to feel him touch her arm. He turned from her.

"My poor camellia!" in a half whisper, picking it up from the fender. "It went far astray this morning. As the heart of its owner," with a deep breath.

The tatting went all wrong: the curled lashes trembled on the chubby cheeks.

"You did not mean to give it to Miss Dundas, then?"

"No."

She looked closer at her shuttle: two big tears rolled from under the lashes. They were too much for Paul Dour. "I meant to give nothing to Miss Dundas, Gerty," bending over her.

"I am sure it does not matter to me if you gave her all the flowers in the world," said Miss Rattlin, drawing herself suddenly up with the dignity of a partridge. "Why should I?"

Paul stared down at her and crumbled the burned flower into bits. "To be sure, why should it?" he said vacantly, and putting on his cap directly afterward, he went out to look for quails, followed by a saucy laugh from the fireside. He was out of temper with himself. What did it concern him if this silly little village girl was full of vagaries? He had taken the first honors of his year: he had made a pilgrimage to Concord to visit Emerson, believing that he stood on the foremost ramparts of thought, side by side with that great seer. Sometimes (especially after reading the books of that great master) he was conscious of original power in his own brain enough to make this whole fallow country fruitful with ideas. And this little jilt treated him as though he were a penny whistle, on which she could blow what tune she pleased. She was nothing to him.

What the devil did she mean just now? Was it possible she did not care for him?

"What are you so glum about, Dour?" asked Colonel Pervis, who was with him.

"A woman, I'll wager."

"Oh, I've done with women, long ago," sourly. "I've outgrown that folly. Nobody ever did understand them since the old Serpent when he managed Eve."

"And even he got the worst of it at last—eh?"

Gerty, for some reason, was by this time quite rosy and radiant over her shuttling. She made half-a-dozen puns, at which Mrs. Duffield lifted her delicate brows in astonishment and smiled faintly. She grew very caressing to Honora, put on her cap for her, and called her a dear little thing, patronizingly, at the end of every sentence.

"What a queer dress, you dear little thing! Quite Polish, isn't it, though? Gentlemen don't like anything so pronounced, I think. Why don't you wear blue? But you can't—I forgot. Your skin won't bear it. I think this is a sweet shade in my poplin. 'Tender and true,' that's the meaning of the color. A gentleman told me so last week."

"Letters!" called Madam Galbraith, taking a black leather bag from a man at the door. "Half a dozen for your sister, Gertrude. All from young men. Tut! tut! Girls nowadays pass about their ideas and feelings at such a rate that they must be tolerably well-worn coin when a husband comes to get them. Here is a letter for Elizabeth, Honora. I wish you would take it to her, child. And speak to her of that matter," lowering her voice. "I will not have her go, d'ye understand? I want to hear no more of it. It's sheer temper in Elizabeth. And the woman has no home but this. I know it."

Honora obeyed quickly, as though the errand pleased her. She looked, as she went, at the big, square yellow envelope, with its direction in a man's crabbed hand, and the queer, written postmark—*Manasquan*. "It's a love-letter," with an authoritative nod. "Maybe she has another home than this, after all." Honora was as nervous and curious in this matter of love to-day as a traveler might be about a new country of which his feet had just touched the shore.

"I've something for you, Lizzy," she cried, tapping at the door of the housekeeper's prim little room and going in. "News from a friend. The best friend, perhaps," holding it over her head and looking archly at Lizzy as she rose soberly, brushing the bits of thread from her dress before she took the letter and looked at it. Surely she blushed!

"Sit down, Honora," gravely placing a chair. She always treated her like a willful child, but Nora spent a large share of her time in Lizzy's room, knowing by instinct how welcome she was to the lonely woman. Honora was the only one in the house who had always treated her as an equal.

"It's a letter from Manasquan," she said, after she had glanced over it, folding it hurriedly. "My old home, you know. It's from a friend of mine—James Van Zeldt; or he's an agent, rather, I ought to say. I have a little house and a lot there, and he rents them for me, and twice a year he writes about them."

"Oh!" with a disappointed shrug. "Now, I had made up my mind it was from a lover, Lizzy. Everybody has a lover."

"He is only an agent, I assure you, Honora," without a smile. "Wait; here is his letter. There is no reason why I should keep Jim's letters secret, as if they mattered anything to me," earnestly, pulling it out of her pocket. "Do take it, Honora. I wish you to read it."

"Well, I will then," ensconcing herself comfortably on the low window-seat. The room was on the ground floor, and the road leading to the door wound past the low windows. The sun shone in pleasantly through the frosted bushes which overgrew the panes, over Honora's bent head. Lizzy stood, square and sober, facing her, looking beyond her down the outside slope. Nora opened the letter slowly.

"I suppose you are thinking of going back to Manasquan, Miss Byrne," she said, her color rising diffidently. "But my aunt bade me tell you you must not say one other word of leaving us. She cannot do without you, Lizzy, and neither can I."

Lizzy touched a bit of the girl's soft brown hair, which hung loose, gently, and then drew her hand hastily away. "I did not think anybody here would care for my going," she said, with a pleased heat and flurry. "It has come to be really like home to me," glancing round at the neat little bed, the rocking-chair, the teapot and solitary cup and saucer beside the fire. She was thinking that it would be good if she could wait here until her boy Dallas came back to claim his own. It would be a very hard wrench to part with Honora. She was fonder than she knew of the girl.

"But I never would go back to Manasquan unless just to die there," she said, solemnly, at which Honora looked up at her with her liquid, dark eyes instantly full of sympathy. She understood it all. Poor Lizzy had buried something out of her life in the old home for which there was no resurrection.

"You will stay with us, and we won't talk of Manasquan any more," she said, gently, and was purposely a long time in opening the envelope and taking out Jim's awkward letter, while Lizzy stood motionless. It was not altogether disagreeable for her to look out into the pleasant sunshine and think that her life had been a sacrifice. She might be homely and sedate and middle-aged, but she was a heroine! Quite as much as the ideal woman of any novel she had ever read. She had acted from the inner truth of things to help others. Now, all hope for herself here was over—all over. She had grown old. She knew "the purple glory of the morning faded."

Since she found she could do nothing more for Dallas at the Stone-post Farm, she naturally had looked about the world for a place to which to go. It must never be to Manasquan. She had been young there and beloved. Her walks with Laddoun on the sands in the moonlight, with the eternal moan of the sea making rhythm for the song in her heart, came back to her. Whatever Laddoun might be, that was the one gleam of poetry in her life. No true woman could love or be happy twice. Some day, perhaps, when she felt the last hour was very near, she would go back to the quiet old village, and, with the moan of the sea sounding in her ears, and the moonlight perhaps shining down on her changed face, make a fit ending to her sad story. For Lizzy, like most women, had drawn much of her idea of the eternal fitness of things from the poems and semi-religious novels which she read.

When she found Honora had opened the letter, she said, apologetically: "It is a very plain letter that Jim writes, and I'm not so sure about the spelling. But he is a good, kind fellow, for all."

He seemed so far outside and below

the living poem in which the sea and her forsaken home and the music of Laddoun's deceiving tongue had share. And yet—

"It is a very good letter," said Honora, gravely, after a while. "I think I would like your James Van Zeldt more than you do." Turning to the first page, she read it again aloud:

"MANASQUAN, *October* 30.

"RESPECTED FRIEND: I take the liberty of stating to you, that the House is lett: to the same parties as heretofore. I remit the rent due. With regard to your inquirees as to repairs: I have to say there is none needed: a new Roof was put on by some of the Neighbors: same as regards a Pump: they desire their names not to mentioned: But then it would be strange if you would wish to make payment therfor: they have not forgot old times, though they fear greatly that you have so done. There is no changes in Manasquan, since I wrote last, except that one or two is gone. Aaron Bent and the mother of your old friend George. She grew feebler for two years, going up and down the beach incessant; watching the far-off sails, thinking they would bring one of her boys: We found her lying quite still there one morning, the sand blown over her: We have not heard news of her son George since you went away five years ago last April: his property was sold out then: I have thought of asking you if you knew of his whereabouts. There have been times when I thought I would ask you to tell me if your relations to him had changed: but I would not hurt you, Lizzy, no matter what my feelings may be. You ask me about my own affairs. They is prosperous. I have a comfortable House and Farm. I have the best poultry-yard in these parts. I find it lonesome at times but I am in no mind to marry, any young girl hereabouts as you proposed to me once. I have no more to say except that if you are minded to come back you'll find them as was friends—friends still. Your taking part with that unfortunate Boy will not set any one against you. Least of all, me. But I suppose you are among fashionable folk and know the World. It is a long time since you went away. Five years last April. I often wonder if you know how long. I am with respect, your friend and well-wisher, JAMES VAN ZELDT."

"I am not so sure as to what you would call a love-letter," said Honora, meaningly, patting the letter on her hand. "But he was a very genuine man who wrote that, I think."

"Oh, Jim is a very honest fellow. But—"

"I would like to see his farm and house."

"It would not differ in any way from any small plot about here. Jim is very commonplace, and so are all his belongings;" comparing, as she said it, little Van Zeldt, his house and poultry-yard, with the flood of moonlight on the great, ebbing tide, and the tender grace and glamour of Laddoun's presence —a presence which had grown very real to Lizzy lately, as she had fallen into the habit of bringing it before her, after the fashion of women, to make more bitter the consciousness that her idol had been but clay. It came so strongly before her now that she scarcely heeded Honora as she rose and gave her the letter, turning to the little oval mirror on the wall to adjust her cap and hair.

"I am going now, Lizzy. I mean to drive down to the village."

"It is a good morning for— What is that?" with a sudden cry.

"Why, Lizzy!" Honora caught her arm. "I heard nothing. Do you see ghosts in daylight? What frightened you?" placing her on a chair.

"I will not sit down. It was a voice I have not heard for years."

"I hear Sam whistling: he is raking the leaves from the path. There is nobody else there," going to the window. "Your letter has put you *en rapport* with somebody who is gone, as the mediums would say, or made you nervous. That is it."

"I could not be deceived!" said Lizzy, huskily, straining her eyes across the field. Her pale, thick skin was damp and her mouth set firmly. "What shall I do if he comes here, Honora? It is all over between us—all over."

Mrs. Duffield's doubt of Lizzy's sanity came to Nora's mind. "I do not think there was any one there, dear Miss Byrne," she said, soothingly. "However, I will go and look."

When she left the room the old musical voice rang out again suddenly and close at hand. The gardener's mumbling tones were heard in reply. Lizzy threw up the window, leaning on the sill with both hands, and waited.

"Get from under the horse's feet, fellow!" cried Laddoun, loudly, snapping his whip over the horse's ear. "Tell old James Galbraith and his wife I want them—both of 'em—without loss of time."

"And who'll I say wants them?" deliberately, dragging a mass of leaves across the road.

"One that can put you and them to the right-about when he chooses," sternly. "One that will be met in this house in a different sort of fashion a year from now, I fancy."

How princely the sternness and courage in his voice used to seem to her! She was older now. She only thought that he must have been drinking, early as it was in the day. The old gardener shuffled by, grumbling and stopping to rake as he went. The horse's slow footfalls came nearer on the graveled road beside her, so near that Moro, the old house-dog, ran lazily by out of his way. She could not draw her breath in all the cold, fresh air. There was a moment's silence, and then, in the full morning sunshine, Laddoun rode up the path. The lover of her youth, with no tender glamour of grace and youth about him, but overgrown and well-to-do; oily and coarse with low successes: vulgar chains strung over his gaudy waistcoat, and a vulgar leer under his thick eyelids. He had set his hat on one side, curbed his horse, and rode with a sort of triumphant pomp for his own delectation, with the bearing which he imagined would be that of a crown prince entering on possession of his kingdom. True, Dallas was the heir,

but what would Dallas ever be but his tool? He lifted his eyes with a haughty indifference.

Lizzy stood in the low window close at his side.

She was squarer and more sober and matter-of-fact than ever. There was the very brown stuff dress which she wore at Manasquan, and her knitting stuck in its sheath. She and Dallas, of all the world, alone knew him to be a forger and a villain.

He put out both hands before him, dropping the bridle, breathless and silent for a moment. Then he hurled an oath at her full of fury, as readily as if he had been her husband all these years.

"Why did you come in my way? What are you here for?"

There was no reply. The bright morning sunshine fell about them. The crackling of the twigs under his horse's feet sounded loud and jarring in the intense silence, and his watch ticked noisily. Lizzy put her hands to her throat. "Is it Dallas?" she cried, under her breath. "Do you want him? How could you think I would harm you, Laddoun! If only for the sake of old times—"

"Bah!" gathering up the rein with a snort of anger and disdain. "What are old times to me?"

No matter what his loss might be, Laddoun, with men, never lost his temper when the cards were against him. But this was only a woman, and the game had been so nearly won! He adjusted the bridle a moment, controlling himself, and then pushing the horse into the bushes which separated them, scanned her from head to foot with a cool, deliberate stare, which took note of, and taunted her, as she well understood, with every mark of age or homeliness.

"Old times have no significance to me, Lizzy," he said. "You forget that I have been abroad in the world, and seen many other women since then, differing from those of Manasquan."

She drew back: the quick change in her face made him suddenly pause.

"I had no wish to remind you of Manasquan, George," she said, with unnatural quietness. " I said the remembrance of it would keep me from doing you harm. It has not lost its significance to me."

But there was a different meaning in these words, he fancied. A covert threat; and Laddoun secretly cowered before it. He thought, too, he understood her game. " There is no room here for you and me both to work," he said, coarsely, "and you've been beforehand with me. You always had 'capacity,' as the Yankees say. You've got the whip-hand of me with Dallas now."

" Dallas is going: he will not be in your way," she cried. " Let the boy alone, for God's sake, George! You've done him harm enough."

Laddoun looked at her keenly in silence. She was not levying black-mail off Galbraith then? At least not for the present. There might yet be time to play his last card.

" You are going to let him start on this wild-goose chase then? The more fool you. Well, my game is up. So, so!" snapping his fingers with a shrug which he had caught from the Mexicans, his manner always being a thing of shreds and patches, gathering as he went.

" Good-bye, Lizzy," lifting his hat and fixing his bold, black eyes on her. " It was but yesterday Dall and I spoke of you. But you've altered. Time tells on us all, eh?"

She was bending forward, her hands resting on the window-sill, steadily looking into his red, excited face. Laddoun moved uneasily. " Do you see that it is the same man as your old lover?" with a forced laugh.

" I see that it is the same."

" Yes, I'm the same old Laddoun. Good-bye, Lizzy." But he bowed again, and glanced back uncomfortably once or twice at the motionless figure as he rode away. He thought that he had played his hand badly. She might have stood his friend. " I fancied the old fire had not altogether burned out when she looked at me first. But Talleyrand was right. She is my enemy now for life. I have called her ugly and old."

CHAPTER XVII.

HONORA came back in a few moments: " I knew you were mistaken, Lizzy. There is no one in sight whom you could possibly know. There is a horseman going down the avenue, a stout, over-dressed man, whose very shoulders assert themselves: I think it is a Colonel Laddoun, whom we met yesterday coming home from church. He is—" an indescribable contemptuous shrug finished the sentence. " He could be nothing to you, Lizzy."

" No,' said Lizzy, " he is nothing to me."

" You're dreadfully shaken by that letter, poor thing. I did not think you had been so nervous. Come out with me: the cold air will make you feel as if you were freshly born."

" No. I'll lie down by the fire, and take some tea. That is the remedy for all middle-aged people," glancing with a miserable smile over the girl's shoulder into the little mirror.

" Middle-aged, indeed! Why look at this," and Honora, with ready tact, pulled down Lizzy's beautiful hair, and let the black, glossy masses fall about her until they touched the floor. " What would I not give for it? Talk of your youth being gone while you have that, and your smooth, pure skin! If you'd only drink less tea, and brood less over the fire, your color would come back; and you ought to take care of your looks for the sake of—your 'friends and well-wishers,'" with a meaning twinkle in her eyes.

But Lizzy refused to smile, cowering on a stool wretchedly over the fire, paler even than before. Honora began to draw on her gloves, watching her doubtfully.

" Elizabeth," she said, with an authoritative nod, measuring her words 'n a miniature imitation of Madam Galbraith, " there is one sentence in that letter about which I think it is my duty to speak to you. I believe that I see in it the cause of your troubles. I inferred from it that you had allowed yourself to become entangled in the fortunes of some desperate character—some abandoned wretch. I think that—well, I think it very imprudent, Elizabeth."

Lizzy turned and looked up at her with a sudden, inexplicable meaning on her face. "You saw the abandoned wretch, Honora, for whom I sacrificed my life. You gave him your hand, and told him you believed in him. He will not soon forget it. The touch of your hand counted for more to him than the work of many of my years."

"Oh, the convict! I remember," growing violently hot and red. "I could not help that. Something in the man's words carried me out of myself for the time. But I draw a line," her slight, stately figure rising to its height: the training and creed of her whole life starting up to give fluency and force to the words. "It is our duty as Christians to hold out a helping hand and to speak encouraging words to that class of people, but to consort with them and make them companions!—It is to touch pitch and to be defiled."

"You forget your Master's work," rising. "He made friends of publicans and sinners."

"That is a different matter," sharply. The little lady, with all her radicalism, did not choose that her housekeeper should argue with her. "He could not be tainted by contact, but a woman like me or you, Elizabeth, should keep herself pure and apart. The Church's ministers were left to preach His gospel," sententiously. "We are to teach it too, but more by example than directly: surely not by mixing ourselves up with the every-day life of vulgar and vile people. I will be very sorry, Lizzy, if I find you have been drawn into any such connection. My uncle and aunt would be very sorry," buttoning her gloves decisively.

"The convict, as you call him, was not guilty. He was punished unjustly."

"That may be," more dogmatically, as Lizzy appeared to yield. "But your own common sense must teach you that five years of prison life would render him unfit for an hour's companionship with women of our position. Think of the vileness which he must have drawn in from the very air! And *I* think a man should be as pure and carefully taught and religious as a woman. Like my uncle, for instance. You need not say a word, Lizzy. Give the unfortunate man money, or whatever kindness you please; but if you lower yourself by associating with him, for however short a time, you are unjust to Mr. Van Zeldt, whose wife you will some time be."

"I will never be his wife! And for the unfortunate man, Honora—" Lizzy stopped abruptly, the indignant, speechless tears rushing into her eyes as she looked at the girl who had usurped Dallas' place; scanning fiercely the delicate figure, the flushed, high-bred face, and the sunshine all about her. "You would give him money and kindness? You!"

Honora drew back quickly as if she had been struck, and was silent for a moment. "You forget yourself, Elizabeth," she said, gently. "I will leave you to rest a while," and went quickly out of the room, without suffering her to reply; while Lizzy sat down on her stool again, her hands clasped about her knees, her back to the window, that she might not see the dainty equipage and the radiant, picturesque little heiress driving off triumphant. She muttered to herself something about bigotry and Pharisaism, and then she turned so that she could look into the mirror; and, twisting up her hair and taking off her collar to leave the yellow crowsfeet in her throat bare, she studied her own age and ugliness, almost forgetting Dallas. She yawned nervously, chafed her wrists, cold and hot shivers creeping out from one spot in her side through her whole body, weak tears dribbling over her cheeks unconsciously; going, in short, through the whole process by which nature seeks to relieve hysteric women of pain which might else be mortal.

And Lizzy's life had suffered an amputation that day worse for a woman than the loss of leg or arm. Back yonder, in the youth to which she had looked steadily for years, there was a gap never to be filled. Moonlight and ebbing tide and the voice whose sorcery had made enchantment of them, and all that these things meant to her, were gone for ever. Instead, there was coarse, every-day sand, a silly girl and a vulgar braggart.

Yet, underneath all, there was deeper dread of another loss. The people at Manasquan had not seen her for five years: would they all think her homely and middle-aged?

Perhaps Jim Van Zeldt had met "other and different women."

Presently she shook out her mass of hair until the sun touched it: it was finer and heavier than Mrs. Duffield's—than even Madam Galbraith's magnificent gray mane; and her skin, too, as Honora said, was smooth as a child's, passing her forefinger over her cheek. After all, Honora was an affectionate, fine-natured little thing, toned on too high a key by those foolish old people, but with wonderfully just perceptions for her years. She was sorry she had vexed her. It was not her fault that she had taken Dallas' place, and as for her antipathy to what she chose to consider vulgar and vile, the child had sucked in such prejudices with her mother's milk: they were a part of her as much as her blood or voice: she would never lose them while she lived.

Honora, meanwhile, being angry, walked her ponies at a funeral pace, aggravating to them and herself. She was not going to be suspected of venting her temper on them! Her uncle, coming through a cornfield up to the road, thought she would make a curious study for an artist as she passed through the solitary landscape, sitting erect in the low chaise in her odd, furred costume, the reins loose in her hands, her face fixed and intent. He had never seen the power in the child's face before. She was a something singularly discordant and out of harmony with the faded November day, in which both the chilly earth and sky betrayed their weariness and lack of strength. The fanciful old man thought that the girl might have better typified some cool spring morning, behind whose faint, beautiful heats and dews lay prophecy of all the passion and storms of the year to come. He leaned over the fence unnoticed, marking the nervous strength of her grasp, the broad, white forehead, the steady, brilliant eyes, the red heat on her cheeks that burned and faded with her thoughts: reading, as a skillful botanist would in a yet flowerless weed, possibilities of which the plant itself knew nothing and which perhaps might never be developed.

As for Honora, she was only conscious that the world had turned the wrong side to her to-day, like a grand piece of embroidery of which she saw only the knots and tangled ends of threads, or like a wonderful harmony, whose shrill treble and dissonant bass only reached her. In church, or after reading certain books, it was very easy to plan out a part for herself in it that would be like a sweet, perfect symphony; oh, very easy: she was quite sure, if she had the chance, she was capable to-day of any of the heroic acts of greatly good women from Madam Roland down.

But when she came out of her shell for a moment, and was even as good and self-reliant as other girls, see the miserable muddles into which she ran! Madam Galbraith scolded her, or Mr. Dour made absurd love to her, or Lizzy insulted her gratuitously, or—and then the angry heat faded into a more meaning pallor. That any convict who had been in contact for years with thieves and murderers should boast of the touch of her hand! "It counted for much to him." There had been a meaning smile on Lizzy's face when she said this, that maddened her: her pity must have made her beside herself, not to see that the man was young. Honora, alone on the road, took off her glove and wiped her little white fingers vehemently. After this she would live to herself. Nobody understood her but her uncle, or if any one came in her way who seemed worth knowing—as a mere study of human nature—they took no note of her. Not as much as if she were a bit of coal or a root, and went away, leaving the dull, commonplace world just as it was before. There was small room for heroism or grand, sweet symphonies of lives there! Plod on, plod on to the end.

But Honora had tried the world through only nineteen clean, sweet-aired years: her melancholy and despair were, after all, rather appetizing: a not unwholesome training with which Nature ordinarily exercises the brains of girls. She suffered her ponies to break into a trot, which grew faster and faster as they reached a level stretch of road, both her eyes and theirs beginning to sparkle. Then the sun came out behind the watery yellow sky: presently she halted, detecting an odd change in the scents of the stubble-fields: then she drove up to the rocks to reach a flaming branch of a gum-tree, taking off her cap to put in a leaf or two. The bit of color suited her altered mood: the road being lonely, she sang to herself some broken snatches of a cheery song to which the flashing hoofs of the ponies kept time. She reached the mile-post in the road where it separated—a by-way turning lonesomely up into the hills, while the common broad plank-road went straight down to the village.

Honora drew her reins and hesitated. She was in no mood for the village women's questions or gossip; or, perhaps (still lashing herself for her sins), she was not fit for it. She had better live alone in future, as far as was possible. The solitary mountain road, shut in by leafless hickory woods, tempted her. She waited, uncertain, a moment, and then turned into it; changing, it may be, as she did so, the whole current of her life. For, jogging down the path, a quarter of a mile in advance, rode Laddoun; and when he saw her coming far behind him, he drew into the shelter of the bushes on one side and waited for her. He had set his face to California on leaving Lizzy. His game was up at the Stone-post Farm, with her there to proclaim him a cheat and forger to the old people. Galbraith might play out the play as suited him. He was on his way to his inn, there to take passage in the evening coach for New York, when he saw the glittering wheels and fiery black ponies coming swiftly up the road, and the slight gray figure guiding them.

He only meant, when he drew off, being a connoisseur in women, to treat himself to a farewell look at the girl, who had a witchery and freshness about her beside which mere beauty was tame. But in the moment of waiting, a sudden inspiration came to him—a scheme which he welcomed as complete and sure of success. Now, Laddoun was a confirmed theatre-goer; his brain was full of hackneyed plots; the garish light of the stage colored all his ideas as thoroughly as religion would those of Honora. When he fell on this plan, therefore, utterly melodramatic and impracticable to anybody else, he took a firmer seat in his saddle, and set his hat confidently upon his oily curls again, his sanguine face beaming with delight and self-complacency.

In the brief space which elapsed before Honora's chaise came up abreast with him, he had to elaborate his plan. Given, a mystery and the chance of being a heroine, and any woman living was ready to throw herself soul and body into the part: he would tell the girl the secret of Galbraith's birth, and either out of love of romance or the chance of winning Dallas, and so saving a share of the spoils for herself, she would seek the boy out.

"Let him meet her again," thought Laddoun, "and the work's done. I saw how he held himself as with an iron curb at the thought of her yesterday. Slow, cold fellows like Dallas come to a white heat under a woman's influence, which men like me never reach. Let him be fairly in love with the girl, and, with all his boasted honesty, I'll wager there'll be no word spoken of Albany to the Galbraiths! That little episode will sink out of the young man's remembrance as if a volcano swallowed it. So? so? When they have been married a few months, it will be time for me, with that bit of knowledge in my hand, to put on the screws."

Honora came closer: the Colonel, unseen, watched her through the hickory boughs. She seemed very untainted and childlike to the jaded roué; and her face, or the healthy mountain air or the pleasant sunshine about him, gave him a sudden twinge of disgust for the job he had taken in hand. "I'd better be off to the ranches and McGill, and let the dirty work alone." But the next moment brought a subtler counselor. "Where's the harm? Dallas is a clever dog and I'm throwing a fortune and a good wife at his feet. There's nobody else would do it for him. Curse it, if I think he deserves it at my hands! Wouldn't drink with me when I took him out of the very gutter, eh? Curse it, if I haven't a mind to throw up the whole business and let him shift for himself! If I do bring him in such a haul as this, he'll hardly begrudge me my—commission. No: Dall's not mean. Commission: that's what it is."

By the time the ponies passed him, therefore, in a slow trot, for the descent was steep, it was with the gracious feeling of a lordly benefactor, and quite the benign air of one, that he sallied out to overtake them.

"You drive well, Miss Dundas," bowing to his saddle as he came up beside her. "Your finger is as gentle and steady as a man's on the rein."

Honora had given a start of annoyance at the first sight of him, but she bowed civilly. "I have always been accustomed to horses," she said, formally, drawing back to one side of the narrow lane and motioning for him to pass her—a motion to which the Colonel was blind, though he smiled under his moustache, reining in his horse close by her seat.

"You are a lover of nature, I see?" with a profound respect in his tone and manner which was unaffected. "So am I—so am I. Though the zest of the matter to me is, that we can put our hand on mountains and sea and say, 'The lord of this is man.' I beg your pardon, but the girth of the off-horse—it is a little loose. Permit me?"

"It is quite secure, I think," said Miss Dundas, dryly.

Laddoun was silent a moment, then began a fresh attack. "What magnificent pasturage this is! I suppose you do not know whether it is included in the Galbraith domain? The estate which you will inherit, Miss Dundas," with another bow, "is larger than many a German duchy, did you know?"

"No, I did not know. The land is my uncle's." Honora's brows were contracting: her temper would bear but little strain this morning. Besides, all the formal reserve in which she had been reared protested against this forced companionship; and there was about Laddoun that insensible air of impurity which surrounds some men, which women breathe with difficulty. He made one or two efforts to talk to her, and was met by cold and colder monosyllables. His black eyes glittered at the unwonted rebuff: he fingered nervously the gold eagles strung over his breast. There was no use in delay, nor reason why he should submit to the insolence of this petted girl: his business with her could be brought to a speedy end: a few sharp words would settle it.

"You prefer that I should ride on, Miss Dundas?" with a sudden change of voice.

Honora blushed when her rudeness was thus brought before her. "I was out of temper this morning, I'm afraid," forcing a courteous smile, "and I came here for a solitary drive to cure myself. I am unattended, as you see."

"Yes, I saw that," coolly. "You will be the better able to attend to a few words which I have to say to you." He turned his horse rapidly, so as to face her, and laid his fat hand on the reins.

Her horses stopped. Honora gave one quick glance down the lonely road, up the mountain-side, growing slowly deathly pale. Then she sat erect and looked him steadily in the eye. "I know of no subject in common between Colonel Laddoun and me. If there be one, this is not the place to discuss it," she managed to say, though her heart was quaking horribly under the Polish jacket, and her own voice deafened her.

"This is the place I choose," he rejoined, insolently. He stopped in genuine admiration, magnetized by the wide eyes, dark with terror and defiance, and the colorless face which the extremity of the moment had vivified with a rare and tragic beauty.

"I did not think there was so much power in you," he said, good-humoredly, after a pause. "Now, see, Miss Dundas," leaning on the edge of the little carriage. "There's no need to be frightened. I'm one that goes straight to the point. I have a hard blow to give you, but I'll make it as easy as I can. I mean well in the end by you, as you'll acknowledge some day."

She motioned for him to go on, not speaking.

"I think it will be a wholesome lesson for you. You carry yourself in a way hardly befitting society in a country where there is no such thing as rank. You learned that from your uncle, I suppose. But that air of distance and hauteur wouldn't go down with an old traveler like George Laddoun!" with an angry pause. "And it is especially unbecoming in you, because you base it on a heritage to which you have no claim. You are the heir of the Galbraiths, the country people say. But if Dallas Galbraith should come to light, what are you then?"

"Dallas Galbraith?" with a long, bewildered breath. "The boy who is dead?"

"What are you then?" persistently. "A poor relation reared by charity. Dallas Galbraith is not dead," his voice rising. "And I—George Laddoun— know the secret of his life. He has been left to work in the coal-pits at Scranton; to— But the rest of his life doesn't matter. He has suffered from hunger and cold while you slept soft and lived warm, holding his place—a place which even now he won't rob you of, humble fool that he is. If you were a man, now that you know the truth, you would bring the boy back to his place. But the usual rules of honor don't obtain with lovely woman," with an uneasy sneer, for he began to fear he had counted too largely on her readiness for heroism.

Miss Dundas paid no more attention to his stream of words than to the neighing of her ponies. She did not seem conscious, either, that he had ceased to speak and was watching keenly her pale face and uncertain breathing.

"Do you mean," turning to him at last, and speaking slowly, "that Tom Galbraith's son is alive—that I can bring him back to my uncle?"

"You've Colonel Laddoun's word for it that he is alive. You can bring him back to-day, if you mean to do it."

She paused a moment, and then gave the reins a fierce little jerk, breaking the horses into a break-neck pace down the hill, bidding him follow by a commanding glance. The girl, Laddoun saw, scarcely knew what she was doing. She was not much better fitted than a baby to master the emergency in which she was placed. He was not at all surprised to find, therefore, when he had urged his horse again abreast of her, that the tears were running down her cheeks, and that she was brushing them off and lashing the ponies alternately with feeble strokes. "They're so slow!" choking back a sob. "They don't heed me a bit to-day."

"Wouldn't it be better to inquire where to go, Miss Dundas?" smothering a laugh, for her energy had put him in high good-humor. "We'll take it leisurely. There's ample time to find Galbraith. He has waited all his life: an hour or two more won't matter, I reckon."

"I wasn't thinking of *him*. I know nothing about him. But he will go to the house if he is so near, and I want to bring him to my uncle. I thought, when you told me, What if *I* could take Tom's son to him? That is, if you are telling me the truth."

"I am telling you the truth, Miss Dundas," gently, looking steadily into the glowing, wet little face. The look of pathetic tenderness in it belonged to a world outside of Laddoun's experience. Nobody but the old man who was so dear to her had ever seen it there before. He did not speak to her again as they rode on for some distance together. It touched even him that her sole thought at the time should be of the only friend and companion she had ever had.

"I suppose, now, the death of his boy was the one great loss of your uncle's life?" ventured the Colonel, sympathizingly.

Honora started and looked at him, on guard on the instant. "I never have heard my uncle speak of his son," she said, quietly, gathering up the reins into a steadier hold. The road which they traversed had narrowed into a mere lane, which opened, a few rods further on, into a wide stretch of pasture-land sloping down to the creek. On the other side the hills were cut by a winding cattle-path. Honora looked at her watch.

"Have we far to go?" she asked, uneasily. "Mr. Galbraith has an appointment in the village at noon, and if he should meet his grandson, he will certainly know him. I shall be too late."

"Dallas is not in the village. Besides, I cannot go with you to find him at all, Miss Dundas. We're not on good terms, exactly. To tell you the truth, he has treated me so shabbily that any other man than I would give him the go-by for life. I'm going to California to-morrow, but I thought I'd do him this good turn before I left. That's my way."

Honora looked at him scrutinizingly, but made no reply. He began to doubt whether the little girl who guided her horses with such a firm hand was altogether the baby he had supposed, or whether, if her uncle had not been brought into question, she would not have been plucky enough to master any crisis in life. He had a mean desire to bring out some fresh emotion, to play on her again as on an instrument.

"Say, Miss Dundas! You are regarded as the heir of the old people yonder. Your position will be altered. You've forgotten your own part in the matter."

"No; I have not forgotten," calmly.

"Umph!" after a pause. "Will you go on alone to find Dallas?"

"Alone! Yes. Where is he? How shall I know him? I wish to take him back before four o'clock if possible. My uncle will be alone then."

"By George! You do mean to block your own game, then?" with a burst of admiration. "There's no compulsion, you understand? Dall 'll never claim the place unless you go after him."

"Where am I to go, Colonel Laddoun?" coldly. "My time is short."

"So is mine. I've to reach the lower ford inn by noon. You know Dallas," his eyes fixed on her face. "You met him once by the quarry in the mountains. A tall, powerful young fellow, with his mind set on slates and coal, I'll wager, far more than on a pretty face."

Miss Dundas drew the reins suddenly, so sharply that the ponies came to a dead halt. She betrayed no other sign of emotion. But she did not speak. "That was Dallas Galbraith, was it? Dallas Galbraith?" she said, at last, to herself.

Laddoun did not answer her. He was peering into her dark eyes breathlessly. So much of his chances for life hung on the thought going on just now in this silly girl's brain. But the face was as inscrutable as Dallas' own. These Galbraiths all had the rare knowledge of when not to speak or act—a tremendous staying-power, in the language of the turf. Laddoun drew back, and put his horse in a trot, baffled. The ponies kept even pace with him.

"You will take the road to the right," he said, when they came to the end of the lane, turning to her. "That will lead you to the Indian Queen. I must bid you good-bye, here, Miss Dundas. Perhaps I may meet you again before next year—who knows? But I'm off to the gold regions now: I'll let things take their course: I can neither let nor forward them any further. You'll find Dallas Galbraith at the Indian Queen."

Miss Dundas bowed—a statelier bow than she ever could have learned from Madam Galbraith.

"I am very much obliged to you, Colonel Laddoun. You have done Mr. Galbraith a great service, and I can answer for his gratitude if you ever choose to claim it. I will inform my uncle of the place where you say he will find his grandson."

"You will not go for Dallas?"

"No;" and with a sudden motion of farewell she turned her horses toward the open common and drove rapidly away. Laddoun looked after her in appalled dismay: then he burst into a loud laugh:

"By the Lord! The fellow's more to her than I guessed! She is afraid to meet him!"

The air grew fresh to Honora when she had left him, but the short saffron grass and zig-zag fences whirled past her blinded eyes. She heard with a feeble terror voices approaching. She was not sure of herself—of a look or word which she would give: the very house at home and the life there this morning seemed far off to her, and never to be regained.

One thing she knew. She had a word to say to her uncle which would heal that old wound in his soul for ever. No one but she ever had known what his dead son had been to him. She was glad that she had never spoken that son's name to him. If she could have been the one to bring his boy to him!—

But— And Honora, being alone, let fall the reins and covered her face with her hands, as if to shut out from her own consciousness the burning heat that rose from her bosom up to her forehead.

Presently she turned her ponies swiftly into the hill road. It was a lonely and direct route toward the Galbraith house. She must lose no time in finding her uncle there.

But fate was against her; for when she had driven some fifty rods into the narrow defile she looked up, and there, coming rapidly toward her in his workman's blouse of gray flannel, was Dallas Galbraith.

PART VI.

CHAPTER XVIII.

WHEN she saw him, Honora pulled the ponies' heads round to turn them backward; anything to escape out of his sight! Then, thinking of her uncle, she turned them directly back again, and suffered them to go on slowly toward him, leaning back, desperately resolved to let matters take what course they pleased. Then she pulled them up to a dead halt, at which one of the poor, patient things looked round at her with mild wonder; but the other, who better knew the young woman's ways, only gave a cynical neigh. Dallas was coming nearer: she had the light of her new knowledge in which to see him. His gray clothes were both sleazy and dusty: as for his face, only savage strokes of ill-fortune could have cut out such spare, controlled features. While she had "slept soft and lived warm—"

The glittering little carriage in which she sat, feeling herself every inch a princess, after all, was his: the jeweled whip she held like a sceptre, was his. They had left him to work in the coal-pits at Scranton, while she— Her very clothes weighed her down and burned in on her a sense of imposture. It was more than she could bear. She threw the reins loose and scrambled out of the chaise, intending to go to him. Instead, she stopped at the head of the nearest pony and put her arms about its neck.

"Stand still, Babe, dear!" in a tone not far from crying. "Don't *you* worry me. I'm worried nearly to death," cramming sugar, with which her pocket was full, into its mouth. "Stand still, I say!" drawing off and stamping her foot. "Don't move till I come back; I'm not so mean but that something shall obey me!" at which Babe, who happened to be the young and favorite one of the two, rubbed his nose into her palm, sympathetically, while his wiser brother stamped for his share of sugar, half shutting his eyes, sardonically.

The little gray figure fluttered along the road with the desperate, uncertain motion of a partridge scared from its nest. There was a fallen sycamore lying half across the way, filagreed over with yellow and black lichen. She stopped beside it, holding by its crumbling branches, while Dallas came nearer—hesitated—nearer—and then stood close before her. The lonely mountain lane, high-banked and hedged, seemed to hold them together with its straightness and silence; the wind had died: the thin sunshine on the faded grass and shelving hill-cuts waited. The hour, for which all their lives before had been but a dull, ticking prelude, struck loud and clear.

If Honora, in all her years of dreaming, had known what was coming, she could have been ready to give the moment its dramatic word of utterance. Many a time afterward through her life she composed the proper greeting which she ought to have given him. As it was, she put out one hand feebly and drew it back again; and finally—

"Are you looking for fossils and—things?" she said.

Galbraith put his hand involuntarily to the empty green bag which was slung on his back. "I have found nothing," he answered.

He had found nothing for days until now; but this was all for which he had looked. Honora was a very different thing to Dallas than a pure, winning maiden is to a society-bred lover. So far, remember, he had humanized his life —not his life him. The genial, divine under-meaning of the work-day world begins to show itself to most young men in their boyish fun, in their home-life, in their glimpses of fairy-land through theatres and circuses, in hymns (not often in sermons), and later, through their love of women, art, society; but all these had always been shut out from him in the coal-pits, in Manasquan and in Albany. Honora, and the wealthy, generous life which framed and made a background, were his first open glimpes of it: they seemed to contain all that he had missed in the past empty years. She held in her hand the magic wine, ready to give him, of which his life had been drained.

So that he had gone about now for days through the hill-roads, in the hope of finding her, with much of the same awed longing, I fancy, as that with which the first of the earth's people looked to meet every day the angels who lived in the near but unattainable heaven. Only that a great, busy, merry household like Madam Galbraith's—culture, books, and a young woman, tempting in her hidden beauty and fragrance as an unsunned rosebud—would mean far more to a healthy, strong-brained man than a whole sky-full of misty angels and rest. As they ought to do.

"I did not think I would see you again," he said, gently. "I am going to-morrow. I did not think I would see you again." He stood far off, as if conscious of the gulf between them, never to be crossed; but he was not conscious of the untamable pleasure kindling in his eyes.

"Yes, I'm here; but I did not come for you," hastily. "I was going home. Oh! that is not what I wanted to say!" with a sudden outburst. "I mean that I know who you are. I know all. You must come home."

"You know who I am?"

"Dallas—Dallas Galbraith."

"You are ill! Sit here, on this stone."

"I am not going to fall," stiffly erect, with both hands on the sycamore trunk; "but I'm worried. The sun makes my head ache." And after a pause: "It was unmaidenly in me to come for you; but the ponies turned down this road. I did not think you were here."

"Why ought you not come? You knew who I was, and you wanted to bring me home. That was right, I think."

Honora, looking into his grave, bewildered face, felt her modesty in some way puerile and false. "Of course it was right," she said, slowly. "Just as any man would have come for another."

"No," sharply; "God knows, not that!" He turned away and walked hastily down the road, leaving Miss Dundas staring after him, amazed. The slow fellow was beginning to realize what it meant that she knew who he was. If Laddoun had betrayed him out of sheer revenge, he had told her the damning secret which he was trying to put out of sight. Then, his whole life was blocked; all chance struck from him of home, work, education, and that something which he dared not name; and, instead, the foul load to carry for life which he had borne so long for another.

But it might have been Lizzy: she

was fond and foolish: she might have used this lovely lady as a lure to compel him back.

He returned with quick steps and passionate eyes. He had not seen before how lovely she was. She had taken off her cap, and the damp rings of brown hair fell loose about her neck, framing her face. There was no gross heat in Dallas' blood. The slight maidenly figure leaning against the yellow trunk did not madden him as it might coarser men, nor the soft rising color in her mobile face. But the pure womanly presence, so unknown to his life, the tenderness, weakness, the very silliness betrayed in her eyes, akin to that of the children who were so dear to him, wrung his heart with a delirious pain such as only men of his nature can feel. He had lived so much with men that the woman in Honora was a new revelation to him: his thought of her already began to change him, as the living breath which once entered into the nostrils of the dull shape of clay, and, passing through its heavy limbs, made it a man.

Honora, meanwhile, had been nerving herself, and proposed now to talk to him of this matter in the exact business-like tone which one man would use to another. That was the way in which she should have begun.

"I want you to go home this afternoon," she said. "My uncle will be in the library. You must go directly in and say to him: 'I am Dallas Galbraith.' I meant to tell him first, but—"

"How do you know me, Miss Dundas? Who told you my name?"

"Colonel Laddoun."

Galbraith did not speak for a moment. "You said," in a strained, unnatural tone, "that you 'knew all:' what did Laddoun tell you of me?"

"Only that you had worked in the coal-pits at Scranton, and had led a hard life, while *I* took your place; that you would not make yourself known; that you were going with Doctor Pritchard never to come back, leaving *me* to defraud you to the end," growing more bitter and emphatic as she went on.

Finding that Galbraith stood thoughtful, unmindful, apparently, of her assault on herself, she added: "Colonel Laddoun is gone. He was not a man to whom I would choose to explain anything. But do you not blame me—do you? *You* can understand?" with an unconscious cadence in her voice which touched him with an electric shock.

"I understand. How could I blame you? Colonel Laddoun is gone, you say?"

"Yes; to California. He said," with an arch smile, "that you had treated him shamefully ill, but that he would do you this good turn before he left. I think," confidentially, "he is a good-natured man, after all—" her look finishing the sentence with an infinite scope of meaning.

"Yes: Laddoun is not malicious," gravely. "He is quite capable of a generous action. And he's gone!" with a deep breath of relief which a freed slave might give. The next moment he remembered that the relief was given by the knowledge that he was free to act a lie, to hide his real life from this girl before him; but he choked down that remembrance.

"We thought you were dead, you know, when I was given your place," Honora urged in an anxious tone, the idea that gnawed her conscience asserting itself again in the first pause. "I am only a poor girl: Mr. Galbraith's niece; and he adopted me. I did not know that I was an impostor. Of course," lifting her head slightly, "I am of as good a family as the Dours—that is, yours: I only meant I had no money when I said poor."

"And Madam Galbraith has educated you as her heir? Kept you from even the sight or name of evil, I have heard?"

"Yes. I believe I have been differently reared from other girls. She is very strict, you see—very strict. She does not understand little follies and faults which we weaker people have, and she counts them all crime. A stain is a stain to her. It might as well be murder as vulgarity in her code." Honora laughed as she said this. She was strangely light-hearted and at ease already with her cousin, for so she named him to herself. It seemed as if they had been friends long ago. Her voice had fallen into the clear, fine accords with which no one but her uncle was familiar, and her eyes, too, rested on his with the magnetic sense of ease and kinship which had only belonged heretofore to her old friend.

"It grows late," she said, looking uneasily up at the sun. "Will you let me drive you to the house—home, I mean? though the ponies and chaise are yours by right," blushing with a sudden humility.

Dallas laughed. "That Cinderella chariot? The ponies would turn into mice out of sheer dismay if such a lumbering weight as I were put upon them."

"Then you shall walk alongside," eagerly. "It is not a great distance. I can walk five miles myself, easily. You must keep on just those clothes. They are so artistic, so picturesque, so different from Mr. Dour's black coats. What if Mr. Dour had been Tom Galbraith's son!" with an appalled little grimace. "And you must wait outside of the library-door, while I go in—I may go in and tell my uncle?"

Galbraith smiled and came closer, looking down into the excited, flushed face and the brown eyes which grew darker and dimmer as she went on speaking:

"He is an old man—it is many years since his son died. I think he is very fond of me. I would like to go in and say, 'I have brought you Tom's son!' I have done so little to please him, and he has been very fond of me." She stopped and quietly brushed away the tears that had chased the smiles altogether from her eyes.

"But Madam Galbraith?" asked Dallas after a pause.

Her face fell with sudden dismay. "Oh! I had not thought of her. I have not planned about her," slowly. "She was very fond of her son Tom, but—"

"But?" He was nearer now. She was as artless and open-hearted as Matt, he thought. But he certainly never had given poor Matt the tender, amused smile with which he bent over her.

"I am not so sure about those clothes," she said, anxiously: "Madam Galbraith does not care for the picturesque so much. They would provoke her inquiry. She likes to turn people over and over. And then she would find out how poor you have been."

"She will know that I have worked in the coal-pits," soberly.

"Would—is it necessary to tell her that?" coloring; adding hurriedly: "Understand me: it is not the poverty which would enrage her, but the chance that you had been in contact with vulgar or vicious people. Her own son was very dear to her; but when he fell among thieves of his own choice, she passed him by on the other side. It is only fair to warn you of your dangers in the new country," looking up at him earnestly.

Dallas crumbled the scaly bark from the trunk that lay between them, looking at the ground with dreamy, speculative eyes. He had not the slightest intention to put his foot into the new country of which she talked. He was going with Pritchard in the morning: he had not swerved from that purpose for a moment. Honora and her world were not for him. "Vulgar and vicious." He, the son and heir, was an illiterate boor: the very names of their commonest books were an unknown language to him: there was no form of vice with which he had not been in loathsome contact for years. He meant to come back from Pritchard's expedition a changed man. Then he would go among them, concealing nothing of the past. But, meantime, there was a subtle enchantment in this unattainable world in which she lived. He could not help but stand at the gate and look in. This sun was bright and this chilly wind bracing: her clear, sympathetic voice, her old-fashioned, awkward, winning gestures, her foolish eagerness, were like alluring music sent out to tempt him to enter. It could do no one harm if he stood and looked in a while. The very careless talk, this surface-touching of matters which imported so much to him, had in it something new and cheerful: a healthy light on what had before been stern and hard.

But if he came back again the man he hoped to make himself—what then? Would he ever be clean in her eyes?

"I can understand Madam Galbraith's prejudices. But you—have you the same?" he said, and then stopped abruptly. The question mattered too much to him to be dragged out so soon and lightly. But Honora shrugged her shoulders and laughed:

"I go farther than she does, perhaps. Shall we walk toward the chaise? Jack thinks it is time for me to go. It's a terrible thing to confess, but I will tell you, honestly, I have an antipathy to the poor. Yes. It's the fashion now to be radical and enthusiastic over negroes and unwashed white people. I'd be kind to them, and give any money to feed and educate them until they stood where I do. But in the meantime I'll keep my own hands and breath clean," with a wayward motion of the delicate little body.

"If you were not so young, or if you had been down in the pit, you would find it no matter for jest," said Dallas, roughly, thinking not of himself so much as the two or three innocent-faced children whom he had meant to rescue from the very door of hell. It seemed to him, while he stood listening to this sweet low voice, he was unfaithful to them. He drew involuntarily away from her.

Honora, startled and irritated, turned to him, with a dignity which in itself she felt ought to settle the matter:

"I speak with more knowledge than you think, perhaps. It is not prejudice with *me*—it is conviction. My experience is, that just in proportion as a man's outer life is stinted and degraded, his tastes lower and grow coarse and his feelings are blunted. It is not the educated class who beat their wives and fill the cock-pits down in the village, or who crowded yelling about the gallows in the county town last week!" with a decisive pursing of her mouth which implied that that argument was closed. Finding that Dallas did not reply, she added in a sharper tone, sententiously:

"I have no faith in making companions of that class. There's nothing so contagious as vice. If we want to help the poor, the firmer we stand on our own ground the stronger we will be to lift them up. That is what I tell Lizzy. Now there is a case just in point. She is our housekeeper. She is entangled with a convict in some way. Poor thing! It has been the ruin of her own life, I suspect."

She caught sight of Galbraith's keen eyes fixed on her face, and grew more bitter and strenuous from his fancied reproval:

"She has ruined her life for him? She loved him, perhaps. I would think any woman would understand that."

"I do not," sharply. "I'm no heroine. I mean, God helping me, to make myself a pure, good woman; and I'll keep out of the slough. I think Madam Galbraith was right in her treatment of her son. I never would let down the bars. If I were Lizzy, and the man were my own brother who was so covered with moral leprosy, I would help him as far as I could with such a gulf between us, but I would never call him brother again. The dearer he was to me the farther I would put him away to save myself."

Dallas walked on beside her in absolute silence. She was hot and angry—more angry that he would not reply to her—but she could think of nothing more forcible to say. Honora was just of that age when the mind is of course quite clear on all social problems, and the creed is fixed irrevocably. But the ideas in the brain, being new and feverish, are apt to rush out and parade themselves tumultuously.

Galbraith never had argued in his life, and most probably never would. He listened with a stunned, sore feeling to what seemed to him puerile, senseless cruelty. It was like the whizz of a lash which might some day draw his own heart's blood. For the moment, their educations coming in sudden collision, the girl's presence was as repugnant to him as the touch of a dainty, malignant cat would be to a rough, stupid dog.

They walked along the road for a few paces, when, just as they reached the ponies, Honora turned on him, her face flushing crimson, her eyes indignant: "What have I done? You did not understand me!" she exclaimed, stretching out both hands. "You thought I included you in that dreadful tainted rabble down below. I never even remembered you had been poor. *You* are a Galbraith—you are one of us. You went into the coal-pits from choice!"

"I was not angry with you," said Dallas, gravely. "I did not myself remember that your words would apply to me. I was thinking of others whom I know, and of how long they must stay in the depths if it were left to you and your class to take them out."

Honora laughed. "Don't be angry with me, Cousin Dallas. I have reasoned that subject out thoroughly, and you have not. If there's one thing I do understand, it is human nature. But you have lived in the woods and mountains so long that you are visionary about men. I understand how that is," as though she gave him a good-boy pat on the head. "That is such a grand life—yours," her voice changing and her dark eyes glowing with enthusiasm. "A naturalist—made so by nature! I thought so the day I met you by the quarry. All other men's work seemed less clean and noble than yours. You have lived many years in the woods, have you not?"

Galbraith swung his bag to the other side, that he might come closer to her. The dogged, honest fellow quite understood now what manner of bigot she was, and intended to show her that he did so. Weighed against the hard realities of his own experience, or with Lizzy's ruined life, or even the narrow bigotry of the Manasquan fishermen, she and her shallow, unfeeling philosophy were weak and paltry. Words like those could hurt him no more, he told himself, than the buzzing of a poor wasp which he could crush in his hand. He meant to tell her for his sole answer where he had lived and how.

If he had but done that, his life and hers would have had a different ending.

But in the instant that he stepped closer to her, Honora blushed and held out her hand. She thought he wanted to shake hands in token of forgiveness. "You know I could not have meant you," she said, smiling.

The hand was warm. The soft pulse beat against his own. Her breath for an instant touched his face: it had a faint milky smell.

That was all.

The next moment the little lady stood apart, friendly and nonchalant as before; but the great lout in the gray flannel turned from her and patted the pony like an imbecile, heaven and earth growing uncertain to him, as though he judged them through the fumes of opium.

To hold her hand in his, to feel her breath on his cheek, to sit down beside her for ever in her life of ease and comfort! He was as little akin to the foul rabble as she, and could put his foot upon their necks as well!

Five years of misery had not moved Dallas Galbraith's integrity, but at the breath of a woman it shook to its foundation.

Miss Dundas sprang lightly into the chaise. "Come!" she said.

Galbraith laid his heavy hand on the low edge: "Wait!" Whatever tumult raged within, his manner was, as usual, blunt and quiet. "I did not mean to go and claim my place when you came to me, to-day."

"No!" eagerly: "you were going as a laborer with Doctor Pritchard. You meant to cede your right to me. So heroes act, I think!"

"I would have come back to claim it some day," said downright Dallas. "But I will go with Pritchard. I have been like a lay figure all my life, dressed in one costume or another by any chance that gained power over me. The heir of the Galbraiths would be as much of a puppet as the others. This is my first chance to make a man of myself."

"You shall not go with Doctor Pritchard!" with vehemence, clasping her hands on her knees, and bending forward. "I will not hold a false place a day longer!" Then her voice fell into that soothing, coaxing cadence which is only given to those women who are Nature's predestined wives and mothers: "Think what you are leaving. You would be welcomed as one risen from the dead. It is your home. Your mother is there—"

"Yes, my mother."

"Madam Galbraith would make herself your slave, and you would be my uncle's friend; and the whole world of books and art would be laid at your feet, if their will could bring it to you. There would not be one shadow in your way. Even Colonel Laddoun is gone, and you cannot deny that he has acted as a friend and not an enemy," with a smile. "Your kingdom is ready. You have only to enter on possession."

"And you? When I had taken your place?"

"My uncle will be my friend always," settling herself back lightly among the cushions. "And I would try to atone to you for whatever wrong I have done you," looking down into his eyes, innocently enough.

There was silence for a moment. "Why, would you turn back from my uncle and—all of us?" in a low voice.

Why would he? Laddoun was gone, all danger of detection was over. Was it a squeamish scruple in him to shrink from the perpetual mask he must wear if he took his place now? Lizzy had been outraged at his unnecessary honesty to Madam Galbraith, and even Honora herself had proposed that he should hide his poverty.

She turned toward him now, holding the reins out: "Will you take them? Will you come with me?" she said.

"Give me until to-night."

"Until to-night? Yes. Of course," with a chagrined, disappointed look, a man could not be expected to change the whole plan of his life with a moment's notice, for anybody. Here is my key of the green-house," taking it from her pocket: "it opens into the apple orchard. I will be in it at dusk and take you to my uncle."

"I will meet you. If I go with Doctor Pritchard, I must see my mother again," he added in a lower tone, to satisfy himself.

"Yes, one would suppose you would wish to do that," dryly. "Unless the study of coal renders you entirely superior to all human sympathies," giving the reins a petulant little jerk. "Come, Babe, it is time you and I were at home. Goodbye, Mr. Galbraith."

"Good-bye," returning her distant bow with a puzzled, anxious face. "How could I have offended her?" he said, as she drove quickly down the hill. "I wish I had Laddoun's insight into women! They are the most unaccountable—" shaking his head once or twice as he walked slowly after her, his hands behind him.

He meant to weigh his whole life now coolly, and decide. Instead, he watched the glittering rings of light on the tan-colored wheels of her little chariot. They were whirling her away into a joyous, affluent life which was his by right, but that the something, which had always been against him, thrust out its shadowy arm to bar him back. For it was clear to him that if he made himself known now to his family, the history of the years at Albany could never be told. He did not analyze his reasons for this certainty. He could have told his story to old James Galbraith at any moment, knowing that he would hear it with a man's quiet moderation and justice. As for the old lioness, his grandmother, Dallas smiled with the usual contempt of a young man for strong-minded women. But—there was not courage in him to declare himself a convict in that house! and then he stopped to drag out a great boulder from the clay and hurl it down the road, as a boy would do to work off some suppressed, gnawing excitement.

When he came back, a gentleman, thorough bred, "the prison smell," as

Laddoun had said, blown off him for ever, it might be different—he could face the world.

But what if he let her take him to-night, with her soft, rosy hand, and lead him in to her uncle? What if he kept his own counsel, and let the current carry him as it would? Into home, wealth and that passionate dream which he did not name. He had gone into the coal-pits for his mother's sake: had gone into the prison for Laddoun's crime. Were these things to hold him down until the day of his death?

He sat down on a patch of bronzed stubble, scratched a bit of scaly rock beside him with his thumb-nail to see if it had iron in it, and then clasped his hands about his knees and sat motionless as the tree-stumps about him. On his right was the cleft in the hills through which her glittering wheels had disappeared, and, as it happened, the sky beyond was suffused just then with a warm crystal yellow, beneath which the far-off mountains lay misty and peaceful.

There was the home to which she called him.

To the left was the road to the west, and his work. Which should he choose to-morrow? Working, he could act out himself, honest, to the last syllable: here he must force himself into a mould set by others. As for concealing that he had been a convict, the question in ethics might have been called overstrained; but Galbraith could not chop ethics about the matter: it did not come before him at all as a question of right and wrong. A church member would have said, perhaps, that God was on one side and Mammon on the other; but Dallas seldom thought of God in connection with his own small affairs, unless, with an insane blasphemy, to name Him as the something strongest "which was always against him." Of Jesus, like most men of the poorer class, he had a dreadful vague reverence; but what had He to do with his going with Pritchard? Old Luther, fighting the visible devil with brain and muscles goaded to their limit, has left the sign of the memorable conflict to this day; but Dallas did not even know that he was tempted.

He sat there during the long sunny afternoon. When it was over, there was a dull dizziness in his head, new to the clean-blooded fellow who never had tasted coffee or smoked tobacco. He had not taken his eyes from that golden haze which wrapped her home. He felt the touch of her fingers on his hand and the sweet breath on his cheek.

Three thousand years ago another Dallas "saw that rest was good and the land that it was pleasant, and he bowed his shoulder to bear, and became a servant unto tribute." The story is an old one.

But Dallas gave to his temptation and defence no high-sounding names. It was—to be himself or some one else. There was an inherent loathing in him for any sort of deception or accommodation. It went against his grain. You might as well hope for a dog to wriggle like an eel through the slime, and relish his employment. But he battled with his nature, keeping his eyes on the motionless, golden haze. "Rest was good, and the land, it was pleasant." A passionate, enervating languor, which his whole life never had known before, stole over from it to him, and wooed him to come.

The rough grit in the man (and, perhaps, the unsmoked and unliquored blood) proved too much for its subtle enchantment. Cover the fact as he would, going back meant to shoulder a lie and live in daily terror of its discovery. It meant to take up a life good for others, but which was not his. It meant, as he put it in his homely phrase, "to go to bed early in the morning and to sleep all day."

He got up at last, stifling a sigh, stretching his arms and legs to rest them. "She is a good, sweet woman, but she is nothing to me," he muttered; and then slung his bag again briskly over his shoulder and set off across the hill. The fight was over.

Long after, when he told his wife the story, she told him that he should have asked the Divine guidance. For Dallas married afterward a good, pious girl, who learned her religion, as her alphabet, out of books.

"I didn't know much about that. But it went against the grain. A man at that age don't take naturally to artificial living. The tiller-rope pulls at a young fellow pretty strong, and generally pulls him right, no matter how the current sets."

"You never will understand, Dallas, the difference between our carnal nature and that spiritual one which comes after conversion," she said, a little testily. "No good action is acceptable in any young man who is an unbeliever. Our own righteousness is but as filthy rags."

"Very likely, my dear," said Dallas, submissively.

It did not occur to her that the same hand which raised the widow's son might now hold the tiller-rope of a wild young fellow's life; or, in Dallas' confused talk of what was natural, or "the grain," in such an one, to remember that He has "many kinds of voices in the world, and that none of them is without signification."

CHAPTER XIX.

DOCTOR PRITCHARD met Dallas that afternoon on the hills going back to the Indian Queen. The Professor was on foot also, and seated himself to wait for him, looking over and smelling some bits of wool.

"Good-day, Galbraith," nodding. "I saw you coming. I knew the stride of your long legs far off. Very fair specimens of Saxony these, eh? Pool's: down in the bottom."

"I don't know anything about sheep, Doctor."

"The more shame for you then, sir— yes," sorting them in his pocket-book and strapping it. "What are eyes, or ears, or any sense given to you for but feelers—suckers, to draw in knowledge of all sorts perpetually? At your age I could class a sheep by a bit of its wool, just as I can a man now by a glint of his eye; though that last needs something more than observation—a keen instinct," complacently, putting his wallet in his breast-pocket and rising.

He walked on, nimbly, beside Dallas, tapping the ground or trees with his pointed stick now and then, and whistling to himself. There was a light-hearted, rugged strength in the young fellow's face which invigorated him. They would have a pleasant companionship by and by. The old gentleman had boasted so much, in the neighborhood, of the lucky "find" he had made in Galbraith, and his own penetration about it, that he began to have a sort of fatherly affection for the lad.

"Is your kit all ready, sir? We start early in the morning, remember. I'll overlook your outfit when we reach New York, and advise you what to take. You're a novice in long marches, and, my word for it, your knapsack will be filled with trumpery. I'll—" he hesitated. "I'll advance your salary for three months in New York, so that you can be all ship-shape before starting."

"I'm obliged to you, Doctor Pritchard," heartily. "I will have use for the money in New York, though not for clothes. I thought that some little business I had to begin there must be neglected until our return. Now I can put it in shape."

"I'm glad I can serve you," said the Professor, with a pleased glance up at the young man's bright face. "New York, umph? I thought you belonged to this part of the country, Galbraith?"

"No; I am a stranger here. I have spent but a few weeks in New York, either, and that was long ago. Five years ago."

His tone betrayed a sudden and great embarrassment, which the little man noticed; and after a moment's curious pause he changed the subject with ready courtesy.

"Do you observe the cinnamon-colored vein in that rock? Now, just beneath that—"

But Dallas had slackened his pace and now stopped, putting his hand on his companion's sleeve. "One moment. I am glad you spoke of New York. I intended to find you this evening, Doctor Pritchard, and ask you if you would not prefer to know something of my history before you took me into such close companionship. I will not go with you under false colors."

"Your history?" with surprise. "It is hardly necessary, boy," with a smile. "A young mechanic is not likely to have met with much adventure; and as for your honesty and the like, I took your face for my bond at first. I know men pretty thoroughly, I fancy."

Galbraith did not reply, and they walked on in a silence which grew more uneasy on the older man's part: he cast shrewd, furtive looks at Dallas' anxious face. "I trust to your honesty," he repeated, with meaning. "If there is any reason why you are unfit for my companionship, I believe you will not conceal it. I could not trust any man farther than that." He had a suspicion that the lad might have contracted debts and wanted more money in advance to pay them. He was annoyed and irritated, and meant to find out the worst at once.

"I am an ignorant man, as you know, but I think I am not unfit to be your companion," said Galbraith, slowly, and then was silent again until they had walked several rods. He stopped then, deliberately. "I prefer to tell you my story, Doctor Pritchard, but there is no necessity for me to do it. There is not a chance that you would find it out in any other way. There is but one man who could have betrayed me, and he is gone. I would like you to understand that, out of justice to me."

"What the devil are you telling it for, then?"

Dallas half laughed. "I hardly know. I did not mean to do it until this afternoon; but I would feel more comfortable if you knew it."

"Knew what?" irritably. He began to suspect his penetration had been deceived.

"Knew that during the three weeks I was in New York long ago I was put on my trial for a penal offence, and found guilty. Stop—hear me out," raising his hand. "I served out my time in the Albany State prison. That is all I have to accuse myself with. I was innocent. You *must* believe me. I was innocent!" for now that he had made the inner self comfortable by his confession, he recognized that his chance for making a man of himself outwardly was slipping from him for ever.

The Doctor was leaning back against the hill-side, his small features full of rage and scorn—not at Galbraith's villainy, but that he had drawn him into a mistake. "Served out your time in the Albany prison! Of course you were innocent! Was there ever a scoundrel who could not pipe that tune? Don't explain to me! I'll sift this matter to the bottom. I'll teach you to foist yourself on honest men. And drawing his salary in advance! By the Lord! Drawing his salary in advance!"

Galbraith made no answer, while the little man fumed and scolded, turning back on his first assertions with renewed zest. "Why, I've endorsed you, sir! I've talked of you far and near. I made myself accountable, as one might say, for you, and I have a jail-bird on my hands! But I'll sift the matter! You need not suppose you can dodge John Pritchard. Who was the man who could have betrayed you, did you say?"

"Colonel Laddoun. You seem to have forgotten that I have betrayed myself, and that voluntarily."

"Colonel Laddoun is gone. You took good care there should be no witness against you. He said, I remember, that he knew you thoroughly."

"Yes. No man could tell the story with more meaning than Laddoun," with a bitter smile, which exasperated Pritchard the more.

"Your sneer is singularly out of place, sir, it appears to me," with what he felt to be telling sarcasm, "inasmuch as he kept your secret. I would have been glad," with an ironical laugh, "if his consideration had extended to me also, before he permitted me to make you my companion for a year."

"It is not yet too late," said Dallas, speaking with difficulty. "You can di*-

charge me now. I—I told you in time." He stopped abruptly.

The Professor eyed him keenly. Against his will, he had felt, through his passion, that the jail-bird, as he called him, stood higher than he—was a graver, more moderate, juster man. He saw, now, Galbraith's effort at control, and knew, in spite of it, that the lad suffered. This chance of work was the last plank to which the poor wretch clung, perhaps.

But what man of sense, he thought, justly enough, would risk a year's companionship with a felon? and what sort of a story was this to get abroad after he had picked out the fellow—talked, boasted of him?

"No, it is not too late," he growled, with a decisive rap of his stick on the ground. "You are discharged. Of course you are discharged. And I am not one to change my mind about it. I never changed my mind in my life. I'm not a woman, thank God! I'll take care that your character is known to honest men. My word for it, Evans never knew it."

Dallas stepped in front of him as he was turning off. Disappointment had hardened his face and lowered his voice; but, after all, the heartiness and strength in them, which had first impressed Pritchard and warmed his heart to the lad, were there, and he could not be blind to them.

"You will not tell my story here, sir," he said, sternly. "If I chose to confide it to you, because I would take no unfair advantage of you, you have no right to blast my name with it."

"Tut! tut! You lay down the law of morality for me, do you?"

"Nor had you any right to believe one half of my assertion and set aside the other," Dallas proceeded. "I would not have been so unjust, if I stood where you do."

"Truly! you would not? The matter's closed, sir," pulling his hat on with an air of determination. "Innocent or guilty, I hardly choose to make a convict my daily associate. Not another word. The matter's closed." He started off down the road, every step ringing out uncompromisingly, while Dallas stood looking after him, leaning against the rock.

At the foot of the hill the Doctor stopped, hesitated a moment and back he came, hotter, more out of breath and angrier than before.

"What is the whole of this cursed story? What do you hold it back for? Have you nothing to say for yourself, eh?"

"I was a boy, and was made a cat's-paw of by another man. I presented a check which he had forged. It was made payable to me."

"Where is your proof?"

"I have none," standing erect and raising his voice. "No matter what manner of man I make of myself, I never can go back to the town where I lived and be called anything but a thief. I would rather those people believed in me as they once did, than— But what is the use of talking about it to you?"

"Don't be so hasty, young man. There may be a great deal of use in it. So they believed in you, did they? That would be a terrible story if it was true. Not that I have the least faith in it, though. Who was the man, by the way?"

Dallas hesitated: "I will not tell you his name. Not that I want to keep his secret. I'd be glad if the whole world knew him for what he is. But what is the use? You would but doubt me the more."

"You are the best judge of the matter, certainly. Well, good-day, Mr. Galbraith. I have quite made up my mind. You are discharged. It's the first time my instinct ever deceived me in a man."

"It did not deceive you now, Doctor Pritchard;" and Dallas gave a low, nervous laugh, so like a woman's that it startled the old man. He only glowered more gloomily, however, and set off again rapidly down the hill; and this time he did not come back.

CHAPTER XX.

WHEN Dallas reached the Indian Queen, half an hour later, Matt met him, breathless, at the foot of the hill. "I've been watching for you all day!" securing a hand. "You're a-going to-morrow, sure?"

"Yes, I'm going."

"They're packing up for you in there." The "they" meant Mrs. Beck and Lizzy Byrne, who came now to the window and nodded smiling, each cheek as red as a poppy leaf. She had a smoothing-iron within an inch of her chin, testing its heat. Peggy had just finished the white shirts she had been making for Dallas, and Lizzy had been helping her to "do them up." The two women had been in a fever of anxious preparation all day; for Miss Byrne had been over at the Indian Queen several times since Dallas' advent, to see her old friend, Mrs. Beck. She told her that she had many friends in common with Mr. Galbraith, and gradually seemed to share in Peggy's fervent interest in the young man.

Indeed, Mrs. Beck had confided to her husband in the barn-yard, while she was milking that very morning, that "if Miss Elizabeth was ten years younger, she thought something might come of it. She was very tidy-looking still, and it was high time she was settling."

The news of her boarder's appointment to go with Doctor Pritchard had put the good woman in an ecstasy of delight and triumph. Evans, indeed! She knew, from the first, he was none of Evans' sort; and now the United States was sending him out on their own especial business. She had no doubt that the President had had his eye on him ever since he came to the Indian Queen. She told Beck that even Miss Byrne, who was so common-sensed usually, was more excited about it than she. It was Miss Byrne who explained to her how high the position really was, and how it would bring his name into the papers, and how the eyes of the whole country would be upon him. "It would be such a splendid triumph over his enemies," she said—"such a triumph!" and was so fluttered whenever she talked of it that she was ready to cry.

When Dallas came up with Matt and sat down on the kitchen door-step opening on the porch, Peggy was putting the last stitches of darning in his woolen socks, and Lizzy was stooping again over the shirt-front, white and glossy as satin paper.

"I took Beck's carpet-bag, Mr. Galbraith," said Peggy, clipping her words because of the haste of the occasion. "Yours is too small to hold a cat curled up. Them jars on the table have to go in yet. They're peach leather—dry, you see. You've got to stew it. It'll be good for a snack out on the Plains, spread on your bread. I've no doubt the Doctor'll like a bite of it too. He's a notion of good living; for, as lean as he is, you ought to have seen him drink my apple-molasses, Miss Byrne, when he come to call on Mr. Galbraith."

"We've nearly done," said Lizzy. "I think these shirts will last until you come back. If you come, as you promised, at the end of a year," looking up at him.

"I'll come at the end of the year," said Dallas.

"I don't know," broke in Matt, meditatively, "whether I'd like a shaggy pony best or not. There's gobs of ponies about hyur. I was thinking of a real crocodile in a box. D'ye hear, Mr. Galbraith?"

"Hear to the child! You'd better ask for a mocking-bird, if Mr. Galbraith means to bring you anything. Crocodile, indeed? You asked me what I'd rather have from them queer countries, sir. Well, I was thinking, since Miss Elizabeth told me of fuchsias there growin' twelve feet high and cactuses in proportion, that if you could bring an original root—you see?—I'd take the premium at the county fair, then, I reckon."

"I'll bring more roots than you'll plant," said Dallas; "and the bird for Matt." For the world was broad, he thought, and roots, and birds, and work were to be found outside of New Mexico. He had not the heart to tell these women that, instead of the honorable work over which they were glorying, he was going out to-morrow without a penny or a friend in the world. He wondered that he was not dejected himself about it—that while he was trying to comprehend the great chance lost to him, he was wrestling with Matt with one hand, and looking into the busy, warm, little kitchen, laughing at Peggy's jokes. It seemed to Lizzy that for years he had not been so light-hearted: all his old, dry, quiet humor, which used to keep Manasquan alive, had come back to him.

"Are you so glad to go?" she said, half reproachfully, when Mrs. Beck had gone out: "One would think you had your fate in your own hands at last, and could make yourself what you pleased."

"I have less reason to be glad than you suppose. But the world is young, and so am I."

"Yes, that is true, Dallas."

"There is no use in moping and whining over a rough tumble at the outset." He had dropped his load somehow, she saw, and was exhilarated as a boy with this odd setting forth so late in life to seek, not fortune, but education.

"I will stay all night, Dallas," she said. "I would like to be the last to bid you God-speed, in the morning."

"I am glad of that, Lizzy," his eyes sparkling. "I have some faith in omens, after all."

"Yes, Miss Byrne will stay," bustled in Mrs. Beck, catching the last words. "Beck's arranged to take a half day tomorrow, and we'll all have breakfast together, and see you off regularly. Maybe now, you'd rather have had the chickens and waffles for supper to-night? They're just as easy cooked as not. It would seem more like a feast; but I doubted if Matt'd hold out so late, and you're never contented without the boy."

"No. I'll not be separated from my chum when the time for the last chicken comes, you may be sure. Besides, I cannot stay at home this evening," rising hastily. "I have a—a person to meet, on business, at nightfall. I will not be late. I have but a few words to say."

"I'll tell Wash to saddle the old mare," said Mrs. Beck, as he ran up the stairs to clean away the dust.

"No, no. I can outwalk Jinny any day," he called back, and a moment afterward they heard him tramping hurriedly to and fro overhead.

"I wonder who the 'person' is?" said Peggy, drawing down her brows over her darning. "He's great at making friends for as silent a man—Mr. Galbraith. There's hardly an evenin' that a batch of the men from the quarry ain't up, talkin' over their affairs to him. People's drawed to him naterally-like. As for Beck, he's told him more of his early life than ever he did me, for as long as I've been his wife. Gracious!" as Dallas appeared again, freshly dressed: "goin' out in gray flannel again! These white shirts is aired as dry as a bone. I'd go out as become me—once. I'd let 'em see you was employed by the government. Them's your quarry clothes, Mr. Galbraith. Jest slip on one of these new ones, now."

Dallas hesitated: "The gray are quite clean, and some people—artists—would like this dress best." But he waited a moment, uneasily pushing back his short hair before he put on his cap. Up stairs he had stood, for the first time in his life, perhaps, critically looking at himself in the square little mirror. There was no help for it! He was hopelessly big, and bony, and homely.

"Well, what does it matter?" he said, cheerfully. "Who will look at the flannel, after all—or at me?" giving Matt a final toss as he went out, calling back good-night, and that they were not to wait for him. Lizzy followed him to the door to look after him, her eyes full of motherly pride: no man ever had so much purity and vigor in his face as her boy, she thought.

"Jest see how he goes!" said Peggy, coming to her elbow. "These young ones think they can carry the world on their shoulders! Dear! dear! Much they know of life! If you'll just take his things in the other room, Miss Lizzy, I'll have supper ready in no time."

Lizzy obeyed, a little annoyed. What right had Peggy to complain and talk about wants in life? watching the hearty little woman going about, swiftly bringing order out of confusion. Hadn't she a husband and child that she loved, and a little house of her own? Presently the table was set, the egg stirred into the coffee, the sausages frying on the side of the fire. Peggy disappeared, and coming back in a new blue calico gown, sat down to rock Matt to sleep in her arms, big boy as he was. The evening light slanted in warmly: Matt was a clean, pretty little chap: his mother's face was young and bright: the picture had a certain homely beauty of its own. It touched poor Lizzy with a sense of hunger and desolation. She had missed her birthright of love, and home, and child. One could bear, she thought, to to be always the broken thread in the web, the solitary looker-in at the home-picture, if one had but a dream of their own to hide and be comforted withal. But her dream, the nauseating story of moonlight and ebbing tide, by this time, made her only sick to remember.

A sudden fancy seized her. What if she went back to Manasquan and waited there while Galbraith was gone? There, at least, was home. She could have her own seat by her own fire, and cozy little suppers, too, which old friends, who knew her when she was a baby, would come and eat with her. Jim Van Zeldt sometimes. Poor Jim! She gave a melancholy smile: Well, well! Every heart knew its own weight; and it would not make her less tender with him to feel that she had made his so heavy. If he came to sit with her, sometimes, they would keep silence for ever on this old wound, and by and by it would be healed, and they would grow to be old, gray friends. It seemed to her very like a poem or a novel, the picture of them both sitting quietly on either side of the hearth, year after year, with this secret between them. This space that never might be passed, and the sea sounding in the distance like a wail over that which might have been and never was.

The melancholy "situation" pleased Lizzy, who was, as we know, sensible and practical beyond all women: it put her unconsciously in a thoroughly good humor. With this vision of Van Zeldt, made miserable for life by her, and sitting night after night until he grew gray contemplating his misery, she did not feel herself utterly cut adrift, or that she had lost her birthright among women. When Beck came in to supper, he found Matt snugly tucked away in bed, and Miss Byrne in the best spirits, drawing the flaky biscuits from the oven, while Peggy made the coffee.

"This is hearty!" he said, giving Peggy a sounding kiss, and then they sat down as snug and cozy as could be. Lizzy quoted to herself something about "harts ungalled," looking at Peggy, and how some may laugh, and some must weep, and that so runs the world away. But she ate very heartily of the biscuit and sausage, being hungry; and was, Mr. Beck said that night, for a wonder, the best of company: he always thought her, before, as dry as a chip.

Familiar as Galbraith was, by this time, with the shortest roads leading to his grandfather's house, it was dusk before he came in sight of the long rows of glittering windows with their background of mountain, and the unrolling, ash-colored drifts of smoke overhead. He stopped at the great gate to take out the key which Honora had given him, and at the moment a man's footsteps came down the carriage-road within, stumbling over first a boulder and then a stump, and Doctor Pritchard's wiry voice broke out in an unwonted oath.

On he came, grumbling: "Just what might be looked for under that woman's management! Slip-shod and violent! If her horses know how to double these snags, they have more wit than herself! So, ho! You're here, eh?" with a sort of snarl, which had in it something of mortification. He stopped, held the open gate with one hand and barred the way, looking up steadily at Galbraith.

"Well, I'm not sorry, on the whole, to have met you. I've made up my mind to say nothing of that matter before I go: I've been thinking it over. I believe you're repentant, and God forbid I'd throw a stone in the way of any man who is trying to get back to the right road." His sandy eyebrows twitched, and his contracted eyes were fixed on Dallas.

"I am not repentant," broke in the young fellow, roughly. "Unless you force me to repent of my stupidity in telling my story to you. The truth must have been rare in your life, Doctor Pritchard, you know so little how to use it."

"So you bandy words about it, do you?" putting out his hand to stop him; and when Dallas paused, remaining uneasily silent for a moment. "I tell you, young man, I have not been vexed in this way for years! I never was deceived before in a man when I relied on instinct. There's not a line in your face that will warrant you in being a humbug. I've been in at the Stonepost Farm-house. I've been talking to old James Galbraith about you."

"You have been there? Did you tell my story to James Galbraith?" said Dallas, in an altered voice, and suddenly standing still.

"I did not tell it. I—well, I cannot rid myself of likings and prejudices so easily as some men. I found that Mr. Galbraith was impressed by you as I had been, though he's crotchety—a phrenologist. I don't wait to rap on a man's skull to know if I trust him or not. Well—good-bye, Galbraith, good-bye!" making way for him to pass as hastily as he had detained him. "I believe you are truly repentant. I will keep your secret. I will leave this place in the morning, never to return, in all probability, and if you can make friends here, I'll not stand in your way."

"Good-bye, Doctor Pritchard." Dallas looked after the jerky, lean figure going down the road with a wrench at his heart. It was the first friend he had gained since he began his new life—gained and lost. The Professor, on his part, walked quickly, uncertainly, a few steps, then slackened his pace: "I do not believe the fellow will stay here when I'm gone, to be disgraced by having been left in the lurch. I wonder if he has any friends in the world. He's reformed—if he ever was guilty. Tut! tut!" and secretly rating John Pritchard for a fool, he hurried on to the brow of the next hill. Then it occurred to him to wish that he had heard Galbraith's story through, at any rate: he hesitated, half turned back, peering down into the gathering twilight. But he was too late· the road was vacant; and the Doctor went gravely on to his lodging in the village.

CHAPTER XXI.

DALLAS, passing among the crooked apple trees in the orchard, came direct to a long, low parallelogram of a house with glass sides that ran along the upper edge. He never had seen forcing or green-houses, but he thought that this must be one. Unlocking the door, he entered, stumbled over the crocks in a dark tool-house, and then—came into fairyland. Two or three lamps made a haze like moonlight over the rising levels of flowers and orchids which stretched into far-off shadows. It was a new experience to Galbraith. Outside was foggy, nipping November: within, the dim, suggestive lights of a damp, sultry summer night, its passionate perfumes and rank green foliage, which here and there took a soul to itself in a sudden flame of scarlet blossoms or white lilies.

Now, it was certainly not Madam Galbraith's habit to light her greenhouse with the chamber lamps. If Honora had not been, in her own opinion, so practical and thoroughly honest a young woman, one might have suspected her of "setting the stage."

Scene—FAIRYLAND. *Enter* TITANIA.

If she had done it, she chose her audience badly. For a moment Dallas stood bewildered with the enchantment of color and fragrance, "over-canopied with sweet musk-roses and with eglantine;" then he pushed his hat back on his head and thrust his hands into his pockets, going about with a puzzled, eager whistle, peering—not at the flowers, but the earth in which they grew.

Musk-roses did not belong to November; and here was the gray moss of the sea-woods, which could not possibly take root in this alluvial soil; and the knobby prickle-bush of the Jersey sands, which never would flower for him, bursting into a glory of red, voluptuous flowers; and those must be the Japan lilies, and that the famous Espiritu-Santo flower, of which he had read, but never hoped to see. All these in summer bloom in November among the Ohio hills! As for enchantment, or a possible Titania, that was hardly within the scope of Dallas' brain.

"So money can do this, eh? *Money!*" was what he said, with a transient fancy that it was hardly worth while to waste years in search of knowledge in Mexico and Japan, when a hand stretched out full of dollars could bring Mexico and Japan under his nose. All seasons of the year in one.

Now, Honora was waiting in the dark behind the little glass door in the corner. She had had time to realize the crisis in life which this night was to herself and him; and I leave it to any woman if it was not unbearable, at the very moment when she was going to appear like the fairy queen to usher him into his inheritance and make herself a beggar, to see this fellow go sniffing and thrusting his fingers into a parcel of pots, muttering, "One-third loam; one, wood-ashes; the remainder—what the deuce is the remainder?"

"The man was a machine—a log!" Honora was not the first woman who had said so.

"He would surely recollect why he had come in a minute, however;" and she waited, smiling, her hand on the latch. But when, so far from recollecting anything about it, he pressed on through the flowers into the forcing-room and prodded and tested *that* earth, and then stood spell-bound over the beds of miserable little sprouts, she opened the latch with a snap and came down into fairyland. He neither saw nor heard her, though he had turned back again and was stooping over an aquarium. What could he find in the forlorn perch and sun-fish to bring such eagerness into his eyes or the hard, compressed look into his mouth?

"Do you understand the language of the fishes as well as of the rocks, Mr. Galbraith? They are mine, but I always found them tiresome enough," with the impatient snap of the latch echoing in her voice.

Dallas started and looked up. He never had seen any vision like that of the young girl that stood before him, her unassertant beauty thrown into relief by the art of rose-colored drapery and delicate laces. She knew that he had not, and that as long as he lived the picture would be one which he would remember. But Dallas had his own old-fashioned, self-taught notions of deference, and after the first glance of wondering delight he bowed to her gravely and turned back to his fishes.

"It is quite new to me—this contrivance for studying their habits," he said. "And there is a balance of animal and vegetable life here that is curious and admirable. It is all a new world to me," with a look which comprised the forcing-rooms, flowers, and Honora fancied, herself.

"Is it?" with a pleased little flutter. "I thought you would like it! You are coming to claim your birthright, you know; coming to take your place for life among us; and it would never do for that to happen in the dining-room among the dishes, for instance, or the parlor. You are a naturalist; so I thought this was the proper place for you to come home. Nature welcoming you back, I thought. Now, if Madam Galbraith knew, she'd as soon as not meet you—well, on the stairs. What were you thinking of, looking at those fishes? Could you tell me?"

To her surprise, Dallas hesitated. "I would rather not have told you, Miss Dundas; but it does not matter. I was thinking of all that money was worth to a man. I never understood it as I have done since I came into this house to-night."

"Money?" said Honora, bewildered. "They are not worth so much—these.'

with a slighting motion of her hand toward the flowers.

"No, I suppose not," thoughtfully. "But it is the facility for study; as if science was mapped out and brought under your very eyes—put into your hand. You do not know how new it all is to me, Miss Dundas," with an embarrassed laugh, which died into sudden silence.

"These plants and tanks, and the knowledge of which they are hints, are commonplace things to you, but they are like glimpses to me of a world where I never have been," Dallas said after a while, in a heavy, unwilling tone, as though the words were forced out by some uncontrollable mental pressure. "A world where knowledge is the very air you breathe. You, and men and women like you, were born in it. I did not know, until to-night, how far outside I was;" and again his eyes turned from the face before him with an indescribable, wistful, hungry look about him, as though measuring the life which he had missed and the few years left in which to master it.

"You—you overrate the distance between us, Mr. Galbraith," said Honora, awkwardly. "These things seem very insignificant to me."

"Because you are used to their meanings. I am a very ignorant man, Miss Dundas. To-night I feel as a man might who had spent his life in making brick, when he sees a great, finished temple for the first time."

Honora understood him. She turned away, pretending to pick the dead leaves from a bush, feeling that he had forgot her presence as soon as he had done speaking. For a man to live to that age and find himself to be ignorant—hopelessly behind all other men—then the sting would enter the soul, she thought. As she snipped the leaves away, this loss and pain of Dallas' seemed to be more to her than any of her own which she had ever known. Her breast began to throb and the scalding tears swelled to her eyes. That frightened her. What ailed her? What was Dallas Galbraith to her? Why should she, with her French ideas of decorum, have met him here alone—have taken his fate into her own hands? It was now as if his soul was her soul, the mere thought of his loss wrenched her with such sharp pain; for the tears were bitter, wrung themselves out of her very heart. She never had made even her uncle's inner self her own in this fashion.

The terror of that consciousness which comes to every woman some time in life overtook Honora. She hid from it. She would not name it to herself. "Dallas Galbraith is nothing to me—nothing to me! I brought him here for love of justice—to give him his place—to make myself a beggar," she told herself, vehemently. Presently she turned to him: she thought he did not look at her, but Dallas knew that all the flush and sparkle had died out in her; saw even the clutch with which her fingers held on the bench at her side. He was as sensitive to a change in her mood or looks, and as stolidly dumb about it, as that flowerless cactus was to the heat and shadows of the sun which warmed it.

It was a lucky fancy, she thought, to bring him here. If he had determined to persevere in his stupid resolve not to make himself known, the signs of wealth in-doors would not have touched or tempted him; but here the grappling-hooks had taken a firm hold of him.

"You understand now," she said, "what wealth will give you. With money a man can educate—can make himself what he will."

"I do understand. It is a great power. The man is a fool who slights it."

He stood in the door which swung open into the orchard as he spoke, looking gravely out into the gathering twilight. Honora, a step or two within, waited. When he glanced hurriedly in, the tempered silvery light, the green distance, the lilies and perfume, the woman's delicate figure draped in rose-colored mist, and her face, which gave life to the whole, all seemed to wait for him, expectant, alluring, eager. It was but to keep silence about that one foul misadventure—to lie, it might be, once or twice, and to enter on possession of what was to him a royal inheritance. Within there, knowledge would come in the very air, breathed in the midst of ease and luxury. Within, there would be a chance—poor, improbable, but yet a chance—to win her.

Without, there was an aimless journey into the world, without a penny in his pocket or a friendly face to meet, to conquer knowledge in poor, meagre morsels, struggling for life at the same time.

There was an undue share of mulish perverseness in Galbraith's blood. At this prospect, without any show of reason, his muscles stiffened and he began to breathe free. Honora and her world became less fair to him.

"Will you come in?" she said, softly. "Home is waiting for you. It will be the old story of the prince found among the herdsmen. But we will keep the secret to ourselves of the coal-pits at Scranton," growing hurried and unsteady when she saw that he did not move. She remembered then that the choice for him to make was for life, and stood silent. Once she half held out her hand, and then let it fall, trembling. It mattered more to her life than his, she thought, after all, whether he went away. When he remained silent, looking out steadily, she spoke to him again: "Will you come in?"

"No," slowly, looking her in the face as he spoke. "It is not home to me. I will come back when I am fit to take my place among you."

She shook her head: "You will never come; or it will be too late. Death may come to any of us."

"And you may be gone. You will do as other women do—marry."

"That may be," with a laugh, but growing suddenly pale.

"It would be but natural," with a long breath, turning away. He was grave and stern, as though it was his own death and not life he was planning.

"If you have decided to follow your whim, then, and go—"

"It is not a whim," slowly. "It seems even to me like the choice of a madman. You suppose I do not know what I am giving up. I do know.

Chances which—which you would never think of, Miss Dundas. These things matter more to a man than a woman."

"You have your own reasons, doubtless," coldly.

"I have this reason," turning to her quickly: "I have not moral courage nor strength enough now to live among you and be myself—to tell my own story honestly and boldly. Later, it may be different. If it is not, I never will return. And then there is a sort of gloss and polish over all the world you live in—an imitation of each other, a hiding of one's self. It is hateful to me; but if I went among you now, I know that I would try to gain it. I would begin to borrow my opinions on this side and on that. I would soon be quite contented to smother up all my past life for ever."

Honora listened intently. "Am *I* false and factitious?" she said, leaning forward in her eagerness for his reply.

Dallas hesitated. But the sincere eyes before him commanded the answer: "I had an odd feeling about you, Miss Dundas, since the day I first met you," he said, smiling. "Something of that with which one wants to strip the husk and silk from an ear of corn and find the kernel inside. But the husk and silk with you—"

"Are borrowed. Now that is true!" earnestly. "I've tried to give myself a good character so long, you understand. I did not suspect you of shrewdness. But no matter! Have you told me all of your reasons for going?"

"No. I have been hampered all my life, and I want to feel my own feet under me. I would rather earn my bread and butter than sit down as your new-found prince to have my lap filled with gold. And I believe I would rather, when it comes to the choice, hammer out for myself bits of knowledge up on the hills yonder than receive it all here without any effort. It is a vain and a doltish feeling, but I must work it out. I am a born boor, perhaps."

"Then that is all. I can do no more," said Honora.

"If it is possible, I wish to see my mother before I go."

"She is not here. Colonel Pervis drove her to town this morning. She will be back to-morrow."

They both were silent after that. There was no reason why Dallas should stay longer. His choice was made. Honora, drawn back a little, her eyes dropped on the floor, waited, he thought, only to say good-bye. But he did not say good-bye. He never knew, afterward, how long he stood there, or of what he thought as he gazed at the downcast face. She knew, without looking at him, and turned from him with a shiver:

"I must leave you now. If you will go?"

"Yes, I will go."

"Do you wish me to keep your secret?"

"Yes: until I come back."

A faint heat began to rise in Honora's cheeks. If she could not take this hero by the hand and lead him in to her uncle, it was something to know that he had gone out like an old Crusader into the world seeking the true knighthood—something to hold his secret in her hand, a tie between themselves alone, some day to draw him gently back to claim his own. It was romance and mystery enough to comfort any woman.

"You may trust me," she said, in a whisper, a precaution which she had neglected before.

Another silence, in which he waited. But still she did not look at him.

"When will you come back?"

"In a year. I will try what strength I have, and if I succeed, I will come and claim my place."

"If you do not succeed?"

"Then I will come to you to say farewell, Miss Dundas, for ever. I will ask you to forget that I ever crossed your path."

He came closer to her, involuntarily, as he spoke. The dreadful constraint and weight which oppressed him whenever he tried to drag his secret thoughts to the light were upon him. He looked down from his grave, square height on Honora where she stood: her hands were clasped and resting on a heap of dead moss. They were so bloodless that he wondered, vaguely, if they were not icy cold, and went on hurriedly stumbling through his words: "You must not think I have not seen the sacrifice you would have made. I am not so ignorant that a noble, true woman—"

There he stopped. Her bosom was heaving, her chin quivering as Matt's did when he choked back the tears. Galbraith made one step that brought him beside her. Could it be that it cost her anything for him to go?

The white, cold hands were very near him. He clasped his own behind him resolutely. He had no thought of her as the beautiful, richly-dressed lady; but he did remember that the taint of the prison was on his flesh, and until she knew it he had no right to touch her.

"I will keep your secret," she said, "and a year from now I will look for you to come back. Good-bye, Cousin Dallas." She held out her hand, and when he did not take it looked wonderingly up at him.

Poor Dallas! All that he knew was the face upturned to his. He had failed to recognize the fairy queen in her elaborate silken sheen. A woman was a woman to him; and in this swift moment he absorbed every trifling detail that set this one apart from others, and gathered it all into his honest, stupid heart, to feed on hereafter. This gown she wore, he thought, was the very color of the inside of the shells he used to find at low tide; and her eyes were dark and brown as the kelp washed up on the shore: the old friendly Manasquan life came up as the echo of a far-off home-song. Her eyes were full of tears. She was very near to him—nearer than any living being. On the night he first saw her he knew that, when, from the world from which he was shut out, she had held her hand down to him. Before he came back, she would marry—in her own class. Not a convict.

But with the quiet assurance of real love, he knew himself to be near to her—nearer to her than any other man could ever be. Now, he was intolerably alone;

—the old stain would shut him for ever into a solitary life.

"Good-bye," she said.

For his answer he took her in his arms and kissed her.

He quickly put her down, white with indignation, and drew back from her. "You think me rude and vulgar. I am sorry. I could not help it." He added earnestly: "It does not seem wrong or vulgar to me."

Honora made an imperious gesture of dismissal: "Go! I—I am sorry."

These words went like a knife to Galbraith's heart. She had trusted him as an equal, and now she thought him a boor. He looked at her a moment sorrowfully enough, bowed without speaking, and went slowly down the hill. "But I was not wrong nor vulgar," he said, doggedly to himself. While Honora, when he was gone, buried her face in her hands and laughed hysterically. Could Colonel Pervis or Mr. Dour have done this thing? But they were thorough-bred —gentlemen. How could one know what to expect from a wild man of the woods? It was as if one had laid hold on Behemoth; and then she sat down among the flower-pots and sobbed and cried until her heart was sick.

The Indian Queen, long before Galbraith's return, was sound asleep in the moonlight. Even Turk, the watch-dog, who regarded robbers as one of the illusions of his youth, was as usual stretched on the porch snoring, his head between his paws. Dallas sat down on the mossy pump-trough: his brain was on fire, the close air of the house choked him. Why should a man be shut up in a box until after he was dead? After all, any house was a jail! He must have the free air to think over his future life clearly. But he did not think at all. That he ought to be miserable was plain enough. No man could be in a worse case. Tomorrow he must go out to face the world, penniless and untaught, with the leprous mark of the prison upon him, awaking suspicion against him in the kindest, broadest, human sympathy. The woman who already counted for more than all the world to him he had driven from him, to-night, irretrievably.

"It is a dark day," said Dallas.

There was heat in the man's long jaws which had not been there since the old Manasquan days. The grave, dark-blue eyes were sparkling and alive. "Hillo, Turk!" he called; and when the dog came sleepily to him he pulled him up and wrestled with him, laughing, and with no gentle hand, as if life, and youth, and good-fellowship were brimful in his heart, and he must find some living thing to caress, if it were but a dog. When Turk went off again, surly, to his nap, Galbraith stood up, stretching his long arms restlessly, looking down the road and then up at the sky. He could not sleep. Of all his strong, brawny body there was but one conscious point —his mouth, on which a touch lay light and warm. Had he found in it to-night that cordial which his hard early life had never tasted? Or was he simply one of those men who never know when fate has worsted them?

However that may be, the Dallas Galbraith who walked vehemently up the hill to the woods, only to throw himself down under a beech tree, was ten years a younger man than the one who had gone out from the Indian Queen this morning. The luck which was against him had vanished out of his sight. As for the disaster that closed in upon him on every side, the thought of it only roused in him the hot, buoyant glow with which he used to fight his way along the beach through the nor'-easters that wet him to the skin. He was going to live out of doors now, thank God! He had done with houses. He began to troll out one of the old fishing-songs, and his magnificent voice echoed through the woods like a trumpet-note of victory. He was so busy with his own fancies and his song that he did not hear the rolling wheels of a buggy on the road.

"Ho, Galbraith! Galbraith! There's nobody fool enough to be shouting in the woods at midnight but that fellow! Galbraith, I say!"

The shouting suddenly ceased, and in

a moment Dallas came down into the road, falling into his usual grave composure when he saw who had summoned him.

"You are late abroad, Doctor Pritchard?" resting his hand on the whip-rest of the buggy.

"Yes; but the night is the same as the day to me. It will be to you when you are as old a campaigner. I—I'm afraid we will have rain to-morrow."

"It is likely."

"Yes; those woolly clouds are a bad sign." Then the Doctor flicked his whip, and finding a knot in the lash picked it out, while Dallas watched him. He could not help it that his heart beat fast or his breath choked him. What if the road was going to open level before his feet? What if, after all the fierce temptation, he had done right and yet not lost his chance?

"I drove over purposely to see you, Galbraith," hesitated the Doctor.

Dallas nodded in silence.

"I was going to the Indian Queen, but I heard you up there. You must carry a light heart, lilting in that fashion in the middle of the night. Well, I've been thinking over that matter—the story you told me, eh?"

Dallas stroked the old horse softly.

"I'm glad to find you are in a better mood, Galbraith. You were angry and disrespectful this morning. A young man, first of all, should master his temper. You prevented me from seeing the thing clearly. Now, when I came to think it over—"

"You determined to trust me," quietly suggested Dallas when the pause grew awkward. "I do not think you will repent it."

"I have determined to trust myself," hastily. "I never found my judgment mislead me yet. And Mr. Galbraith has formed the same opinion of you; though that weighs but little with me. He's a phrenologist. There was Colonel Laddoun—as clever, gentlemanly a fellow as ever lived—yet the Galbraiths would have none of him. No: James Galbraith's opinion does not count for much with me. But I've determined to risk it all on my judgment of your face, Galbraith. Convict or not, I'll take you with me to-morrow, if you will go." The respect which he felt for the young man betrayed itself involuntarily in his tone more than his words.

"Yes, I will go. I am glad you trusted me." There was a heartiness and feeling in his voice which took the Doctor by assault.

"Give me your hand, boy!" suddenly, stooping forward. "I believe your story, every syllable. Some men have damnable usage in this world. I'll do what I can to set it right for you."

The men shook hands, and then, as men do when a word of earnest feeling escapes them, began, in a hasty, ashamed way, to talk of the horse and the chances of rain. "We'll make an early start," said Pritchard. "I'll take this road and call for you at the Queen by eight o'clock—sharp. Well, good-bye," pulling his reins. "Don't leave your voice behind you, either. It's good company on a long day's tramp—a tenor voice like your's. I know; I have heard good music in my time. Well, good-night!" looking back, after he had driven a little way, with a nod and smile again to reassure the young fellow.

CHAPTER XXII.

MR. DOUR, the next morning, rose as usual with the dawn, for the young man was in reality a hard-plodding student. Gerty, as fresh and sweet as a spice-pink, always was the first of the household to break in on him in the library; but to-day Miss Dundas came in for a book. Paul sprang to meet her, persuading himself he was glad of the rare chance, for his suit was lagging in this quarter; but Miss Dundas was preoccupied and grave, in haste to get a book from the top shelf, which proved to be Humboldt's "Cosmos," and two or three others which she thought she would need for reference. She was as worn and her eyes were as sunken as though she had spent all night over them. She was a very homely young woman, Dour thought, as she went out loaded, and he took up his book again; and then he dropped it, considering whether brain-power did or did not tend to injure the ideal woman, and whether women were not, after all, only meant to furnish the element of repose in this hurly-burly of life, to caress away care from their husband's brows, and to bring up children.

Mr. Galbraith laid down his paper when Honora came into his little study and began to sweep the sewing from her own table in the corner and to pile up her books. He could read the titles from where he sat.

"Are you going to study, my dear?"

"I thought I'd try and learn—something," with a despairing energy, sitting down with her chin in her hands, and beginning at the first chapter. The clock ticked for half an hour before she spoke.

"I've laid out a system for myself, uncle. Do you think, if I read and took notes, and all that, I could make myself worth anything in—well, in a year?"

"It is probable. Have you had an especial call toward the natural sciences?"

There was a little pause: "One must begin somewhere. That seems to be the only knowledge of weight. Languages and metaphysics—that sort of indoors learning makes men like Mr. Dour."

"And farming and hunting, men like Colonel Pervis."

"I would be very sorry for the world if they were the only types of men—very sorry, indeed!" tartly, dropping her forehead in her hands and going to work again.

Mrs. Rattlin, at breakfast, suggested that Honora "looked poorly. Most young girls had something in their spines. A white of egg, now, beaten up in raw whisky, was excellent before meals." Madam Galbraith growled assent, and looked keenly at her niece from under her shaggy brows, as though she saw a change in her deeper than the dark scoring under the eyes. The eyes themselves were full of meaning, steady and reticent as never before. The shy awkwardness had given place to a languid grace, which had a subtle charm for the eyes of the old lady. When she spoke to the people about her, she neither stammered nor hesitated as usual, but it was as indifferently as if they belonged to a world to which she had long since bidden good-bye. Her very voice was new to Madam Galbraith—natural, and with clear, fine cadences.

"What has altered Honora?" she demanded sharply of her husband, after breakfast. "There's a peculiar steadiness that comes to a woman when she is married or betrothed. I see it in her now. She has done with copying others. She is herself for the rest of her life. What has she been doing?"

"I do not know, Hannah. Studying Humboldt, I believe," tranquilly.

"Some one ought to know," anxiously. "I must take better care of the child."

The old gentleman lighted a cigar and went out to the garden walk, looking in each time that he passed the window at the light flickering over his darling's head, bent again over the books. The change in her face was that of a beautiful life dawning out of chaos, he thought, and went on turning his wife's rough idea over in his fanciful way. Love coming in to a woman's nature was like the last stroke of an artist's pencil to the landscape; there was the background waiting—a bit of heaven and a bit of earth: promise of summer or promise of storms. Then the solitary human figure came in, and the motionless drama took instant life, shape, meaning. The picture was finished for ever. Time would make no essential change—only to dim the hues, perhaps. Having finished his cigar and his meditation together, he went up to the window and opened it:

"Are Babe and I left out of the plans for the year? Come and ride with me, Nora."

"I don't think I have time. You see, uncle, I have been living in a world where knowledge was the very air I breathed; and you have no idea how dumb I am. My head does ache horribly!" giving the "Cosmos" a push and coming to the window.

"Yes; go put on your habit. I am going down the river-road. I will meet Doctor Pritchard somewhere there, and bid him good-bye."

Honora put up both hands to shelter her face from the sun. "No, I will not ride this morning," in a low voice.

Mr. Galbraith pulled his spectacles down over his eyes to look at her. "The air is from the mountains," he persisted. "I thought it would be but friendly to meet Pritchard and bid him God-speed. It is a long, dangerous journey the foolish old fellow has undertaken."

"You had better go with your uncle, Honora," said Mrs. Rattlin, who came up just then, patting her on the shoulder in her motherly way.

But, to her dismay, the tears began to roll down the girl's pale cheeks. "I wish you would not worry me, uncle!" she sobbed. "How could you ask me to do that? How could you? I did not know it was a dangerous journey."

"Go take your ride, Mr. Galbraith," said Mrs. Rattlin, quietly. "Don't be uneasy about Honora. It's her spine. Girls are all weakly, nervous things now-a-days. Go and lie down a while, Honora dear."

But Honora slipped away from them both, and went down, slowly, to the garden—to the orchard—into the greenhouse. As she watched her uncle's horse coming to the door, ready for him to mount, the tears dried and her face began to burn hot as the cactus-blooms behind her. In a little while he would be on the hill-road, where Doctor Pritchard must pass.

A quarter of an hour afterward, when Mr. Galbraith stopped his horse to unfasten the gate, there stood Miss Dundas waiting, eyes and cheeks aflame.

"I cut some flowers for you, uncle."

Mr. Galbraith saw that his greenhouse had been altogether rifled. "But I like out-door flowers best, you know, Nora."

"You need not keep them then," eagerly. "Give them to your friend, Doctor Pritchard, if you choose."

"From you, Honora?"

"No, uncle. My name must not be mentioned there," with sudden emphatic gravity.

After Mr. Galbraith's horse had trotted down the road, she leaned a long time on the gate, thinking. She was sure that Dallas would guess that she had cut the flowers for her uncle. She pictured him, gaunt and hollow-eyed, this morning, at the thought of her displeasure, manœuvring to possess himself of one—hiding it, wearing it, as a knight of old was wont to wear his lady's colors, until he came back at the end of the year, having won his golden spurs, to claim—his own.

Dallas at that moment was finishing his breakfast. He always liked a hearty breakfast. It was a question whether he or Matt had done most justice to the chickens, and waffles, and cream-gravy. As for Lizzy and Mrs. Beck, they ate but little, and with that little Peggy literally mingled her tears. Mr. Beck, last night, had given them vague ideas of the vast wildernesses waiting to be explored by Dallas, and they had sat up until near dawn to talk of it.

"Miss Byrne took it worse than my wife," said Beck, when they went up for Galbraith's luggage. "One 'ud think your road was beset by cannibals, by the way she watches you. Women beats all. If you stick an idee in their heads as bare as a broom-stick, they'll have it up and flourishin' like a green bay tree in no time."

"I don't know much about them," said Galbraith, indifferently. He had no time to speculate on women or their idiosyncrasies. There were some bits of rock which he wanted to take with him for comparison, and he had not yet chosen them. He began to choose and pack them now.

Now that he had his work in hand, it was curious how the image of Honora, over which he had been brooding for days, faded far into the background. A beautiful dream, to be summoned in lonely hours, perhaps; but now the spar must be packed. There were no hollows about his eyes. Ten minutes after he had found his work for life was ready for him last night, he had lain down and slept soundly. It made Lizzy angry to know that he was sleeping like a log in the next room.

"Now, that is the difference between men and women," she said.

"Why, it is only for a year, Lizzy," he said, wringing her hand good-bye, when Doctor Pritchard came at last, and Beck and Washington were storing away the valise in the buggy.

"Only a year! Oh, Dallas! But a year is nothing to you. You will inherit a great fortune—you will marry—"

"No woman would marry a convict. There is no need to remind me of that," sternly.

"There is no need to tell her," eagerly.

"I've no time to be thinking of marriage now, Lizzy. Good-bye—God bless you! I don't forget all you've done for me."

"Time's up, Galbraith!" shouted the Doctor. He was looking down with dismay at Mrs. Beck's store of luncheon and jam jars.

Dallas nodded, packing them in. "Hush. Humor her. We can throw it out easily enough. One moment;" and he ran back to leave a package in his room for Matt.

In that moment Doctor Pritchard saw Mr. Galbraith ride up, quickly, over the brow of the hill, and he drove on to speak to him. He fancied the old gentleman was curiously distrait and anxious. He looked beyond the Doctor, at Dallas when he came out on the steps again and they all gathered about him.

"That is your assistant, Pritchard?" he said.

"Yes; that is my young friend. I use that word advisedly," with a half-defiant tone. "I take him on the responsibility of my instinct, sir. His history is nothing to me."

Mr. Galbraith hesitated: "You have heard his history then?"

"From himself. Without reservation."

There was a strange lightening in Mr. Galbraith's face, which struck even the unobservant Professor as odd. He found, too, that one or two remarks which he made were unheard by the old gentleman, so intently was he regarding the group on the porch, and listening to an occasional word from Dallas.

"The lad," he said, at last, "has the gift of attaching all kinds of people to him. It belonged to—to another of the Galbraiths."

"Yes; but he has the gift of attaching himself to his work, which is better. I have been pleased to see how, since his proper profession opened to him, he has taken hold of it—like a tree that finds itself in its native soil. Friends nor women will not hold this young fellow back, sir. They will be outside matters to him. His work will be the air he breathes."

"You think the discipline good for him, then?" anxiously.

"It is not good—it is necessary. As air to breathe," crustily.

Mr. Galbraith turned his quiet, critical eyes on the irritable little man beside him, as though sounding his nature in reference to some secret thought of his own: then, satisfied, they went back to the tall figure on the porch and the face of the younger man. There was an odd likeness of meaning between them. He wondered if there were any virtue in the earth's secrets that kept the souls of men, who were born to dig them out, clean and honest.

"It is better the boy should go," he said, slowly, as Dallas, having bidden Matt the last hearty good-bye, came toward them, and for the first time saw his grandfather. Mr. Galbraith pressed his horse forward a step and half held out his hand, but seeing that Dallas stopped, he bowed without speaking.

"Now, that fellow does not mean to be uncivil," said the Doctor, quickly. "He will not shake your hand because you don't know his history. There is no sham about him."

"I understand." Mr. Galbraith spoke nervously, with an unusual repressed excitement in his thin face. "But I should like to have taken the boy by the hand. I hope you will be kind to him, Pritchard?"

"No fear. Well, good-bye. That is a new specimen of acacia in your bouquet. Oh, many thanks! Good-bye. Come, Galbraith."

As Dallas sprang into the buggy and they drove away, the spare military figure on horseback was the last that he saw. It seemed to typify the life and kindred on which he had turned his back. We see ourselves and our neighbors as we are but two or three times in life, and then with electric, irrevocable insight. This old graybeard, with his delicate fingers and sad, sensitive eyes, that would look on the wealth and education for which Dallas schemed with long-used indifference, was a something which the young man never could become. He sat silent beside Dr. Pritchard until they had driven a mile or two, and then, stooping, began to finger the package of tools without which the Professor never traveled.

"You like your trade, Galbraith? Not sorry to give civilization the good-bye for a while, eh?"

"I suppose a man cannot serve two masters?"

"Not such a man as you."

"Then I like my trade."

He took up the flowers which the Doctor had let fall. He was sure that Honora had cut them for her uncle, and touched them with a blush like a boy, as though their leaves had been her cheeks and hair. She might belong to the same world as her uncle, but, if he came back, she would come into his, he thought, with quiet assurance. After a while he pulled one or two of the blossoms to pieces to find out to what class and order they belonged, and when they all drooped in the heat, he threw them away. Dallas never had a keepsake in his life.

Crossing a ridge of the lower hills, Doctor Pritchard drew up his horse. "There is the Galbraith homestead. Take your last look at it. You are a branch of that stock, I believe?"

"More of kin than of kind," said Dallas, under his breath.

But the Doctor caught the words: "Oh, of course. But a man's no less a man on account of difference of rank. That is a noble old house. It sits upon the mountain like a crown." He waited to allow the horse to breathe, for the pull up the hill had been hard.

Now, the domestic instinct was strong in Dallas, however wanting in sentimentalism women would have thought him. He had given to even his prison cell a home look. He could not forget that the solemn mountain-landscapes and the house yonder in their midst were his home—had been the birth-place of his ancestors for generations. He alone was cast out—a vagabond upon the earth. Doctor Pritchard broke the silence with words that oddly jarred upon him. He put his hand on Dallas' knee, and said, earnestly:

"I heard you promise to come back here in a year, Galbraith; and I meant, as your friend, when we were alone, to protest against it. What can you have in common with these people? Why would you give up your work when it was just begun?"

"There is something in common between us," said Dallas, but vaguely, for a moving object on the road before them had caught his eye: a low phaeton, with two figures in it. At the sight of one of them, his heart stood still. "There are reasons why I should come back—there are reasons," he repeated, slowly, looking at it.

"I do not ask your confidence, of course," testily: "I only give you practical, common-sense counsel. You have told me your story: you say there is no way for you to prove your innocence, and I tell you your only chance is to devote yourself to-day to your profession, and to rid yourself of every vestige of your past life—make yourself new aims and a new world. There is no hope for you there," motioning to the mountains and homestead. "There is not one man or woman there who would believe in you as I have done, with the story clinging to you."

Dallas did not answer. He could not take his eyes from the delicate woman leaning back in the phaeton which rapidly approached them.

"No!" pursued the Doctor, energetically, motioning toward the great western valley which opened before them. "There lies your true path. I don't want to see the man in you spoiled by the influence of people whom you have left here. Take your work and go out with it. Let there be no looking back to the flesh-pots of Egypt."

"It is not my work that keeps me from them," cried Dallas, the fair, laughing face of his mother coming nearer and nearer. "It is the stain that is on me; and it was no fault of mine."

"But it will shut you out from them for ever," coolly. "What if you had gone to any of them, as you did to me, and said 'I am a convict'?"

Dallas did not speak, but he took off his cap, and, leaning forward, looked into the woman's face that was now close upon them. The Doctor noticed that he drew his breath heavily: his face became the poor vehicle of some great emotion. What could Mrs. Duffield know of the man?

Colonel Pervis, who drove her, pulled up his horses with a jerk: "Off, Doctor? 'Westward the star of science takes its way,' eh?" with a furtive, inquisitive glance at the workman beside him.

Mrs. Duffield also saw Dallas, but without looking at him. It was a noble, singular head, she thought; and the rolling gray collar and bare throat were wonderfully artistic. She stretched out her pretty little hand to the Doctor. "We will miss you so much!" she said, gently. "But you will find your way back to us some day, I am sure."

"Will I find you here, if I do?"

"Yes. I am at home now. This life suits me." Her hand lay on the red cushion, close to Dallas. For years he never had slept without holding it close to his breast. The brown hair—there was a little gray in it now—how he used to tug at it and tangle it while she sewed at the slop-shop work! How patient she was, laughing when he brought the tears to her eyes! He could see a faint scar across her forehead: it was there that Duffield struck her that night when she held him in her lap to keep off the savage blows. That night he went to the coal-pits. He knew that the only chance for life for her was to be rid of him.

If he could but touch her! She was not a dainty lady to him: she was only—mother—mother. His hand, holding his cap, was near to hers. The strong, brawny man grew weak and blind. He dared not touch it.

The stain was between them.

She looked beyond him, as though he had been vacant air, to his companion.

The Doctor's kind heart could not bear that any one should be neglected. "My young friend goes with me," he said. "You must wish him God-speed. He is one of your own people."

Colonel Pervis mumbled some commonplace, and Mrs. Duffield promptly held out her ever-ready hand. She looked up with a smile, and their eyes met. A strange, confused trouble came into her face; it grew pale: she drew back the outstretched hand.

"Shall I tell her that I am a convict?" said Dallas, in a quiet whisper, turning to the Doctor. But the boy's look made Pritchard think that he had suddenly gone mad.

"Tut! tut! I will drive on, Colonel Pervis. Good-day, Mrs. Duffield. You are insane on this matter, Galbraith."

"Stay!" Dallas laid his hand on the Doctor's wrist and brought the horse to a sudden halt. He looked at the phaeton which was driving rapidly away. "I may never come back," he said, with a loud uncadenced laugh, "and she—she is—"

"What is she, Galbraith?"

"This life suited her." Should he bring his disgrace on her?

"She was a friend of mine once," he said, loosing his hold on the reins.

"You had better sink all friendships.

There lies your work. I warn you," pointing forward.

Mrs. Duffield was silent and pale so long as to alarm her companion. "Do you know that young man, Colonel Pervis?" she asked at last.

"No. But we can easily hail the Doctor again," with uneasy solicitude, for she was a woman whom every man was anxious to serve.

"No."

"He reminded you of some one?" anxiously.

She bowed, her face turned from him.

"A friend, perhaps?"

"A friend who is dead."

Colonel Pervis was silent. As they turned toward the Galbraith homestead, she looked hurriedly back, and in the rapidly widening distance she saw the two adventurers going down into the valley of the west, whose rising mists enveloped them, making them dim and shadowy to her sight as the image of the dead boy who would come no more, nor send her tidings.

PART VII.

CHAPTER XXIII.

APRIL. The conventional April—bright-eyed and tearful, "with flesh-like columbine bedight, beneath whose feet the curled streams soft chidings kept,"—was shut up between the leathern backs of some old English books on Mr. Galbraith's favorite shelf of the library.

This was her American sister. Mud and dyspepsia, lagging brains and heavy feet announce her coming in lieu of hawthorn blooms.

The winter months, Honora thought, looking out of the library window, had been tedious enough, but spring had thawed out and dragged to light all the uncomely background of the heavens above and the earth beneath. The world had quarreled with both winter and summer, and would be reconciled to neither. The insolent light bared all the dirty patches of snow on the mountain-sides; the sullen creeks bogged with the winter's ice; the gaping clayey land-slides; the trees stood like black and pulpy sponges, motionless in the sickly cold wind. A veil of vapory green had fallen pityingly on the great slope before her, but beneath it, she knew, was mire.

Her uncle came to the window outside, his long boots covered with mud, from a tramp through the hills: he held up a bunch of red maple buds and the pale emerald cups of the water-arum for her to see, and then looked up at the sun glinting through the saffron waves of smoke which the wind drove about overhead. Honora tapped impatiently for him to come in. She wondered that he could always be busied with such trifles. Did nobody but herself see how awful a thing it was to be alive? She had been dabbling in Carlyle lately.

Beside this, the winter months had left some vehement, hard lines on Miss Dundas' face. Her secret had proved heavy and galling; and since the rough fellow, in his laborer's dress, had turned his back on her that night and left her to keep his place, she had been conscious of a gaping vacuity in her life unfelt before. If she had been a man, she would have had politics or a trade or profession—some interest below and broader than her own petty cares—to sink them in. As it was, she sewed. She did not find in the needle that infallible medicine for a woman's mind diseased which men consider it. Cosmos had proved a failure. On the third day of trial, Mr. Galbraith found her asleep over the first chapter before noon. Then

Honora took to religion. She went to the church to pray every morning; began to meddle with the Irish housemaids, and to shake their faith in the Virgin; tried to bring Lizzy, who was a staunch Baptist, to a confusion of spirit about the truth of Episcopal succession. It was a matter of deadly earnest to her; for it was a real void in her own life she was trying to fill with her prayers and proselytings and thirty-nine articles. Perhaps she found most comfort in her secret nightly supplications for Dallas. For was he not a poor wanderer? Should no man care for his soul? In church she used to put his name into the prayer for the President. She was very sincere, thinking it was only his salvation she cared for.

Her uncle silently noted it all, and felt a deep, tender pity for her. There was no career open for women but that of wife and mother; and until that came to them, he thought that even the least morbid among them suffered from unused power and mental hunger—sat alone and gnawed their own flesh, as the woman in that horrible tale of the Flemish prison. But he would have been ready to strike any one who would propose that Honora should find work and happiness outside of this tardy husband. He had a most delicate appreciation of woman's sphere, and drew the limits narrowly.

Honora saw him a few moments later come into the adjoining room in his dressing-gown and slippers, and put the buds and calla in a vase upon his wife's table. She took them up and sniffed at them. "Very pretty, James, but scentless."

"Now, to me they have a delicate perfume."

"Your senses are keener than mine. I wish I could find the comfort in such things that you do."

Mr. Galbraith did not reply.

"But I never could. A frog could not find honey even in a field of clover," forcing a laugh. "So—" taking up her pen again; but she dipped it in the ink two or three times before beginning her writing, looking thoughtfully at the poor buds.

"Is it the old work, Hannah?"

"Yes; it is a description of the oil-wells and site for the town. That which young Dour wrote from hearsay was too flattering. I want to deceive nobody. I want no capital put into the concern on false expectations."

"Capitalists have not come forward very promptly, have they?"

"No. But they'll come. Dour has brought me notices of the undertaking, clipped from the New York papers. Very favorable. I suspected him of writing them; but he protested that the thing is talked of widely. I'll have no puffing," driving her pen energetically across the broad sheet, while Mr. Galbraith settled himself in his easy-chair, drawing his gown over his knees, folding his thin hands and falling into his usual dreamy scrutiny of the fire.

She looked up presently: "Dour came last night, James."

"I saw him. It is a long journey. What is his object?"

"Honora, I fancy," with an abrupt laugh. "Ostensibly, to offer his services in the laying out of the town. I may make use of him: he's shrewd and governable. It's hard to find men who are governable," without observing the quizzical glance which her husband shot at her. "He has made up his mind to address Honora, I suspect. Not that he cares a straw for you, child," raising her voice as Miss Dundas came in. "But he thinks it an easy way to turn a penny. Send him to me: I'll put him to the right-about properly!" turning her paper, with a snort of defiance. "If I'm wrong, though, and he marries the little Rattlin girl, I'll make his fortune for him."

"I would think, my dear, you would find quite enough occupation in your derricks and town without playing Providence to all the lovers you stumble over."

Madam Galbraith vouchsafed no direct reply. Presently, stopping to consult a map, she put her pen behind her ear, and said that "Dour was a fair-enough specimen of a mediocre New Englander, clear-sighted and shrewd, if he could rid his brain of the smattering of Transcendentalism which it never was made to comprehend. That's the trouble among any people when a great thinker like Emerson goes from among them into his own path on the mountains. All commonplace men feel called upon to follow him, and there they go scrambling about in the darkness like silly sheep."

"I think," said Honora, anxiously, after a pause, "it is only fair to set good as well as evil before Mr. Dour. I will bring Gerty up on a visit."

"Just as you please, child," indifferently. "Don't talk to me. I have these lots all confused. Give me the pins, quick. I can do nothing without pins."

Honora came closer, giving her, from a hard, square cushion, red and blue-headed pins, which the old lady stuck viciously into a square, parti-colored map, stopping to ponder over each as it went in.

Everything in the room was growing hard and square, Honora thought, looking drearily around, under the spell of Madam Galbraith's new hobby. It was her especial sanctum, and used to be warm, genial, disorderly—the very heart and core of the house. It had fallen under line-and-plummet rule now—was as blank as the maps of her proposed town on the wall, or as the ground on the river flats on which it was to be built. It seemed to be the old lady's fancy that her office should wear a business-like aspect, severe enough to awe the largest capitalist, if that tardy man ever appeared. The worn, old Turkey carpet, on which Tom Galbraith had played when he was a child, had been replaced by hempen mats; piano, sewing, portraits and flower-pots had been swept away as useless lumber; the square, white ceiling stared down at the square, earth-colored floor, with only a table, squarer than either, to break the blank between; and at the table sat the stout, brawny old woman, bending over her maps, as though it were the one chance between her and death.

Her mass of silvery hair, which used to be framed about her face with a curious artistic effect, was skewered back in a tight knot, and the face itself reflected in its unyielding mould the figures over which she had been brooding for months. One could hardly believe that a baby's fingers had ever touched that hard hawk's beak; for in the fierce energy of even her repose there was something of the traits of a bird of prey.

She pulled out and put in the pins slowly, rubbing her knobbed forehead, bewildered: "District A, that is the rolling-mill; C, dwellings; D?—there is assuredly a mistake about D—"

"Can I assist you, Hannah?" Mr. Galbraith rose reluctantly, hesitating before coming closer.

"It is the first time you have offered to do it, James," with grave reproach. "The whole country-side has taken part in my great work, while you have been dreaming, as usual, over your Dante and Jean Paul."

"But I know so little of oil," sitting down and picking up the map as daintily as though it were greasy.

"I am very sorry, James, if you confound my undertaking with a vulgar oil speculation. To be sure, I saw no reason why the Dour lands should not yield oil as well as any in the country. So the wells were sunk: there they are—red pins. I've no doubt they'll yield three hundred barrels a day. I do not hold them as a means of selfish aggrandizement. We have enough. So will Honora have. The town is laid out as you know: the cotton and rolling-mills are nearly built. The oil-wells will be a sort of support—backbone to the whole. I see no reason why there should not be a town on the Dour lands—I mean, why Western Virginia should not be developed."

"No—certainly not," abstractedly, examining the maps, while Honora watched his face anxiously.

"I am glad," pursued Madam Galbraith, with complacency, "that you allow me at last to explain my scheme to you. I'm no reformer, James, but I'd like, before I die, to look at a community of people who owed their advance in well-being entirely to me. To me. I'd like to leave such a community on the Dour lands. You understand? I bring here industrious emigrants, furnish them with comfortable dwellings and remunerative work: they repay me the money advanced as they earn it. I have drawn into the scheme as many of the neighboring farmers as I could: the hands in the house and farm have put all of their savings into it."

"But the large capitalists?"

"Well, to be honest, James, I have made use of no means to bring them in. I don't want them. Then we should have a board of directors, with their delay and fal-lal. Why, *I* should not even have a vote. As it is, the men I have employed are controllable. Quite controllable."

"A is the rolling-mill? Is it stocked?"

"Yes. I drew on the Western lands for that."

"You have not sold the Western lands, Hannah?"

"Certainly," sharply. "You signed the deeds in March."

"You bring so many papers to me to sign," mildly.

"I sold them at a sacrifice, I confess. But I required the ready money. I found the undertaking more costly than I expected. Stocks and mortgages were readily transferred, but with land and cattle, of course, I parted this season at a disadvantage."

Mr. Galbraith's cheeks flushed under the gray whiskers. He was silent for a moment: "Do I understand you that you have invested all your property in this scheme?"

"Excepting the Stone-post Farm and homestead. Why, it is but throwing out minnows to bring in whales. It will bear an interest of a hundred per cent., though I did not think of the profit. You appear surprised, Mr. Galbraith?"

He delayed his answer for an instant.

"I did not know how extensive your plans were, Hannah," quietly. "Here is Mr. Dour. This map will be more intelligible to him than to me, perhaps," ceding his place at the table to the young man, who returned his old-fashioned bow but slightly. A henpecked scholar was a creature with which Paul Dour had no sympathy. Finding that he could not catch Honora's eye, he bent zealously over the maps. He had come back intending first to win Madam Galbraith's favor: when the fairy godmother was secured, he could bring himself to marry the stupid Cinderella.

"The plat marked D is incorrect, Mr. Dour."

"We will amend that, madam—we will amend that," with oily fluency. "But about the proposals that I brought with me, as we are upon the subject. You positively reject New England colonists? That appears to me a singular prejudice. They are the very leaven of any settlement. These men, too, will pay their own way—"

"Precisely. *I'd* rather pay their way. Debt's the surest yoke on any man's neck. I'll have none of your headstrong radicals. Sir, if you please, I'll leaven my colony in my own fashion."

Dour forced a complaisant smile.

"A German population, such as that which already forms the nucleus of the settlement, is what I would prefer. But moral—moral. I'll have neither man nor woman who cannot show a fair record. We'll have no room for prisons or courts, so we'll start with an honest brotherhood. I have not left this matter to Mr. Rattlin's oversight. I've made a point of knowing the antecedents of every settler myself, and if he cannot show a clean record, as I said, I make short work with him."

"Certainly. Indubitably you are right." His truckling assent flowed in ready chorus to every dogmatic sentence.

Honora, meanwhile, stood looking down at them with an appalled, helpless dismay. While she had been brooding all winter over her secret, deaf and blind to all that went on about her, the royal robes in which Dallas was to be clothed on his return were being changed into flimsy rags. She had an unutterable contempt for Madam Galbraith's business knowledge; and it was Dallas' inheritance with which she was gambling, in order to rule over a herd of Dutch laborers. It was Dallas' rights against which the foolish old woman and this truckling, time-serving Dour were conspiring.

She had a knightly, chivalric sense of protection for the hardly-used fellow, obstinate and unmalleable though he had been in her hands. In her own chamber, with maidenly blushes and tears, she prayed night after night that he might be brought into the fold of the church; and now she was ready to fight as vehemently for his acres and stocks.

But her secret? Her lips were closed.

Mr. Galbraith had gone back into the library and seated himself at the window, beside the chess-board, on which he had left an unsolved problem. He spent many silent, happy hours every day working out variations of the same old gambits: now, however, he was looking absently over the board into the bare woods outside. When he heard Honora's hasty step following him, he began hurriedly to move his pawns.

She put her hand on his shoulder, standing behind him, motioning him to listen to the murmur of voices inside. "Do you know what that means, sir—all that mad scheming and flattery? It means ruin—beggary."

"No, no, child," promptly, as though he had expected her attack, but without looking at her. "Madam Galbraith has great skill in affairs—great skill. You should have confidence in her."

"I? What is it to me? I am not thinking of myself. *You* have no confidence in her business judgment. You have no faith in this new scheme, sir—none."

Mr. Galbraith looked up at her: "Honora!"

"No, you have none," steadily; "and yet you suffer her to undermine the ground under our feet, until at a touch we will all sink into ruin—we and these poor wretches at the wells, and—and— Oh, if I could but tell you what I know!"

Mr. Galbraith averted his eyes from her face, moving a red knight slowly to and fro.

"I am in a sore strait, uncle," in a calmer tone. "I must stand and see a great wrong done, and I dare not speak the word that would stop it. - I beg of you not to slight my warning. I am not a child."

"No; you are a child no longer, Nora."

Some graver thought was in his mind than the ruin she prophesied. She drew back as though she understood it. They both were silent.

"You must remember," he said, at last, looking at her with a shrewd smile, "that you base your fears upon your own contempt of my wife's skill in business. I do not know how that may be. You women are always the harshest judges of one who undertakes a man's work, cry out for a career as you will. Eh, Nonny? But I have not been so blind and deaf to this scheme as you suppose, though I had no idea that all of her property was involved in it. No; I did not comprehend its extent until to-day." He paused abruptly.

"You comprehend it now?" eagerly, "and you mean to interfere?"

"No; I will not interfere, Honora."

"Not if you believed as I do, that it would end in beggary?"

"No, my dear; not even then."

Miss Dundas bent on the slow, gentle eyes a look of amazed pity.

"If—" she hesitated—"if there were a natural heir to whom the property would revert? In that case—"

"In no case will I lift my finger to thwart my wife," replacing the chessmen with the quiet, indolent motion habitual to him; and then turning to her: "The property is hers, Honora. I was a poor young fellow when I met and loved Hannah Dour. I had but a small annuity—enough to feed and clothe me—to buy a book or print now and then. I have the same now—no more. When I asked her to be my wife, it was with the condition that I should gain nothing through the marriage other than her great love. The Dour estate—its income or its privileges—was to be no more to me than to the merest stranger crossing its boundary. Our marriage has, therefore, been a very true one. But if I had not enforced that condition, I should have been a pensioner upon her bounty;" and the thin, high-bred features colored painfully.

"I understand," said Honora, gently.

He opened the box and began to carefully set the quaint old figures in their velvet case.

"You did not solve your problem, uncle?" stooping to help him.

"No; my head aches. This southerly wind, I suppose." He took hold of her busy fingers with a half-quizzical, half-sad smile. "Money weighs heavily in hands as young as these, Nora. You think life ought to be like an English novel, in which virtue is always rewarded in the end by a shower of gold? When one is an old graybeard like me, one knows that it is only the surface-crops in life which wealth can buy. The real treasures lie far below." He closed the box and pushed it from him. "Now, as to that imaginary heir of the Dours"—falling into his favorite, speculative tone—"if there were such an one, there are many better gifts in God's hand for a young man than large property. Discipline, for instance, or hard fortune to wrestle with, until every thew and sinew is strengthened, and—but what is the use of defining the good and ill of the world for young people? It is a lesson which every man has to learn afresh in the bitterness of his soul."

"Discipline?" Miss Dundas thought the heir of the Dours had secured his share of it. When she would have spoken Mr. Galbraith avoided her eye.

"Tut! tut! Where have I mislaid my book? You did not see it, my dear?" putting on his spectacles and peering about on tables and book-shelves.

"Ronsard, uncle? It is here."

"Ah, true. Thank you. It is a book you must never read, Nora. As false a guide in literature as in love." He composed himself, however, in his chair, put his slippered feet to the fire and opened the squat, black volume, with an air of tranquil enjoyment. Miss Dundas, with an impatient glance at him, wandered uneasily back into the other room. The progressive party there had received a reinforcement. Mr. Rattlin was pacing to and fro, his hands clasped under the tails of his thin black coat, a satisfied smile on his face. Beck, from the Indian Queen, sat a little apart from the table, in a suit of Sunday black clothes and a wide expanse of shirt front, which altogether appeared to have unmanned him. He sat bolt upright, swinging his hat between his wide-open knees. Madam Galbraith was writing.

"There is your receipt, Mr. Beck," she said, handing him a slip of paper. "It is not a certificate, because there is no company yet formed; but your dividend is secure. I am good for it."

Beck read the paper, took up a pinch of white ashes from under the grate to sprinkle on it to dry the ink, and then stowed it carefully away in his wallet. "I reckon I'm satisfied with my backer," he chuckled. "Them's my savin's since I first did a stroke of work. I was afeard of banks, and we kept 'em in an old tea-pot. That's so. They growed very slow; especially as Matt's a'most raised an' 'll be needin' schoolin' soon. I'd like to give him a start ahead of what me and Peggy had. So it seemed kind a providential when the madam opened up this way for us to make a fortune out of hand. But it cost Peggy and me a tug to give up the old Queen, for all, sir," for Mr. Rattlin had stopped and was listening patiently.

"No doubt, Mr. Beck—no doubt. I had no idea that we were so attached to our own little house until we left it last week: we quite forgot that the roof leaked, and that the children have grown so big that they threaten to split it open like a locust's back. It was just adapted to my wife and me when we were married. But there are eleven of us now, all told."

"You've given up your old place to go to the wells, Mr. Rattlin?" said Dour, joining them, with an embarrassed effort at ease.

"Yes. The whole country is in a ferment. Emigrants are arriving daily and going to the wells. There is great work to be done there—the field is white for the harvest. When Madam Galbraith summoned me, I hesitated long before going. The responsibility will be heavy. It ought to have been laid upon a different man. I doubt often, now, if I was not presumptuous," anxiously.

"You have no reason to doubt," said Dour, putting his hand heartily on Mr. Rattlin's stooped shoulders. His heart warmed to Gerty's father. It would have warmed to the very dog of the house in which she lived; though she was but a silly girl, and his life lay quite in another sphere from hers.

There was no sham in the humble fear of the little man, but he quickly checked its utterance. What right had he to be chattering of himself or his fitness? "It is a great work, Mr. Dour, which Madam Galbraith has undertaken so late in life."

"She is a shrewd woman. At the present price of even doubtful oil stock—"

"She had no eyes upon oil, sir," eagerly, "nor profit. It is a care for souls. She was frank with me as to her motive. 'Let me feed the bodies of these men, Mr. Rattlin,' she said; 'give them work, cheerful homes, education, and they are much more ready for you to lead into the kingdom of heaven.' She may be right," meditatively. "Ascetic religion was pushed very far—very far—by the Papists. I doubt its efficacy. Now, we Protestants—"

"She is a shrewd woman," repeated Dour, quietly.

"You think she is right, then? Well, there is a great deal to be done," cheerfully. "Church, Sunday-school and weekly lectures to be inaugurated. I'm glad our friend Beck here has moved to the town, and put his shoulder to the wheel. His example may do much."

"I've put my shoulder to because *I* mean to rise ile," said Beck, sturdily, buttoning his coat. "My dooty is to Peggy and Matt. As for the Dutch and their souls, that's a horse of another color. I don't know it. No disrespect to you. Mr. Rattlin."

"No, Beck, certainly not," watching him make his bow and exit with a good-humored smile. "Beck is a neighbor of mine in our new village. He has put all he has into the scheme."

Dour was looking down at the little cheerful cricket of a man with a nervousness singular in the self-possessed, trig, ready youth. "Is your new home as pleasant as the old one? That was a very peculiar house, I think."

"Why, my dear sir, there are a dozen like it within a stone's throw! The new one is infinitely superior. And I have bought my mare back—Jenny—from Whitcross. You've heard me speak of Jenny?"

"Is Mrs. Rattlin well? And—the children?" with a quaking in his narrow chest for which he could have scourged himself.

"Well, no. Tony has a weakness in one leg—a fall, we fear—and the baby is just over the measles. There have been changes among us since you left us, Mr. Dour, and there will be greater soon, I fear. Come down. I would like to show you Jenny. We felt as if an old friend had come back again—"

Madam Galbraith came up, and, beckoning to Mr. Rattlin, led him away for consultation. There was a grave respect in her manner to him which she showed to no one else. Mr. Dour was left alone, more startled than he chose to own. What changes could be coming among the Rattlin brood? Tom was going to school, perhaps, or the twins were ailing. If they were not so cursedly healthy and such hearty feeders, a man need not be afraid of marrying the whole family.

He turned sharply around on pretty Mrs. Duffield, who had halted in the open door, taking in the hard, earnest room and hard, earnest people in it, with an amused, placid glance: "Mr. Rattlin spoke of impending changes in his family, just now. Do you know what they are, Mrs. Duffield?"

"One of his daughters is to be married, I believe. Rosa, Gertrude—what are their names? If you will close that window, Mr. Dour, I think I will come in," composing herself in Madam Galbraith's chair with a little shiver.

The old lady turned on hearing their voices. "If you are persuading my daughter-in-law to join in our scheme," she said, sharply, "your efforts are wasted, Mr. Dour. She is the only member of my household who stands aloof. I was much gratified, by the way, to-day"—to Mr. Rattlin—"when a woman whom I have employed for years put her earnings into my hands. A canny Jersey woman, too—my housekeeper. She had, apparently, entire confidence in my judgment, as, I must say, even the business men of the county appear to have."

But Mrs. Duffield, quite unconscious of being lashed over Lizzy's shoulder, drew back her soft lilac dress, lest the fire should fade it, and putting up her dainty feet on a footstool, leaned back and surveyed them all with the critical good-humor of the spectator of a comedy.

Mr. Rattlin came up to her. "Madam Galbraith hopes to do a great work among these people," he said, anxiously. "I still think you will help us. If you would try to make one soul among them purer and better. At your age, and childless—"

"I ought to be laying up treasure in heaven," with her pleasant, indolent smile. "But I object to helping you, personally, on principle, Mr. Rattlin. It hardens one terribly to work among the poor. Your managers of almshouses and asylums always degenerate into machines. They've no sympathy with the sensitive, acute pain which you feel, looking on misery from far off. I grew calloused enough when I lived among the poor unfortunates. I took in washing during my first husband's life-time, you know. I was quite convinced then that I had no call to be a reformer."

Madam Galbraith brought her ponderous body between her and the fire. She had been watching the insouciant little lady with angry eagerness from under her heavy brows. It gave her little comfort that the whole of the county acknowledged her leadership, so long as this Mordecai disregarded her within her very gates. "One would think you would wish to see your native State developed," she said, in an acrid tone. "Your patriotism—" and there stopped.

Mrs. Duffield waited courteously for her to finish. "I have no call to be a reformer," she repeated, with vivacity. "As for patriotism, I have not an atom in my veins—not an atom."

Mr. Dour, who had been standing gloomily by the window, roused himself to join Madam Galbraith. "But you must have some *esprit de corps*, Mrs. Duffield," he said. "You are one of us. We have put all we have into this venture. We are in the same ship together—"

"Then I'll—'paddle my own canoe,'" sang the sweetest and most liquid of voices. It was one of her attractive little ways, to embroider her talk with snatches of songs (with no high notes to show the crack in her tones). But she was too indolent to be vivacious or winning long. She bent forward with a steady look, as if determined to put a stop to her annoyance for ever. "I wish Madam Galbraith success," with a grave little bow. "May she find her subjects submissive! But, my dear Mr. Rattlin, never talk to me about the poor. There is a class of people to whom such talk is jarring and morbid. Their religion comes to them through good clothes, good music, gentle, æsthetic emotions. I think I am one of them. We are the right hand of the world; and if you are the left, you should not let us know the good you do."

Mr. Rattlin looked bewildered at the ironical smile on her lips. It disappeared as she turned to Mr. Dour: "My little property would be of no value in your great undertaking. But it is invested in State securities, and yields me six per cent. in gold. It is very comfortable to have it in gold."

"But in oil—"

"The flow of brine will not account for the late stoppages in your wells," a keen glint in her eyes. "When the pulse is uneven, the man is sick—sick, Mr. Dour."

There was a sudden silence as this bombshell fell. Dour looked anxiously at Madam Galbraith. "Paraffine!" she growled, contemptuously, taking up a map.

"But the paraffine cannot clog my six per cent. in gold," retorted Mrs. Duffield, arching her golden-brown eyebrows significantly. "Come, Honora, let us go. We are without the camp," putting her arm about Miss Dundas.

She did not speak again until they had reached her own room, and she had given Honora a chair near her softly-cushioned lounge. Then she walked restlessly to the window and back again, a look of almost anxiety on her fair face. "I can read defeat and disaster written on the very walls of this house," she said, at last. "It seems as if it were God's will that no family should stand long secure in this country. There is a sort of leprosy attacks all large fortunes. After a generation or two they all moulder—moulder. But one does not care to be in the falling house." She seated herself a moment after, arranging herself comfortably with her usual good-tempered calm.

There were no signs of defeat or decay in the wide, dainty room to which the firelight gave such warmth and snugness. It was curious to note how Madam Galbraith had gradually sacrificed to it the best which the house could afford of beauty or taste. Not that she had any fondness for the little woman, who sank into her luxurious home as naturally as a bird into its nest; nor that the said little woman would have given one shrug of discontent if they had lodged her on bare floors.

The room had taken meaning, also, since she came. There were engravings, sketches, rare pieces of glass, all manner of delicate souvenirs from guests who, when gone, had sent back some trifle to give her pleasure. Yet they all loved Honora better.

But Honora was not one of the world's bits of useless porcelain which it delights to set aside and guard.

"You have no faith in my aunt's foresight, then?" Miss Dundas said, gloomily, after a long silence.

Mrs. Duffield gave a most expressive wave of her fingers. She had drawn her work-basket toward her and was twisting a cord about a blue velvet Normandy cap, which was the only covering which she permitted on her hair. "Pah!" she said. "But what of that? She is like an old, untamed animal. It would be death to her to balk her." After pausing a moment to look critically at her cap, she continued, gravely: "But these poor souls for whom she intends conversion! Now, positively, Honora, I would as soon be gored into heaven by a herd of wild buffaloes."

Miss Dundas sat motionless, her face toward the fire, for some time. When she spoke, she did not look at her companion. "If I could tell you all that was at stake, you would interfere. There is a secret—"

Mrs. Duffield gave her a quick, searching glance. The girl's great and suppressed agitation would have made any other woman curious; but Mrs. Duffield put up her hand with positive alarm. "My dear girl, choose anybody for your confidant but me. I really cannot be annoyed by this matter; and as for secrets, I never had one of my own in my life. They are childish, silly."

"You will not interfere, then?"

"Certainly *not*," taking up her work again. Honora had risen and stood regarding Dallas' mother with impatient scorn. "Then I wash my hands of it!" she said, bitterly. "What can I do alone?"

"Very little, my dear," tranquilly. "You are quite wise not to vex yourself." After a pause she looked up: "When you are as old as I, you will have learned the sense of being a mere spectator in the world. This dear old lady did not control her nature in her youth, and it is sweeping her headlong to ruin in her age. That is inevitable. Why should I throw myself in the way? Now, why should I, Honora?" with a gentle appeal. "When you meet that which is inevitable never make a single struggle against it—not if it brings your own death to you. Die if you must, but there is no need that you should be weak and foolish. I have something for your uncle here," changing her tone, and bringing from a closet some bunches of foreign grapes, which she heaped on a plate, with leaves under them. "Now give me that rose, my dear. An old friend sent them to me. There. Will you take them to him? They will give flavor to his book, perhaps."

"I will take them," said Honora, understanding that she and the trouble of the house were dismissed together.

When Honora had left her uncle, he dropped Ronsard on his knee as though he had suddenly lost all relish for his monstrous welding of bad Greek and French, and sat listening intently to every inflection of his wife's harsh voice. He had studied her voice for forty years: he had learned through it her secret thoughts and passions as surely as men measure the far-off heights and depths of a mountainous, unsafe country by a breath of vapor. No man ever brought to such study the patience and strength of this meek, gentlest of gentlemen; and having found the mastery over her, he had held his controlling hand steadily. Only Hannah Dour knew from what pitfalls and gulfs of passion that inflexible hand had saved her.

He understood, as few men do, a certain ebb and flow in the souls of some women, half physical, half spiritual—an abnormal swell, a flood-tide of the mysterious life within, which, in a woman of Madam Galbraith's age, nervous and childless, drifts the body like a weed close upon the boundaries of life and death. He had noted lately the signs of its rising: the dead, inactive lassitude of brain, alternating with unnatural vigor. Listening now to her inarticulate tones, he judged her more justly than those who heard her words, or than she did herself. It was not greed that possessed her, as Dour thought, nor love of power, nor the hope of saving souls.

"She must not be thwarted," he said at last, rising, decisively. "If the end be beggary, she must not be thwarted. Unless—" Going into the room, he found her alone, the maps pushed from her, and her hands pressed into her forehead.

He sat down beside her. "You are tired, Hannah?" he said, quietly.

"I am very tired, James!"

"I wish you would rest. What if you put this whole tangled business aside and forget both it and yourself for a while? A sea voyage, or that exploring journey through the West we used to plan when we were young—"

"We are not young now, James. It is not far from the end." She took her hands down and looked at him. "If I had been a man, I would have made my mark upon the world. But when I am gone, there will not be a sign on the earth that I have lived."

"Does that cost you so much?" with a strange smile.

"There is not an hour of the day when it is not present to me." She stood up pointing to the distant mountains and broad river: "I will do what I can. That is the Dour land. I am the last of many generations. I will write my name on it so that time itself shall never wipe it out."

Mr. Galbraith hesitated before he spoke, as if the words he meant to utter were a forlorn hope which he threw in her way: "If our boy—if Tom were here you would not care for this work."

"How can I tell," wiping her forehead. The old tenderness had gone out of her eyes: they were firm and grasping as a hawk's swooping on its quarry. "He was but one—I am going to save many souls. I am called to do a great work. I must have something to fill up this gap," hoarsely, laying her hand on her broad breast. "Do not stop me James, do not stand in my way."

"I will not stand in your way, Hannah," he replied, gently.

CHAPTER XXIV.

WHEN Mr. Rattlin made his adieux to the stern old woman bending over her maps, Mr. Dour followed him out. "I'll walk down the avenue with you," he said. But he went no farther than the door. When they were outside, he glanced up at the massive house and then at the wide sweep of landscape, repeating a lesson he had taken pains to learn, that when he married Miss Dundas all this would be his. What was it to him which of the preacher's little daughters was to be married!

Yet, when Mr. Rattlin had gone, he followed him to the brow of the hill, looking after him, with a homesick longing which shamed him. That Gerty should marry! Why, there had not been a moment when he was gone that she had not been in his thoughts, a winning, tender presence. And, at the very moment she had been giving her soft lips to the touch of another man!

In the few days that followed, Mr. Dour became prime councilor with Madam Galbraith. He was so deferential to her, so regardless of Honora, that the old lady accused herself with injustice. "He has no folly about marriage in his head," she said. "And he will make a very fair business man—under control, of course." The truth was, there were certain gaps and weak places in the schemes of her own imperial intellect, the patching of which she left to meaner minds, taking it for granted that they knew their place.

Paul, on the contrary, wrote to his mother: "Many persons prophesy disaster, being prejudiced by the old lady's visionary, violent character. But oil is oil and capital is capital. They are secure. She has the sense, too, to leave all important arrangements to me and others, comprehending the difference between a man's intellect and a woman's. I think she has a plan for marrying me to her niece. I would have the business capacity, and she the capital—a usual partnership. But marrying is very far from my thoughts." He had no mind to take anybody into his confidence. As soon as he could see his way clear he meant to marry Miss Dundas.

Honora, meanwhile, had driven down to the wells to bring Gerty up, as she proposed. The Rattlins swarmed, at present, in a half-finished house full of raw carpenter-work and wet paint. "You need not wait for me, Honora," said Gerty, loftily. "Papa will take me up if I determine to go." Then she went into her mother's room, and sat down: "There is no use in bringing out my clothes, mother. There's only the faded old merino with the patch on the elbow. That's the beginning and end," with a laugh which brought the tears into Mrs. Rattlin's eyes. For Madam Galbraith, in her great scheme, had forgotten her usual box of spring clothes, which imported so much to the poor preacher's household.

Mrs. Rattlin did take down the faded merino, and turned it over hopelessly. "If it had not been for the dresses we had to buy for Rosy—"

"I don't begrudge Rosy her few little things or her happiness," said Gerty, pushing back the hair from her pale cheeks. "I didn't mean that, mother. But it's hard that my whole life should depend on the want of clothes."

"If your dress makes any difference to him, he's not worthy of you, Gerty," rejoined Mrs. Rattlin, hotly. "In my day, true love didn't come and go with gowns."

"I suppose Honora wants me there as a foil," said Gerty, spitefully. "But he never cared for her when I was there, as lovely as her things were this winter. He cared for me." She came and put her arms about her mother's neck, and cried there silently. She had grown quiet and gentle as never before during the winter months, while Rosy was making ready for her wedding. Her mother was the only one to whom she talked of Dour or her hope in him. The two women had waited day after day since he returned, for him to come, the aching pain as sharp in the mother's heart as in the child's. They had walked together every evening beyond the derricks to the point where they could see the Galbraith house on the hill-side. Even that was some comfort to Gerty, her mother fancied. The girl raised her head at last, and taking the old merino, hung it up quietly. "I cannot go. It's all over," she said, under her breath.

"Oh, my darling! your day will come. Cannot you trust a little in the Lord?"

"What does He care for a girl's shabby clothes? No, mother; Rosy shall be married and happy, and I'll stay and help you with the children. I'll be an old maid and sew and do kitchen-work on to the end, as I've begun, and grow old and die, and wake up in heaven alone—alone!" sitting down on Tony's trundle bed and hiding her eyes, sobbing. "I think I'll go and walk a while," she said at last; and putting on her worsted hood, to hide her eyes, she went out, while Mrs. Rattlin sat down to patch Joe's trowsers, with a great weight at her heart. When a girl like Gerty misses her chance of marriage, what is there to give her to fill up her life? What is there?

It was a cheerful morning. Down by the muddy meadow-creek the willows began to look like pale-green mists held motionless in the air, and here and there under her feet a bluebell or dandelion peeped up from under last year's grass; but Gerty hurried on, blind to them, into the crowded lanes, which crept outward, crooked as a spider's claws, from the oil-wells. She passed under the shadow of the great derricks, stopped to look at the green mass in the enormous tanks, and then walked more slowly through the rows of unfinished wooden houses and the swarms of workmen and Dutch emigrants, all chattering, eager, busy. She crept along still more slowly by the towering, half-built factories, the tent-like roofs of the rolling-mills, bitter speculation in her chubby, doll-face. For Gerty was weighing the value of mills and oil against that same doll-face. They were Honora's fortune. Gerty was dumb when her father talked of the love of God shown in Madam Galbraith's gigantic scheme of philanthropy; but its percentage the girl could understand well enough. It was her rival. There was not a sign in the long battle between Paul Dour's avarice and love that the giddy, kittenish cherub (as he thought her) beside him had not keenly seen and noted. She passed drearily out of the town, and looked back into the crowd and heat, with its overhanging cloud of black smoke. It was only to Gerty a great engine, which dragged the triumphant car of the brilliant little heiress. Then she thought of her one faded dress, and her soul was bitter within her.

Outside of the nucleus of life which had suddenly appeared in their midst, the hills fell back into their old melancholy silence and solitude. Gerty, leaving the town a few rods behind her, was utterly alone. It was a narrow cattle-path which she had followed, through a cleft of the hills. She sat down on some dry rocks which shelved down on the banks of the creek: there were the ruins of an old mill below her, the sun shining brightly on the broken, mossy wheel and charred rafters. Dour, walking down the same path an hour before, on his way to the town, had stopped to notice the picturesque beauty of the place; but Gerty saw nothing, unless it was the clinging folds of the ill-fitting yellow dress she wore and the faded, cherry-colored hood which she took from her head. Her clothes were only the sign of her life—all faded and worn out together. She crouched down, remembering the dinner uncooked at home, looking wistfully at the bright water's drip, drip. To the poor little Rattlin girl, forced back from love, marriage and motherhood to unending sewing and kitchen-work, life was as vacant, and the rest of "muddy death" as alluring, as to Ophelia. But Gerty only stood and looked at it. After an hour she stood up to go back to the sweeping and dish-washing. Then it was that she heard a quick, decided step on the beaten path, and sat down on one of the mill logs until the intruder should pass on. The step came nearer: the man gave a hoarse cough. She got up, put out one hand, as if she would have fallen, and then cowered down lower than before, forgetting her clothes, her misery —herself.

It was Dour's first visit to the town. He knew every dollar invested in it through Madam Galbraith's books, and the probable capacity of each well from Mr. Finn, the expert whom she had employed to oversee their opening—had gone over maps and accounts with the lingering tenderness of an heir-at-law taking stock of his future possessions. But he had not before found courage to see, touch, handle them. This chubby figure in the yellow dress would not be thrust from the secret recess of his heart, though it was more terrible to him there than any skeleton.

He had pushed through the crowd, smelled the oil and surveyed the mills and the drays loaded with pig-metal, with the same light shining on them all which Gerty had seen. They were Honora's fortune. They were his price.

He had not seen the golden shekels before for which he meant to sell himself. Their ring and glitter touched him home. He was no longer Madam Galbraith's feed clerk: he was an absolute dictator. He was quite satisfied to stand off from oil and iron and accept Finn's fluent assertions and the mill-master's guarded estimate. Dour told himself that his was the controlling faculty which enabled him to use the brains of these men as tools—to convert their knowledge into capital for himself. While he was tip-toeing complacently through the street, swinging his cane, his nattily-brushed coat buttoned about his narrow chest, Mr. Rattlin hailed him: "Why, bless me, Dour! Come over, man; I want you to see the mother, and Jenny, our mare. Did I tell you I had got her back from Whitcross?"

Dour followed him only to the stable: he would not be drawn farther. But through the window he saw the shabby dining-room, the huddle of unwashed children, the meagre dishes upon the table, and a flood of disgust rose within him, and quite overwhelmed that old love, he thought.

He made short work of it with Jenny and her light-hearted little master. Mr. Rattlin never thought of his daughters but as children, nor introduced them into his conversation; and when Dour would have asked with indifference which of them was going to leave her home, something rose in his throat and choked him.

Yet he was awkward and silent while Mr. Rattlin dilated over Jenny, held the little man's hand a moment at parting, as though bidding to him, or something which lay behind him, a last good-bye, and when he left him, did not go back to the town, but turned to the mill-path and walked hurriedly toward home. The sooner he was out of danger the better, he told himself. He would propose to Miss Dundas to-night.

Looking up with the thought, he saw a plump little woman, in a faded hood, shrinking behind one of the beams of the mill, as if to avoid him. Inside of his tact, philosophy, measurements of pig-metal and oil, there was a sudden terrible throb.

He walked straight to her.

Paul Dour knew a hundred women prettier, more companionable, more winning than this untidy girl in yellow: what nerve or cord or magnetic fluid was there between his heart and hers that gave him that wrench and brought him to her against his will? Who will tell us the history, before we were born, of that living creature within us which goes about to find its mate in all impracticable places, deaf to reason? It dragged Paul close to Gerty: it spoke through his eyes and mouth; it tried to drive his calculations out of his head, as though they had been vile money-changers in the temple.

"Gerty!" he said. "Will you not speak to me, Gerty?"

"I am very glad to see you, Mr. Dour." Her dignity would have impressed us, perhaps, as much as that of a pullet, but it forced this astute fellow back with actual pain.

"Why do you hold your hands clasped?" putting his fingers on them. "Will you not trust me? In memory of our old friendship."

"That is dead and gone."

"It was not killed by me. You are as—you are the same to me that you ever were. You are the same, Gerty." He held her closely-shut hands and drew her slowly, passionately toward him. Whether from art or real despair and jealousy of Honora, or physical weariness from her hysteric sobbing, Gerty remained cold as marble—her fat cheeks pale, her wide, brown eyes meeting his, sad and fearless. The bird was not in his reach; and, after all, it was the only thing in the world which his heart had really coveted.

He pushed her from him: "You have found some one who is more to you than I. I know that you are to be married."

"No; it is Rosy. There was a man who loved me very much," with a certain childish gravity, "and he would have made me his wife this winter; but I would not choose that degradation."

"Why is it degradation?"

"I did not love him." She was holding back the tears under her strait lids, and did not see the effect which her quiet words had upon her hearer.

"Poor Gerty! Your ideas of honor are out of date," with a cynical laugh. "A woman has only her hand to sell: she ought to make as good a bargain as possible with it. See; your clothes and bread and butter for life depend upon your marrying. That is the result of our admirable social system. And mine also," he added, secretly, warning himself back from the precipice.

"I know that," simply accepting his sneer as truth. "But I did not love him," and again her eyes were raised to his.

"Perhaps he would not have given you a comfortable home?"

"Oh, yes; he is in a good business—John Stokes. I should have lived in an elegant cottage and been dressed very nicely. But he was nothing to me."

Dour balanced himself against a fallen log, looking with keen, not untender, speculation into her silly face. "And yet you have hard lines down there, Gerty? Eleven of you? Little to eat and less to wear? Don't be angry, child; I don't mean to hurt you, God knows."

"It is a poor home. We are tired and overworked—all of us," with some spirit. "But I love them all there. I will not marry a man whom I do not love."

There was nothing very new or magnanimous in Gerty's words, but they struck Dour as a lofty strain of music belonging to a life higher than the one he had chosen. But then the little woman, with her brown hair and appealing eyes, her rounded, peachy-tinted figure, in its miserable dress, down to the very feet in the worn shoes, was a something different from anything else in this vulgar world. And, beside, he was enraged at John Stokes to the breaking of his head if he had been a fighting man. As he was not, Gerty's scorn was grateful to him.

"Catholics can go into a nunnery when they're tired and lonely; but we Protestants must drag on at home, where we are not needed. I am going to do that, to help with the work and the children. It will all come to an end some day," said Gerty, with the old, quiet, forlorn gesture, pushing back her hair with both hands. Dour could not speak: he looked down at her in silence. If he had not loved her, there would have been something terribly pathetic in the sight of this poor little woman, cast out of any rightful place in the world because she would not marry for a home. If he had not loved her, he would have used the case as a telling argument in favor of giving to girls trades or professions as well as boys—have argued that there was less indelicacy in a woman selling goods and groceries than selling herself for a livelihood. As it was, his soul was dumb within him.

She looked up at him at last. "I must go now. Good-bye, Mr. Dour."

"Good-bye, Gerty. Am I never to see you again?"

He meant to give her up, then? But she was too tired and worn-out for the certainty to bring forth more than a low sob. "It would be better if I did not see you again, I suppose. Good-bye."

But he did not move. "Will you give me your hand?"

She hesitated and then held it out. He clasped it hard in both his own, standing motionless, his face bent on the ground. When she would have moved, he said, with a frown: "Give me a moment. I do not want to repent hereafter." She looked wonderingly at him, not knowing that within that oddly-shaped, narrow head, curiously flat a-top, her future life was being decided—his reason, habits, ambition on one side, and that incomprehensible, living creature on the other, who would not be thwarted.

Suddenly it dawned upon her that it was her own fate which hung uncertain before his half-shut, calculating eyes. She did not move nor speak.

How hot the sun glared! Paul, looking up presently, gave a pitying smile when he saw her face. "Poor Gerty!" he said, gently.

"You have no right to pity me!" she flamed out. "You belong to Miss Dundas. You mean to marry Honora!"

"I did mean to marry her," he said, quietly. "Hush, child. Do not talk to me. I am trying to do what is best for you and me both." He left her and walked uneasily down the road: then, coming abruptly back, he said, with more passion and fire than his meagre, thin lips seemed capable of expressing: "I think you have no right to doubt me. I mean to give up this great chance of my life because I love you, Gerty. I mean to marry you. You *will* marry me?" remembering that he had not asked her.

Gerty had often planned her coy, reluctant consent, but now she said: "Oh, yes, Paul," meekly enough, and then fell into an ignominious sobbing, with joy as sharp as pain.

"Why, what are you crying for, child?" sitting down and taking her in his arms, and for a moment forgetful of anything but the womanly beauty and softness and tenderness with which he meant to fill up his life. The distant sight of the gallows-like derricks over her shoulder put him in mind, however, of all which he had given up for this beauty and softness.

"Of course," releasing her, "I must turn my back on this part of the country. There's no chance for me now here."

"Shall we go home now?" timidly. "I'd like to tell mother and ask her blessing."

"Oh, time enough for blessings, dear. I was going to explain to you, Gerty, that having lost this chance, I have nothing tangible to take hold of. If you'll look over this book"—pulling out a leather-covered pass-book—"here are my last year's expenses put down to a cent. Just run them up. What, with teaching for six months and five magazine papers, I covered them. You see, just covered them."

"Dear Paul, if you were a beggar, in the worst of rags and tags, I would love you just as well," energetically, patting one of his hands between her own.

"Oh, I've no doubt. But love don't pay board-bills, darling Gerty," looking impatiently over her head.

She had no conception of the sacrifice he had made! None whatever!

"What I wished to say to you was, that it must be a long time, perhaps, before I could claim you as mine. I'll go West. I'll make a comfortable home for you before I ask you to share my lot."

"I would live in a hovel," whispered Gerty, trying to make amends, for she had a vague consciousness that she had been found lacking in some appreciation of her lover's perfections.

"It will not be necessary for us to live in a hovel, Gertrude. Very good land can be pre-empted in Kansas, and a snug house built for a couple of hundred dollars. We'll try Kansas. It will need but a few dollars to set us up in kitchen ware. We will go to your mother now for our blessing," with an indulgent smile down at her.

"I've no doubt mother would divide the parlor things with us. I shouldn't like to have only a kitchen. Though I suppose we would not have many callers in Kansas," said Gerty, wistfully.

Paul stopped—held her off at arm's length, and laughed nervously, as this woman never could have laughed. "What a baby you are!" he said. "Kiss me, Gerty;" and then strained her to him passionately. He had made his choice: he must make the best of it. They walked on in silence: he paused again: turned her round, facing him: "You do not doubt my love, Gertrude?"

"No, Paul."

"Never doubt it. It is real," with one forefinger on his shirt front. "I have sacrificed much to it. It is a wonderful study. It is not you who are in my heart, as the vulgar phrase it." After a meditative pause: "It is a foreign element within. Underlying and antagonistic to the *ego*. You merely called it into action. There is no limit to the heights of heroism and self-abnegation to which it may lead. Different triumphs from those achieved by money."

"I thought you considered money a very good thing?" said Gerty, anxiously.

"There are two sides to every great truth," said Dour, snappishly. "Money helps me to develop my inner self, and is good. But if love and poverty develop it also and lift me higher, they are better."

"Oh!" said Gerty. So as they walked along she leaned on his arm and looked up in his face, and Dour felt the development of his inner self a very pleasant process, although the oil-wells lay behind.

"Young man!—Mr. Dour! Halt!— a word with you, if you please!" Dour stopped with a guilty start as the well-known large figure in gray came out of a by-lane and beckoned him toward her with her staff. She nodded kindly to Gerty with a glance at her flushed, tear-stained face. "Stay where you are, child. My business is with this lad. If the girl's mother is unfit to take care of her, I will take her place," lowering her voice when Dour came up: "What is that young woman to you, sir?"

"My friend."

"Tut! tut!" with disgust. "You are too sensible a man to prate of friendship with a young, attractive woman at your age. She must be something more to you or nothing. Stop!" when he would have spoken. "I have watched your course with Gerty. I had a plan that you should marry her. It is perhaps my habit to lay plans for others," with a half smile. "She is a good girl and a pretty girl, and for her father's sake I mean that she shall not go penniless to her husband. I thought that you would be a very proper husband for her, though you have your faults. You need training. But I will not have her trifled with. There must be no more strolling through mountain lanes. I will not have her name or her affections tampered with."

A proper husband for Gerty? Verily here was an end to his vision! "Miss Rattlin is my affianced wife," said Dour, with a distant bow, making the best of it.

"Eh? How! I think well of you, Dour," striking her stick unto the ground. "Come, give me your hand, little one. You are an honester fellow than I thought you, sir. I tell you, candidly, I had my eye on you. If you had given this little girl the go-by, you would have left my house as penniless as you came into it. But from to-morrow I appoint you my overseer—secretary—what you please. We'll not quarrel about names. But you shall have plenty to do, and no cause to complain of your salary. I give it to you for Gerty's sake. Mind that. I'll give the child an outfit myself. Now, off with you both, and talk it over."

"Why, she did not want you to marry Honora after all," said Gerty, glancing up shrewdly under her curly lashes.

"It appears not." He did not speak for a long time, and then stooped and kissed her heartily. Gerty knew that in the kiss he accepted her and the situation for ever.

CHAPTER XXV.

SLOW spring: slow summer; and at last—November.

Honora, absorbed with the one thought which possessed her whole being by this time (because of her anxiety for her uncle, she told herself), keeping up her incessant watch for a gray-coated figure coming over the hills, who was to deliver him from impending ruin, could not see that Lizzy too grew uneasy and restless, until one day, when Elizabeth, grown desperate for the want of definite knowledge about Dallas, attacked Mr. Galbraith in the library while Honora was within hearing.

"There was a man from the Indian

Queen, sir, who went with Dr. Pritchard on his expedition. He promised he would return in a year. Can he do it? We do not know about the railroads down there."

"It is most unlikely that he could do it, or that he will," with an unwonted impatience in his tone. "If his work suits him, it is more probable that he will return after three years than one." After Lizzy left the room, he looked up and saw Honora standing by the window. "No doubt those two silly women look for the fellow to turn his back upon his work and post from New Mexico to report himself, like Lord Lovel, a year from the hour he set out. As if a man allowed his life to hinge on sentimental promises like a school-girl!"

"But he will come," said Miss Dundas to herself. On Wednesday of the next week the year would be over. She fancied Dallas returning; counting the hours as she was doing, taking out the flower which doubtless he carried with him constantly, feeling that its faint perfume brought him close to home and—to her.

Madam Galbraith had by chance fixed upon that very day for the celebration at once of Gerty's wedding and of the success of her colony. She chose that the little girl should be married from the Galbraith house, and the whole neighborhood was bidden to rejoice with her. The town also was to hold a holiday. There was to be a dinner for the workmen from the wells and mills (all of which were in full operation), and at night a dance in the town-hall and a public meeting outside. She scattered her money like an Irish king: gave unlimited orders for feasting and drinking: the speechifying and the praise of Hannah Dour necessarily would follow; and whether it came from her equals or from Dutch or Irish laborers, praise was sweet in her nostrils. "It is not only the happiness of the little girl's life I want to commemorate," she said to her husband, "but the success of mine. I have done a great work for Humanity. I have scored my name deep. It will last as long as the land endures."

The day came.

The sun, she thought, never had flashed over the mountains and valleys of the Dour lands with such victorious splendor. Surely God saw a great work done and approved it—set his seal upon her as one of the leading spirits of the age. The petty, joyous excitement in the house jarred upon her. She ordered her carriage and prepared to drive down to the colony, feasting her eyes, as she stood on the steps, with the great column of smoke rising from it to the skies, as though it were a thank-offering to her, going up perpetually.

"I will go with you," said Honora, joining her.

Madam Galbraith was annoyed, but the girl looked ill and restless, and she did not refuse her. But she wanted to be alone. Even her husband was in her way lately. He was weak, idle, inefficient. He was no help-meet for her in this her enduring work. She had no companion: she thought, with a vague remembrance, of the lion who was born alone.

She drove in absolute silence—Honora, rousing herself now and then to look at the stately figure in its purple dress beside her, the imperious, hard face, the gray crown of hair shining in the sun, wondering what welcome she would give to Dallas when he came. For to-night he would be here. At dusk, when the moon rose, he would come to the door of the green-house and bid her remember that the year was over and he had kept his word.

They reached the town. It had grown rapidly as a fungus. Streets and lanes of the snug, four-roomed wooden houses had sprung up as by magic. Madam Galbraith alighted and walked slowly through her dominions, her eye brilliant, her wide nostrils dilated. If the black mills and great tanks of oil had been the beautiful Utopia of a dream, her triumph could not have been greater.

"It is a noble work for Humanity!" she said to Mr. Rattlin, trotting by her side.

"Yes, when the school-house is finished and a good teacher secured—"

"All in good time! Don't begin to worry, I beg," impatiently. "Yes," surveying the crowds surrounding the tables spread in the woods, "I think I have the faculty of managing men in masses —hereditary, probably. The Dours are of German descent, accustomed always to the control of large tenantries."

Honora's eyes were dull: she could not see that the men about her differed from any other laborers, or understand how their two or three months' residence on the Dour ground had advanced either them or Humanity.

"I hope the mills and oil may turn out well," she said. "Otherwise it will be worse for these poor creatures, who have risked their all."

Madam Galbraith turned on her. "What is that, Honora? Do you think the Lord will not protect a work for Him? You had better look over Gerty's cottage while I continue my walk." Miss Dundas turned gladly enough into a pretty little house, which the old lady had furnished for Dour and his wife, and Mr. Rattlin managed to join her. They went from one room to another, the little man saying nothing, by which Nora knew how full his heart was. She did not know why the little ménage—meant for two—the two easy-chairs on either side of the fire, with their prophetic, happy meaning, even the little cooking utensils and cozy table, thrilled her with such tender warmth. Nor why she blushed and started when Mr. Rattlin spoke to her, as if she were the bride and the beloved! They could hear the cheering in the woods when Madam Galbraith entered them.

"They are roasting an ox whole and two sheep. It is a regular barbecue," said Mr. Rattlin. "Gerty will be very happy here, I think? You must come another day and see how snugly our own house looks now. Madam Galbraith promises positions for the boys in the works as soon as they are of age to fill them. I think the hard times are over for us now, Miss Dundas."

"I'm glad," said Nora, holding out her hand, with sudden tears in her eyes.

"Yes, it has been a long fight," he said, under his breath. "Shall we lock up the house and go back to the farm? I do not believe Madam Galbraith will miss us. Gerty will want me."

It was noon before they reached the house again. Gerty was watching for her father—ran to meet him and hung on his arm. As the time for her marriage had come nearer, she clung like a baby to both mother and father, was petulant with Dour, and scarcely gave a look to the pretty dresses with which her wardrobe was filled.

Honora looked drearily at the slow-creeping shadows. "Evening will never come, I think," she said, with a sigh.

"It comes so fast to me!" said Gerty, looking up into her father's face and drawing him off for a solitary walk, telling him how much she meant to do for Tony and Joe and the girls, and that perhaps it would have been better never to have married, and that no home could be as happy as this one that she left. Mr. Rattlin, seeing Dour coming to find her, waited for him and gave her over to him, trying to joke, with a choking in his heart. But he never forgot those words of Gerty's. Years afterward the old father and mother used to talk of what it cost her to part from them. They had not thought the child loved them so much.

At any other time, Nora would have been in the thickest of the heat of preparation—the very spur and life of it; but now she went restlessly through the halls and reception-rooms, which the women were hanging with evergreen and flowers—into the state dining-room, where the long table was glittering with silver and glass—into the kitchen, where Peggy Beck and two other amateurs, with the regular cook, held highest carnival of all. Everywhere that she went was Lizzy, in her brown dress, her face hot, busy, eager and silent. It was no wedding or success of a colony for which she prepared: it was the coming home in triumph of her boy—the heir. Her years of patient waiting were over. He had conquered a name and was coming to take his rightful place. There was not a flower she plucked or a dish she cooked which was not meant to take its part in doing him honor. Perhaps the dishes filled a larger part than the flowers in her mind; for Lizzy had grown more and more into the housekeeper's mould.

"I thought you would have come down to flavor the creams, Honora. No one can do that like you. Did you see the tables? There will be a light collation and a hot supper afterward. Madam Galbraith left it all to me. What with flowers and confectionery and colored ices, the table will look like fairies' work. What do you think of the supper-rooms? I want to make the house an utter contrast to the dreariness out of doors, to please—the bride."

"I'll see if those creams are right," said Honora. There was no reason why she should shut herself out from life and its business because a man was coming home who most probably cared nothing for her. She stopped, too, to give her opinion with regard to the stuffing of the turkeys, at which Peggy laughed when she had gone.

Then she went up again to the library, where her uncle was pacing to and fro, as if he, too, waited and watched. Honora looked out of the window. What if a storm should come? But Dallas would not heed a storm, and the sky was cloudless. Her uncle did not notice her. He had brought in that pretty curly-headed boy of Peggy Beck's, and seated him with a picture-book, and then forgotten him. He had made a pet of the child lately. She wondered if, in this turmoil and rejoicing, his thoughts had not wandered away to his own dead son, who never would wake to merry-making or love again. If he only knew that Tom's boy was near at hand—coming to him to-night!

The day lagged, slower and slower, as evening approached. The house, the people about her, passed before her feverish, exaggerating senses as pictures in a vivid dream. She caught a glimpse of Dallas' mother from time to time as she passed her room—a room in which there was perfect quiet. She lay on a lounge before the clear, red fire, turning over the crisp pages of a freshly-cut book. Whatever storm of joy or sorrow might rage about her, Mrs. Duffield remained, like Gideon's fleece, miraculously dry and white and cool.

Evening was here at last. To Honora a strange hush, a waiting pause, seemed to have fallen on the great house and the darkening landscape without, though it was only, in fact, that lonely silence which precedes dusk in solitary mountain countries. Yet even when, later, the house was lighted, so that it shone like a beacon over the hills, and filled with guests, the laughter and crowd and music seemed to her but a prelude for that which was to follow. She had been foolish in her prophecy of ruin: it was a great inheritance to which Dallas came home to-night.

Gerty was married. The plump little body wore tulle, which moss roses caught and drew back from her white neck and arms, and Mr. Dour stood there, sallow and black-coated, beside her. Rosy and Mrs. Rattlin, who sat sobbing in the big arm-chair, with half of the Rattlins quartered on her lap, thought there never had been such a pageant before; but the little cricket of a preacher who married them, standing on his tip-toes, leaning on the back of a chair, his voice choking as he talked, carried his child's life to the very feet of God, with every word he spoke struggling for a blessing upon it.

But to the rest of the guests the commonplace little girl and her marriage were secondary affairs. Everybody knew that the wedding was but an opportunity to celebrate Madam Galbraith's success and chant pæans thereon. She knew it herself: her very dress unconsciously asserted triumph—the clinging purple velvet showed the grand poise and motion of her limbs. In her very coarseness and rugged strength she seemed better fitted to be the product and exponent of the land she meant to develop. Her old friends, perhaps, missed something of the old heartiness in her welcome: it was an ovation to which they had come, rather than a feast.

The supper-rooms were open, though

Lizzy had delayed until the appointed hour was past. Honora met her wandering uneasily through the corridors, but hurried on without a word. It was her first chance of escape. The broad hall was darkened. At the far end there was a window and balcony without, which commanded an outlook over the Dour lands for miles. At the other end, the open door framed the wide, brilliant room, the flowers and feast, and the lion-headed old woman who made the centre of the picture. There was a man standing on the dark balcony when Honora went out. It was her uncle, who made room for her silently. Who could *he* wait for? She forgot that he was there, however, in her eager scrutiny of the dim slopes and winding road. But no gray-coated figure coming over the hills rewarded her.

It was a dark night: the moon was obscured by a wet, ash-colored mist that covered the heavens, the wind soughed shrilly through the far defile of the mountain with a melancholy, foreboding wail. They stood silent side by side. It was long past the hour when Dallas should have come. She could see the door of the greenhouse which she had set open and the ray of light streaming out through the dark orchard—all in vain.

If he were living, he would have kept his word. She pictured him lying dead in the long, rank grass of the Plains. Dead!

"It grows late," said her uncle, turning in, she fancied, with a sigh.

Colonel Pervis stepped up behind them: "Where have you been in hiding, Mr. Galbraith?" touching him on the shoulder. "I just rode up from the wells. They are holding a regular carnival there—have adjourned to the woods to hold the meeting, and kindled fires of pine-knots on tripods. It is not often a woman can reap such success from her work. What is that singular light? There, down by the river. It changes place."

"I see nothing."

"A dull, red point in the fog. Too low for the moon. Ah! I perceive that they are about to drink Madam Galbraith's health within there!"

Mr. Galbraith turned and through the glittering vista saw his wife's swarthy, powerful face kindled with a flush such as he never had known there before. She stood up and bowed silently over the glass which she held to her old neighbors and friends. She did not miss her husband in this crowning moment of triumph, or look for him to share in it. Yet if the consciousness of the difference in wealth between them, which day by day had put her farther from him, gave him any fierce pang, there was no sign of it in his mild, observant face.

The red, luminous point in the far river fog kindled and shot up into the sky a swift stream of light which broke into a shower of starry sparks. Colonel Pervis hastily crossed the hall. "They send you greeting from the colony, Madam Galbraith," he said. "They have signal rockets. Will you look at them? The effect is wonderfully fine in the mist."

She rose, followed by most of the guests. She was greedy of every token of homage to-night. "That was well done—well done," she said, smiling, as she swept through the darkened passage.

As she looked toward the window, the western sky burst into a horror of flame.

"Keep her back! For God's sake, keep her back!" cried Colonel Pervis.

There was a moment's silence; and then, in the distance, a low foreboding roar, as the winds from the defiles of the mountains rushed in to fill a sudden vacuum. Her husband drew her gently away.

"The oil-wells are on fire!" he said: "May God have mercy on the women and children to-night!"

Fire! All through the long night the valley to the river gaped open in the darkness, a bed of seething, surging flames. Madam Galbraith alone, on the balcony of the house, set like a watch-tower far up the mountain, looked steadily down at the end of her work. Her friends had forgotten her in this hour of terror. She saw Honora hurry to her uncle's side as he headed the men and set off hastily through the night. Mrs. Duffield calmly bade farewell to the last guest, then changed her dress, and summoning Lizzy and the servants, quieted them with a look. "There will be lives lost yonder," she said, "and there is no place for those poor wretches but this house. It must be made fit to receive them." She worked quietly all night, and the first wounded man that was brought in was laid on her own bed.

Madam Galbraith heard through the night, from time to time, the slow tread of men carrying a body into the house, and the rush and whispers of the women as they received it: even the silly little bride was at work among them. But she had no help to give. She shut the door behind her. She must be alone to see the end of her work.

From its first centre the fire went creeping, creeping, in rills, in pools of bloody heat reflected bloodily from the sky. Pillars of flame of a ghastly greenish hue rose where solitary wells burned and threw a spectral light out to the very horizon, where the mountains circled in their awful shadow, silent and solemn spectators. She fancied they knew how poor and mean her work had been. For the light laid bare the little settlement like a mere fleck on the vast landscape: a paltry thing seen far off and in the glare of the devouring tide that had been sent to sweep it away: the great derricks and tanks stood for a moment bars of shadows like black straws before the flame and then vanished: the shed-roofs of the mills crisped and crackled, as though made of paper, in the first sweep of the terrible flood, disappearing in the shower of fiery seed that sowed destruction in far-off fields. For wherever they fell, the ground, saturated with oil, slowly smouldered and sent forth its tiny, creeping stream of fire. The very Dour land had turned against her to burn out her name, which she would have written upon it.

She was too far removed for even the roar of destruction to reach her, and the meaning of the scene stood out in fiercer characters against the intense silence. She thought that the Hand that traced upon the wall the fate of the idolatrous king wrote her ruin on her own land in these letters of fire.

If, in her old age, she had set aside the simple duties of home to make herself a name; if she had driven out the love of husband and friends from her heart, and given it up to a hard, inexorable power, which she called the love of humanity and of God, God himself brought her to-night to sudden and terrible reckoning.

As the night passed the fog deepened, but the horrible gulch of heat and light through its centre assumed new and fantastic forms in the slow, silent fury, opening vexed depth after depth, as though the fountains of the great deep of hell were to be bared at last. Her eyes were fixed on the dark mass where the town had stood, and about which the crowd swarmed, looking like black ants in the glare. Then they disappeared. The fire had touched the loaded rafts that lay along the shore, and in a moment the river, covered with oil, was a winding stream of flame, and cut its way through the darkness to the far horizon.

No trace of her work was left. It had all gone down into the night and silence. The very springs, which were to have been the life-blood of her schemes, were ebbing to feed the fire that had defeated her. Over all, the stench and soggy, sulphurous clouds drifted and settled slowly and heavily.

The damp north wind gave sign of morning; a sickly light struggled up the east; the flames paled before it, but did not lose in strength or volume.

Madam Galbraith went out into the hall. Lizzy met her and stopped, not saying a word, when she saw what one night had done: it was an old, broken, feeble woman who stood before her. Hardly knowing what she did, she put both her hands pityingly on the gray hair, wet with the night dews. Her sober eyes were full of tears. The old lady rested one heavy hand on her shoulder.

"Yes, child—yes. The men you

brought here last night—were they—were they—"

"No, not dead. There are no lives lost, but many wounded. But—all is gone, madam."

"He has not laid the charge of murder on my soul," she muttered.

"Take heart," said Lizzy, hotly. "You purposed a noble work. You shall not reproach yourself with an accident."

"You talk like a child. There's no such thing as accident," with a touch of her old asperity. But that momentary flash in the gray embers died down. She stood motionless, looking about her with dull, aimless eyes.

"I think I will go to my own room and sleep," she said, and sat down heavily as she spoke. The incertitude and uselessness of old age seemed to have fallen upon her. Honora came up the hall, and, running to her when she saw her, put her strong little arm about her. The girl's countenance was pinched, but strong, new meanings had come into it. She looked at Madam Galbraith, and then at Lizzy:

"I will take her among the people. That is best for her."

She led her passively down the great staircase and suddenly out into the court, crowded with outcasts—a mass of miserable, sooty, half-clothed men and women, who were thronging up the hall and into the barns and out-houses, carrying their children and the wretched, greasy beds, quilts, clothing—poor bits of débris—they had saved from the wreck. Overhead the pale dawn brightened slowly, hesitating before it unveiled the full desolation, the unclean ruin of that night.

Her husband, Mr. Rattlin and Dour, their clothes torn and blackened with the night's work, hurried toward her: she, standing on the dirty stones of the courtyard in her royal purple and rich lace, seemed to curiously belong to a different life from them all. She did not reply to them when they spoke to her again and again; but Honora saw that the vigor and incisive insight was coming back into her hawk-eye. Her jaws were stiffening into their accustomed stern set. She looked at the little preacher suddenly:

"Your house is gone, sir? Your occupation's gone? Just as life was beginning to clear for you?"

"Yes, the house is gone. But, thank God," rubbing his hands, "the children were here with their mother; and I saved Jenny, too; though I ought not to think of a beast in the face of such suffering as this."

"And this was your wedding night?" turning sharply on Dour. "Your chance of fortune is lost—"

The young man put his hand gently on her withered fingers. "Gerty and I are young. There's a long life before us."

"Yes—yes," slowly. "James, I have a word to say to these people. Call them." Mr. Galbraith beckoned, and in a moment the crowd had turned and began to gather into the court-yard. She went forward slowly, her full strength coming back to her, apparently, as she noted shrewdly every miserable, discontented face. A level ray of morning light fell full on the commanding figure and the silvery hair; but a subtle loss and defeat in her face rebelled against her old air of command, and gave it the lie.

"My friends—back, back; don't crowd on me: I have difficulty in finding breath—my friends, this has been a hard night for you. I know that all you had you put into my venture. You shall not lose it. I think there was a Jonah in the boat, or it would not have gone down. God knows the secret thoughts of us all. He knows who was false to his duty. It is right the punishment should fall where it is due. I wish to say to you that it is my intention to fulfill my promises to you, whether oral or written, to the last farthing. I gave my word that your capital should be forthcoming, whether the experiment succeeded or not. You were to lose nothing. I renew the promise now—"

"Madam Galbraith—"

"Stand back, Colonel Pervis! My friends—"

"This is sheer madness," laying his

hand on her arm. "These people have no legal claim upon you. Give them what you will out of your charity, but you shall not beggar yourself with any such Quixotic promise while I stand by. The law will not hold you bound by mere verbal engagements which you may have made."

"It is *my word* that you scoff at. I pledged it to these people. What is the law to me?" Her voice was unnaturally gentle, and her eyes fixed upon his were dangerous. Pervis drew back. "You forget yourself," she said, quietly. "My old friend," turning coolly to the people, "underrates, probably, my resources. You shall be fully repaid. You shall have what temporary shelter and aid we can give; and as your claims are made out, present them. They'll be verified to the last shilling, however," sharply; "I'll have no cheating. Remember that."

She waved her hand, dismissing them. Beck, who had stood closest and most eager, threw up his hat as she moved back, giving a hearty American cheer.

But the majority of her hearers, from lack of comprehension of the language or disheartened with the night's horror, scarcely understood her meaning, and began to gather up their loads again, apathetically.

Colonel Pervis, his bluff face red, stood in her way: "It is not yet too late. You must hear me. You do not know how far your estate is involved, Madam Galbraith. You cannot fulfill this engagement you have made. The sale of the homestead farm, even, and the house itself, will not suffice."

"Has it come to that? The sale of this farm? Do you mean that I must alienate the Dour land?"

"If you keep your promise, you leave yourself not six feet of ground in which to make your grave, and then it will not be enough."

"Alienate the Dour land? And for such a rabble as that?" She stood a moment while they waited about her: once or twice she looked into her husband's face, as if for counsel. But he gave none.

She looked up, slowly scanning the wide sweep of valley and mountain, over which the rising sun threw steady light and broad shadows. There was not a far-off peak, a misty water-course, a green pasture, which she did not note. Never, even to the alien eyes about her, had her heritage seemed so fair. Then, standing in the court-yard, she glanced up at the massive, mossy walls of the homestead.

"I will keep my promise. Let it go."

Honora broke into a low, exhausted weeping and crept away, but the old woman's wrinkled face, though bloodless, did not flinch. They all stood apart from her, until she turned and looked into her husband's face:

"James?"

"You did right, Hannah."

She put her hand on his arm, and leaning on him, he led her into the house. It was a sight which even their old friend Pervis had never seen before: they usually walked side by side, but apart.

"I am a beggar," she said, when they stood alone in the great doorway.

There was a new expression on his thin face. "Then, my wife, there is nothing between us now," he answered, looking down at her.

CHAPTER XXVI.

THE mountains threw their great melancholy evening shadows over the dreary landscape: here and there, where wells stood apart, the fires burned unappeased, continuous volumes of foul smoke drifting away east, west, north, south to bear tidings of disaster.

Mrs. Duffield, who had been looking gravely from the library window, closed the curtains and turned to meet Colonel Pervis. "The new expression of wretchedness on the grand face of this landscape is curiously out of keeping," she said. "Have you succeeded, Colonel Pervis?"

"Yes. I have found shelter for the

majority of the people on the other side of the river. I have made, also, a rapid résumé of Madam Galbraith's affairs."

"And they are in as hopeless a condition as you thought?" taking down a boxwood screen to shelter her face from the fire.

"Worse—worse! She brought all she had to this hobby and toppled it in. By the Lord Harry! When a woman goes into business—I beg your pardon—but, now, you must have seen, Mrs. Duffield, what women in business are. Screws or spendthrifts."

"Pray, sit down, Colonel. It tires me to see you tramping up and down in that manner."

"I'll take a glass of wine," going to the sideboard. "I'm fagged out. Try a little of this hock, Mrs. Duffield. It's very delicate."

"I have had my tea. I never omit taking my tea at the regular hour, happen what may." She waited tranquilly until he came back and drew himself up on the hearth-rug fussily, his back to the fire, tucking his coat-tails under each arm.

"Well, there is no chance of escape. If the estate was brought to the hammer to-morrow, it would not cover her liabilities and relieve half of the absolute suffering of these people. There is a young fellow down at the fire who gave me some practical hints to-day. He advises buying land for them out West. Shipping off all but those who are not able to make their way in a new country."

Mrs. Duffield nodded approvingly.

"He remarked that there seemed to be no capital to run the mills again, and the land is too poor to support so large a number as small farmers; and as for the infernal wells—why, even if they don't burn themselves out, their yield, it appears, has been but half that which Finn stated. This young fellow got the truth from him to-day. He's a cool hand! And he's posted: he only needs to look at the soil or oil to know all about it. He's at work down there all night and to-day. Those poor people have quite made a leader of him."

"To the West?" thoughtfully. "Does Madam Galbraith consent to that?"

"Why should I speak of it to her? How can we send them to the West? When her liabilities are paid, after the estate is brought to the hammer—" stopping to cough.

"Yes. I understand," hastily.

"But you do not understand the extent of that absurd engagement. These people were, in general, respectable mechanics, with more or less means. They are left without a stick to shelter them. She has engaged to restore them the full amount that they lost—the full amount."

Mrs. Duffield changed her position and lifted the hand-screen again before she spoke. Her cheeks were flushed a little, even with its use. "There is a small sum of money," she said, "which I would be glad to appropriate to carrying out Madam Galbraith's wish, Colonel Pervis; provided that you will not mention to her, or to any one, indeed, that you received it."

"Certainly not—assuredly not—if you desire it. I am sure you would give to the extent of your power to these poor creatures, Mrs. Duffield."

"I want to help them—well, yes. And I wish Madam Galbraith to be gratified in fulfilling her promise. You will have no difficulty in converting these into money," handing him a sealed envelope.

Colonel Pervis withdrew with the package to the lamp: then hurried back, stammering, with excitement, "Why, madam! these are bonds. This is the bulk of your property!"

She made no answer, other than an annoyed frown, which knit her placid brows for a moment. He stood staring curiously at her:

"It is incredible. I never was so astonished in my life! Why, positively, do you know, I have fancied that you were even a little hard on the poor sometimes? And as for Madam Galbraith— I did not know that two women ever had so deep a feeling for each other. You must pardon me, but this is so extraordinary a—"

She hesitated, and then said, calmly:

"You forget that I am Tom Galbraith's wife. It was for me that he left his mother; it was for my sake that he did not return to her to die. I know now what the loss was to her. I think if I can make her old age happier and more honorable by this sacrifice, it is but a small atonement. Besides, I know a dozen ways of earning my own living. I've been used to doing it," with an indolent smile; "and, after all, one needs but a trifle. Tea and toast and fruit—I eat very little more than that; and one can dress in muslin quite as becomingly as in silk."

But the Colonel tapped the envelope stupidly with his thumb, as if he had been deaf to her explanation. "But it is all you have—all," looking down at the fair, perfectly well-dressed little woman. "And this will not be enough. A mere drop in the ocean—"

"Let it go as far as it will, then," rising and laying down the screen. "I think my husband—" she stopped, and was silent so long that he looked wonderingly at her. She went on, with an effort: "Tom would wish me to do it for his mother. I thought last night that he—No matter! We women have our fancies, you know, Colonel." He thought a nervous quiver passed over her face; but so used was he to its constant, careless calm, he concluded it must have been but the flicker of the firelight. She took up her book, and bidding him goodnight, moved to the door. But he stood before her:

"But you don't consider, madam! Don't put this responsibility on me. You'll be sorry for it to-morrow, and then you'll think I've robbed you. Why, you haven't even got a receipt! 'Pon my soul, I never was in such a strait in my life. Take back the cursed thing, there's a good soul! You'll be sorry for it to-morrow. You haven't considered."

"I will not be sorry," looking him full in the eyes. "I never did anything without considering it. Tom would wish me to help his mother. And—I loved my husband, Colonel Pervis," in a low tone.

The bluff old fellow was silent. He bowed low to her as he opened the door, the hot, generous blood dyeing his face as if it had been the secret of his own heart which had been dragged out. He buttoned up the package in his breast-pocket, and then absently walked to the sideboard as Dour came in:

"Take a jorum of brandy, Dour. No? Here's a mess of sweets and cake—women's stuff. Have nothing—'m? Well, here's luck! I'll be hanged," he broke out, "if women aren't the infernalest contradictions! Cake and tea and muslin—there's the objects of importance to them. And they'll fling around fortunes like half-pence."

Dour assented, sitting with his legs stretched out, looking sourly in the fire. He could not but be gentle with the worsted old woman up stairs, who had been his ruin; but he could not forget that he was here with a penniless wife on his hands and his chances gone.

The Colonel took up his hat and looked out through the darkened hall, which was as silent as the grave. A gloom, heavier than death, had fallen on the house. "Lord! Lord!" he said, with a miserable yawn; "the good old times are gone for ever here, I reckon. I must go home and put something in the safe, and I'll ride down to the wells and hunt up that young fellow. I've taken a monstrous liking to him, Dour. Queer where I've seen him before. I can't remember. I didn't like to ask his name." He went out, taking the shortest way to the stables.

As he opened the hall-door, a man came up to him in the darkness. A horse stood a few paces off, from which he had apparently just dismounted. Something in his manner roused the colonel's quick suspicion: he held his military cloak closely about the lower part of his face, concealing it, and stopped a few paces back in the shadow. The voice, too, was strained and unnatural.

He bowed with a sort of flourish: "You are one of the family, sir?"

"Well, no; not exactly. But I can take that place, I suppose."

"There was a wedding here last night?"

"Yes, there was a wedding."

"It was that of young Galbraith, I presume?"

The Colonel hesitated, perplexed: "There is but one Galbraith—the old man. Any one belonging to this neighborhood should know that," with a keener look of suspicion.

"But the heir? James Galbraith's son—grandson?"

"Tom Galbraith is dead years ago, and his son died when he was a boy."

The man had pressed closer in his breathless eagerness, leaning forward, where a stream of light fell from a side window, unconscious that the cloak had slipped down on his shoulders. It was a gaunt, hollow-jawed face that was exposed, marked with purple blotches, the flat, dead black eyes unnaturally bright. "That fellow's been a hard drinker and had his day," the Colonel had time to think in the pause that followed; "but Death's got a hold on him now." So slight and unwholesome, in fact, was the tenure by which the man seemed to hold upon the world that the Colonel drew back with a vague, uncomfortable dread. The dark, wretched night without seemed to have taken shape in this darker, more wretched shadow.

"Do you mean to say that Dallas Galbraith is not here?"

"I do mean to say it. I know no such person."

"Then I am too late." He stood erect, fumbling, a moment after, uncertainly at his breast, as though in pain, and was turning away, when a thought seemed to strike him. He caught Pervis by the arm. "For God's sake, don't deceive me," he cried. "Dall may be hiding from me. I've dragged myself back from California to see him. Look at me!" thrusting out his bony, emaciated hands: "they are like birds' claws. That fever did for me, they say. Bah! I've got the strength of a dozen men yet, and, living or dead, I must see Galbraith. Don't deceive me."

"I've no wish to deceive you, my friend," gently. "The man you want is not here."

He drew back incredulously: "I'll soon verify that. If he's not here, I'll find where he is. I've laid my plans, and I'll end them in my own way. A man who fights with Death, as I've done, and gets the upper hand, is not to be balked like a boy."

There was something in the melodramatic tone and stride of the man, as he went back to the horse, that struck Colonel Pervis as not unfamiliar. "If that braggart, Laddoun, were dead, his ghost would come bullying back in that fashion," he thought. "But no living man could so alter. This fellow looks as if he had been down through hell."

Going for his horse, after the man had disappeared, he stopped suddenly. "Why, Dallas Galbraith is the boy who is dead!" he said, aloud. The Colonel was a brave man, but he quickened his walk to the stables. The events of the previous night and the jorums of brandy had no effect upon him, he told himself; nor was he superstitious. But when men, with the mark of death on them, came at night searching for dead men in a house as cursed with calamity as this, evil must follow. There were signs which no wise man would slight.

PART VIII.

CHAPTER XXVII.

"WHY did you not bring the young man here, Colonel Pervis?"

"Well, really, Madam Galbraith! I—I wouldn't risk presenting him to ladies without permission. He has not that —that certain gentlemanly ease—that *je ne sais quoi*—you understand?"

"Bah! Gentlemanly ease! I understand that the fellow has common sense and information, which I need. What is his ease to me? The wisest practical advice we have received in this matter are these hints which you have brought us from him. I desire that you will bring him here immediately, Colonel Pervis."

The Colonel took his slippered feet from the fire, glancing out at the driving storm of sleet and hail that hid even the near mountains from sight. "Well, to tell you the truth, madam, there's no use in going, for the man won't come. I saw him last night (after I had that talk with you, Mrs. Duffield, you know), and I asked him to come up and explain to Mr. Galbraith about that Western land. But he was too busy among the people. 'I intend to go up,' he said; 'but my first duty is here.' And really he had a quiet, cool, hearty way with him which brought order out of the confusion in a miraculous manner."

"He had no business to meddle with the people without direction and approval from me," said Madam Galbraith. She sat before a table heaped with maps and account-books, which she had been turning over all morning with a secret feeble bewilderment.

Colonel Pervis laughed: "I fancy this young fellow puts his shoulder to any cart that is in the mire, without caring whether Hercules approves or not."

"What is his name, did you say?"

"He did not mention it, and I didn't ask him. He is not a person whom one would annoy with curiosity. I've an indistinct impression that I saw him before somewhere. By George! Mrs. Duffield, I know where I saw him before! The young man who went with Pritchard! We met them on the road. You remember?"

"Yes, I remember." With the remembrance an uneasy shadow seemed to fall on her. She never had forgotten the chance encounter: the thought of it chafed angrily an old sore wound carefully covered from sight for these many years. She could not endure that any living man should bear a likeness to her dead boy. It violated and made common that which was beyond all else sacred to her.

She rose and went to her own room presently, fearing that the man would appear unexpectedly, and wishing as usual to spare herself unnecessary pain.

But the Colonel was excited about his discovery. He waited impatiently, hearing Mr. Galbraith's light, measured step in the hall. The two men had been at work all night, estimating the losses and drawing up schedules of the property for sale. Land, houses, stock to the last implement, were inexorably noted down, and the lists quietly despatched to the printer's. In the morning, at Mrs. Duffield's suggestion, they gave the books to Madam Galbraith, hoping to employ her with fancied usefulness.

Colonel Pervis hardly waited until Mr. Galbraith entered the room: "The young man whom I mentioned to you so favorably last night—I have discovered who he is, Mr. Galbraith!"

"Ah? Who, Pervis?" indifferently, for the colonel's heats and enthusiasms were of daily recurrence.

"A young fellow who went with Pritchard to New Mexico. I remember his face perfectly."

Mr. Galbraith, who had advanced half-way across the room, stopped, as though the words had been a blow, looking fixedly at Pervis a moment: then turning suddenly he went to a bookcase, and stood with his back to them while he took down and replaced uncertainly volume after volume. A few moments after, Madam Galbraith closed her great folio decisively:

"What is the use of it? It is like reading the log-book of a ship after the vessel has gone to pieces on the rocks. When this storm abates, Colonel Pervis, I desire that you will bring that young man up. I will consult him about the soil out yonder and the direct routes, should we decide to purchase."

"Hannah!" She looked up, rising quickly, when she saw her husband's changed face.

"What is it, James?" hurriedly. "Have you heard of any good news? Is there any chance for us to save the land?" adding, with a feeble apologetic smile when he did not reply immediately, "I'd be glad to think the old ship was not a wreck after all."

"I was not thinking of the land. I only had a word to say to Pervis in reference to this young man."

"Oh!" She walked to the window, looking out at the storm with gloomy indifference.

"I wish, Colonel—if my wife consent," glancing nervously at her—"that you would not convey to him any desire of ours that he should come here. We did not accept him in the days when we had position and wealth to give, and now that we are destitute and apt to be a burden in our old age, we will force no man into our—our misfortune. But I think he will come of his own will," he said, looking out into the plains and high drifts of unlightened snow.

Both his wife and Colonel Pervis turned and looked at him silently, so great was the unwonted agitation in his voice and the causeless brightening of his thin face. The same thought suggested itself to both: the quiet scholar had grown morbid and jealous, dragged, as he had been, from his long retirement and forced to face the coarse realities of the past few days.

The Colonel rose. "Of course, my dear sir, I will do as you wish," soothingly. "But the lad is a very simple, genuine fellow—the last sort of person with whom one would observe ceremony. No polish—you comprehend: none at all."

Madam Galbraith came back to the table and drew her books hastily up again: "It surely matters little whether the young man comes or not," her irascible, black-browed face lowering. "Loss of property can hardly sink us so low, James, that the opinion of any man can affect or touch us." Mr. Galbraith said nothing, but paced up and down the long apartment in his old manner; but his step was nervous and quick, and there was a health and light-heartedness in his frosty face and blue eye new to them.

Colonel Pervis uneasily went to the

door: "I'll go to the stables. Those fellows have come to appraise the horses. You wish them all sold, madam? There is no exception?"

She raised her hand impatiently and shook her gray head. When he had gone, she growled: "They ought to be told that the breed is a famous one to draw the horse-jockeys," with savage bitterness. "They have been in the Dour stables for generations. My father would have sold his child as soon as one of them. *I* have swept them all off—for that drove of paupers yonder!"

Defeat had not metamorphosed Hannah Dour into a weaker or sweeter-natured woman. The vase was broken, never to be the same again; but the fragments yet lay useless, rough and unsightly. Some kindlier element than her life yet knew was needed to bring them into harmony again. Her husband came up abruptly to her side and pushed the books away from her.

"No, James. It is better for me to study my loss," looking up irritably at him. But he had turned from her already, and his eyes again wandered over the gray wastes outside.

"Your power and your loss are both dead and gone. That story's told. But there may be another chance, Hannah—" She did not answer, watching his abstracted face with a startled wonder. There was something in it which she had not seen there for many years; the look that belonged to Tom, and Tom alone. Before she had taken the boy into her own charge as the heir of the Dours, and thrust his father back from him. Many a time she had seen that same forbearing, amused, tender smile lighten through the reserved face and betray the boy's heart underneath, when he and Tom romped on the hay together, or walked hand in hand over the stubble.

Tom was dead—in a profligate's grave.

"There is no chance in the future for either you or me, James," she said, in a low, forced tone. "You might as well hope for that decayed old trunk yonder to break into fresh leaves again and to bear fruit." She walked rapidly away from him as she spoke, and stopped as suddenly, her great, gaunt body cowering over the fire.

Mr. Galbraith did not speak: he waited patiently by the window till the driving wind lulled, and the noonday sun glinted feebly upon the white wastes, over which came no sign of moving figure. The sun was lost in an impenetrable distance of gray and cold as the short winter afternoon wore slowly on into evening; and yet no shadow had crossed the fields; but still the wistful, thin, white-moustachioed face which old age had touched only on the surface waited patient behind the dim pane. Before nightfall, he thought the shadow would be seen upon the snow, and then— Why, that lad's simple, grave face, alive with unsuspicious strength and kindliness, over which there was no polish—that was his own face when he was a boy; and the clear, genial voice—that was Tom's: when it would ring out again in this dreary house to-night, all that had been lost out of his life would come back to him. Tom's son, coming over that vast waste of snow, seemed to come up from out of his long-ago youth, to bring from that old enchanted land the days of hard work, sound rest, silly, happy jokes and laughter. The days before the shadow of a great fortune tamed and cowed him, and faded all the zest and pleasure out of life. The fortune was gone, thank God! At last, in his old age, a man's portion of wife and child was coming to him.

As the sun went down into inexplorable regions in the west of gray and cold, toward the close of the winter afternoon, a little skiff put across the river, from the point where the houses were in which the people had found refuge, to the flat where the town had stood. When it grounded on the beach the two men who were in it sprang ashore, and after making it fast walked slowly over the burnt district, halting by the black gaps in the snow where the fires still raged with horrible fumes and stench.

"This was the best of the wells," said Mr. Rattlin by one of them, smelling some of the soot, with a funereal shake of the head. "Dear, dear! You are going up to the Galbraith homestead this evening, I think you said?"

"Yes; I am going there." He had been looking earnestly at the distant heavy pile of building ridged blackly against the white mountain-side; but when Mr. Rattlin spoke averted his eyes from it quickly.

"They must be kinsfolk of yours: there are innumerable Galbraiths hereabouts."

"They are kinsfolk," quietly. They left the wells and turned into what had been the town, as the masses of charred, black rafters told them, and here and there the unsightly ruin of what had been a cozy little dwelling not yet decently buried beneath the screening snow. Mr. Rattlin grew more and more silent.

"This cottage was built for my daughter Gertrude," he said, touching with his foot a sooty heap of boards and plaster, on which could yet be seen a bright, pretty paper. "She was married that night. It was not a happy beginning of life."

It was the first time he had spoken of his own loss to any one; but his heart had warmed strangely to this quiet young fellow, who had thrown himself into this pit of suffering as if it were the simplest, naturalest thing to do, and had helped so many out with his cool head and strong hands. Perhaps his boyish credulity had made him too pitiful—an easy dupe to imposture. But Mr. Rattlin was not the man to see that, or to blame it if he saw. There had been something in the boy's manner also for which no pity could account, as though he felt himself in some way guilty of their misfortune and bound to atone for it.

Mr. Rattlin stopped a few paces farther on, glancing up hesitatingly at his tall, grave companion: "This was our own house, Mr. Galbraith. We are not young people—my wife and I—yet this was really our first true start in life. We had a great many plans laid. We have had to abandon them."

Dallas watched the little man steadily, measuring him apparently by some mental scale, while he stood looking down at the ruin as though he had walked over a grave.

"You have no church now, then?" said Galbraith.

"No; my old place is filled. It was but a small country parish. But it is filled. I have work enough ready to my hand among those people yonder, as you see."

"Yet I am disposed," Dallas said, with hesitation, "to ask you to undertake more. There are some children—three or four: I took them a year ago to try to make decent men and women of them. Baptist, Methodist or Catholic—they can settle that matter for themselves when they're older, but my plan was to give them a home: to let them see a mother in her home and hear of Christ. They're out of the New York slums—you understand; they were going very straight down into hell. But they're fine, brave boys at bottom." He stopped, breathless.

Mr. Rattlin did not smile at his ignorance or contradictions. "I understand!" catching the breast of Dallas' coat and looking eagerly up into the homely, flushed face. "You want to save them. I'll do what I can to help you—I'll do what I can."

"There are only three or four, and there are thousands left. But my salary was not large. Out of it I gave a certain sum to pay for their boarding. I can be sure of the same amount next year. Now, will you take it and them? I paid for them last year—" naming a certain sum.

"Why, that would be enough for me to rent one of those little farms back on the McDowell hill!" and Mr. Rattlin's eyes sparkled in spite of himself. "It is productive land and cheap. We could live comfortably on it. I'll do what I can for the boys, with God's help."

"There's good stuff in them, or I wouldn't ask you to try," said Dallas earnestly, as they walked on together

"I've had the plan at heart a long while: ever since—a time when I was thrown in contact with them." He gave another quick, doubtful glance at the towering house apart among the mountains and became suddenly silent.

Mr. Rattlin spoke at last with embarrassment: "I think I'll go and tell my little woman the good news. You don't know how good this news is to us, Mr. Galbraith. I had plenty of work in view, but really there was no good prospect of food or clothes. And there are eleven of us. Very hearty eaters, too, thank God! I can work among these emigrants all the same now."

"Look out for your farm to-morrow, then, and let me know when you have secured it," said Dallas, heartily. "I'll send for my boys when you are ready. We'll make good farmers and mechanics of them some day." But when he had done speaking, he fell, as before, into thoughtful silence, as though some darker shadow than this old helpful fancy rose before him and darkened his thoughts. They passed out of the town.

"There lies your road." Mr. Rattlin pointed to the line marked by the fences through the snow. "You can reach the homestead before dark." But Dallas, after a slight hesitation, walked on slowly by his side. "It is like going into the house of the dead to me," pursued the little man. "There has no such utter ruin fallen on any family in my knowledge. Though they could have saved a comfortable fortune if it had not been for this last sacrifice to fulfill a shadowy sort of engagement. But that washed away every stain on their honor. It was worth the money."

"They are a family who cling closely to their honor?"

"With reason. It is a matter, indeed, in which we all take pride for them. They were the first white settlers among these hills, and since old John Dour there has never been one of the name who would cheat an enemy or betray a friend. Hard drinkers and fighters sometimes, but clean-blooded—clean-blooded."

The prolonged silence of the young man caused Mr. Rattlin to look at him curiously. "You came here from New Mexico on this pilgrimage to the Galbraith homestead, I think you said?"

"Yes."

"It is not often we find a young man so persistent in purpose," smiling.

"It is an old purpose with me." He stopped, with one hand on the fallen bars leading into the road. "I think I will leave you now. It is time I was on my way," in the same slow tone, which gave to his hearer the constant impression that, for some reason, he held his natural, boyish impulses, his tastes and fancies in a hard, inflexible leash until the time should come to loose them.

"Good-bye, Mr. Galbraith," cheerily. "You've given me good news to carry home. God bless you."

"I am glad you said that," quickly. "Good-bye." He stepped over the bars and struck into the road. Another man, irresolute as Dallas as to whether, after his long journey from New Mexico, he would after all finish his pilgrimage, would have stopped to deliberate, left alone in the untrodden road while the little black figure of the preacher disappeared over the snow. But he, deliberating, went steadily on with his swinging, unhesitating gait. How old was the purpose which he came now to fulfill no man but himself could ever know.

To come to his mother when he should have made himself fit to say—I am your son.

The record of his daily, hourly struggles to that end, in the mines, in prison, out in the free, healthy life of the last year, she would never read. It belonged to that inner chamber in the breast of this man, where, as in that of every other, the soul, whose face no friend has ever seen or shall see, sits alone inside of tears and laughter, and keeps silence. The day had come when he could speak the word so long held back. He was a man among men. He was the last of the Dour race; he could throw his young, healthy strength into their sunken fortunes and bring them to firm ground again. Out on the Plains at night, when all in the corral were asleep, how often he had planned this final home-coming of his life—to Honora, to the old people, to his mother. It seemed easy to him then, when they would all be together, to tell them of that first mischance of his life, caused by Laddoun's villainy. It would be as simple and indifferent a matter to them as it had become to himself.

But here—with the prestige of the old house before him and the awe of the clean-blooded, untainted race—he hesitated, with the long-ago sick loathing of that fall of his wakening from its sleep. He had gone through his long journey only to find the same foul slough waiting for him at the end: the clean name he had won for himself must be dragged through it before he could reach his mother and Honora, who stood waiting at the other side.

Mr. Galbraith from his window had seen Dallas, a mere black speck in the distance, growing distincter as he came across the snow: a tall, broad-shouldered figure now—the boy at last. But at this point he stopped irresolute, his hand on the gate; the breath of the poor old watcher in the window came heavy and thick. Why, thought Galbraith, should he drag back the old infamy on himself? A good part of his solitary life was gone: why not let the rest be solitary? That free life in the woods had suited keenly to his taste, and was shameless. Why not go back to it?

As he looked up, an odd procession met his eye: the horses, carefully blanketed, were being led down the hill, and outside of the stables stood the wagons, carriages, the cumbrous old family coach, ready to be taken away for sale. Carts were heaped with tools and farming implements and the trunks and rubbish belonging to the servants: the cattle were gone, the doors of the empty outhouses swung to and fro in the wind. Mere hints of the ruin that lay beneath, of how utterly dead that affluent, beautiful life was which had awed him a year ago. But one object touched Dallas with real pity: a small, tan-colored pony chaise, swathed in sooty cloth and being dragged away by a stolid Dutchman. It was Honora's own especial possession, from which she used to look down like a princess: now the poor little girl was dethroned, beggared. And within there was the old man and woman who had come to want in their days of feebleness and gray hairs; and he, Dallas, was about to skulk off like a coward and leave them to their fate! His own flesh and blood.

"Hillo! I knew you'd come!" shouted Colonel Pervis' breezy voice, as he clambered heavily down a ladder from a toolloft, wrapped in a shaggy coat. "Here's a wreck for you! Here's desolation! I've put in the day taking stock of this infernal iron-ware. Where are you for now? Going in to see the family?"

"Yes, I'm going in."

"I'll follow you directly. There's a lot to be done here, and having no son, you see, they depend on their friends." He stopped, with one hand on the ladder, looking after Dallas and pointing him out to old Henkel, the coachman. "Do you see that young fellow in the gray overcoat going up the steps, Joe? He's been out among the Indians— farther in a year than you and I in our lives. His very walk and talk has a whiff of the prairie in it to me. I relish it. It's quite outside of this regular life of ours."

"He kerries hisself like Mr. Tom, sir," leaning round the fence to catch the last glimpse of Dallas.

"Tom! Stuff and nonsense! You're as blind as an owl, Henkel!" But afterward, as he went through the dusty granaries, paper and pencil in hand, he muttered occasionally to himself: "Tom Galbraith? What if the old woman takes that notion? Tom Galbraith, eh?"

Dallas went up the broad stone steps, and pushing open the weighty hall door, entered without touching the lion's head of a knocker which scowled at him. It seemed natural for him to go in and out there: it was his home. No more skulking through dark side-passages or green-house doors: he was done with concealment. He carried his story with him: it was not his fault if it was fouled and blotted: that was done by a Hand outside of himself: where he had written it, it might be weak and paltry, but it was well-intentioned and honest.

The light was dim in the broad, high-roofed hall, for the November afternoon was fast merging into dusk: there was no sound within the closed doors on either side; but from the barn-yard without he heard the rattle of the windlass and a man singing some old country ditty as he drew water from the well. The sound grated strangely on the melancholy silence and the choking weight which oppressed his breath. Moro, the old house-dog, got up from the wolf-skin on which he lay asleep, and came drowsily up to the stranger standing motionless by the door, sniffed about him critically, then rubbed his approval against his legs, looking up at him. The very dog, Dallas thought, had the anxious shadow of disaster upon him. "Poor fellow! Poor fellow!" stroking his shaggy head. But his voice was hoarse and unnatural, even to himself: he was suddenly silent.

He waited a while without moving, but no door opened: only the ticking of the great clock that stood on the dim, broad stairs yonder told off the minutes. Moro crept back to his wolf-skin and lay down again to sleep. Dallas, after another moment's pause, chose the farthest door at random, and going toward it with his slow, steady step, put his hand upon the lock. But he did not open it.

What was it that waited for him at the other side of that thin oaken plank? The mother he had lost so long—a home—the only woman he had ever loved? Or the old solitary life, with the damning disgrace on his head, heavier to bear than before?

It was his mother who sat inside by the clear, red fire. She came often to this quiet little room: not for the books on the hanging shelves, as she asserted, but because of a picture which hung over the mantel-shelf. It was little Tom Galbraith in his boyish finery of velvet trowsers and blouse, his arm over his pony's neck. "It is very like my son Dallas," she had told Madam Galbraith the first time she saw it, looking at it with steady eyes. "Only I was glad to dress him in corduroy. And Dallas had no pony: many a mile he trudged barefoot to carry home the clothes I had washed." It was the only bitter reproach the old lady had ever heard from her lips, and she made no retort to it. After that she never saw Mrs. Duffield glance toward the picture. Yet there was not a day when she did not come and sit alone, looking at it with her calm, unfathomable eyes, as she was doing now. Her trunks were packed, her arrangements all made to go to-morrow quietly, and, far out of the knowledge of Madam Galbraith, begin the world over again.

"I have no regret for what I have done," she told Colonel Pervis an hour before. "I beg that you will consider the matter as settled," and going into this room, closed the door behind her. Yet Colonel Pervis—none of them—could know, as she did, what this life was to which she had chosen to go back.

Dallas knew. Her boy, who was dead.

She, too, heard the clock ticking through the dreary November afternoon as she sat, her hands folded, her eyes on the child's eyes, a different meaning upon her face from those which even her nearest friends had ever found there. She stood up at last at the sound of a step outside, and with her hand on the back of her chair, gave it a quick, parting glance, as if she asked for pity. She was but a weak little woman after all, and in heart, perhaps, was miserably solitary.

"I shall be quite alone out there, now," she said, putting her fingers up to her pale lips. "I will not have you, my little boy, now."

She turned as the door opened on its noiseless hinges, and a tall man, in a gray coat and planter's hat, who stood without, after a quick glance through the room, came in and paused in the shadow, looking at her. It required a moment's breath to bring Mrs. Duffield to her ordinary calm composure. The room was not light enough for her to detect the likeness which had troubled her, but her quick glance recognized at once the finely-shaped head, the homely, noble features, which had first pleased her artistic eye.

"You are Doctor Pritchard's friend? You wish to see Madam Galbraith?" recovering her ordinary shallow, pleasant voice.

The man closed the door behind him and came toward her, removing his hat.

"No," he said, slowly, "I did not come to see Madam Galbraith."

She began to speak again, hesitated and stopped. Her nerves were unstrung, and some old echo in the hoarse, choked tones sent the blood with a frightful throb to her heart. Dallas stood silent, his hat in his hands, looking down at her. He would not frighten her. She was so weak and frail! He could see the gray hair and sunken temples. How long they had been apart!

O God! Mother—mother!

But he did not speak a word, holding his hat tight clenched, the burning tears welling up slowly into his eyes. He came out, now, trembling, into the clear firelight, where she could see him plainly.

"I am one of the Galbraiths," he said; "and I have been told that I was like your husband."

She leaned with one hand lightly on the table. The dulled grating of the well-chain was heard without: the cold November daylight fell through the windows in a square patch beside him upon the worn carpet. He saw and heard even those trifles in that moment as he waited.

"Like my husband?" as one in a dream. But her keen eyes read his face. There was a sudden, strange change in her look, as though some vital chord within had been roughly jarred. "No; you do not resemble my husband," she said, with a strong effort to regain her usual calm courtesy. "But—I will go out, if you will pardon me. There is a likeness to some one whom I have lost, and it—it pains me." Then she lost herself utterly.

"It was my little boy!" she cried, flinging her hands up toward the picture. "He is dead now—dead!"

He kneeled down at her feet in the blaze of the firelight: he pushed his hair with both hands from his face. "Mother!" he said, in a whisper. "He is not dead. It is I, mother."

She made no sign or cry: even in that moment her habit of self-control bound her strongly: she put her cold hands on his cheeks, drew his head closer, looking steadily into the long-ago familiar eyes, until her own grew slowly blind.

"Dallas?" the name was wrenched at last like a sob out of the heart where it had been so long hidden. "Dallas!"

Then she stooped and would have kissed him, but her head fell a dead weight on his shoulder. He took her in his arms and placed her on the chair rubbing her hands, her arms and forehead like a frantic man, but without saying a word. Neither mother nor son ever found the ordinary relief in words or outcry for the deeper passions in their hearts. When her eyes opened at last and the sense came slowly back to them, he brought her a goblet of water from a side table. "It's not as clear water as that from our famous well in Chester, mother," he said cheerfully, to reassure her.

Her face lighted at that remembrance of every-day life: she drew him down with one hand beside her as she lay back on the chair, but then did not speak to him for a long time, her eyes hungrily wandering over his face, her hand passing with a pathetic anxiety through his thick hair, down his close-shaven cheeks, examining his hard, muscular hands, while she shook her head with a sad smile. "Why, this is a man, and I don't know him. Dallas, I don't know him! And yet—it's the same old Dallas, after all."

"Yes, mother, the same old Dallas." If there were any way to make her feel and believe that before the story was told!

"And you remember the well?" with a laugh, the tears in her eyes. "Where you planted the gourd-vine? We were very happy in Chester. I think that was our happiest time, Dallas?" Again their eyes met with a meaning which no bystander could have understood. There was a history between them which neither of them had ever yet put into words. Nor would they ever do it.

"That is all over now, and I have come back to you, mother. To-morrow we will begin the world afresh." He stood up as he spoke: he thought he could tell the secret better standing: he was conscious of a heavy constraint upon him, paralyzing his thoughts, his tongue and very limbs.

"Sit down, dear, sit down," putting her soft hands on his sleeve. "Do not go to the others. Let me have you to myself for a little while."

"I am not going. There is something I must say to you—"

"Anything you will, Dallas. You've the same odd turn in your voice still, my son, though it's coarser. It makes me feel as if I were a young woman, with my boy helping me with the work again, to hear you talk. Oh dear! I thought that sort of feeling was dead and gone for ever for *me!*" with a nervous, almost girlish laugh.

Was this the time to open to her the disgrace which she would count as worse than death? "What were you going to tell me?" she asked, presently recollecting herself.

"Nothing, mother. It can wait." He brought a chair and sat facing her, while the clock ticked slowly through the hour. They talked very little. If she had been curious and anxious out of very excess of tenderness, as other women would have been, some chance word might have broken the spell. But the past or future always had but small place in Mrs. Duffield's life. Dallas was there. The power of laughter and tears in which the heart had some share, which used to belong to Mary Jennings, had come back with her boy, she thought, to her. That was all the reference she made to the past.

He had been out with Doctor Pritchard? She knew when he was a boy that he was born a naturalist: no wonder he had preferred his present profession to the law or medicine. He would go on with the same sort of work, she supposed? If she might advise, he would do so: a man should never slight a true vocation.

"And there's nothing here, Dallas, for your future—nothing at all. If you had come to us a year ago, with your strong sense and coolness, you might have put a check to your dear grandmother's pig-headedness. But as it is, it has run her into the mire," with an odd, downward gesture. "Me, too. All paupers alike!" with a merry little laugh. "Only that now," with sudden revulsion of feeling. "*I* have—I have—" putting his hand up to her eyes and holding it there quietly. The hot tears that wet it, she speaking not a word, gave to Galbraith the idea of unutterable depths in his mother's love. But when was a woman so wanting in curiosity? As though it were altogether the natural and proper thing for a boy in the coal-pits to be offered the choice of the professions! Poor little mother! What did she know of the world? and Dallas kissed her, a twinkle of amusement in his blue eyes, and, being a man, loved her a hundred times better for her innocent silliness.

But how could he tell the truth to such silliness and love? Besides, by some instinct, he felt that with all her tenderness she was the coolest, most impartial critic, as far as her knowledge went, that he had ever faced. Her son was here, a man and a gentleman: that she seemed to accept as a matter of course. But—what order of man and gentleman? He felt that she was testing the coin to know if it were genuine. She did not recognize him by intuition, as Honora had done. He grew painfully conscious of his hardly-learned accent, his long legs and arms, and blunt manner, as he used to be when he first left the prison. He knew the moment when her anxiety on this score gave way to satisfaction, even to triumph.

"You are not like your father except in mere outward feature," she said, when they stood together, surveying him from head to foot. "That is, not after I knew him. Poor Tom frequented places which you know nothing of, and low company and habits had left their mark on him. You are like your grandfather. Dallas, there are but few gentlemen of that class—but few!" touching his breast with her white hand, her eyes growing soft and brilliant with pride. "Why do you draw back from me, my son?"

"Did I? I was not conscious of it. I think I will go to my grandfather now. Perhaps he will recognize me for what I am. But you, mother—it is an ideal Dallas that you see in me."

He looked from side to side with a fierce impatience, like an untamed horse, that recognized eternal servitude in the light touch laid upon his neck. Why could he not be himself, tell his commonplace story in a few straightforward words to this soft, loving, well-bred little woman? Because she had a factitious theory about what constituted a gentleman, was he to make himself a sham and a lie? "You don't know me, mother. I'm afraid you never will," he repeated, with an attempt at playfulness. "I will go to my grandfather: men are keener-sighted than women."

"Do you think so, Dallas? But we have so few opportunities for studying human nature, you know," she said calmly, yet she held him by the lappel of his coat as she spoke, looking searchingly into the strong, sterling face before her, with eyes as earnest as his own. "You must not think I do not know you," she added meaningly, after a pause. "You are the same boy that left me. You never gave me an hour's pain or anxiety then, and you have not come back to do it now."

"There is nothing which ought to give you pain. But—"

"You can go to your grandfather now, my son," after waiting for him to finish his sentence, touching the bell as she spoke.

"You will come with me, mother?"

"No. I will follow you in a little while. Madam Galbraith—" with a slight arching of her brows. "Indeed, my dear boy, I always avoid witnessing any emotion on her part. She ploughs too deep for me—it tires me. And they will leave me but a little share in you. You are the last Dour, you see: you are Tom's son: you are the forlorn hope of a fallen house, as well as my little boy," buttoning his coat and smoothing it down with both hands. Then she drew back quietly, the color rising to her face. "It is a long time since I did that for you." Nothing could be more simple than the action and the words: why should they unman him as nothing had done before?

"I'll never give you pain, mother, as God sees me," he said, hastily adding within himself that to-morrow, when they had learned to know each other better, he would so set the matter before her that it should seem of no more importance than some childish disease of which he had long been cured.

"Ah, Henkel! how came you to answer the bell? Take this gentleman to the library: Mr. Galbraith is there, I believe."

"What name shall I give, sir?" said old Joe, edging curiously closer.

"I will announce myself," said Dallas. His mother went out of the door with him.

"I will follow you in a moment. Be kind to them, dear," pausing with her foot on the stair to watch him cross the hall and disappear in a side corridor. Then the expression of her whole face altered. "Why could he not have trusted me with his secret," she thought, going up the stairs. "Why could he not trust me? Whatever it be, he will find there is no one who knows him like his mother, after all."

Honora, coming in from a long tramp through the snow, caught a glimpse also of the retreating figure. Henkel, when he came back, found her standing just where she entered, Moro nuzzling at her hand without more notice than if she had been cut out of stone.

"Who was that man, Henkel, who went into the library with you?"

"I dunno, miss," solemnly. "He said he'd announce hisself to yer uncle. But if so be that Mr. Tom had a're a son, I'd say that's him."

She pushed the dog away, muttering to herself: "No. Dallas Galbraith would never come back in *that* way—not in that way."

"You're nigh onto froze, miss," said Joe, anxiously. "You're face 'pears as blue as if you were dead. I'll send one of the gals to you with somethin' warm."

But she passed him swiftly and steadily up the stairs. The poor little thing had been so faithful with her secret, and knew herself now to be slighted and neglected so cruelly. She rushed into her room and locked and double-locked the door. She could dully hear voices in the room below. Dallas was there.

It was she who was to have brought him home. He had forgotten her and her silly plans! And she had been wasting her prayers and her tears on him! She had thought of him as lying dead on the Plains. *He* dead on the Plains! She doubted if he had ever been there at all: in all probability he had been in business over in Ohio. He was as unfeeling, cold-blooded, as a frog —a stone! He was their heir—their son: now that he had come she was to be left out and forgotten. He was in his rightful place, beside the very hearth where his father had played when a boy; they were giving him all the sacred love they had kept for him, and she was a poor outcast, up here, freezing to death. She lay on the hearth-rug, sick with her disappointment and rejected love. She would not answer when Lizzy knocked at the door with her hot tea; nor would she get up to put any wood on the fire, until it went out. What did it matter? What did anything matter any more? Life was a great mistake, a misery. For the current of the little girl's wishes in life had been checked, and all of God's great world of order was but mocking, blind mischance in her eyes. And through all, the kiss he had left upon her lips was there, bitter as gall. Had he not forgotten her? Cast her off?

CHAPTER XXVIII.

IT was not into the library that Henkel brought Dallas, but, by orders, to Mr. Galbraith's especial room beyond. The first sight of it, as Joe threw open the door, gave him the idea that it was prepared to welcome some one. There was an indefinable air of expectation in the glowing fire, the early-lighted lamps, the bright-tinted geraniums and roses in the windows, making a frame for the winter landscape without, over which the gray, cold evening was closing. A tall, spare old gentleman, carefully dressed with gray hair and moustache trimmed in military fashion, shading his pale, aquiline features, turned to meet him as the door opened. "That is my grandfather—the man whom I resemble," thought Dallas, with an inward laugh at his mother's partial eye; yet he went toward him, with none of the embarrassment which, despite his love, separated him from her. The clothes, habits, education, out of which women make such impregnable barriers, are slight matters between men who choose to meet.

"A gentleman, sir," said Joe, lingering under pretence of stirring the fire.

"That will do, Henkel. I am glad to see you," motioning him forward with a courteous bow; but Dallas noticed that the attempted smile faded on his nervous jaws, and that the withered hands trembled as they rolled a chair nearer the fire. They both stood silent until the door shut behind the tardy servant. In the moment the remembrance came back to Dallas with a sudden force of the night when he, a convict, had stood in the library watching this old man, with Honora, and feeling a secret kinship and equality with them, deeper than blood and apart from all the others. He had come back to claim it now.

When they were alone he went up to the chair beside which Mr. Galbraith stood. He held out his hand to Dallas mechanically.

"No, not yet," putting it aside, smiling. "There should be something more than mere ceremony when we meet, I think. When I have told you my name—"

"Why should you?"

Dallas drew back startled. "You

knew me from Doctor Pritchard to be a Galbraith?" after a bewildered moment.

"No."

Their eyes met for the first time.

"There is but one of the Galbraiths whom you resemble," said his grandfather, with a strong effort at his ordinary composure. "But I perceived that resemblance when I met you—on the mountain."

Dallas was silent, listening. But his cheerful, candid eyes, the rugged simplicity of his face and manner, even in repose, seemed to be like a fresh well opened to the old man, so visibly did he gather strength and spirit with each moment's scrutiny of the boy. He came forward a step, looking at him in absolute silence.

"I have been waiting for you to come ever since that day," he resumed, controlling the agitation in his voice. "It is a long time. I knew if you were the man I thought you, you would come at last. Now that I see you, I know how much I have all my life wanted you—needed you—" He lost all command of himself here. "You're very like your father," he said, putting his hands on Dallas' broad shoulders for a moment, and then he turned away and walked hastily to the window, standing with his back to the room.

When he came back he took the boy's hand: "You are welcome home, Dallas. Not for your father's sake alone, understand. Blood is a bond that won't last if there's no other. But I've learned to know you since that day on the mountain, and I welcome you for your own sake, as well as—as his who is gone."

Dallas colored, like a boy, with gratification, having an old-fashioned fear and reverence for gray hair. But he did not reply directly, any kind of sentiment being a foreign language to him, which he spoke with difficulty. "I'm glad that you have felt the need of me," he said, heartily; "though I don't see how that could have been until now. Now, I think, I can be of use," glancing out at the miserable signs of ruin, from the disordered outbuildings to the yet smouldering fires.

Mr. Galbraith drew the great chair in front of the fire and seated the young fellow in it: "Before I take you to my wife, I wish to show you something," fumbling with one hand in his pocket. "I have never allowed even Honora to look at it. But you—I thought all summer that I would show it to you as soon as you came." His fingers shook as he placed a small morocco case before Dallas and opened it, disclosing an ivory miniature, the likeness of a handsome, ruddy-faced man. "You know who it is, dear boy?" lowering his voice.

Dallas bowed gravely. He had no very tender remembrance of his father: it was the old man's sorrow laid thus bare before him which made his eyes dim as he looked at the face. Mr. Galbraith took it from him gently, polishing it with his hand. "Whenever you wish to look at it, Dallas, come to me. I carry it with me. There is no other likeness of him after he was grown and —he was my only child." He glanced once or twice, before he put it away, from the face of the son he had lost to that of the one who had just come to him, with a quiet tenderness passing that of woman.

Dallas was not blind to it. He sat, with a hand on each knee, looking steadily into the fire. There had been but little sign of emotion in this meeting with his grandfather, but something in the few words and shake of the hand had stirred his honest soul to its depths. The strong domestic instincts of the man asserted themselves. All his life he had been a vagabond: to-day he had reached home. These people were his people: the blood in the veins of this old man was in his veins; but they were old, and poor, in need of him: he was strong, had the world freshly in his grasp. His niche was ready. As for that old, hard Luck of his, let it pass: surely it had had its day. When he thought fit to tell them of it, they would know his innocence—as he knew it. There was so much weight in the instinct of the same flesh and blood. But now, when disaster closed in on them on every side, should he bring this dis-

12

grace, unknown before, to level them with the dust?

Mr. Galbraith, turning, saw that the young man had risen, and was following him in his walk up and down the room with a pained, far-reaching look, that went, he saw, into something far beyond the present moment. He halted, then came up to the fire, resting his arm on the mantel-shelf, and his chin on his hand. "You have some trouble?" he said gently, though he was not able to conceal the latent anxiety in his voice. "You must remember that you are with your own people now, Dallas. Your troubles are theirs."

How could Dallas know the effort which the words cost the man who had held himself apart all his life, morbidly afraid of intrusion? "I have no secrets but those which would be the heavier for sharing," he said, turning away with a dogged shake and something of his grandmother's surliness. "It would be hard indeed if your boy's son brought trouble to your door now! Shall we go to find Madam Galbraith?" with a hasty change to an indifferent tone.

"Yes." But he did not move, though Dallas stood waiting; his powerful figure and grave, sincere face in relief against the gray window light. Perhaps because it was a picture that pleased him the old man watched it with such breathless intentness. As for Dallas, he hardly noticed the silence. The secret burned in his heart, where he tried to conceal it, like vile, extraneous matter in healthy, quick-growing flesh. If he could but utter and be free from it! He had almost forgotten it, it had so dwindled into insignificance in the free, hearty, natural life of the last year, but once back among these stifling houses into which men boxed themselves, it assumed its old, unwholesome, foul proportions. He knew his own strength better now: it could not make him less a man; but what would it be to his mother—to these old people, whose good name was the only tower of strength left them? Was it a gift for Tom's boy to bring them in their day of calamity? At least let him have a day to consider. To-morrow—

"You have nothing to tell me, my dear boy? Nothing?" The gentleman's great love for and hope in his son seemed with this eager question to come from his heart out into his face, and to animate his whole body, showing themselves in a strained, painful wistfulness very pathetic to see in any old man. But Dallas, still pondering over his miserable secret, did not see it.

"No; I have nothing to tell," he said, gravely.

There was a moment's silence. The clock without began to strike the hour slowly in a hard, metallic clang. Dallas raised his head, listening with an anxious, boyish fancy in his brain. "If I do not cast off my burden before that hour has struck, I will carry it for ever, and bear its weight alone to the grave," he thought. His grandfather watched him, as though he saw and understood the vague fancy from its birth.

If in that moment, when the eyes of the old scholar and gentleman, grown clear and sad as Truth in their long experience of life, were upon him, Dallas had dared to be true; if he had been brave enough to meet the earnest faith that silently summoned his own, the ghosts of all the dead years of his loneliness, of his prison, would have vanished with the striking of that hour, and returned to vex him no more.

But he was silent, and the chance slipped by him. "To-morrow"—he thought, with guilty haste, pushing by his fancy as childish—"to-morrow," and the last note rang with a reverberating, melancholy peal, and died away.

Mr. Galbraith took his arm down with a stifled sigh. "We will go now," he said. But the pathetic tenderness had gone from his face. They crossed the hall together. He paused, with his hand on the library door. "My wife is a strong and nervous woman," he said. "I do not wish to give her a sudden shock. It would be better that she should discover you herself—if you are willing?"

Dallas bowed, and they entered, the young fellow feeling the same half-pity, half-dread of the woman he was going to meet that he might for an old toothless lioness. She was walking slowly up and down the dim, long room, her hands clasped behind her, but halted for them to approach. Discerning, perhaps, some agitation in the stranger's movement or gesture, and fancying it proceeded from fear of herself, her old, hard-scored face softened and kindled into that rare look with which, differently from any other woman, she was wont to welcome strangers.

"You are the friend of Colonel Pervis, of whom he has told me?" without waiting for them to speak, and holding out her hand in the genial Virginian fashion. "I thank you for coming. You are very welcome." It was her whim to be gracious, and the cordial tone, the sensitive, fine smile on the grand old face, the indescribably winning manner, affected Dallas, long unused to educated women, like a strong, sudden note of music from an unknown instrument. Who had been so blind as to call this woman coarse? Mr. Galbraith fell beside his wife, passive as usual.

"Our friend belongs to our own family, Hannah," he said, quietly.

"The Dour? No, Galbraith. It is a large stock and a strong one," smiling, "But I am the last of the Dours. That fire has burned down to a single flame, which a puff of wind may extinguish forever."

"It is a fire which has burned clear to the end," rejoined her grandson, emphatically, feeling himself in every grain of his big body a Dour and an honest man. He met Mr. Galbraith's eyes bent steadily on him.

"I thank you, sir," she said, with a stately bow. "I perceive that you have heard the story of my family. It is well known in this neighborhood." They walked together up the room, Madam Galbraith, when they came within the glow of the firelight, inspecting the stranger with her usual keen scrutiny. She remained silent while they seated themselves, and Mr. Galbraith rang for lights —silent so long that he leaned forward and looked in her face anxiously. She drew herself up erect in her chair, with a long breath.

"It is nothing, James. There is a strange family resemblance among you Galbraiths, and—it is nothing." But she averted her eyes from Dallas and listened when he spoke, as though beneath the courtesy of her manner she concealed pain.

"You have taken much interest, Colonel Pervis tells me, in my poor colony?" she said, with an effort. "There was the ruin there of the most promising scheme ever developed in this country."

"I doubt that, madam," promptly. Dallas felt his own ground under his feet now, and was himself again. "From all that I can learn, the elements of failure were always there. The fire only hastened it."

"I do not understand you," coldly. "Pray explain yourself."

"That oil is of the poorest quality," blundered on Dallas. "The mills should have been supplied with fuel from the neighborhood to enable them to compete in low prices with those higher up the river, and your coal was suffered to be untouched in the hills."

"True. I did not think of that," she muttered. "But that is a small matter. I was in haste to gain the great end."

"There was the trouble," bluntly. "There was no one to direct the small matters which ensure success. No one. There were hands, capital, and, I suppose, a visionary enthusiasm. But any one can see there was no scientific or practical knowledge. It is a terrible calamity to have brought upon those people. There has been great suffering among them—great suffering!" speaking in a stern undertone and looking fixedly in the fire, his thoughts being with the people far more than with her.

The angry heat had been rising slowly in Madam Galbraith's face. "If I have unwillingly brought suffering upon them, I have atoned for it," she said. "You do not understand, probably, being a stranger in the place, what I have done to atone." She sat fiercely silent and motionless, the firelight shining on her pale face and gray hair: she was proudly conscious in every throb of her heart that she was a beggar, that she had sacrificed her all to keep her honor unspotted; but she was too proud to boast of it.

"I did not intend to reflect upon you personally, madam," said Dallas, gently. "I did not know even that you were the only originator of the scheme. I understood you had given up your property to liquidate your debts to these people. That was all proper and right, of course. But unfortunately real estate is not money, and does not supply their immediate need. Their distress has been extreme, as no doubt you know."

She rose impatiently and began again her restless walk up and down the room. Now she knew the fire had been sent expressly from God to humble her—Hannah Dour. Great had been her punishment, and her atonement not small. But this man set aside both as of the same import as the lack of clothes and food among those stolid Dutch boors. Any other young fellow she would have dismissed contemptuously; but a vague something in this man's voice and words touched her with a mysterious power, as though it was herself that met her in another form.

"My friends," she said, with ironical gentleness, "have not pressed home upon *me* the wants of these persons. They thought it better to convince me that the amount of sacrifice I made for them was Quixotic and unreasonable."

"It appeared to me only just," said Dallas, simply.

"Your ideas of honesty are singularly strict, young sir!" with a short laugh.

"Honesty!" Dallas rose to his feet, the blood rushing to his heart, leaving his face deadly pale; again he caught the sight of the wistful, mild eyes keeping their steady watch upon him. In a moment they restored him to himself. He answered them with a smile. "I never tested my honesty," he said, in the dry, humorous voice which had become lately habitual to him. "It never was strongly tempted. But I inherited it, and the quality should be good."

Madam Galbraith made another turn, and then beginning to fear that she had been inhospitable, she came back and resumed her seat as Mrs. Duffield entered the room. Dallas glanced hastily at the opening door, his color rising: it was not his mother whom he expected to see.

"Colonel Pervis mentioned some of your views as to the future establishment of these people to me," she resumed, with a distant gravity. "They showed excellent judgment for a person of your age—excellent. Have you considered the probable worth of the coal-beds? The Dour land is a mine of wealth."

"It is good arable land" said Dallas, thoughtfully: "very good. As to the coal—it hardly ranks so high as that a few miles farther up the river. I can bring you specimens of both, and explain the difference."

"You appear to have made the subject an especial study?" dryly.

He hesitated a moment. "Necessarily," with a half laugh: "I was a miner."

She was turning over one of her books of maps as he spoke, and continued to do so, but a secret significance in his answer seemed, in the silence which followed, to creep gradually into her mind: with her finger on the book she looked up slowly like one who hears a far-off call. Then she glanced at Dallas with a terrified, wild doubt, a wild denial in her face. The book fell from her trembling hand to the floor: her husband came quietly and stood behind her chair.

"Galbraith?" she muttered to herself, "Galbraith?" Then she raised herself slowly and leaned with both hands on the table. Dallas rose and came toward her where the light fell full upon his face. "You were a miner? Where?" she said.

"In the coal-pits. At Scranton."

"James!"

"I am here, Hannah."

"Who is this man?"

He looked at her as a physician might have done before he answered her. The hard contour of her face was harder than ever before, yet there was a certain terrible womanish pallor about the fierce eyes and stern, set mouth. It deepened as she looked at Dallas, and at his mother's fair, beaming face as she came to him and put her arm about his neck.

"Do you not know, Hannah? I told you there was a new life coming to us which would atone for all the past. I have brought you Tom's boy."

"Why, *I* told you he was not dead!" loudly, with a flash of triumph.

There was an embarrassed pause. "He is very like our son, I think, my dear. Before he—went from us," said her husband gently.

Madam Galbraith's dry lips moved, but she did not speak. She motioned Dallas closer: "You are sure there is no imposture in the young man, James? You have received a proper account of his life from him? He should have brought—brought credentials." Then, without waiting for a reply, she held out her hands to him: "My son!" she cried, feebly, "my son!"

When she touched Dallas and saw clearly her dead boy again in him, she pushed him away, trembling violently—"Go, go, I want to be alone."

At the door Dallas turned, looking back at the woman who, through all her life, had played a man's rough part, and he saw that she had fallen on her knees to the floor, but her face was covered with her hands and hidden from him by her gray hair.

CHAPTER XXIX.

COLONEL PERVIS walked up and down the brightly-lighted library late that evening, rubbing his hands. "Where is the boy? God bless him! Where is he? I little thought who I was bringing to you!" stopping beside Mr. Galbraith, his red face beaming down on him. "And you think he resembles his father, eh? Now—do you know?—he seems to me altogether different. Tom was a yielding fellow, yet not easily read; he had a light, playful way of slurring and glossing over his own opinions, so that you never could be sure of them. But this boy is like a bit of limestone rock. You know him all through when you see his face. That singular downrightness strikes you at once in him. He has it from Madam Galbraith, I think."

Mr. Galbraith listened eagerly, and with evident great pleasure: "You're right, Pervis, you're right: no man could doubt a face like that. Yes, he is like his grandmother," with an almost boyish laugh of keen amusement. "And there will be a little rubbing between the rocks, if I am not mistaken, before long."

"All the better! all the better!" beginning his walk up and down again. "She needs something to rouse her. She'll live her youth over again in this boy, and so will you. By George! It seems as if the old times had come back to this house, after all. The very servants are wild about it down below. The fire's forgotten. I ought to have been here at the discovery. But I was called down to the village suddenly, and when I got back it was Lizzy that told me. The murder was out. She has got up a supper fit for a prince, and when I stopped at the door, getting a sniff of the partridges, she came out, her face red and the tears in her eyes for joy: she said, 'It is the heir that has come back, Colonel Pervis. His name is Dallas. I haven't seen him yet, but they say he's different from any of the Galbraiths. Better than any of them, quite different. Like a king among them.' By George! you might have knocked me down with a breath!"

Mr. Galbraith listened to the story with a curiously grave attention, but made no answer. The Colonel's excited brain went off speedily on another track. "This boy has no money, eh? Oh, of course not, poor fellow! What a cursed beast that Duffield must have been! Only if he *had* happened to have a few odd thousands, they'd have come in luckily just now. Where is he, by the way?"

"In his own room. His grandmother

is with him. Pervis," he continued after a pause, with the embarrassed manner in which he always broached a subject, "there is a matter of business which I would like arranged before Dallas comes into the family councils. It will be his wish that Madam Galbraith's engagement shall be kept: the land must go. But the house in which my wife and son were born I cannot part with. You shall bid it in for me, with two or three acres immediately about it."

The Colonel's face brightened. "Can you do it? Your annuity—"

"It will take it all. But it will be our home now, to the end—*ours*," with an unconscious emphasis on the word. "And I'll go to work. I can make enough by my pen to support us. I never had a wife and boy to work for before."

Pervis listened attentively without the expected outburst. "Thank God!" he said, after a while, with a good deal of quiet feeling. "You don't know what it cost me, Galbraith, to see the old house taken from you, and to think I had been such a poor, thriftless devil I had no help to give. I'll attend to it. You want it kept quiet between us, I understand?"

"Yes: Madam Galbraith would doubtless object."

"Hush! she is here!" opening the door for the old lady, who came in with a stately step. One point in her dress caught the eyes of both men as soon as she entered. It was a shawl which Tom had given her—one of his few presents, for he was not thoughtful about such trifles. The day he left them to marry Mary Jennings she had folded it away, and it never had left its hiding-place until to-night.

"I thought you would be with us to-night, old friend!" she said, as the Colonel shook her hand, looking into her radiant face.

"Why, you are yourself again, Madam Galbraith! It reminds me of the days when Hannah Dour in her stiff brocade and I in knee-breeches led the dances in this very room; or the night when Master Tom was baptized. I think that was the crowning-point of your life. Lord! what a night that was! I never sat down to such a supper. What an inheritance that child was born to!"

"My son Dallas," with a proud lingering on the words, "has no inheritance but honor. And that he gives to us, as we to him. I have had a long talk with the lad," as she seated herself, with a certain majestic port not used of late. "He is not altogether a Dour. That is better," with a half sigh. "I was glad to find *you* in him, James," looking at her husband. "But he is headstrong—headstrong. He needs control. Well, well, the boy is young. He has been giving me the history of his life." Mr. Galbraith turned suddenly toward her, but did not speak.

"Poor fellow! He has had hard times, no doubt," said the Colonel. "And he gave you the history of his life?"

"Of course; I asked it from him. It's a sad story, though he makes the best of it. In the coal-pits, in Philadelphia, among medical students, down at a fishing village on the coast, and in the stone-quarry here. I imagine he offered a strange contrast to the poor people with whom he was thrown, everywhere—like a prince in disguise. There are some other particulars which, he said, he would give to us all to-morrow. The village, by the way, was Manasquan, and he knew Miss Byrne there. He asked to be shown to her room to see her. I liked that. The Dours were always noted for their gentle consideration for the poor. Where is Honora?" looking hastily around, as if she missed something.

"She is not well," her uncle replied. "She will come down later in the evening. Has any one remembered to order up wine? We will drink the lad's health in some of the old hock we put away when Tom was born, Hannah."

"I've been thinking of that," the Colonel broke out, eagerly. "I'll go myself. I know the very bottles."

It was Tom's room which they gave to his son. The largest and warmest chamber in the house, always kept in perfect order, as though its occupant might return to-morrow, but in which no one had slept since he left it. For days before Mr. Galbraith had been busy in it, adding to it such fanciful, dainty furnishing from his own store as he thought might please a young man's fancy.

Dallas, when Madam Galbraith left him alone, took quick, observant note of it all. His valise, which they had sent for, lay on the floor, and he proceeded gravely to dress in a fine suit of gray cloth, the shirt collar turned down from the shapely throat and knotted with black ribbon, remembering how some one, whom he did not name, had thought such a garb artistic.

The mellow light of the room, the soft carpet, the luxurious toilet appointments, had a strange effect upon Dallas. They were his, and they barred him inside of a new class. Out on the Plains he had been with gentlemen, and met them as their equal; but that was under the broad sky, where all God's creatures stand on one plane. But this was in civilization, where the invisible lines were strictly drawn. The long fight was over: he stood on a level with educated men and women: inside of their world at last, however little fitted for it. When he had dressed, he went out through the long halls to find Lizzy, one or two servants escorting him, others peeping at him through half-open doors—a welcome on every face. It was home—his home. Through the windows he passed he could catch glimpses of the wide moonlit sweep of valley and mountain. It was the Dour land. He meant some day to buy it back again—every acre. There was nothing which he was not strong and patient enough to do to-night.

Yet under all was the picture of a group of fishermen's cabins: in one of them a little homely chamber, opening out into pine woods, the sound of the sea far off—a chamber whose rude furnishing had been made for him by friendly hands. There was not one of these cabins whose threshold to-day he would be suffered to pass: not one of these men's hands which would not now point at him for a convict and a thief. No money, no strength nor patience, could buy back the power to enter that poor little room again as he had left it. Lizzy met him outside of the housekeeper's room and drew him hastily in, shutting the door.

"Why did you come here? Why did you seek for me? Oh, Dallas, you have risked it all!" But she could hardly breathe in her joy and triumph. "It's all over—what I've worked for so long. You have come home at last."

"Yes, I've come home at last," quietly.

"There is little to inherit," looking anxiously into his face. "But this is your rightful place."

"Do you remember that little room at Manasquan, which the people fitted up for me, Lizzy?" abruptly.

"Yes."

"I never can go back there. Never."

"What does that matter?" angrily. "You are ungrateful to God for all He has given you. Why, the whole house is filled with joy and thanksgiving because He has been so good to you, and you cry out for that trifle, which you cannot have."

"I know. There have been times, even to-night, when, because I could not have it, this house has been intolerable to me. I'd rather go back once more to old Graah and the fishermen, and know they'd clap me on the shoulder and make the friend of me they did then, than inherit all this estate that is lost. But I can never do that."

"No, you can never do it. So, for God's sake let it go! It is better that all remembrance of it should pass out of your life. It's the sight of me that has done it. I will go back to Manasquan."

"No, Lizzy, you shall not leave me."

"Yes, I will go. There is not an hour which is not fraught with danger, now that you have acknowledged your acquaintance with me. Any chance word may betray all."

"You do not think I am going to live always under cover of this lie? I will tell my whole story to-morrow. I wanted to draw my breath first. It is a hard blow to give them—my mother."

Lizzy stared into his face aghast. Then she recovered herself. "It is a blow which you will never give, Dallas Galbraith. I know you better than you do yourself. You are dogged and obstinate, but you never hurt a worm. That old Manasquan life is dead to you—dead. You will not bring up its ghost for no purpose but to torture these women?" putting her hand on his shoulder.

Dallas drew a heavy breath, and presently wiped his forehead, looking down at the little woman from his height in despair.

"I wish to God I had stayed out on the Plains, and not tangled myself up with a parcel of women! Why can't they look at a thing in a common-sense, practical way? There is no reason why it should torture them. I am innocent. I feel like a baited bull with women, Lizzy! I don't understand them."

Lizzy bit her lip. "Oh yes, you do, Dallas! You've great power over women. There is Honora. I do not know when you knew her; but I know this," she paused, lowered her voice, and ended the sentence in a whisper.

Dallas blushed, as Honora would have done. "Whether it be true or not, *you* have no right to tell me that," quickly. "It is her secret."

"Oh, of course, I am wrong. It is no difference whether it is my love for you that makes me anxious or not. Take your own way," holding his wrist in both her hands. "See, Dallas! I've come to love you as if you were my son in all these years, and now you will undo all that I have done. But go on—go on! It does not matter to you if you break that girl's heart," watching him furtively. "She has grown thin and pale waiting and waiting for you. But what of that? Your whim will be gratified."

"I would rather you did not speak again to me of Miss Dundas, Lizzy," with the old quiet authority, which nobody resisted. But Lizzy saw the red spot burning in his cheek, and knew her purpose was gained.

"Go on, now; they will be impatient for you. You had better tell them to-night," giving her nail an additional blow on the head. "It is a pity to give them even this little glimpse of happiness after all their trouble. Oh, Dallas! if you but knew what you were to your mother or — Look at poor Honora's worn face to-night, and see what you read there."

"I shall not tell them until to-morrow. Good-night, Lizzy," holding out his hand.

Lizzy's eyes sparkled when the door shut behind him. "He's safe," nodding as she pinned her working napkin in front of her again. "The whole estate waiting for him last year would not move him, but that silly girl's pale face will do it. Dallas is as stubborn as a mule against fate, but he's a fool in the hands of a woman."

Meanwhile Dallas, going through the wide halls, felt the pulse throbbing in every vein of his body. He had not a doubt of Lizzy's story. He had never learned the conventional rule that women must be sought, pursued, wooed. The man was born for the woman—the woman for the man. Honora loved him. That seemed to him natural and right. Did he not love her? And the poor lonely girl had watched and waited for him? Well, had he not thought of her constantly out on the Plains?—constantly—quite forgetting the digging and the hard study and the buffalo hunts, and Pritchard's stories, and his own frolics with the younger men, which had put her out of his head for weeks together.

"Pale? Worn?" He hurried forward, his hand almost trembling when he turned the latch of the library door. He would go to her before them all and claim her as his. She never should know sorrow or pain again.

But when he opened the door, her face was not among those which turned to meet him. The room had taken on itself a new cheerfulness to-night, never seen there before, Colonel Pervis thought as he bustled about, making himself high master of ceremonies. Even Dallas knew what happy hearts he had made among the group gathered about the bright fire. They were all there: Madam Galbraith triumphant in her chair of state; his grandfather examining his famous old fowling-piece, which he meant to bestow on Dallas, listening with a quiet smile to the Colonel's jokes; his mother, for once thoroughly alive, cheerful, saucy, winning; Dour and his chubby little, over-dressed wife; and Mr. Rattlin, first in one corner and then another, telling the story of his good fortune.

Madam Galbraith stroked her heavy chin when she heard it, trying to conceal her gratification. "Half of his salary, eh? I am very glad this immediate relief has come to you, Mr. Rattlin, and that it has come through this source. I recognize more and more of the Dour traits in my son Dallas. Have you heard this story, James?" raising her voice and repeating it for the benefit of the whole party. "I will assist you in your choice of a farm, Mr. Rattlin, and advise Mrs. Rattlin how to set matters in order," she added aside at the close.

They all waited for Dallas, watching the door, and there was a sort of thrill and hush among them, as though they had not seen him before, when he came in among them. An unusual, powerful face, Dour thought as he rose to meet him, full of Nature's original meanings: even the clothes seemed to have less power to diminish the natural expression of the free, athletic figure than they had upon men in town. The contagion of excitement had roused Dour into unusual heartiness, but he shook hands with Dallas the second time with cordial pleasure, because he found him to be the manner of man he was.

She was not there, Dallas thought, glancing around. She was too ill to come. This was his doing!

Supper was announced. "We are waiting for Miss Dundas," said Madam Galbraith, rising. "Send to her room to know if she is able to come down." A colder chill crept to Dallas' heart. Before the servant could obey her, however, the door opened.

"I am here, John," said a sweet, clear voice, and Honora, radiant as youth itself, a rose in her hair, and the richest and most dazzling of robes setting off her piquant beauty, came floating up the room. "Will nobody present me to my cousin Dallas?" she said, stopping with outstretched hands before him, and looking up into his face like a bewildering fairy.

Dallas gave one quick glance over the little figure—saw the cool, observant eyes, the healthy pink cheeks, the little, soft, peach-tinted hands held out steadily: then he took one of them in his own cold fingers, and let it fall, as though it had been a hot bit of iron.

"Honora is so frank and cordial," whispered Gerty, admiringly, to Mrs. Duffield. "It is sweet in her to dress her hair with flowers and to put on her Paris-made dress in honor of Mr. Galbraith. It's the very apple of Honora's eye—that brocade." For Gerty, who wanted now with all her heart to see all the poor young girls married, thought she might speak a good word for Nora with this new hero's mother. Mrs. Duffield gathered herself up from her lounging attitude and favored Miss Dundas with an unusually keen survey. The red on that young lady's cheeks was oddly stationary, and she had put on with her brocade a certain gayety and aplomb which were as foreign to the simple girl as would have been the cruel suavity of Lady Macbeth's welcome to her guests. The mother's jealous eye found in it miching malicho for her stupid boy.

"You are late in welcoming your cousin, Honora," said Madam Galbraith, severely.

Miss Dundas had walked toward the fire, and was engaged in teasing a Maltese cat on the rug with the toe of her slipper: she looked up brightly at this, however. "Oh, *I* welcomed him long ago. Down, Barba! Poor pussy! Cousin Dallas," she added, indifferently, as she stroked the cat, "was here a year ago, and I accidentally discovered who he was."

"Dallas made himself known to you a year ago!" exclaimed Madam Galbraith, towering fiercely over her, while his mother sat listening, her eyes on the floor, but growing suddenly very pale.

"Oh, no; I discovered him. I remember that I urged him quite earnestly to remain with you, dear aunt. But he declined. He was going on an expedition for—coal, I believe, and when he had done with coal he intended to come back to his mother and family. Go away, Barba. I can't play any more," knitting her brows anxiously as she brushed off the marks of his paws from her skirt. There was a painful silence.

"I hope you found the coal successfully, Cousin Dallas," said Honora, courteously, smiling and turning her hard, brown eyes full on his. "I used to be very anxious about you—dreadfully anxious! It was quite a relief, I assure you, to hear to-day that you had arrived safely," with a civil little bow as she turned to Gerty; and, dismissing the matter as finished, began to explain, in answer to her queries, that the pansies on her sash were embroidered and not woven.

"There is something here that I do not understand."

"It is nothing, Madam Galbraith," said Mrs. Duffield, rising. "Did not John say that supper was served? Dallas, give your arm to your cousin Honora." Which Dallas did, walking stiffly down the hall in grave silence, while the little girl's silk rustled and glistened at his side, and her civil voice went on chattering what he called unfeeling balderdash, and now and then a milky breath touched his face. He would like to have struck off the soft, round arm and the hand that peeped out from its laces and nestled on his wrist, and have rushed away where he would never see her again. Out on the Sierra Madre, Dallas had stood his ground with a hearty cheer when the Comanches attacked their little party and the odds were hopeless, and had come out of the fight as fresh as though he had been taking a plunge in the breakers. But the light touch of this little hand, this shrill, polite, treble ringing in his ears, unmanned him. The old hurt, neglected feeling of his boyhood choked him: he knew himself to be ignorant, a boor; the tears of mortification and self-contempt were not far from his eyes. Loved him? This pure, dainty lady, whose every new word or motion marked more and more sharply the gulf between them! Why, in spite of her courtesy, he saw plainly that she had forgotten that he was alive. And he, like a vain puppy, had believed her ill and pining for his sake!

When they were seated side by side there were one or two points which Honora made clear for herself, taking advantage of the first buzz and noise about them. She had not forgotten that he had come back at the appointed time. There was a hope in that. Perhaps she wronged him altogether!

"You have been down at the wells for several days, Colonel Pervis tells me?"

"Yes; I came back the night of the fire. I would have come to the farm sooner to see—my mother. But I was needed down there. To-day was the first time I thought I could be spared."

The hard glitter went out of her eyes. "The night of the fire? That was just a year since you left us," her voice faltering a little.

"About a year, I believe," indifferently. Why was she trying to make civil talk for him? He ought to thank God if he never saw her face or heard her voice again!

"Lizzy," she began again, writing with her fork nervously on her plate—"Lizzy and Mrs. Beck said you promised to return in a year. They were quite certain you would come."

"It was exceedingly foolish in Lizzy to keep any such arrangement in mind," impatiently. "A man cannot hold to such visionary plans out in the wilderness. One has not steam-cars there to come and go at his nod."

"Yet you came?" with a timid, shy smile.

"Yes," in his solidest, most matter-of-fact tone. "Doctor Pritchard secured an appointment for me in this part of the country, and I came back to accept it. It happened to bring me back at the end of the year, otherwise I should hardly have been so punctual. I did not tell you, sir," to his grandfather, "that I am to assist in the geological survey of some of the Middle States. It will give me steady employment for several years."

Honora chipped at the white slice of pheasant before her, as calm outwardly as any ideal fine lady, but for a few moments some inward pain made her blind and deaf to all about her.

After a while she looked up, her unflinching eyes going slowly around the table. They were all changed; she felt that. This long-lost boy had wakened a genial, deep life in the house that had never been there before, with all its cheerfulness and hospitality. It was like the kindling of a Christmas fire in a cold, bright room.

The wind was howling without and the sleet and hail beating against the windows, but they only laughed when the storm drowned their voices, looking toward Dallas—always looking toward Dallas, her new-found idol. Whether he spoke or moved, she could read the quick response in all the attentive, loving faces.

She could tell them what their idol was! Stone—stone; like any dumb and deaf image of a man that the heathen set up for a god. A woman might wear her heart out in his service, she could tell his mother: she might sacrifice her life at his feet, and he would stare over her head stolid and blind to' the end! She would like to give his dull heart a stab! She would like to do it now—now. To test if there were any life or feeling or love in it for anything beyond his roots and ores.

Mrs. Duffield, who kept a quiet watch upon the girl, saw an indescribable weariness stealing over her face, strangely at variance with the gay, unfading patch of color in each cheek. She poured out a glass of wine and sent it to her by a servant; but Honora left it untouched before her, looking at it in a moment with eyes whose brilliant defiance rivaled its sparkle. She was strong enough: she did not need it to keep her in accord with them, though they were warm and cordial and happy, and she was shut out.

How delicious the supper was, and was there ever so cheerful a room? The very old smoky landscapes in their frames seemed to glow and brighten: Madam Galbraith was subdued and gentle as never before—the old scholar, on the contrary, full of life and quiet humor, telling some of those old stories which it was Honora's rare treat to hear; and Dour was genial, proposed Dallas' health in an apt little speech, to which Gerty listened with her heart in her throat. She had quite a matronly, composed manner now—poor Gerty—with a sunny stillness in her eyes, at which Honora turned to look again and again. At the door, Honora saw Lizzy's face from time to time: she, too, was looking at Dallas. Dallas seemed to fill up the measure of life for them all to-night! Even the servants gave him their allegiance at first sight—stumbled over each other in their zeal to wait upon him, until old Henkel put them all aside and took up his own station behind his chair.

Dallas' conscience, meantime, began to harass him for his rude neglect of the brilliant little beauty beside him: he took heart o' grace, therefore, and told her that she wore the flower which he cared for the most in her hair. "Though it has a half-sister, which is called by some Indian name, that I like even better than the jessamine," he added. "I used to find it under the dead pine needles in the woods when I was a boy."

"You have associations with flowers, then?" said Honora, with a sudden hopeful flurry. "I have kept flowers to mark every part of my life. I have them all pressed and put away."

"I have but one; but that is very precious," he rejoined, in his deliberate, grave way. "I have kept it for a long time. I have it here, I think," putting his hand in his breast pocket. She half turned her head toward him, a soft color stealing over her neck and throat different from the flame in her cheeks. "It is a specimen of a Scotch heath, which

I found on the top of a mountain in Colorado. There can be no mistake in it. Doctor Pritchard called it a freak of Nature, but I consider it a hint of a law not yet understood. There are no freaks in Nature. Would you like to look at it."

"Yes. It is very curious, very curious, indeed!" She let the brown little wisp fall on the cloth after the most indifferent of glances, giving it a twist with her fingers which crumbled it to pieces. Dallas did not touch it and said nothing. What unaccountable tempers were these of which women were possessed! What possible harm could the poor little heath have done to the woman? But it was the heath without doubt: a moment after, as they rose from the table, she affected to perceive for the first time what she had done.

"I'm sorry to have destroyed the one thing you held as precious, Mr. Galbraith," she said, laughing, and took pains to brush the bits down on the floor with a virulent haste, as though it had been a live thing which had hurt her.

When the house was still that night, Mr. Galbraith heard an uneasy step stealing up and down the corridor outside of his door, and presently Honora's knock. She came directly up to him and began, without stopping to take breath: "I have made up my mind now, uncle: I must go away. I must go at once."

He took off his spectacles without looking at her, folded them, put them in their case more deliberately than usual, she fancied. She herself took his book and pushed it far over on the table. "That is the Bible. I've tried it. It has no meaning in it to-night for me."

But even this blasphemy, which chilled her as soon as she had fairly spoken it, did not discompose Mr. Galbraith. "So you are going away? Sit down, Nonny."

But she preferred to stand. The fine tint was off of her cheeks; instead of the delicate embroidered silk, she wore a dingy gray wrapper: it was the dead chrysalis from which the butterfly had escaped for ever, she thought.

"I am going to earn my own living, uncle."

"You are going to éarn your own living, my dear? In what way?"

"You don't mean to oppose me, then?" stopping short in her sobs.

"I mean to oppose you in nothing that will give you happiness, Honora."

"I thought," after a chagrined pause, "you would have been distressed—surprised, at least. But one would suppose you had been sitting here waiting for me to come and say just these words."

Mr. Galbraith bent forward suddenly to stir the fire. She could not see his face. "I thought it not improbable that you would come in to-night, Nora;" adding, after a pause: "As for your making your own living, that idea is a common epidemic now among women. In old times they worked off pain or discontent in a pilgrimage to the Holy Sepulchre, or hied them to a nunnery, but now they rush out of doors to try and turn an honest penny, or sometimes to obtain the right to vote in the fall elections."

It was some time before Miss Dundas answered him. She felt that she had in some way been effectually balked in mid-career, and could not readily find her way again. "It is selfish in me to desert you now, when you need me most," she began, "after all our life together. I know it wounds you."

"It does not wound me, Nora. I shall not call it selfish. Study your own happiness first, my child."

"Of course, I know I'm not at all fitted to make my own way. I don't know what I could teach, and I am not acquainted with business. Gerty knows more of that than I. She has been in town shopping many a time. I never was. But I will do what I can," gulping down the sobs heroically. "The very air of this house is insufferable to me."

"I hoped it would have been cheerfuller for you, my child, now that Dallas is come. He seems to be unusually fresh and youthful in his feelings. His hearty laugh makes me feel like a boy again."

"Cousin Dallas?" with an effort of recollection. "Ah, true, he will be here this winter. He will be a great comfort to you, no doubt. He is so tender, so full of fine sensibilities. But I don't think he would feel much interest in me. I am not a relation, and neither a frog nor a fish. No, uncle, I've made up my mind. Let the consequences be what they may, I'll go."

"You shall do as you will, Honora. When you have discovered your vocation, I will make your way clear for you."

The tears were dried in Miss Dundas' eyes, and, though she knew that miserable she was and ought to be, they would not flow again. "I thought you would have tried to control me. But I would not have been controlled. I owe it to myself not to remain where I am suspected of feelings which I know nothing of."

"I never controlled a woman in my life, my dear."

"I may as well say good-night. I suppose it is all settled now," with a sigh. "Here is your book again."

"Good-night, my child. Honora!" as she reached the door, "of course I desire that you will take time to assure yourself of your own wishes. In a month we will talk again of this matter. You must give me so much time."

"A month? Yes, dear!" She ran quickly back and put her arms about his neck, kissing his gray hair with the fervid, bright tears in her eyes. "Of course I'll wait a month, as you wish it. But I am quite determined to go. You mustn't oppose me. Yet I—I—did not wish to leave you and the dear old house just at once," holding his head on her breast, her face all tears.

Mr. Galbraith, when she was gone, opened his book again, laughing quietly to himself. But after an hour had gone by, there was a sound in the far side of the house, at the first hearing of which he rose anxiously, and with unusual haste, put on his overcoat and hat and went out. There was a long sheltered walk along the western side of the house which the drifting snow had left bare, and up and down this a heavy step kept regular, monotonous time through the keen whistle of the wind. Mr. Galbraith stopped, waiting for the dark figure, which was at the farthest end of the stone pavement, to turn and come toward him. The steady timed footfall, the heavy build of the man, a certain business-like decision in his movement, came in sudden contrast in the old man's mind to the vehement heat and passion of the girl from whom he had just parted.

"Dallas!"

The young man came toward him, hastily drawing him into the shelter of the house. "I am an unlucky dog," he said: "I am afraid that I have kept you awake. Whether I wake or sleep, I seem to run my head against some dead wall of civilization."

"Why can you not sleep, Dallas?" As soon as the involuntary question was asked, he seemed to repent, and turned hastily to look down the grayish-white slopes of the valley and up at the black forests on the mountain-side, as a man might do who seeks to avoid the sight of a dreaded spectre near at hand.

"It is the payment for my vagabond habits," said Dallas. Assuredly there was no spectre of aught that was dead or unclean in this face or hearty, spontaneous voice. "I have slept so long with nothing between me and the sky that I wake at night now, in a house, stifled : the ceiling, I fancy, is my coffin-lid." They had turned the corner of the house, and came to the open side-door. Dallas paused within the entrance. "I ought to tell you," he added, trying to preserve the same careless tone, but making it, in spite of himself, strenuous and artificial, "that I came to the conclusion to-night I was an irreclaimable vagabond. I am going back to my old life again, and at once. There are many reasons," laying his hand on Mr. Galbraith's arm, when he would have spoken, "which make me ill at ease with even the kindest and most loving human beings. There is a repugnance between us which is no fault of mine. I include you, sir, and my mother."

The old man, standing in the shadow of the doorway, bowed his head attentively.

"I prefer speaking of this to you. Men can understand men. I have thought it over coolly to-night, and I feel that I have reached that age when a man cannot afford to temporize with his life. Whatever path he chooses, if he would accomplish anything in it, he must pursue it doggedly to the end. It is time for me to be done with looking back and vain regrets."

"You mean to leave us, then, my son?" It was noticeable that, wander where his eye would, it never even now rested on the face of the younger man, though the moon, rising between two mountain peaks, threw it into strong relief. "You have chosen your path, Dallas?"

"I think I have chosen, finally." Yet even as he said it there was doubt subtly conveyed in the grave tone. "I was born for my work. I seem for any other purpose to be dull and incompetent. When I turn from it I am thrown back. I don't complain. It is a man's work, and I have had delight in it—a keen delight. But other men, young men, starting with me, have been able to live out a man's whole life. They are citizens, sons, husbands, fathers. I am shut in upon myself." He paused, but Mr. Galbraith asked no question and made no sign. "When I stretch out my hand for any share in these things, there is a shadow at my side which bars me out from them. I am not talking with a young man's exaggeration," he added, hurriedly. "It is a real power—as real to me every hour I live as Death will be some day. I mean to yield to it. It is a boy's part to fight and struggle and whine for what can never be mine!"

"It is a boy's part to yield! Drag your enemy to the light. It will prove to be but a shadow after all." But the energetic appeal, wrenched as it seemed to be from the old man's tranquil lips in spite of himself, did not move Dallas. He shook his head quietly as he drew Mr. Galbraith back into the screen of the wall.

"I know what is against me," calmly. "And, after all, I'm no more fitted to be a husband or father than a buffalo is to live in a farm-yard. I would grow tired of any home and any wife in a month, with the old gnawing hunger to be digging in the woods again. Roots and earths I can understand. I do not need to be a sham to them."

"There is no use, then, in fighting against your nature."

"No." Yet he stood irresolute, looking into the dark hall. Within there lay the home and wife which he had come back so far to find; and if he turned his back on them now, it was for the last time. "If a man dared to be himself in there," he said, thoughtfully. "I'll tell you!" with his finger on Mr. Galbraith's breast, and blundering out the words, for any kind of speculation was new ground for Dallas. "Out there on the frontier, gentlemen and trappers and roughs used to camp and eat together and ask no questions. You take a man for what he is: he's a good shot, or he's a plucky devil, or he's free with his whisky and corn-bake—you take him at best, you understand? And as for what went behind, what does that concern you? But here in Society, as you call it—Christian Society—a man is weighed and measured and marked, and, it seems to me, by narrow scales, sir—narrow scales. There's not an opinion he may have, or a whim of temper or ignorance of manner, that is not carped at and noted and set down," bitterly. "And if he has made a slip in his youth—" He stopped abruptly.

"Yes, my son?" laying both hands softly on his shoulder.

"Or if, not being guilty, there is a doubt upon him—such as has come upon many men—I know such cases—when there is no way to shake it off and prove his innocence—"

"Then, Dallas?"

"There is no hope for him," after a moment's silence. "There is no Christ among us now-a-days to look below the hard luck or below the guilt."

The storm was rising with the moon, driving the wind with shrill sighs down the defiles; the sallow clouds overhead rolled and heaped themselves in bulwarks along the west; the sharp grains of sleet began to strike against their faces. "Let me take you in, sir," said Dallas, with a change of tone. "This wind is piercing."

"One moment, my son, I will not argue with you as to this matter of which you have spoken to me. I am not fitted to argue with or to influence any one, I fear. Do I understand that this feeling has prompted you to leave us, and go back finally to your old course of life?"

"That seems to me best, and I have thought it over coolly to-night."

"It shall be as you wish. You are a man—you are a stronger man than I. I cannot judge for you. But give me a little while longer to learn to know Tom's boy," taking his hand as a woman might have done. "You say there are reasons which make it painful for you to come in daily contact with us. I ask you, Dallas, to bear the pain. Stay with us a month—a week longer." They had reached the door of Mr. Galbraith's chamber.

"I will stay for the time you wish," said Dallas, pressing the delicate, wrinkled hand in his own blacksmith's fingers. "Perhaps for a week or two I can be of use to you." He opened the door and bade him good-night, repeating cheerfully, "I'll stay." He was glad the old gentleman had not attempted to argue with him. He was wise to see that Dallas was the best judge of what was the right course for him. But he would humor the old man's fancy. He was weak and old.

As for Honora—and here Dallas put his arm across his breast—she could not hurt him again: he was quite willing that she should despise him, know that he was a convict. He saw the difference between them now. He would remain the boor that he was; and she—she was the finest, frailest work of—Society.

As for his secret, they all might know it now. He was done with them —done with the world. Let them think as they would of him.

He would tell them the story—to-morrow.

PART IX.

CHAPTER XXX.

"AND that was the end of John Dour!" And Madam Galbraith, as was her wont at the close of a long story, cleared her throat, jerked down her stomacher and brought herself generally into stately order.

"But Nicholas? You said there was a brother Nicholas?"

"How?" with a pleased chuckle. "You're an insatiate fellow for old family gossip, Dallas. I never could induce my son Tom to listen to any of it. Well, Nicholas—" and she went on, her listener following her intently. It was a cold winter morning, the sun sparkling on the frozen creeks and rivers below, and giving a glittering edge to the bellying, bronze-colored vapors about the horizon. There was a long balcony across the upper part of the house, from which the Dour landscape, as she called it, with its mountains and hollows, in all its changes of light and shade, could best be seen. It had been her daily habit, since she could walk, to walk there. She could give you the age of every tree within a year: when the crops failed on the Dour land, that year of our Lord was set down as a defaulter in time—the sun was delinquent in the chief work he was sent to do. It was the land of the Dours: there were they born; there they lay buried. As for the United States or any world outside of it, they were of as much value as the rim to the cup—so much and no more.

She and Dallas stalked up and down there side by side—their hands behind their backs—every morning, whether it rained or shone. He always went to find her and bring her out for this walk. These dead Dours were *his* people, and for so many years he had stood alone. He never tired of them. When they had done with the dead Dours, they took up their land.

"There's no better soil than that strip of bottom east of McGruger's, in America," nodding toward it. "Why don't you speak, Dallas?"

"Because it's made ground, and badly made. In five years it will only be fit for sheep-grazing."

She rapped angrily with her staff: "Sheep-grazing! That is on a par with your saying there were no indications of gold on the North Bluff. Quite on a par! Why don't you speak, Dallas?"

"There are no indications. There's lead in the hills beyond, or I'm much mistaken."

"Lead? There never was lead heard

of on my land! I'll go in, if you please; I'll go in. I cannot bear this perpetual contradiction. My son Thomas never contradicted me. Young people in those days knew their position better and their information. It is in my old age that I must be taught my ignorance. Ignorance of the Dour land! You'll be sorry for this, boy, when your own hair is gray."

"I am sorry now," earnestly, holding her as she was entering the door. "You know, madam, I have no wish to oppose you, even in this trifle."

"Trifle? You have strange ideas as to what constitutes a trifle! You mean to acknowledge that there are indications of gold, then?"

"No, madam. There is no gold there, and never will be;" and Dallas' jaws shut as tightly as the old woman's before him. "How can I say what I know to be false?"

"As you please, sir; as you please," and, drawing her breath heavily like a horse, she went into the open door of the upper hall. Dallas continued his walk to the window of his own room, and going in, shut himself up and sat down with his feet on the table. "Gold, indeed?" picking up certain bits of ore that lay scattered about. "I'd like to buy back the land and prove that there is lead in it, and that that bottom is fit for nothing but sheep-pasture. It ought to be mine. We Dours are all buried there," looking down at a little enclosure on the same mountain as that on which the house stood.

There was a tap at the window: "Hillo, Dallas!"

Dallas took down his feet, and said, "Hillo!"

"There's the last deed, thank the Lord. When a thing's dead, let's bury it out of sight—the sooner the better," said Colonel Pervis, throwing down some papers on which the letters ranged themselves square and black as mutes in a funeral procession. "And there goes the last of the Dour land, except these half-dozen acres about the house. It has gone for a song."

"It could be bought back again as cheaply, you think?"

"Have you a mind to buy it, Galbraith?" quickly. "That would be a noble task to set yourself now in your youth."

"I? No. I'm but a vagabond, living from hand to mouth."

"You persist in your determination, then, to turn your back on the Dours and the Dour land before long, do you?"

Dallas did not speak for a moment: "I promised Mr. Galbraith to remain for a month, and it is nearly over now. It is time I was gone."

The Colonel folded and squared the papers before him, keeping a sidelong watch on the young man. "A month only? It seems as though you had always been here. Your niche was kept so vacant and so ready for you, you see! You fitted in like a keystone to the arch. It's an unaccountable move for a young man to turn his back upon his home—a man in your case."

"I could almost believe I had been always here," said Dallas, under his breath, glancing around. Some people stamp themselves at once upon their surroundings. Tom's room was changed; had taken on itself the impress of its new occupant in a curious degree. Colonel Pervis, having tied up his documents with red tape in what he considered a thoroughly legal manner, his head knowingly on one side, began wandering about, his hands in his pockets, staring up at the hanging-shelves filled with ores, the papers tacked on the walls, gummed over with lichen and shavings of different woods.

"So you're going just as you've got things ship-shape about you? Though you could pick up this rubbish anywhere. But it's your meat and drink. A woods now is a completer thing to you than the best furnished parlor, I reckon!" with a subdued awe. "And you're going never to come back, Dallas?"

"I did not say that. I'd be glad to think of this room and my place here always kept vacant and ready for me, and that I could come back to it when I pleased, from year to year." He too got up and went around from shelf to shelf, but in a lagging, lethargic way, setting straight and dusting his specimens.

The Colonel's curious questions had taken, as it were, the life and color from all that was around him. He felt himself to be suddenly heavy and dull as the lump of mud mixed with iron that he held in his hand. He was going. Had he not determined to go that night, in spite of his grandfather's entreaties? Nothing had occurred since then to alter his position. Nothing. When the time came to say farewell, he would tell them his story; and after he was gone, perhaps the sting of it would grow less sharp to them, and they would be glad to have him come some time, convict as he was, and sleep in his own room for a night, and to remember how, if Fate long ago had been juster to him, this might have been always his happy home. The month would be over in a few days. He had not told them his secret, thinking he might surely be free from it for that little time—time enough only to take breath in this sweet, pure air of home before, like the Wandering Jew, he took up his curse and began again his solitary pilgrimage. He had something of the feeling of a man whose days are checked and counted off, measured out by some inexorable disease; less pity for himself than yearning tenderness for those whom he must leave behind—a hungry longing to be dear to these healthy, fortunate people who were so dear to him. In the little time left him he thought they should feel that he was their son, bone of their bone, in every word or action by which he could bring them near or show the affection that choked his stupid heart and brought the tears to his grave blue eyes.

At that moment the thump, thump of Madam Galbraith's staff was heard outside, and then a single authoritative summons to the door. Poor Dallas had it open almost before the knock, and met her with a heated, anxious countenance and outstretched hand. Her face, which was black as a thunder-cloud, instantly cleared:

"Why, how's this? Glad to see the old dragon, hey? Well, I'll come in, though I only was in search of Colonel Pervis. He has some papers for me to sign, I suspect. What are you hiding them for, sir?" sternly, taking her seat, bringing up an inkstand and putting it down in front of her with a bang that made the Colonel wink. "I know it is the last of my land I am to sign away. Am I an hysteric girl, do you think, that the news must be broken to me piece by piece? Give me a pen, my son."

Now, the truth was that the Colonel had stopped in Dallas' room from sheer cowardice before he took the papers to her. Nobody knew in what mood she would complete her sacrifice—whether in fury against herself and Fate, or gloomy silence. Pervis, behind her chair, drew a long breath, and rolled up his eyes thankfully when the *Hannah Dour Galbraith* was scored in free, deep characters across the whole bottom of the page. She threw down the pen and looked up at Dallas, her hard, long upper lip trembling as she laughed hoarsely:

"Tut! tut! why it is only so much earth and water gone," rising as she spoke and putting her hand on Dallas' shoulder. "But I have something left which nothing can take away."

Even Colonel Pervis, whose observation was as headlong as his tongue, noticed the singular silence in which Galbraith received this half appeal. He was unusually gentle with her, however, after that, leading her down the stairs to the dining-room, where the usual cozy luncheon-table was set, and Mr. Galbraith and Honora awaited them. So gentle that Madam Galbraith, who did not usually dally long in regions of tenderness, presumed on it. She always had an irresistible propensity to lash a quiet horse to find what spirit was in him.

"Dallas was surprised, James," she said graciously, glancing at the pale face of the young man on the opposite side of the table—"very much surprised, when I mentioned to him Edward Dour's theory that there was gold in the North Bluff. He doubted it, in fact; but I have no doubt from his manner now he is convinced of his mistake, and regrets that he differed with me."

The horse was alive to the lash. His

secret, his affectionate resolves all forgotten, went whistling down the wind. "Edward Dour or any man who tried to convince you of that was worse than a fool, madam: he was a knave. It is preposterous. Look at the formation of the soil—"

"Now, Dallas," said Mrs. Duffield, putting her blue-veined little hand preremptorily on his lips, "if you bring your hobbies on the table, nobody can eat a mouthful, and this custard of Honora's is delicious. Adjourn the soils, my dear. Cannot you yield to your grandmother?" she added in a vexed whisper.

"I hope to the Lord he'll not: every blow brings them closer together," ejaculated the Colonel in the same tone, while Dallas sat obstinately silent. The storm, however, soon passed by, clearing the air. It was an old matter by this time: there were such storms between them at every meal. After a while Dallas began to notice how cheerful the fire was, flashing over the snug little room, while the winter landscape lay drearily outside. Then the little party about the table drew closer together when he began to talk, and ate and laughed with fresh enjoyment. They were careless and happy and sure of each other, as they had not been before they were shipwrecked together.

Otherwise, the shipwreck had made but little change. The great Dour landscape yet lay without, no matter what hold the flimsy bank-notes of other men might affect to lay upon it: the house was unchanged; there were still the chairs placed at the table for the friends who might happen to come in, and the friends were always there to fill them; there were one or two quiet old servants instead of the old crowd and confusion; but the dishes had a flavor beyond any which spices could give. Honora had taken Lizzy's place. And it is wonderful what human interest and poetry one finds in a beefsteak if hands we love have seasoned it; especially if it be a tender cut and done to a turn.

There had been so much to tell and show to their new-found son, to make him familiar with his home, that the great loss and consequent changes had been slurred over every day until they were almost forgotten. His grandfather had haunts and walks which he must know; Madam Galbraith had her legends of each to tell when they came home; there were the old neighbors and friends —neighbors and friends for many generations—who were clamorous to know the boy and to hand him around through a long succession of dinner-parties and oyster-suppers. There was a thoroughness of geniality in the old fellows and their wives with which Dallas struck a quick accord.

"The boy's one of ourselves, sir!" cried Squire Pool, enthusiastically to his grandfather, giving the verdict of the county. "He fell into our ways from the first day as if he were born among us, and wasn't chock full of such queer, out-of-the-way learning. The county has cause to be proud of him, sir. He's healthy and hearty, sir, as few of our young fellows are now-a-days; and he likes a joke, Dallas does," confidentially, "as quiet as he looks. Now, some of them stories he told at our house was capital. When you'd think 'em over, you'd see how keen they were."

They gave Dallas no time for thinking of himself. He was up before dawn and down among the emigrants with his grandfather and Pervis, serving as an interpreter between them and these coarser folk, with whom his sympathy seemed, Pervis said, as close as that of blood. The Galbraith funds were all exhausted: homes and employment in the West had been found for the larger number of the colony, but there had lingered a crowd of wretches, the most unable and helpless. For them, until Dallas went to work to plan and contrive, there was apparently no help. Madam Galbraith had given all she had, and now washed her hands in innocency. Her husband, when he was among them, stripped himself of his very clothing in his nervous trembling compassion; but at home, with his feet to the fire and his book in hand, he was apt to philosophize about them coolly, regarding them as a vague abstraction—one of the unclean masses that make up this dull, unanswerable puzzle of a world. Colonel Pervis God-blessed his soul, and grew hot and cold, and rode madly about the neighborhood, drumming up baskets of provisions for them, and then, conscience-clear, sat down composedly to his whist and jorum of brandy. "What more could he do? Wasn't he a shiftless devil, that never had taken care of himself?"

But there was not one of the sordid, hungry faces which this healthy, hearty young fellow, whose laugh was so infectious and whose jokes were so capital, did not carry with him night and day with a motherly tenderness—an aching at heart that could only grow out of his own hard mischance in life. With this weight to carry, he had been living altogether outside of himself, and until to-day, when the last man was comfortably settled, he had no chance to go back and probe and speculate upon his old foul secret, and how he should reconcile it to his new life.

They used to ride back from the wells to breakfast, and then his mother claimed him for long walks or visits to the neighbors: she lost all her apathy when he was beside her; went about fair, smiling, triumphant, quite content to be silent so long as he would speak; or his grandfather established him in an arm-chair in the library beside his own. The old gentleman had gathered Dallas' books on geology together, and was studying them with a boy's freshness. Honora used to stop outside of the door and listen to their eager voices and Dallas' occasional hearty burst of laughter, and go away a little colder and stiller, and with dryer eyes than before. For, whatever he might be to others—whether she saw his eyes full of pity or twinkling with amusement at Madam Galbraith's absurdities; whether she donned her dazzling little dress and enacted the dazzling little rôle she first played, or sat humbly stitching in the corner, like the poor dependant she felt herself to be—Dallas stood aloof from her, cold, grave, regardless.

He had forgotten the stain upon him with others, but with her he had never forgotten it.

She sat opposite to him at the table to-day, the light from the window at his back throwing the delicate little figure and thoughtful face, so full of sweet, untold meanings, into relief, while the others were in the shadow of the dull wintry day. He looked at her alone as he talked, her figure being thus in relief, and for the same reason, perhaps, remembered how he had stood apart from her, never forgetting the stain. He was very thankful that he had done this.

As the firelight burned redder and warmer, and the home within grew more and more homelike and familiar, he looked out at the driving snow and the solitary wastes sloping toward the west, where his path lay: the feeling of thankfulness strengthened within him. Luxury would not have tempted him. But it would have been so easy to rest here, in this homely old house; so easy to forget that he was a solitary outcast, with these two or three people who loved him to work for; so easy to have been tempted to strive with all the strength of his manhood to draw this pure little girl to him—to win her to lay her head on his breast, to lie there for ever, his wife.

She looked up at that moment, laughing and blushing, when her uncle spoke to her. Because his life lately had been so healthy and vigorous, and free from all morbid pain, the shadow of the Albany years lay the heavier now on Dallas. It lay like some foul disease, with which his healthy self had nothing to do. The old heavy throbbing began in his breast, with which his heart used to count out the slow hours in prison, each one nearer death: he looked at her a moment, and then rose suddenly. He was very thankful that he had never crossed the space between them—very thankful!

Mr. Galbraith followed him to the window, where he stood with his hands behind him, leaning his head against the pane. "We will have heavy snows this winter," he said, cheerfully. "It will be long before I can go with you on your tramps, Dallas. But in the spring you must let me take my hammer and chisel and follow after you. I'm a good walker for my age. Very good," glancing down at his thin legs complacently.

"You forget, sir," speaking slowly, "I gave myself but a month to remain here, and that is nearly over."

He had not turned his head to look at the old man when he spoke, and for a little while he heard only the sleet beating against the window-pane: then his grandfather put his hand on his arm: "There is nothing here which could cause you to alter your purpose, Dallas?"

"Nothing."

"There is no effort which I could make that would do away with this necessity which urges you? Consider, my son."

"I have considered. There is no chance of any change while I live. None."

Mr. Galbraith stood beside him quite silent, but Dallas moved away restlessly. He could not bear the reproach of the presence of this old man, not one of whose days had been tainted even with suspicion.

"Ho, Dallas!" called the Colonel, looking up from his newspaper. "By George, my memory's going! Beck asked me to desire you to ride over to the Queen, on particular business, early this morning."

"I will go now. It is not yet too late," glad of the escape. But when he reached the hall and had shut the door behind him, he halted. Honora stood in the large bay-window at the farther end, quite alone, her hands clasped above her eyes, watching so intently the driving snow that she had not heard his step.

He was going: he meant to put a barrier between them that never could be passed. But before he went? Other men drew the women they loved to them for life, made them their own, body and soul. If he could but hold her hand once in his! But once! It was not much to come near her in these few days, before they parted for ever, to take away a few kind looks and words.

So thankful was he that he had never forgotten the bar between them that he felt he deserved a reward. He laid down the cloak that he carried, and went toward her with quick, resolute steps. It was the first time he had come near her of his own free will since the first day he came; yet, being a woman, and hearing him behind her now, she did not turn or look at him, but drew aside with a smile, to make room for him in the narrow recess, as naturally as though they had been hourly companions, though he noticed that an uncontrollable shiver passed over her. It was she, too, who spoke first after they had stood for some time silent, side by side.

"You are going to ride over to the Indian Queen, I think you said?"

"Yes."

"Lizzy is there: she is going to-morrow. I bade her good-bye; but will you give her my dear love? Will you tell her again that I know what a good friend she has been to me?"

"Yes. I will tell her."

The silence between them, which these surface-words did not seem to break for some strange reason, seemed full of meaning to Miss Dundas—her color, her ordinary strength and vigor left her: it was as though she saw a warning presence which held them apart; the ghost, the shadow of a something of which the reality was never to live, never to be known to them. She tried to thrust it aside with any sound of words, without caring for their meaning:

"I will never see her again. I never have been outside of these hills. Friends who go away are lost to me for ever. But you will see her? She is going back to Manasquan, and you have lived there. You can go back again to see the mists come up over the marshes, and the sea break on the beach: Lizzy has told me of it. It is good to be a man, to come and go where you will. There is nothing to keep a man from his friend unless death part them."

"No, I can never go back to Manasquan."

She glanced quickly up at him There

was no morbid shadow in the face turned to hers, nor feverish discontent. It was that of a resolute, young and strong man, with great possibilities in it for happiness and achievement, looking down calm and uncomplaining upon the friend from whom death had parted him. He had accepted the death. There was in his look the memory of much that had been, of all that might have been; but there was no promise of anything to come.

She understood the meaning of the look fully.

"I am a man free to come and go as I will," he said. "Yet I can never go back to Manasquan. I meet men and women who I know can only be my friends after I am dead. There are hands which I can never touch," and his eyes, she thought, rested on hers, where it lay close beside him.

"A man," said Honora, with a slight pause upon the word, "can do what he will. His life is in his own hand."

"I thought that when I was a boy," said Dallas. "But there is something which goes before you through life, and rules your way, Miss Dundas. It is not tangible, even as the pillar of cloud. But you follow it. You follow it, if it leads you through the fire or the sea." He was silent, not waiting for her to speak, apparently, but because the subject was closed and ended, and there was as little use in farther words as in moans over a grave.

The dry white flakes fell without steadily. Honora, who was never to be his wife, from whom he was thankful he had held himself as a stranger, was beside him; her soft dress touched his foot, her breath clouded the panes. Once he had felt her breath, and knew how sweet it was.

"A man," he said deliberately, as though reciting a lesson, "will learn to obey and keep within the lines ruled to him. He will not come near the woman he loves if he knows it is forbidden, though no other can take her place to him. He would not come near her. He would not touch her hand, though it lay beside him."

She drew away her hand involuntarily. His whole countenance changed at that: he caught it in his own with a breathless, half-famished look, smoothed and stroked it as it lay in his own tanned palm, narrow and fine and milky-tinted.

"I am going away, Honora," drawing her toward him. "I want to hold your hand once, and hear you say that you are my friend. I want to remember that when I am gone."

"You may remember it. I am your friend," in a measured voice.

"How can you be? How could you know me? Other men have been able to come close to you and try to show you the best that is in them—to change their tastes and habits to suit your fancies. But I—"

"I know you better than any other human being does, Cousin Dallas," with a dry, bitter tone.

"What do you know of me?" hurriedly letting her hand fall, which had rested in his as passive as the handle of a machine. She adjusted her disordered sleeve with it as mechanically and precisely as if it had been a machine.

"We are cousins, you know, and you have been the object of interest in all eyes: it is not unnatural that I should have noticed you curiously."

"No; it is not unnatural. What do you know of me?"

Honora gave an abrupt laugh, in which there was no sweetness, and which seemed to rob her cheek of its slight color. "I know you to be earnest and zealous in your work. You ought to be. What heart or soul you have has gone down into it."

"Into my work? And my mother and kinsfolk?"

"God gave them to you, and you make the best of them. They were none of your choosing. You do your duty."

"But I do not go out of my path to find love or friendship?"

"No. You go out of your beaten track only for ores and reptiles. Where they are concerned, I have seen you eager, or angry, or glad as other men. But only then."

"And if love came to me?"

"You would receive it as that stone wall does the poor creeper yonder. You would give it support and protection. But an answering life, never. A few moments ago, before you came to me, I was thinking of you, when I looked at that rock and the miserable vine—"

Dallas, always blind as a mole to any but the barest meanings, studied the passionate little face before him for a while, finding nothing but the indifferent contempt of her words in it. He began to button up his coat slowly.

"Well!" stifling a sigh in his big breast. "It doesn't matter; though I did not think you would judge me so hardly, Miss Dundas. I know you so well that I thought you would be just to me, perhaps, when I was gone."

"I am just. I am your friend."

"No! no! I know what friendship is better than you. After all, I would have been a tenderer, more loyal woman than you."

"You are going, Cousin Dallas?" seeing that he took up the cloak.

"Only to the Queen. On Monday I will go to the West." The fastenings of the cloak were intricate. She watched him for a minute, and then turned her head, looking out of the window.

"I—I have not vexed you. You are not going the sooner because of what I have said?"

"Not a day sooner. I intended to go on Monday." The cloak was fastened at last, and he came up to her side again. She turned quickly, and held out her hand. He took it, holding it an instant and looking in her face steadily. "I could make you think differently of me, Miss Dundas. But I will not. Why should I?"

The little hand which had laid in his passive as a machine, was alive now, burning and trembling, but he released it quietly and drew back.

"You do not intend to try to alter my opinion, then?" with a quick breath, that sounded like a sob.

"If I could change it by the turning of my finger, I would not do it," vehemently. "I hold my life in my own hands, as you said: I will not be dishonest."

A moment after she saw him riding down the avenue through the snow—a black, powerful, obstinate figure, against which the wind blew and the soft flakes drifted in vain.

"If I could take her to my arms to-morrow, I would not do it," were the words which he said again and again to himself. "I hold my life in my own hands."

CHAPTER XXXI.

MATT was perched in the window of the stable-loft, among the hay, watching for Dallas, when he rode up, and Beck himself came out from the door below, his green wamus on and pitchfork in hand, and gave him a cheer. "It's Lizzy that sent for you, sir: she's got a sudden notion of bein' off to Manasquan. But I'm mighty glad you're here to look over things, now that they're in order. What do you think of them pigs, now? Genuine Berkshire, *they* are. Well, sir, it's a relief to get back to the Queen, bless her copper-colored phiz—a relief. Peggy and me got the money the madam give us changed into specie, and it's back in the tea-pot. I kin hardly get the smell of them infernal wells out of my nose even yet," rooting among the pigs as though inhaling the odors of Araby the Blest. "Hyur's the old woman now."

Peggy came bustling out, her apron over her head. "Lord bless us! is it you at last, Mr. Galbraith? In with you, Matt, and ask Miss Lizzy to put the coffee on the boil. Beck's been on the tenter-hooks all day, clearin' up and watchin' for you to inspect the place. The Queen don't seem the natural Queen without you, sir, for all. We've got a nice turkey-poult for dinner, waitin' an' ready."

"I'm very glad to hear it," said Galbraith, heartily. "I did not eat any luncheon for some reason or other, and this ride through the snow makes a man ravenous. Good-day, Wash. How are you, Lizzy?" sitting down on the porch to unstrap his leggings. But, in spite of his noisy greeting, Lizzy lingered in the doorway, looking at him. She fancied the heartiness was artificial, and that there were unusual dark hollows under her boy's eyes. She followed him closely when he came in, swinging Matt on his shoulder, and beginning to romp with him, evading her, while Beck made his toilet outside by pulling off his boots, and Peggy hurried up the dinner, peeping in the lids of various stew-pans:

"The tomaytoes is done to a turn; but the potatoes is dried, I'm afeard. But this celery— Oh, you know they were goin' to sell off the celery the day after Beck come up to take the house agen? Seemed kind o' providential; throughout it's bin providential since the day you set foot on them there steps, Mr. Galbraith." Peggy stopped in the middle of her neat little kitchen, tapping off her words with a shining pewter spoon in one hand, the stove at her back, with its half-dozen savory steams rising in a cloud. "I often says to Beck, 'Do you mind the day when Mr. Galbraith first come up them steps, and wrote his name in our register?' There's been changes since then. Changes!"

"I would like to look at that register, Peggy," said Dallas, suddenly lowering Matt on the floor. "Have you it there?" She gave it to him, dusting it on her apron, and he turned over the leaves to the page where his name was written in unsteady characters. It was the first time he had taken his name and place on leaving the prison. Next week he was going out from them again, and, beyond the name, what had he gained? The stain was on him heavy now as then.

"What is it, Dallas?"

"Nothing of moment, Lizzy," closing the book. "Only that for some of us the chance of change is over."

Lizzy turned away hastily. "That is better, Dallas," she said. "I want no change, but rest now." She went into the other room presently, and Mrs. Beck whispered to Dallas that she had been "low" ever since a letter came last night Dallas thought rather that the long season of anxiety and work was beginning to tell on her. She had been worn and listless of late: the salt sea-air and drowsy sun yonder would revive her again. She came out again in quite a glow of cheerfulness, however, and helped Peggy place the dishes on the table, and sat beside Matt, joking with him as she cut choice bits of turkey for him. He must come and see the cozy little house where she would live quite alone, where you could see the white surf roll in on the beach, and the fishermen drawing their nets along the edge. Wouldn't she be afraid to live there alone? How she laughed at that! Why she had been alone these many years— many years. Would she be afraid of the sea or of the woods? Very few people there in Manasquan remembered she was alive: they would soon forget her altogether in her queer brown house in the trees: she would live on, she told Matt, and on, till she got to be a little, white-haired old woman, and then some morning they would come to find her, and she would be gone.

Perhaps somebody would say then, "Why, we used to know her when her cheeks were red and her hair was black." Though, perhaps, they would have forgotten to say even that.

They did not join very heartily in her laugh after this, and Beck fell to work slashing fiercely at the other side of the turkey, and piled up all their plates afresh. Then Lizzy, in another tone, told Peggy she was quite serious in wishing Matt to come and spend the summer with her, and she wanted her and her husband to come; and then she glanced at Dallas with a sudden white face, and was silent.

He looked up at her quietly, and smiled. She had carried his trouble a long time. His shoulders were broad enough to bear it all now.

Peggy's dinner was so good that it blinded her to anything beyond. "Beck, give Mr. Galbraith some cranberry-jelly; his plate's quite clear. I kerried over a pot or two of my apple-butter to Mrs.

Rattlin yesterday, knowin' all her stores went in the fire. Dear! dear! but they're snug over there. It ud do your heart good; and Miss Gerty, she declared she'd take a crock for herself. She's getting ready to house-keep. Her man has gone into business in Ohio. He's a thin-blooded feller, but he's mighty clever."

"He's ahead of the telegraph, that Dour," said Beck, with a significant shake of the head, his drumstick in hand. "He's shouldered the Rattlins heartily, though, with all his sharpness. Now, Peggy, my woman, whar's yer puddin'?"

The pudding disappeared to the last crumb. The table was cleared, and Peggy seated by the clean hearth at her sewing, when Lizzy beckoned Dallas out to the little porch. "I sent for you to say good-bye, Galbraith."

"You are going back to the old place, Lizzy?"

"Yes. Every hour I stay here adds to your risk of detection. Besides, I'm not well. By night or day I hear a sound like the roll of the surf, beat, beat. It drives me mad. I think it must be the homesickness, as Peggy calls it," with a faint smile. "I had a letter from Father Kimball yesterday, and since then the surf has called louder and louder." She took an enormous yellow envelope from her pocket as she spoke, and opened it.

"May I read it, Lizzy?" She stood beside him as he sat on the bench poring over the old-fashioned writing, smiling now and then to himself. A single name belonging to those old Manasquan days had a curious power over him, she saw; brought out his hidden self—the old Dallas, who used to go rooting through the woods, trolling out fishing songs. He had forgotten, in his eagerness, the gulf that lay between himself and them.

"So Becker has added a room to the smithy?" muttering as he read. "And Tim Graah's mate on a schooner? So! so! Tim's almost a man by this time; and the railroad's looked for next year. To be sure, and will be till the day of judgment. There's a salt smell in the very paper, Lizzy," turning it over with an odd homesick look. "I am glad for you that you are going back to Manasquan. There's no other place in the world so quiet and so friendly. No other." After a little pause he read to the end: "Kimball says that Van Zeldt is married, Lizzy. Do you know his wife?" as he carefully folded the letter, and gave it back to her.

"Jenny Noanes? Yes, she was a rosy-cheeked little girl, who used to come to the Point to pick huckleberries in the fall. Very pretty! Oh, very pretty!"

"Too young for Jim, then, I would say."

"Just the right age, Dallas; just the right age," emphatically. "Men don't grow old as soon as women. They like fresh roses and fresh hearts," with a laugh that stopped too short, looking over the unending white slopes growing gray in the twilight.

"You are cold, Lizzy, and ill. Go in. I am glad you're going home."

"Yes; it *is* my home."

"I do not forget that you never would have left it but for me. If it had not been for me, your life would have been —like that of other women. I have not many words, Lizzy, but I never forget."

Lizzy did not seem to hear him. She walked to the end of the porch, where the wind blew freely on her sober, colorless face: one would have fancied some raging fever burned under the pallor and steadiness which sought some outward storm to contend with. "You are going to remain here, Dallas?" she said, suddenly.

He hesitated. It was not easy to tell her that her sacrifice had been in vain— that after all he was to be the vagabond and wanderer, to save whom she had given her all.

"No, Lizzy, I am going. The ship yonder is low in the water already. I will not stay in her to make a wreck of her altogether."

"Thank God!" with a long breath of relief. She hurried toward him, and caught his wrists. "Will you go at once, then?"

Dallas stared down on her. "Go? Why, you brought me here. You would have had me marry—"

"That is all over! There's no hope for you, do as we will." As she spoke she glanced again and again over her shoulder into the darkening twilight. There was a leafless forest stretching its black and grim phalanx down the hill to the frozen creek below: up the road were scattered bare trees, lifting their dusky, spectral arms with a mute appeal. She watched them as she spoke, as though some shadow she dreaded would appear from them. On the hill-road, down which Dallas, once standing where he did now, had seen Laddoun's black horse striking out fiery sparks in the night, the snow lay deep and soft. But in the strained silence he fancied he heard muffled footfalls coming closer, closer.

"Is it the dead you fear?" he said, half smiling, touching Lizzy to rouse her.

She rubbed her hand slowly over her forehead. "I do not know. We people from the sea hear voices and see faces which no one else can know. He is on your track, Dallas. He is on your track."

Dallas drew back. "There is but one man who can do me harm. You mean Laddoun?"

"I mean Laddoun. I do not know whether he be dead or alive."

"It does not matter. Death will make small change in George, I fancy. Is he here?"

"I heard to-day that he had been seen here a few weeks ago, looking for you. Do you understand, Dallas? Looking for you. And there is a rumor of his death, last summer, in California. However he comes, dead or alive, he has a power which you cannot fight against. Oh, Dallas, I could not live to see you trodden to the dust here! I thank God that you are going."

He turned on her: "You think I would turn my back on Laddoun?" and then began walking up and down the porch in the slow, swinging gait which she well knew.

"Now he's winding up his soul in obstinacy, and all the powers in heaven or hell would not move him," she muttered in appalled dismay. She caught him by the sleeve as he passed: "Dallas? Dallas?"

He stopped. "I have my life in my own hands. I am an honest man; and, by God's help, I mean to take my place and marry the wife I love, as other honest men do. I'll be baited and bullied by no ruffian, though he rise from his grave to do it. The matter's closed, Lizzy. We will not talk of it again."

She leaned against the railing of the porch until he had gone in to bid Peggy and Beck good-bye, and, coming out again, had mounted his horse. Then she went down and put her hand up on the pommel: "Dallas!"

"Go on, Lizzy," kindly. But a new expression in his usually patient eyes reminded her how many years he had been baited by that old ill-luck as by a hound from hell, and that now he had suddenly turned upon it. But his manner to her was very gentle. "What is it, Lizzy?" he said again.

"I only wished to say to you, dear boy," trembling as she said it, "that discovery now is sure, and that with Honora's prejudices she never would marry you with that old stain upon you."

He sat erect on the horse, perfectly motionless while she spoke, and then said deliberately: "I mean to have my right, my home, and wife, and position, as other men. I shall not consider the cloud over me or Honora's prejudices. They are matters for which I am not responsible."

"And Laddoun?"

When he did not reply to her she leaned forward to see his face: the blood forsook her own. "There is murder in your heart, Dallas Galbraith!"

He put away her hands with unnatural quietness: "You vex yourself with vain terrors. I see my path quite clear to the end. Laddoun will never cross it again."

There was a thin flaking of ice about the horse's mouth—he stooped to clear it away: the gentler his touch to the dumb animal, the more Lizzy, with a woman's keen instinct, shrank before the secret purpose hidden beneath his grave calm with a clear but unnameable terror. She saw him and his life with a keen flash of insight—how long he had worn the halter about his neck; that Laddoun had pressed him hardly, was riding him down to death; that beneath the Galbraith credulous, gentle temper the Dour blood ran in his veins untainted, fierce, relentless, untamed in him by any religious teaching. She remembered his old grandmother's words: "I have crushed many a snake under my foot that threatened to sting me." And this man, genial, hearty, single-minded, would do the same if driven to the wall, with a gentler face and colder, more steely will. She looked again and again from him up to the hill-roads drifted deep with snow and growing gray in the twilight, listening for muffled footsteps. What if they came now? What if they met him yonder in the solitude of the night among the mountains?

There was no surer sign of the terror with which his inflexible will had inspired her than the fact that not by word or motion did she seek to interfere further with his purpose. When he drew up his rein and held out his hand to her, she only sobbed over it, holding it close to her wet face, praying to the God of whom he knew so little for her dear boy. But she said not a word beyond good-bye.

"Good-bye, Lizzy." He put his fingers for one moment on her head. Long afterward she remembered the touch. It was different from anything Dallas had ever said or done to her. It made her wonder whether, dull and insensible as she thought him, the years gone and the kindness which lay between them had not borne a deeper meaning to Dallas Galbraith than even to her, woman as she was. She would have been glad to think it. But what did it matter? He was gone. The soft echo of his horse's steps had died out speedily: no others came to fill the silence, though she listened until late in the night, trembling as she listened. They were all gone on their separate paths. She was left behind. The world was full of crossing paths, whereon love, and pain, and danger lurked; but she had only to creep into her quiet corner now and wait for the end. No steps came and went in which she had a part. There were now no voices in the distance calling on her to follow.

CHAPTER XXXII.

It was Honora to whom the muffled steps came that night up through the snow, heavy and firm, tending to their end, she thought, steadily as Fate itself. When we are young as Honora there is a meaning in every passing step to us: we know not in what disguise the lictor will come—who brings to us the royal robe and crown of which we dream. Some legend lingers with us of the world from which we came, by which we know that Fate touches us in the fingers of every beggar—that every hand holds out to us the leaves of healing or of death. It is as we grow old that we grow wise—or blind.

Dallas, coming into the library, found it vacant, though he had seen Honora's slight shadow passing to and fro behind the curtained windows as he came up the walk without. He closed the door behind him and laid down the cap which he still carried, and then, after a moment's pause and a long breath, he went to the door of the little breakfast-room beyond and opened it. She was there, and alone, dressed in some soft crimson stuff, standing by the fire, her sewing in her hand as she had hastily gathered it up when he frightened her, for she had fled from him, she did not know why; yet in the moment that elapsed as he crossed the floor to her side, some sudden instinct told her that the man approaching her was himself pursued.

He took the work from her hand and laid it down: "I have a few words to say to you, and I wish nothing to come between us until you have heard me." She bowed and seated herself in a great arm-chair slowly, to gain time, while he leaned with one hand on the table, regarding her through his half-shut eyes. There was no flash of sultry passion, with which a young man might look upon as fair a woman as Honora when he loved her. But there was a keen appreciation in the homely, nobly-moulded face of all that was true and beautiful in that world of which she was to him the secret and only portal. The clean blood in his strong body might flow temperately, unquickened by her touch; but there was a hunger in his eyes that told how his nature cried out for her; how all the singular, life-long desire which possessed the honest, loving fellow, beyond other men, for a home, for children, for the something genuine and pure denied to him and given to all others, had found its issue in her; how his secret soul, kept closely covered and difficult of access, had been reached by her, was alive, kindled to the quick at last with that enduring, sturdy affection, that jealous honor which a man feels but once in his life, and then for his wife, and for the woman whom he loves.

Yet Dallas did not speak. The beautiful city was before him; but he did not forget that to gain it he must creep into it like a thief in the night, disguised and false.

"You gave me your verdict upon me, to-night, Miss Dundas," he said, forcing a careless tone, which he lost at the outset. "I wish you now to know me as I am. I would be glad if I could open my heart for you to read, and all of my life."

There was an under-current of thought with these words.

Was it showing her his true self to drag out the vile character which society had put upon him? Was it the justice to himself which he would have shown another man? Let it sleep for a while. It was Dallas Galbraith who wooed the woman he loved, not Laddoun's victim.

He continued, his face lightening after this curiously: "You thought me unfeeling and colder than other men. Perhaps that may be so I do not know other men: I only know myself. You will pardon me if I speak of myself a little longer?" coloring.

"I will pardon it," without raising her eyes.

"The old life I knew before I came here, Miss Dundas, was different from yours," choosing his words slowly, keeping down, she saw, beneath their moderation, a strong emotion. "Its weight has been upon me: it is upon me still. If you knew it all, you would perhaps forgive those deficiencies in manner and speech in which I seemed to you less deferential than other men."

She would have spoken, but he put his hand up asking for silence: it seemed as though the constraint once broken which he had enforced upon himself, his only safeguard was gone:

"I have dragged that old life about with me like the dead seed which clings to some living plants." He did not see the smile which she hid at this under a nervous cough, but went on with such a pallor in his firm face, such terrible vehemence under his deliberate tone, that she, looking up at him, felt the smile freeze upon her lips. This was no love-making amidst summer and roses. The man led her, behind him, into the narrow straits which lie between life and death, where his soul, she knew, had already fought through many a combat, and had sometimes been worsted.

"It hangs over me like the dead, ill-smelling seed upon the living plant," he repeated. "Though I owed that old life nothing, I did not grow out of it. It was foisted on me by others. It is unjust that it should cling to me and poison the air about me for ever."

"Let it go," she interrupted him. "What is your past life to us, Cousin Dallas? You come to us as you are. Besides, I know more of it than you think, and what is it? You were miserably poor—you are self-taught."

"Yes."

But it daunted poor little Honora that this encouragement, which came with many maidenly blushes, roused in him no answering heat. On the contrary, it cooled him: he turned away even to the window from which could be seen the snow-covered mountains, up which the distant roads wound, and the sombre speculation in his eyes was something in which she had no share. The next moment he was by her side:

"I have been ridden by a spectre long enough!" countenance and voice full of vehement fire. "To-night I have done with it," with a curious gesture, as though he threw a yoke from his neck. There was a heap of cushions on the floor: he sat down on them at her feet, and looked up in her face.

The old locust tree at the window beat with its bare branches against the pane, impatient of the silence: the hot coals fell in red showers and grew gray and cold, but Honora did not speak. The Dallas Galbraith at whom she glanced shyly through her veiling lashes was a man whom she had seen before, but as through a glass darkly. It was as if he had brought his soul into his face for her to read. The spectre was gone, and whatever pure meaning lay between them secretly came out now, not dreading the light. The man and woman seeking each other in soul and body, met, and were not ashamed.

What words they spoke were hardly conventional. When her flushed cheek and quick breath showed that the silence grew painful, Dallas took the nervous, trembling hands in his:

"You always knew I loved you, Honora?"

"Yes, Dallas," in a weak little whisper.

"But you? I know how rough and untaught I am. And yet I thought you cared for me."

"I could not help it," putting her hands over her face with a stifled sob or two.

There was a bit of fine, reddish-brown hair which in some way curled itself about Dallas' fingers just then. He suddenly drew her down to his breast, and putting away her hands, kissed the dewy red lips again and again.

The wind sighed its warning, the dead branches beat the pane, and the fire flashed and faded in vain. The one rare, healing cordial of the world had come to Dallas' lips at last—the life of this life, and the only thing of which we are sure when we are dead. The poor, stupid naturalist, who had blundered over it unlooked for, had power to drink as deep a draught as the crowned Cæsar, or the divine Florentine who sought it through heaven and hell. God's wine of love, as of sunshine, waits on the roadside for the beggar who is willing, for the murderer on his way to the scaffold.

But Dallas, finding it, saw no scaffold or shadow beyond: sitting beside this woman, reading in her soul that it knew no world outside of his, his life seemed to him suddenly full and complete. There was no pain or danger coming, no change lurking in the distance. He traced the outline of the small, purely-cut face with his forefinger as if learning a sweet lesson by heart, kissed the closed lids to waken the liquid light of the brilliant eyes; and when he looked into them, thought the world a summer-garden, secure, warm, beautiful. A delicious, childish feeling—a security—which had never come to him in his life before. The home in which he had rooted himself so firmly, his mother, the fond old people who made the home complete, his friends outside, Matt, the boys he was trying to help,—they all came vaguely into his consciousness, framed the picture of his wife, and made it more tender and more real.

He had been conscious of the rough grit and clay in his own character—Honora would take it away. He knew how ignorant and irreligious he was; yet sometimes, when at his work, he had been on the verge of awful visions, wherein God and His world had almost been made known to him. His wife, with her pure, holy touch, would lead him within the veil.

He said something of this to her. It was when she rose and asked him to take her to her uncle. Dallas pushed back the hair from her forehead, and turned her face up to his. "I put my life in your hands, Honora," he said solemnly. "When you are my wife you must lead me in the right paths, here and hereafter," lowering his voice. "I will be guided by you."

"Oh, Dallas! as if I could find

fault with you. There is nothing I would have changed. Though I often have thought," knitting her brows anxiously, "that if you would go into business, and only break rocks and pull plants to bits in your leisure hours? You will not be vexed with me? It is a noble work to interpret the rocks; but when it comes to frogs and fishes—"

"Of course, Honora, I shall never give up my work," with emphasis. "You must marry my hobby for plants and frogs, if you marry me," forcing a smile.

She changed color, but laughed: "We will talk of that some other time, then. But now you will come to church with me, and read a little book I will give you? Only an explanation of our belief. Our faith must be the same, Dallas."

"Well—yes. I'll read it," with a perplexed frown. "In fact, I have read it: I saw how you valued it. It was but a show of opinions to me, Honora," in his doggedest tone. "Out in the woods yonder I have seen something at times altogether strong and good under all the beauty and contrivance; but I do not see Him in those opinions of the preachers. He is both narrow and cruel, according to them. As for church, the crowd, and the dress, and the forms drive good thoughts away from me. It is in quiet and alone I would find Him, if at all; and I would rather not receive Him second-hand through the brains of other men. I'm afraid I never will be a church-goer, Honora."

Honora looked at him steadily. In that early moment there reached her the consciousness which generally comes after years of married life, of the insoluble differences of character and of creed which love can never destroy. She had a foresight keen as intuition: there was not a struggle which might come between her prejudices and his obstinacy which was not plain to her. She hesitated a moment, and then with a loving faith, different from any that yet had shone in her eyes, she held out both hands to him. "After all, we will go to Him on the same path," she said quietly.

Dallas opened the library door, and at the same moment Mr. Galbraith, his tall figure tightly buttoned, and blue with cold, came in from the outer hall.

"It's a nipping night, Dallas," rubbing his hands as he hurried to the fire: then he stopped suddenly on seeing their faces as they stood together. Honora ran to him. "So, little one?" he said slowly, putting his arm about her. "So?"

Dallas stopped in the shadow by the door. There was not the keen flash of pleasure in his grandfather's face which he had thought to see there. It was anxious, almost stern, as he stooped over Nora with his old habitual motion, stroking her hair.

"You know the story we have come to tell you, I think, sir," said Dallas.

Mr. Galbraith turned to him with quick attention, but made no answer.

It happened that Dallas had stopped in the same place where he had stood a year before, a convict. The fire, as then, burned low, and the light was dim. It brought the scene back before him so real, that the old sense of being condemned and trampled under foot returned as bitter as it had been before.

"The first time I saw you and Honora together," he said, boldly, "I felt that if I had no weight to carry unknown to other men, I had a right to be a nearer friend to either of you than any man beside. If I have justified that right to you, sir, I ask you to give her to me."

Mr. Galbraith's silence lasted so long that Honora, in a frightened, pale flurry, began to pat his cheeks and put her arms about his neck, and with womanly tact to fill up the pause before Dallas should notice it. "You know, uncle dear, when first we met Dallas in the mountain by the quarry. He seemed quite different to me then from— I mean—" blushing crimson. "I— Though I don't suppose he noticed *me*."

"In the mountain by the quarry?" the searching look still upon him.

Dallas was silent. He had crept over the wall like a thief in the night to win his prize, and the sense of meanness and defeat secretly dragged his soul in the dust. But was this a time to bring out his secret? To thrust her from him when she was in his hands?

Honora, after trying to read her uncle's face, gave an audible sob.

"Yes; Nonny, yes," hurriedly. "I have no right, Dallas, to keep you from the wife whom God has given to you. But she has been my darling so long! I could have wished—" interrupting himself hastily. "If you can touch her hand to-day feeling that you are, as you say, worthy of her love, in God's name take it."

For a moment Dallas did not move. But Honora, with a swift motion, at once indignant and shy, which brought a smile from both men, went to him and put her hand in his: "Worthy! worthy! Why, he is your own son Dallas! You are cold, cruel! I did not think that you would turn against us and make everything wretched, as you are doing."

Mr. Galbraith answered with a sad smile: "I am not cold, God knows, Honora. So be it, then: I think God will bless you." He turned, and was passing them to go out, but suddenly stopped before them. "I'm an old man, Dallas; but I have never known a happy marriage where there was not perfect confidence. The world has no right, perhaps, to your secrets. But your wife should know the worst which is within your breast before she lays her head there." He wrung the boy's hand, and left them.

Dallas gave a short, surly laugh: "Are you afraid of any secret viper which I have hidden, Honora?"

But Honora did not laugh: "I suppose every one will give us advice. I thought he was going to say whose duty it will be to give up when we differ."

"Differ, Nora! There will never be a thought on which we will not be one! Do you not feel that?"

"Oh, of course I feel it," with a queer little smile. "Still, it is as well to know that it is right for the woman to give up in case of emergencies." But she spoke as if she was tired and jaded. Her uncle's coldness had hurt and disappointed her perhaps more than she chose to tell. "And I was startled, too, by an odd feeling which I had, Dallas," she said, thoughtfully; "though one often fancies that we have gone through parts of our lives before, long ago. But when you stood there in the shadow of the book-cases, and I went to you and put my hand in yours, it seemed to me as if it was not for the first time. It confuses me—" passing her hand wearily over her eyes.

Dallas took it down. "Such fancies are common, my darling," he said hastily, and began to tell her how dear she was to him—how in all the days of that wild life on the Plains his heart had cried out for her. But even while he spoke he glanced uneasily over her shoulder to where the mountains lay gray and spectral in the night, up which the deserted roads wound. There was not an hour in which the chance of detection did not dog him: it had its voices echoing Lizzy's cry, "He is on your track—on your track!" It would lay in wait for him even here, in his wife's love.

As the image of his old enemy rose up before him, his face hardened, and an ugly look came into his eyes that boded ill for Laddoun. Whatever of good there was in the man that had raised him above all the vice and folly of his early years, was, under the present temptation, the strongest element in him for evil. The very persistence and obstinacy that had beaten down the demons that would have held him fast, would now beat down to death the man who stood between him and the bountiful, more generous life that opened before him.

The time for revenge, if it had ever been, had gone now; but the determination to suffer no more was more cruel in him than any spirit of vengeance could have been.

And all the worse for Laddoun.

CHAPTER XXXIII.

"AND when is it to be, my son?" Madam Galbraith patted Dallas' hard hand with her own bony, wrinkled fingers, looking at it as she might have done at her baby's long ago. She broke into a hurried, abrupt laugh now and then, but the water stood in her eyes.

"To-day, if Honora is willing."

"To-day! Upon my soul, boy, you carry on your wooing as they did in the days of the old Indian-fighters! To-day? James, do you hear the lad? Call Honora. She shall consent, she shall consent! I will take your part, Dallas!" with smothered delight. She rapped with her hickory staff on the floor, and sat up erect in the bed, the white nightgown, with its broad frills, making the swarthy countenance and gray hair more strong and unwomanly. Since the failure of her great scheme a singular disease mastered her now and then—a sudden, uncontrollable weakness and lack of nervous power. It was the price she paid for the savage control with which all her life she had held her body down: when it refused to serve her now, she uttered no complaints, but stretched herself out without a pillow on her hard mattress, and lay there in silence, looking not unlike the grim, hard-beaked Crusaders in the old churches, stiffened into stone on top of their graves, waiting their call.

"I must get up," pounding more vehemently with her staff. "I am myself again. It is the thought that I shall keep you with me always, my son, that has cured me. When your children come to put their hands on me, I will grow young again, and the old dragon may live for ever. Who knows?" with a nervous laugh.

Mrs. Duffield came in with Honora. There were dark hollows under her eyes, as though she had not slept through the night. Early this morning she had gone into Honora's room, and dressed her according to her own taste, putting the little bunch of mignonette, which she wore every morning the year round, on the girl's bosom instead of her own; and then she herself had donned a cap. Only a square bit of lace, but significant to her as a nun's veil. When Dallas came up to them, she watched him and Honora, blushing like a girl, so forgetful of herself, her eyes so full of happy tears, that it was his mother to whom Dallas gave his good-morning kiss, and not his bride.

"Honora," going straight to his point as usual, "I know nothing of the usual customs, but I do not understand why a mob of strangers should come to hear us say we love each other, nor why we should not say it at once if it be true. I wish you to allow me to send over for Mr. Rattlin this evening, and he will say a prayer over us to keep away the ill-luck for ever. And so our story will end." He would not even touch her hand before them all; but his look was a caress before which she drew back.

Now Honora had meant to spend two or three months in fasting and preparing, making herself inwardly pure before she began her new life. It was an old fancy she had.

"It is all arranged, Honora," said the old lady, impatiently, reaching over for her dressing-gown. "I want to see my boy happy. I like his manner of wooing; though of course, if you object, we will hear what you have to say."

Honora said nothing.

"You shall do as you wish, my darling," Dallas whispered.

"I wish to please you," after a pause, with a subjugated sigh.

"Then it's all settled!" Madam Galbraith grew purple with delight and excitement. "Honora is generally biddable. Go out, good people, all of you. I must be up and dressed. A wedding in the house at a day's notice! Ah, Dallas, so the Dours used to carry it in the old time!"

Mrs. Duffield touched Honora's cold cheek when they were outside, and then kissed it—a most rare sign of feeling: "Go now: you want to be alone, child. I will attend to your dress—everything. I am your mother now."

In ten minutes Madam Galbraith recalled her. "*I* dress in military time, my dear." Already she had the floor and bed covered with the contents of sundry presses and enormous closets. "We must see what we can do for the young people, eh? Glorious, sunshiny weather! I think my plans were tolerably successful," chuckling, as she unlocked drawer after drawer.

"You do not mean—"

"That I brought them together? Assuredly. *I* saw the propriety of it the very day that Dallas arrived. I wanted him to marry among his own people. And Honora is very suitable, very easily controlled. What do you think of these cameos? I'll give the child all my jewelry. Only a married woman should wear jewelry. And I have some silks and velvets, never cut, here. But, tut! tut! velvet and silk! the poor children will be paupers!"

"Dallas will be quite able to support his wife," proudly.

"Yes; he's as solid as granite. A very different character, my dear, from my other son, Thomas," stopping with an awkward cough as she remembered to whom she spoke, and ringing the bell violently: "Send for Mrs. Beck immediately. The house must be set in order and supper prepared. And good Mrs. Rattlin. I'll feel more at ease when I have my staff about me. Come, my dear, and see what I have laid away for Honora."

Mrs. Duffield followed, nothing loth. Any true woman finds a press full of fine linen as fair a sight as a field of daisies. Up and down the old woman dragged her, nothing slacking in her zeal, bringing to light great stores of which nobody knew but herself, repeating again and again: "I put by for the child as if she had been my own. I little thought it would all come back to Tom's boy."

Mr. Galbraith found her seated at noon, exhausted, before a heaped table of old lace, which she had been sorting. There was a light in her face which had not been there since the days when they were first married. She made him sit down beside her, putting her hand on his knee, chattering gossip like any girl.

"The fellow has your desire to shut out the world when he is in great pain or joy, I see. Morbid, but I understand it. Well, we'll have the county in another time. I've nothing to give the children but this poor housewifery, James."

"There will be the old house and bit of land when we are gone, Hannah."

"Yes. That is yours." She sat thoughtful a long time, and then turning to him, said: "I am glad it is yours. I never have spoken to you of it before, James, but the happiest day of my life was that when I first slept under my husband's roof, and knew that I was dependent on his work for the very bread I ate."

The old scholar stroked his gray beard softly, and made her no reply. But walking up and down the room in his accustomed habit that evening, he hummed a tune—some gay old song which he used to sing in the days when he was a gallant young fellow, and meant to conquer the world, giving furtive, proud glances toward his wife. Never, in her fairest days, had she seemed so womanly to him as now.

Of course, the house was in a ferment all day long. The sun outside shone brightly—within, the fires flashed and crackled. There was not a woman, from motherly Mrs. Rattlin to Jinny the scullery-maid, whose heart did not beat fast as though she was the bride, and who did not find time in the high-tide of preparation to run in now and then to Honora with some tender offer of service. Mrs. Duffield wandered about the house, for the first time in her life irresolute and incapable.

Colonel Pervis found her toward dusk in the dining-room. He had taken charge of the whole affair, and with the glee of a dozen boys in his red face, was going in and out, and up and down the country-side, under high-pressure power, scattering the news far and wide. He steamed into harbor for a moment to the sideboard, and finding the pretty little widow alone, leaning her head on her hand, thought, as he drank off his hastily-made cobbler, that whatever heart she had was bound up in that boy, and that she was cursedly cut loose from her moorings to-day.

"By George, madam!" wiping his moustache, "I think when poverty came into the door of this house good-luck besieged the windows!"

Her eyes sparkled. "With Dallas? But I wished to speak to you, Colonel Pervis. It must be evident to you that

I cannot stay with the good-luck. I cannot be the drone of the hive. We count the cost here now from day to day necessarily, and my son will have enough weight to carry with a wife, and half of his income gone to the orphans with Mr. Rattlin."

The Colonel concocted another cobbler, and muttered something about infernal folly. "I mean," he added hastily, aloud, "that there is a drop of Quixotic blood in Dallas. Very remarkable in so practical a fellow."

"There are very few persons who can comprehend my son," complacently. "But I must go. I trust to you to make the explanations here as easy as possible for me."

"I'll smooth matters over for you," putting down his glass and corking the bottles, with his back to her, in silence, as if at a loss for words. Then he came up to the table by which she sat, and stood, balancing his portly body on heel and toe, twisting the end of his whiskers. "I'll smooth matters; but it must be in my own way. I've a conscience of my own, Mrs. Duffield. I'm your friend, madam; and you know when you were a child your friends crossed you for your own good." Here, his courage oozing out altogether, he stopped to cough.

"I do not know what you mean, Colonel Pervis," coldly.

"I mean that I've carried these cursed bonds until they burned my pocket, and I'll carry them no longer!" throwing the envelope on the table. "I beg your pardon, madam; but, upon my soul, the flesh is wearing off my bones with the responsibility of them."

"Do you tell me," rising haughtily, "that you have not applied my money, as I desired, to the use of the sufferers?"

"Not a red cent of it! I say now, Dallas and you may play Don Quixote if you like, but you'll have to find another Sancho Panza. It's not in John Pervis. Now, don't say a word!" backing to the door, his hand up. "Get somebody else. Dour's your man. But, thank God, I've washed my hands of them!"

"You had no right to thwart me, sir," her fair flesh flushing to her very bosom, red with anger. But the Colonel was gone, and the door shut hastily behind him. The next moment she saw him hurrying to the stables, and laughed nervously. She took up the envelope presently, which smelled horribly of tobacco and brandy: she tore it off, and turned over wistfully the blue-lettered papers. Then she went slowly to her own room, looked out of the window for a while, and then, in an absent, careless way, unlocked a private drawer and put them in their old place, hanging the key to her chatelaine.

She went down a few moments after, and was sweeter and more sunny-tempered than ever before. Madam Galbraith had never known her so affectionate. She even put her peachy cheek to the old lady's hard jaws, and whispered, "Don't be uneasy about the children. There'll be a little to give them when I'm gone, you know."

The secret, however, burned Pervis' brain as the bonds had his pocket, and before night he confided it to Madam Galbraith. "She did not care for the poor wretches a picayune," he said. "It was to gratify your whim that she would have beggared herself."

"To satisfy me, eh? I did not think it was in Tom's wife." The old woman made no other remark. But she went away hastily to find James. She never told Mrs. Duffield that her secret was known; but she called her "Mary" that day for the first time in her life; and to the day of her death she gave Mary the daughter's place which she had never held before.

The sun went down redly, leaving long bars of ruby light arching up the sky. The snow was crisp under Dallas' feet as he came slowly down the hill-road and stopped in the gate leading into the woods, looking at the house before he went in. The long rows of windows shone warmly in its massive front against the mountain-shadow, as they had done on the night when he first came to this gate, haggard and shaven, from his felon's cell in Albany. Now he was going in as a master, to be a helpful citizen, caressed and obeyed in his home—the fairest woman, he thought, that God ever made, to nestle in his bosom as his wife. He had gone, on this, the day of all days of his life, to the poor wretches at the wells and to the children whom he had tried to save, as some men would have gone to church, and now was coming home.

Now, Dallas was no thinker: he never speculated on the meaning of his own life or that of others: he was very seldom conscious, until he saw their effects in his action, of the deep, vital forces that had their ebb and flow in his soul. But a strange thing happened to him to-day. As the sun went down he glanced about the horizon to find indications of snow, and then going through the woods, mechanically broke off, as he went, bits of the twigs or bark, examining them. There was a space blown bare of snow beside the trunk of a dead ash, and turning up the ground with his foot, he picked out some seeds of weeds, and stripped off the scaly layers in which they were sheathed: in the dead wood, too, breaking off the bark, there were the larvæ of a dozen different kinds of beetles and moths waiting for the snow to be gone to spring into life.

As Dallas threw them down carelessly, something—the red sunbeam, perhaps, flickering in his eyes—brought before him, as by second-sight, the vision of the great world in which he lived, whose bosom was filled with illimitable myriads of seeds and larvæ waiting for summer to begin their appointed lives, the least of them to be ruled, useful and instinct with beauty—of the long procession of animal and vegetable lives since Time began, whose most trivial feature was governed by law. He stopped, sat down on the crumbling trunk. Perhaps both his brain and heart were quickened and tender to-day, for with electric force an insight into the meaning of all the knowledge he had ever gained came to him: as an artist brings his ideal from the canvas, and oil, and paint—a thought that has always been in them, but not of them. For the first time, Dallas saw the order beneath the life of the larvæ, of the snow that killed it, of the summer that called it into being. The old Jewish account of the creation had always been to him a child's fable beside the story written on the rocks. But to-day he seemed to catch a glimpse of an infinite truth that underlaid these gropings after God of the world's earlier days, as well as the clearer insight of later time—an eternal Right, of which the order and disorder of the world were but chance glimpses that came to us. A living something behind the dead stone, the birth of the animal and its decease—the something in which this dead wood would live again. Crumbling it in his fingers, even he could see creative skill in it—justice, and a terrible human element, beyond justice.

What if this Right held human lives also? His own, with its paltry, every-day chances?

Dallas Galbraith rose and bared his head. His face was pale, and awestruck as the savage who sees his God in the sunshine. What if his own life had been underlaid by the same eternal strength? What if there had been in it no wrong, no chance, which was not ordered by the same loving purpose? He went on slowly, his lips set, his thoughts turned inward, as never before, to find what manner of man he was, and to test what Circumstance had done to him.

If it had not been for the bitter poverty without, would he ever have clung so desperately to his real work, and made himself a man by mastering it? If it had not been for those years in the convict's cell and the stain on him now, would he have met fate with such stubborn endurance? would he have known the patient tenderness for the wretched and the guilty which made him now like a woman before them?

Never. He could see the uses of it all now. He raised his head and walked on, his step elastic, his heart throbbing, full and light. Immeasurable content wrapped him as the beautiful world floated to her rest in the sunshine. It is so easy as we enter heaven to understand the discipline of earth; and Dallas, with his hand upon the door of home, thought his final reward had come. If Laddoun never crossed his path again, he could see how the ill-luck which he fancied had always been against him had borne its part in this all-embracing order, this good, which you could call God if you would. If he came again— and the old cloud came into Dallas' eyes. One can so much more readily see God in the flood that destroyed the world than in the accident which crosses our own purpose.

He went in with a softened, gentle step. The open rooms were lighted and dressed with evergreen; but there was a great silence in the house. He met Mr. Rattlin, who wrung his hand with all the heart that filled his little body. He met his mother, placid and lovely, in a pure dress of white, and she put her arms about his neck and kissed him. He ran lightly up to his own luxurious chamber, bathed and dressed. It was his wedding-night. Every sight and sound, the far-off laughter and voices, the very cold water, as it touched him, wakened in him a keen sense of delight. His feet had touched ground at last. Under all thoughts of home or the sweet woman's life which was to run henceforth in the same channel with his own, was a deep, abiding sense of security, of good.

Provided, Laddoun never returned.

They were all gathered in the library when he came down. There were no shadows in it now. The last rays of the red sunset looked long through the western windows this evening, with their kindly good-bye—soft astral lamps, like globes of moonlight, shone here and there. The great, many-colored coal fire burned cheerfully. Otherwise, there was no change here; only the little home party that gathered about the fire every evening; and Dallas went in and sat down among them.

"Of all the weddings I ever have seen," Mr. Rattlin said to him, with suppressed feeling, "yours, Dallas, seems to me to be the tenderest and most solemn; as if it were from the every-day, home life here that this new, beautiful flower of love had bloomed."

Presently her uncle went to bring Honora; and then Peggy, and Beck, and old Henkel, and the servants silently came in and filled up the background. When Mr. Galbraith opened the door again, Dallas went to meet him and the pure little girl dressed in white that he held by the hand. They said afterward that Honora never looked so like her dead mother as she did on that night.

"You are not afraid to give her to me?" Dallas asked in a whisper, his blue eyes meeting the old man's steadily.

"I am not afraid," he answered, but with whitening lips, and detached his hand from her fingers. "Go, Honora. God make you true to each other, my children."

It seemed to Dallas that then the prayer had been said which made them one. He scarcely heard the words which Mr. Rattlin uttered over them. The invisible something which held them all was warm and close about him as the sunshine to the bird that floats in it; and the old man's love had in some way spoken for it and made it real.

The rosy glow died out of the west while they were crowding about Dallas and his little wife, kissing them, laughing and crying, joking foolishly as people with over-full hearts will do. The sudden winter twilight came on. "Close the shutters, Henkel," said Colonel Pervis. "I've no faith in omens, Dallas, my boy, or I would be vexed by a shadow that seemed to peer at you from that window at your back when you took Honora's hand in yours—a man's mocking face, white as death. I see now that it was but the waving of the branches outside in the lamplight. By the Lord, there it is again!"

"I see nothing," said Madam Galbraith.

But Honora clung to Dallas with a cry of terror, for he had pushed her behind him, as if to save her from some peril that menaced them, and bent forward, going to the window slowly, step by step—following, one might think, some ghost that had beckoned him and disappeared in the night.

They crowded to the other windows. "I see nothing but the shadows of the woods; there is no foreboding in them. Why do you prophesy ill-luck for Dallas?" cried Madam Galbraith angrily, for she had faith in omens.

Dallas turned quickly. "Why, it is nothing," he said. "No, you shall not go out to search, Colonel Pervis. If it is ill-luck that haunts me in the shadow you have seen, why, then it—is but a shadow."

He laughed, and after a moment laughed again. But they, looking at him, seeing such strange matter in his face, and how suddenly cruel the eyes had grown, did not laugh with him. Honora, feeling how cold and clammy was the hand she held, drew it the closer in her own; and she and the grave old scholar, whose love had made their insight deeper than the others, knew that the young husband had also seen the shadowy face; and they knew with unerring instinct that Dallas Galbraith, hunted down, stood at bay.

PART X.

THERE was a little toll-gate about half-way down the hill from the Galbraith house. Old Potter, the keeper, had let fall the rail, and fastened up doors and windows for the night, and, with his wife, was brewing a whisky-stew over the fire, to cheer their hearts before they betook themselves to bed, when the door was roughly shaken, and through the moaning of the wind a man's voice was heard outside.

Potter thrust his gray poll through the square window: "Who's abroad in this storm?"

"Open the door, Dick, curse you! and let me in. Can Bessy give me a place to sleep? I—I'll go no further to-night."

"For God's sake, Colonel!" He opened the door, and catching hold of the dark figure that lay half helpless against it, helped him in, his wife pushing up the cane settee in front of the fire, exchanging significant glances together as they took off his dripping cloak and wet leggings, and seated him in the hottest place. The man swore savagely at them and at the storm, with a fierce cough between-times, that racked and tore his breast, wringing out great mouthsful of blood. When the paroxysm was over, he fell into a silent exhaustion, holding his knees with his hands, his head fallen on his breast, and his eyes set on the fire. The fleshless, sunken face, with its ghastly blotches, was adorned with black, glossy hair and whiskers, carefully trimmed, and the white teeth and hard, black eyes shone at times with a jaunty, cruel sneer. His clothes, of fine mulberry-colored cloth, worn threadbare, hung baggily on a bulky, emaciated figure: a purple ring flamed on his forefinger. Old Potter scanned him from head to foot meditatively, and then shook his head, turning away:

"You're welcome to a bed, Colonel Laddoun. But you ought to be in the hands of your friends, accordin' to my thinkin'."

Laddoun burst into a loud, hollow laugh. "I'm a hale, hearty young fellow! It needs more than doctors' croaking to kill George Laddoun these twenty years! I've been with one of my friends. He's a gallant young bridegroom to-night."

"You've been up at the house? Did you see the heir?" cried the old woman.

"The heir, eh? Yes, I saw him. I'll drink his health with you, if you like," looking toward the steaming saucepan. Potter poured him out a bowlful, and he drank greedily, without waiting for them, smacking his lips as he set it down. "The heir!" with a chuckle. "You'd not believe I crawled here from Panama to see that friend of mine, so dear he is to me? They told me I was going under: every cursed quack croaked death to me, and I meant to settle with him while I was above ground. I'm loyal to my friends— loyal!" swelling and flourishing his bony hand with something of his old swagger. A terrible trembling seized him before he had done speaking.

"Have you settled with him yet?" said old Dick, steadying and seating him again.

"No. When I'm stronger I'll bring our story to an end. I'm growing stronger. You think so, Dick?" holding his shirt-sleeve and looking breathlessly at him, as though a sudden doubt wrenched him like a spasm.

"Of course, of course, Colonel dear," whined Bessy. "Go to bed now—that's a good soul. Don't you fash yourself about gettin' stronger."

But Laddoun looked sharply into the old man's face. "What do you say, Potter? Why, I've gained two pounds in the last month, eh?"

Dick turned away from the pitiful attempt at a smile. "Come to bed, Colonel," soothingly. "You're a man. You oughtn't to be afeard to face the truth. If you owe no man nothin', why need you be afeard?"

Laddoun was silent, staggered to his feet after a while, and suffered old Dick to lead him out of the room; but when he regained his breath, Bessy heard him between his chattering teeth cursing Potter as having linked himself to the rest to drag him into the grave. He went to sleep in good spirits, however, having drunk another bowlful of liquor, telling them he was a hearty young dog, as he would prove before long.

But in the middle of the night he was heard crying feebly for Dick. The two men were closeted together for a long time; and when Potter came out he was very pale and carried a small copper case in his hand, which he stored carefully away. "The Colonel thinks it's nigh over with him," he told his wife, "and he gave me this. In case of his sudden death, I'm to deliver it into Madam Galbraith's own hand. Living or dead, he says he will be square with her grandson. I doubt there's a shameful story between them, too, that don't belong to common day."

CHAPTER XXXIV.

THE winter which followed Dallas Galbraith's marriage seemed to have gathered into itself the rage of many years. Old men in that region tell strange tales even now of its fierce and unprecedented storms—how for weeks together the sun was lost from the heavens, that lowered in a leaden, unbroken plane over the great Valley of the Ohio; how the wind cut a way for its mad fury through the vast forests, gorging the hill-passes that had barred out the besieging storms of a hundred years; how by night and by day it went wailing and shrieking, like some mad, damned soul let loose, through the mountain defiles, over the desolate stretches of snow, the frozen rivers— past the windows of the lonely farm-houses, making the dwellers within shiver and creep closer together, as though some human creature in deadly straits cried to them for help which they dared not give.

For weeks no living being could venture abroad, so deep were the pitfalls beneath the soft, dazzling, treacherous waste. The great Galbraith ruin, colony and wells, was blotted out from the landscape. Nothing was left but the vast volume of snow that threatened to bury once and for all the solemn mountains, petulant rivers and commonplace farm-houses under its calm monotony, gentle and inflexible as death.

As Christmas drew near, however, and the storm abated for a few days, the men in the hills began to creep out and dig paths from one dwelling to the other. There was a sort of hilarious warmth shut into every farm-house. The snow augured well for the crops of next year; and then the poorest log-house in these mountains had its smoke-house filled with pork and onions, its stores of dried fish and fruit. It was good to have a respite from work, to sit down and enjoy their keenest delight in life—well-cooked victuals: the ox-faced men sat knitting blue woollen socks with the women about the kitchen hearths until early dusk, when the fires were slaked, and they went to bed, full of the same sort of happiness as the bears in their burrows yonder.

Colonel Pervis and Mr. Rattlin, with Dour, forced their way up to the Galbraith homestead one day, arriving late in the afternoon, when a threatening tide of cloud, rising from the north, foreboded a fiercer outbreak of the storm. They were powdered with snow, their faces red as blood, and the icicles formed on their beards; but they shouted like school-boys on a frolic when they reached the massive, warmly-lighted pile of buildings half-way up the mountain, and began to thunder at the outer gate. The whole family came out to welcome them. Two weeks had passed since they had had a glimpse of the outer world.

"We fought our way up inch by inch," said Colonel Pervis, as they stopped to breathe and stamp off the snow. "We were determined to bring Dallas the treasures he gathered in New Mexico. The box arrived weeks ago. Gently, Henkel, gently! Mr. Dallas' fame and fortune may lie in that case." He pushed Joe away, and anxiously helped Dallas carry it in.

One would have thought the fame and fortune of the whole party lay in the case, to see the breathless zeal with which they dusted the snow from it and hung over Dallas as he pried off the boards. They lifted it on the great hall table; and the Colonel and his companions, warmed by a visit to the fire and sideboard, crowded up with the others.

Dallas' color went and came as he put the boards on the floor. "All my specimens are here," he said. "There are some I never could replace. I can hardly hope they are not broken."

"Henkel, you can call the people in to look, if you wish," said Madam Galbraith, as though speaking down from a height. "These are things which your young master collected for the instruction of the government, you understand?" The people, not very far off, speedily appeared, open mouthed.

There was a moment of silent suspense. Dallas stopped, with his hand on the first wrapper, and looked about uneasily.

"I am here," said Honora, touching his elbow.

He smiled, drew up a chair for her, and then lifted the wrappers. Mr. Rattlin, who knew no more about the stones or dried plants than if they had been Indian hieroglyphics, came up close, the heart in his spare little body beating hot and fast. It was the faces of the little home group that touched him. The intentness, the awe, the pride with which they looked at Dallas. The breathless anxiety with which they followed every motion of his fingers as he unwrapped each specimen; the buzz of relief when it was found safe; the reverence with which they listened to his explanations. As he laid each one down, his mother and Honora (their sleeves pinned carefully up for fear of breakage) carried them up to another table nearer the fire, holding their breath until they laid them safely down. Mr. Galbraith, his spectacles on and a pile of books before him, was at his elbow, with pencil and paper, noting every word down eagerly.

"I have been studying lately under my son," he said to Mr. Rattlin, by way of explanation. "But I have only mastered the rudiments of his profession, sir. I wish I could have advanced a little farther before this box arrived;" and then back again, with renewed zeal, to the case, to his books, and to Dallas as supreme and final authority.

Madam Galbraith sat stiffly erect in her purple dress, troubling herself very little about the box, but greedily drinking in every word that Dallas spoke—one minute swelling with triumph and pride, then turning sharply to watch if the others were listening—even to Henkel and his troop. It was not enough that her ship had come home to her for ever in this boy: she wanted the whole world to see how fair and good a ship it was, and to envy her the freight it carried.

As for Dallas himself, he must have been a very log if the fond, admiring glances that followed him had not roused him out of his ordinary gravity. Besides, this was his own ground, which he had conquered for himself, of whose wonderful richness they knew nothing. It was not strange that he used forcible, apt words as he talked, or that his whole countenance became transfigured with a magnetic, whole-souled energy which they had never seen in him before, and which kindled his enthusiasm in them all. There were a hundred adventures, too, that the specimens brought to his remembrance, which, when told with all his queer, dry humor, brought down peals of laughter.

Dour watched him with unusual respect. "I never knew the real man before to-day," he said aside to Mr. Rattlin.

Night closed in suddenly, with a low, foreboding sough of the wind through the defiles. "The storm's risin', sir," Henkel said once or twice, under his breath, as he came in to heap the fire with coal, shying carefully back from a dried infant alligator which lay stretched upon the hearth. But nobody heeded the warning. Doors and windows were barred fast: the great boulders of jetty coal broke into miniature volcanoes, spouting jets of flame that rushed up the wide chimney, carrying defiance to the night without. What did the storm matter to them? This mysterious knowledge of Dallas and his former life, of which they had gained but shadowy glimpses, was made real to them to-night, and every one of them felt that they had a share in his glory.

Supper was announced just as they unrolled the last package. "I wish the empty box taken to my room, Henkel," said Honora, whispering to Dallas that it had been made by his own hands, and that she had an odd attraction to anything that belonged to the time when she was not his wife. "I am jealous of the story of every moment of those years," she said, passionately, at which Dallas only laughed, stooping to sweep the paper and dry moss into the box. Some new insight into life, which in the last few weeks had come to him, had done much to blot out his morbid fears. The danger, delayed so long, was almost forgotten: he was a citizen, a man who would be of weight in his State—a husband: these things were real—the shadowy face that threatened him had been but an unhealthy megrim.

Colonel Pervis announced once or twice that the pheasants would be cold. He had been out secretly to watch that they were properly basted. But Dallas and Honora must arrange and label their stones, and alligators, and jointed snakes. Mr. Rattlin brought them coffee, but had to take it back again untouched.

The others sat long over the brilliantly-lighted supper-table. No great gala-night in the old house had ever been so full of triumph as that homely supper, with the toast given in a low voice by the Colonel: "To our boy, who would bring higher honor than wealth to the old stock."

Madam Galbraith replied to it formally, standing. She said that Dallas was a Dour—that the field of physical science was one on which the Dours had never before entered. But wherever they went they won renown. That this night, if she might be allowed to relate a family tradition, reminded her of that on which old Major Peter Dour came home, wearing the sword which Washington had given him on the battle-field for a charge which no other officer would have dared to make. The trophies which her son Dallas had wrested from Nature, through perils as extreme, were as honorable as that sword in her eyes. Though she was an old woman, and must be forgiven if she talked feebly. She was resting heavily on her knuckles. She stopped abruptly here, her swarthy features contorted, and sat down without finishing.

Meanwhile, the wind moaned unheeded over the white plain down in the valley, where the power and wealth of the Dours lay buried, and beat fiercely against the walls of the old house, as with wild warning of worse disaster. At times, when the wail of the storm drowned their voices, and shook the very foundations of the house, which were built upon the solid rock, Madam Galbraith looked around with a complacent, reassuring smile. She knew her walls to be impregnable.

But Honora (who was sadly lacking in the old woman's kind of stamina) felt her heart quake and her teeth chatter with every fresh blast. She looked out of the unshuttered window at the far end of the hall with a great show of courage, and drew back hastily. The Northern Lights flamed up the sky with a red, unnatural glow: black, spectral shapes moved through the driving storm from horizon to horizon — whether mist or avenging spirits who could say? The old trees near at hand waved their branches with shrill moans like ghosts in pain; but the mountains, beaten by the tempest, drew farther back with their secret, which no man has ever known, and wrapped themselves deeper in their eternal, melancholy calm.

Honora had no idea of secrets in storm or mountains. She found herself alone in the wide, dimly-lighted hall; and Dallas, who had gone to his own room to wash the dust from his hands, heard her little feet pattering quickly after him, and laughed to himself.

The chamber was large, cheerful, softly lighted. "I was afraid," she said simply, and knelt down on the rug to wait for him.

When he came to her she got up, standing on tip-toe to gravely adjust his cravat. "You bare your throat like a sailor," she said.

It was a foolish little chance. But years afterward, when the great change had come, and he knew her as a different woman, the little brown figure on tip-toe would seem to stand before him again. The scared face and beautiful eyes close to his—the cold hands seeking this silly pretext to steal about his neck and cling there. Years afterward the picture remained as of one whom he had lost on that night, and who would never return to him again.

They found the whole party gathered in the hall when they came down. Being in the centre of the house, the storm was less audible here than in the outer rooms: "Besides," added the Colonel, "we cannot separate Dallas from his treasures."

It was a great gloomy hall, with a heavy, arched ceiling of unpainted beams, the curtaining shadows of which were scarcely disturbed by even the noonday sun. The walls were hung with branching antlers, lynx and bear skins, Indian quivers and tomahawks—an index to the old histories of the Dours.

They had all made up their minds, however, that it should be cheerful: they dragged in easy-chairs, carried in lamps, heaped up mountains of coal on the fire at the far end; yet, after all, the illumination was but a nebulous glow, that only threw heavier, flickering shadows into the dark cavity behind. But in the perverse, gay humor which had taken possession of them all, they turned their backs on the darkness and storm, and told stories and sang songs—Dallas and Honora together, while the Colonel growled out a bit of bass now and then, and Henkel and the women loitered in the dining-room to listen. When they came to some old Scotch ballads, the whole party joined in the chorus, Mr. Rattlin's shrill treble piping over all. The beat of the sleet and hail and the wail of the wind were so incessant without that they had ceased to notice them, and looked up in surprise when Dallas suddenly grew silent, and, rising, walked uneasily to and fro.

"Does the storm so disturb you, my son?"

"No wonder if it did," said Colonel Pervis, stooping to the hearth to drop some apples he had roasted into a great pitcher of toddy, and anxiously watching them swim in the golden-brown, steaming liquid. "The moan of that northeaster is almost human to-night. I could have sworn a while ago, if it had been possible, that I heard a voice without. I saw by your face, Dallas, that you heard it."

As if to give meaning to his words, a hoarse, inarticulate cry broke into the muttering of the storm, far off and discordant.

"It comes from the northern pass," said Madam Galbraith: "the wind in that gully has a voice like the Banshee, full of incomprehensible pain. No living being could be abroad to-night. Come, Dallas, let us have another song."

"In a moment. Go on without me: Honora will lead you." He went hastily through the dark hall to the window.

Dour looked after him sharply: "Mr. Galbraith's face is ghastly. One would think that he believed in the Banshee, and had heard his own death-note."

"He is like all persons who live close to Nature," Honora rejoined sharply: "his whole system is affected by slight atmospheric changes." She began at once to sing some careless, ringing air, where the voice turned back on itself, as it were, and made a sudden refrain of a clear, triumphant note, dropped before, so contagious that they all caught and echoed it. But her eyes never left her husband.

Dallas glanced back as he heard the joyous catch: a colder, heavier weight came with it to add to whatever dread or pain it was that oppressed him. He paused a moment, then pushed aside the curtain and looked out.

There was the plain of deep snow, sheeted with ice; there was the storm sweeping steadily by, white-winged, moaning for its prey; there were the black, bare forests, bent dumbly before it, and the gigantic shadows of the mountains bracing each other in the far horizon. There was nothing more.

He waited a while, and then, recovering from his stooping posture, stood for a moment curiously erect. He was turning to go back to them when a shadow, in a deep pitfall of snow, which he had thought was a log, moved.

It was no log: it was a broad, powerfully-built man.

His back was toward the house: the hail had blinded, and the faint echo of the song bewildered him. He had fought his way thus far, nigh to death as he was, to sink down at the threshold. There was no cry now—not even a moan: his hands stretched feebly out, and the paralyzed motion of his head, showed that his strength was nearly gone. If it had been Colonel Pervis who saw him, and the man had been his worst enemy, he would have rushed out breathless and carried him in tenderly as a child. But Dallas Galbraith drew the curtain close, that no light should escape, and, with his hands clasped behind him, leaned his forehead against the pane and watched him in his last struggle. He knew, as though he saw them, what bloated features were those under the broad-brimmed hat—what black, flinty eyes.

The song within went on gayly. Without, the sky darkened and sank heavily overhead; but a chance ray from the low, watery moon fell on the black, broad figure that every moment sank deeper, inch by inch, in the snow, and grew more still.

Dallas Galbraith had never been more cool and warily self-possessed than now, when his life hung in the balance of a moment. The thoughts even came to his brain moderate and deliberately. Deepest of all, there was the fact that, end as this might, there was no God— no good. Nothing but the inexorable Something, which all his life had forced him deeper, step by step, into ruin, whenever he had been true to his best self. There was no power outside of himself to whom he could look up.

He pushed back his fair hair, and looked in at the group in the circle of ruddy light about the fire. There was home for him—warm, loving, healthful, until death: there was a man's place among men. His wife's voice at that moment came to him in a pleading little air, which she had sung to him so often that it had grown full of tender, secret meanings to them both. He watched her steadily with his quiet blue eyes, while a clammy sweat broke slowly on his body. He thought he could hear Laddoun's jeering voice telling her that it was upon a felon's breast her head lay last night—that it was a felon's lips which she had kissed with such passion. There were some old words of hers which he had never forgotten: "Though he were dear to me as my own soul, if he were guilty I would put him from me."

There was no way now to disprove his guilt: his long concealment would but make it sure.

He turned from her.

The man's head had fallen heavily on his breast—he had ceased to struggle. It did not need that Dallas should even raise his hand to thrust him back, and be done with the peril and the old foul life for ever. Let him but drop the curtain, and go quietly back to the cheerful fireside.

The night and storm were doing his work for him. The cry would never be heard again. In the morning there would be but a stiff clod of matter—harmless: that could tell no tales.

He waited in silence. The wind had lulled; the snow fell heavily, softly; he could detect but faint resistance in the dark figure, which it strove to bury, flake by flake.

Yet if he drew yonder bolt and let the beacon-light stream through the open door? In another moment Laddoun would be in their midst.

He clasped his hands more tightly behind him, and stood as motionless as a stone; but he closed his eyes: he had no wish to see him die.

Then there was a lightning flash and heat through Dallas' veins—a throb of the sturdy, honest, gallant heart, that had made him what he was. He put his hand out, drew the bolt, and let the flood of red light flash out into the night; and then, after he had seen the man look up, and with a desperate struggle gain his footing, he went quietly back to the fire, and stood among the others, for one brief moment more, their equal and companion.

Let the old hard Luck that had followed him always, that now struggled into life at his door, enter and do its worst.

CHAPTER XXXV.

BEFORE they could speak to him, the fierce blaze of the fire, quickened by the cold entering air, flashed up into a sudden and more powerful brilliance, illuminating the great hall, and chasing before it the sombre shadows that had lurked in corners unseen and unfelt. It threw into strong relief the figure of a man, framed in the massive portal of the door.

So wan and gaunt he was; so strangely unreal, ghostly and pallid; so worn with disease, battered of Fate and abused by the storm through which he had dragged himself, that the questions with which they had greeted Dallas died suddenly into silence; and, as if each one there confronted visible Death in his most spectral shape, they rose in confusion, and stood regarding the ghastly figure of the guest who came to trouble their enjoyment.

The fire shot up into a triumphant gleam—then fell apart in drifts of saffron smoke, and the shadows filled again the heavy arches overhead, pictured themselves upon the walls, and made still more unreal the living shadow which the doorway framed. He came forward, dripping and staggering as he came, until he stood among them, leaning with one hand on the table, while the other, upon whose thin forefinger burned a gaudy purple stone, toyed feebly with the glossy black beard that grew on his lean, colorless face, luxuriant as lichen upon dead wood. Madam Galbraith hastened toward him; but before she could speak he had turned to Dallas, upon whose arm Honora had laid her hand, with no look of fear now, but of a quiet protection for him against an evil of which she already knew the depth and danger.

There was an effort, piteous to see, for the old grace and swagger in Laddoun's sweeping bow. But his smile had lost the mellowness of youth now, and was a hard, stage-grin, and the rotund voice was but a hoarse quaver:

"You do not know me, Dallas?"

"I know you, Laddoun."

"I am not welcome?"

"No, you are not welcome."

They faced each other in silence. Then Laddoun turned his back to them all, with a peculiar choking in his throat which chilled their blood as they heard it: "I saved your life there, in Scranton," he said. "And it's almost up with me now. But no matter! I regret—I did not mean to have intruded, madam." His jaws fell weakly open and his eyes were glazed; but the ringed hand waved with the old suave flourish.

Madam Galbraith, her countenance red with anger, put her hands on his elbows and gently seated him in her own chair. "My son was not bred in my house," she said, her stern eye on Dallas, "or he would know that its doors were never closed upon a man ill and needy, were he my worst enemy."

Laddoun tried to reply, but the words failed him. He pointed dramatically to his deathlike face, made a feeble effort to tear open his thin, soaked coat and waistcoat, and then sank down in a helpless, soggy mass at their feet.

When Dallas stooped to lift him, Honora stood before him, her eyes flashing and her features pinched. "You shall not," she said: "I know who he is. If *I* could bring him to life with one touch of my finger, I would not do it, Dallas."

He put her gently aside, and, with the other men, laid the bulky, inanimate body on a lounge. "It's that poor braggart, Laddoun," muttered Pervis, as he poured out a goblet of the hot liquor. "He was on your trail before, Dallas. What's the grudge between you, eh? If I could get a mouthful of this down his throat, it would bring life to him again."

"He has been lodging at the toll-gate with old Dick Potter," said Mr. Rattlin, tugging at his boots. "He came there late one night, weeks ago, and has been too ill to be removed. He must have been mad to dare the storm to-night."

"He is not mad," said Dallas, quietly. "His errand is to me, and he thought he was near the end. But he will not die until it is accomplished."

The other men worked in silence after that, with furtive, grave glances at the young man's patient, stern face. Something in it, more terrible than death, awed them, and made them wish that the morning had come.

The man was so emaciated and so exhausted by his long fight with the storm that they thought it best not to remove him to another room. Madam Galbraith herself made a bed upon the lounge, while Dallas, helped by the others, stripped off his wet garments and wrapped him in blankets. Honora alone was idle. She was, like all women, tender enough by instinct. But when their prejudices are roused, they are, unlike men, pitiless as death. She watched the poor wretch struggling for breath, and Dallas' resolute efforts to help him, as though she had been a bar of steel.

Then she went to the window and stood there, where she could not look at him.

He did not revive as they had hoped. The long, dark hours crept by: the storm without had grown silent; there was a vague consciousness upon them all that it had done its worst when it drove this poor, human wreck to their door, to work out what evil yet lay in him before the end. But as the night deepened, and he yet lay unconscious, the firelight flickering upon the livid face and glossy beard, they began to move with more hushed footsteps, to watch uneasily from time to time for the first gray hint of dawn. The awe of that inevitable Shadow which waited to claim them all had fallen upon them: conscious that it stood now in their midst, and that its victim did not know that the call for him had come.

It seemed best to them that his last hours should be quiet: they sat around the fire, therefore, gravely silent or speaking only in whispers. But Dallas worked with him unwearied—at first to drive out by force the remembrance of the murder that had been in his heart. But when he felt the hands and feet grow cold under his hold, and saw the gray, unmistakable shadow steal over the face, the memory of these later years was blotted out. He was the boy Dallas again. For how many years this man had been his open-handed friend, his hearty companion!

"George!" he called once, when he thought the eyes moved. "George!" But the silence of the grave mocked him, and after that he did not speak again.

When the sickly light of the first dawn glimmered through the window and struck the roof, however, Laddoun's torpor was broken: he stirred and opened his small, black eyes, and after staring dully around, they rested on Dallas.

"My errand was to you," he said.

Madam Galbraith moistened his parched lips, and they lifted him up to a sitting posture, and then drew back and left Dallas alone before him. Laddoun began to speak, but pausing, motioned to a bottle of brandy on the table. Dallas poured out a glassful for him.

"Hah!" wiping his lips, "that has body to it. I'm not as strong as I should like to be, madam," to Mrs. Duffield, slowly, as though the words were drawn from a well that was nearly dry. "I need bracing. If I had seen you, I should have certainly drunk my—my old toast—Lovely woman. George Laddoun has been a gallant man in his day— devoted to the ladies."

Mrs. Duffield bowed and drew farther back, very pale.

The black, shining eye, missing her, wandered restlessly, and fixed itself on Mr. Galbraith.

The well was nearly dry now, but the old ceaseless rattle and jingle went on. "It is the walk, sir, that made me require a stimulant. The fatigue was severe. But I am rewarded by the honor of your acquaintance. It is an honor— long-deferred. My business was with your son—"

"We will leave you, Dallas," Mr. Galbraith said to him aside, hastily. "We can do nothing for him, and it is more fitting that you should hear the last words of this man alone."

Laddoun's jealous eye was on them, reading Mr. Galbraith's words by the motion of his lips: he raised his hand authoritatively.

Dallas detained them by a sign: "Let no one go out. The secret has been kept too long," he said. "If the end is to come, let it be now." He gave one quick look around for Honora, but she stood still motionless by the window, her back toward them. He took a glass of water and drank it slowly, and then, leaning with one arm upon the mantel-shelf, looked down at Laddoun.

The slow, patient years of endurance and toil were over, and the sum of it all was placed in the hands of this half-drunken, dying wretch, to make or mar for ever, at his pleasure.

God's justice!

Laddoun, with the blanket gathered about his throat, nodded critically as he inspected Dallas. "A pale, dramatic face, and lights up well with passion!" he would have said, but his breath was gone. He was considering the scene with regard to its stage effect. He had often planned it, but not so well as chance had done. He looked up at the wan glimmer of dawn on the high, dusky arches, at the woman's figure by the window, at the silent group in the glow of firelight, at Dallas; then with a smile of content stroked his jetty beard, and glanced down at it. Then he sipped the brandy slowly, and so gathered, as it were, and nursed his strength.

"Will I fill your glass?" asked Colonel Pervis.

He looked into the goblet doubtfully: there were but a few drops left. "No more, sir. Do you know I believe that will be the last drink for George Laddoun? And he's been a jolly dog!" with a sorrowful quaver. "No—no more. Dallas!"

"I am here, Laddoun."

"Dallas!" he said, struggling to sit erect and to form his words after some coherent plan long in his mind. "There are some men who go out of this world with their accounts unsquared. But it seems to me that life should end like a play. When this cursed fever got the better of me in Panama, I determined that it shouldn't cut off George Laddoun's life as commonplace and meaningless as a dog's. I've been trying all my life to write a play, but the managers wouldn't take it. This is a better play than any I could write; it brings us all in—all of us. Why are your faces all so cursed white? Do you think that old Death has come to drop the curtain now? Death and justice at the end! Yes! it's like a play. Like a play!"

They saw that the man's mind had wandered away into incoherency, and that he had lost the thread upon which he began.

Dallas stooped and touched his forehead: "Do you know me, George?"

"Yes, Dall, I know you. Will you give me the brandy again?"

"It is in your hand."

A weak smile trembled on his lips as he slowly sipped it, measuring the amount with a melancholy shake of the head. "It's the last—the wine of life for me, sir!" to Colonel Pervis; "and it runs low," looking at it in silence, as if he told off by the remaining drops the minutes of his life. It seemed as if by this tawdry, dramatic symbol alone the narrow space of sight and sound which barred the man from the eternal Silence beyond was made real to him. He turned to Dallas at last, still holding the goblet in his hand.

"For you, Galbraith," with a sudden, loud energy. "I came here from Panama to fulfill my purpose for you. McGill told there that I had grown insane in brooding over it. Curse him! Who's Joe McGill, to judge a gentleman? I mean before I die to take the mask off that you've worn—to show you as you are to your friends and your wife. It's proper work for George Laddoun. The Dours are a genteel, high family."

"The man speaks with great good sense, though his meaning is obscure," said Madam Galbraith, aside.

Mr. Rattlin suddenly came before them all, and put his hands on Laddoun's shoulders. His natural solemn voice jarred strangely against the incessant cracked hectoring of the other. "My friend, in God's name be silent! Dallas Galbraith is known to us all. Nothing you can say will harm him here. But, for yourself, Colonel Laddoun, the time is short."

He blenched for a moment: "Well, my little man, I know that," rallying with a good-natured, miserable laugh. "I'll be found game when the time comes. Don't chouse me out of my plan. I've known this man as you never knew him. He would have turned me out to-night to die like a beast. Yet I took him out of the coal-pits. I clothed and fed him! For years he had no friend but me," with a sort of hysterical sob.

"Is this true, Dallas?" Madam Galbraith touched him on the breast as she spoke.

"It is true."

The sudden flash of strength gone, Laddoun had sunk back in a heap as though he were disjointed, covering his face with one hand. Dallas went up to him and took it down, holding it in his own: "George, the play's almost over, as you said. Is it worth while to ask you to be just? In an hour it will be too late. I've borne this weight many years without complaining; but—" he grew so hoarse as to be almost inaudible—"the truth will matter something to me now."

"You've no proof of your innocence," a flash of cunning in the black eyes.

"No. I have no proof." He looked slowly around upon their faces, resting on his wife at last. "I don't try to move you, Laddoun, but you are taking something from me to-night which will never come to me again." Some hidden meaning in the quiet, moderate words made their hearts stand still, as though they heard the cry of a soul for its life to God.

Laddoun looked up, and the eyes of the two men met. The sickly morning light glimmered down the walls, touched the strange birds and beetles into brilliant hues, and dimmed the red flame of the fire, but the silence was unbroken.

Then Laddoun wiped his mouth with the back of his hand, his eyes wandering guiltily. "What would you have me do?" querulously. "Damn myself? Here—now? I will leave the world an honorable man. As I've lived."

Dallas went back to his own place without a word. "It was the last chance," he muttered after a while, and stood alone, apart from them all, looking at no one.

Laddoun lifted the brandy and tremblingly wet his lips. "I have more to tell," he said, loudly.

But Dallas' hand was already pressed to a warm, steady little breast, and a woman's voice filled the silence, rational and quiet: "Why should you say more, Colonel Laddoun? Did you drag yourself here, a dying man, only to tell us that Dallas Galbraith was ignorant, poor—was for years a convict in Albany? Is that all? Is that the whole of your poor revenge?"

"Honora?" Dallas dragged his wife round until she faced him. It was no longer the silly, petulant, lovable girl whom he saw. She was gone, and never after this night returned. It was a woman, beautiful, with noble patience, that met his gaze, her great brown eyes brilliant as with new life. She caught his coat with both hands, and spoke to him. Alone. Laddoun was forgotten.

"I know it, Dallas. I have known it a long time. I have so loved and trusted you that I never asked you whether you were innocent or guilty. What did that matter to me? I know you as you are now, my husband!"

She would have kissed him, but he did not move to kiss her: he stood breathing heavily and staring blindly down into her face, parting the hair on her forehead mechanically. Looking into his eyes, she had a glimpse, for the first time, into the soul of this log of a man whom she had married. She knew something then of the pain he had borne there, the awful tenderness and patience which lay hidden there, never to see the light. She saw there, too, the strength she had brought to him. It was well she had that comfort, for he spoke no word of it to her.

He looked up at last. "He is dying, Honora," he said, and putting her aside, went toward him.

He was dying. He lay back on the blankets, the hand fallen by his side which held the goblet, the brandy dropping slowly on the floor. Mr. Galbraith was gone, but the other men were busy about him. Dallas felt rather than saw the constraint and cold civility with which, as by one impulse, they moved aside to let him pass.

Madam Galbraith was on her knees before Laddoun, with no gentle purpose of ministering to him, but intent on dragging by force the secret from his miserable soul ere it took its flight. Her gray hair and proud face, that spoke in that moment, as never before, the clean blood of generations, were brought close to his foul breath as he whispered huskily.

"I cannot hear you," her black eyes flashing savagely. "Give the man a stimulant. Is that the tale you came to tell, that my son was a felon?"

Laddoun nodded, and tried to pull the blankets over his shivering feet.

"I must have the whole truth," making no effort to assist him.

He began to speak, and, making but an inarticulate sound, pointed apologetically to his throat, trying to smile courteously. With the Shadow that waited behind him, its blindness and chill upon his eyes and lips, Laddoun could not forget that this was a great lady—a woman who led society—who spoke to him.

Madam Galbraith rose and looked down on him, fierce and hungry as a balked bird of prey. Mr. Rattlin would have put her aside: "He is near death, madam. Let me pray with him."

"What Popish folly is that? Do you think a life like his is to be glossed over by a twinge of fear at the end? What is the soul of a wretch like that compared to the honor of my family, that is at stake?"

Mrs. Duffield stood before her. "My son Dallas," she said, in a hard, metallic tone, "will tell you that this story, which Honora has accepted so readily, is false—false. You will not refuse to credit him?"

"Why should I credit him?" in a voice which, from its low key and concentration of bitterness, was audible through the whole apartment. "The time has passed for Dallas Galbraith to speak. He has stolen his place and his wife. It is too late!"

Dallas, who heeded her words no more than a stone the wind that blew against it, had lifted Laddoun into an easier posture, and, in obedience to his signs, was loosening the gaudy, red cravat and wetting his lips, ceasing when he found that he shut his eyes drowsily, as though for a quiet slumber.

But Madam Galbraith stooped nearer to the closing eyes, pale as though Death had touched her also. "The truth before you go!" she cried.

The soul seemed to come back to the graying, rigid features, and linger in obedience to the imperious summons: "I—I came back from Panama to tell you. But I lost the cue to-night somehow. It was better than any play I wrote. But I never could finish my last act successfully. Take this lump off my breast, Dallas. It's cold."

The Shadow was so near, its inexorable hand so open and visible now upon its prisoner, that even the fierce old woman drew back awed and dumb.

Laddoun's eyes rested by chance on Dallas, and brightened into a look strangely foreign to them—both genuine and cordial. The boy's nature, asleep so long, wakens again, according to the old superstition, and looks through the most hackneyed, vilest face at the last, when Death comes to bare all secrets.

"I've been a good friend to you, Dall. I'll—I'll drink with you." He lifted the glass which, according to his fancy, held the last wine of his life, with an effort to his mouth, but the last drop had dripped, untasted, on the floor. He looked at it. "Spilled, eh? And now—for my secret!" But the weight was too heavy on his breast, that never should be lifted: the last act would never be finished: he turned his head to one side. "No matter! You know—down there at Manasquan, Laddoun was—was a jolly dog."

The morning light shone in blankly. They waited a moment, but the soiled linen and ruby buttons on his breast did not stir. Mr. Rattlin bent over him and took the glass from his hand; and, if, as he closed the black eyes, still with the pleasant smile in them, he followed the soul of the jolly dog with a prayer upon its for-ever silent journey, who can blame him?

CHAPTER XXXVI.

THE softest morning light is melancholy when it falls into a room disordered with last night's work or pleasure. But it was a cold, unflinching day that suddenly bared the great hall at whose end the little group were huddled. They had suffered the fire to go out, and the hearth was strewn with blackened cinders and soot: plants and ores, the poor trophies of Dallas' life, were scattered underfoot—their previous proud significance gone from them for ever: the dead man lay in their midst, stiff, on his untidy blankets.

They left him neglected for the time, watching the living figure which had for them a sadder significance—the gaunt, gray old woman, who stood on the ashes of the hearth upon which for the first time had fallen dishonor. Even Dallas, forgetting himself, looked at her with pity. But Honora, though sick to death at heart, began to pick up the scattered plants with proud composure, as if she could show by that means that her husband was the same to her. She chose to ignore altogether the dead man and the blow he had struck.

Mr. Galbraith came in, nervously turning his head from the body on the lounge, going up to his wife, who stood beside it. She did not move when he spoke to her. She held her hand on her whitening, bearded upper lip, and drew heavy sighs, as a man does who struggles to control some cleaving pain within. There was an ominous silence, which no one dared to break. At last Mr. Galbraith's mild voice was heard:

"I was a coward to desert you, my dear boy. But I knew what this man came to tell. I have known it a long time. I could not see you degraded on my own hearth. I do not know how much was told to-night. But I am sure, Dallas," trying to speak cheerfully, "that you can make it all plain to us now?"

Madam Galbraith did not raise her eyes, but she waited motionless, holding her breath. Honora stood quietly listening. But Dallas was silent.

"You believed in his innocence?" said Mr. Rattlin, anxiously. "You had, doubtless, proof of it, sir?"

"No! I have but his word. That is enough for me."

"It is not enough for me," said Madam Galbraith, in a hoarse thunder. "Poverty and death find lodging under this roof—I cannot keep them out. But crime—never!"

Colonel Pervis stepped forward to Dallas with a forced heartiness and cordiality, more galling than open suspicion: "It will all come right," clapping him on the shoulder. "Many a man is sent unjustly to those Eastern prisons by the cursed blockheads of jurymen. Dallas has proof that he was unjustly sentenced, no doubt."

But Dallas stood, bigger, more immovable, more dumb than ever. The light fell directly upon him, and the wind from the open window blew the fair hair back from his broad forehead, his blue eyes turned gravely from one speaker to the other. But with the first sound of Madam Galbraith's bitter voice, her own fierce obstinacy rose to meet her in his cooler blood. His lips were sealed.

His mother came up and shook his arm violently: "Speak to them, Dallas!"

He stooped and kissed her dry lips, and held her with one arm close to his breast. When he looked up he found they all stood waiting. Even Madam Galbraith had come forward a step, her eyes upon him.

He turned from them to his own mother's. "I have nothing to say," he replied, in a clear, quiet voice. "The only proof of my innocence was with the man who lies dead there. I shall find no fault with him now. He *is* dead. I have no proof. I ask no man to trust my word."

The stern old woman was for a moment stunned and breathless. If he had succumbed to her, if he had but once acknowledged her as either judge or mother, the heart of her within might have spoken through the flinty pride. But she looked into his cold eyes and obdurate face, her own growing each instant more wan and hard. At last she raised her hands and motioned him back: "Let him go, James. He has deceived me once. I do not trust his word. When he can prove his innocence he will find home ready for him."

Then she sat down by Laddoun and covered her head with her hands, more cowed, more defeated in her life than he in his death.

The next moment Dallas stood without the door, a little brown figure close beside him. Mr. Galbraith had followed him: he was the paler of the two. He chafed his thin, long hands unceasingly together: "You shall not leave my roof, dear boy! This is your home!" repeating the words again and again, until they lost all force.

But Dallas answered loudly, his eyes unnaturally bright: "No, it is not my home! What! are you here still, Honora? Go back! You are no wife of mine. It was not a felon that you married!"

"We are going together, Dallas," quietly.

"I have no home for you. I am branded like Cain. I know what my ruin is, now that I have brought it on you!"

"We will make a home. Come, let us make ready and be gone."

Mr. Galbraith stood apart, looking dully at her, leaning against the stone wall of the house, unconscious of the fierce wind that blew his gray hair back. "Honora!" he said, feebly, "my child, will you leave me?"

"When Dallas can prove his innocence we will both come back," she said cheerfully. "That will be in a little while! Only a little while, uncle!" smiling, as she gulped down her tears.

But her hopeful voice roused no echo in either of the men, who had fought against Circumstance longer than she.

"You are very right to go with your

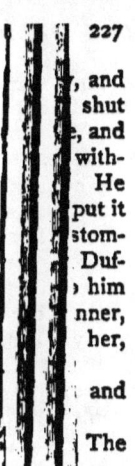

"Follow Laddoun. I will trace him back and find the proof. I am Dallas' mother. I'll not tire."

Her head fell forward. The Colonel caught her as she sank down, her flesh very cold, and the heart quite still within.

He rang the bell: "Take Mrs. Duffield to bed," when the women came. "'She'll not be apt to leave it for some time," he muttered to himself. "'My son is innocent,' eh? God help the women! How they do hang on to the last!" and he resumed his miserable lounge through the room.

Honora and her husband were left a long time alone. When they were almost ready to go, there was a tap at the door, and Mr. Rattlin came in. His insignificant little face was like a cordial to starving men. It broke down that iron-faced little Honora, who, after the first glance at it, began to cry quietly over the valise she was packing.

"Well, children, I have the sleigh. Are you ready? We will just reach the farm in time for lunch, and then we can talk over our plans."

"We are not going home with you, dear Mr. Rattlin. We will not bring our disgrace to *you!*" sobbing out loud now.

But Dallas had risen and held out his hand: "You think me innocent, then, sir?"

"I know it, Galbraith! Our religion is not that of our Master if it does not teach us to have faith in each other as well as in God. I know you are innocent."

"Does your religion teach you that justice always comes in this world?"

He hesitated, and shook his head: "We will not talk of that. Your mother is ill. It is best for you not to see her. You will come home with me?"

"No."

"Have you any plan? I will not urge you. Do what will give yourselves most comfort."

When they did not answer him, he walked away to the window to give them time. "I will go to my work," Dallas said at last. "Something can be done, even before spring. Unless I lose the appointment when this discovery is made known."

"I have a letter here which I neglected to give you last night." He laid it on the table and went out hurriedly, fearful that even his kindness would be jarring and intrusive.

"Honora," said Dallas, as she folded her little keepsakes; "how did you know—that—"

She blushed crimson, and did not reply for a moment: "I remembered—the convict that Lizzy brought here."

Dallas was silent. Then he took her head between his hands and turned it toward him as she knelt on the floor. "If you had known it before we were married, Honora?"

She looked at him steadily with both a laugh and tears in her eyes. "I remembered the convict that Lizzy brought—long ago."

"And you married me?"

"I loved you, dear," burying her head in his breast.

It was only when they rose to go out that Dallas remembered the letter. It was square and large, with the postmark *Manasquan* scrawled in one corner. He opened it, and found on the thick sheet of paper within only these words, in a formal hand:

"TO DALLAS GALBRAITH:

"SIR: Elizabeth Byrne desires that you will come to her without delay. Of her claim on you, you are the best judge. Her need of you is a matter of life and death.   JOSEPH KIMBALL."

"Who is Joseph Kimball, Dallas?" touching him when he stood silent.

"A good old man, Honora. A friend of mine before I lost friends."

"Lizzy is ill or in great trouble. We will go to her."

"Yes." But he stood folding the letter slowly, a deeper shadow on his face. The world outside to Dallas was blatant with his shame. He was going out to meet it. But it gave him a keener pang than any he had borne to think of carrying back his old weight of disgrace to the simple people to whom his perverse affection yet clung. He roused himself in a moment. "We will go to Manasquan," he said. "I know what Lizzy's claims upon me are."

Honora saw that the halls and chambers were curiously vacant when they passed out. The very servants avoided them. Her uncle stood at the doorway to bid them good-bye. He held Dallas' hand and tried to speak, but the words died on his tongue. Mr. Rattlin ran alongside of the sleigh as it dragged heavily along, talking fast and cheerfully, until he sank hip-deep in snow. Then he stood watching them, waving his hat, his little face red and his eyes wet.

So they went out, quite alone, into the waste of snow.

The gray-headed old gentleman watched the black spot creeping out of sight across the white plain. If he had been a less unable, unready man, he thought vainly, he might have commanded their fate to a different ending.

Mr. Rattlin, who had joined him, sighed when they were no longer to be seen.

"Justice will come at last," he said.

"It may be. Yet Justice is slow. I fear that I shall never see my son again."

CHAPTER XXXVII.

SOLITUDE: every hour deeper solitude and silence. It seemed to Honora that the mountains of the West and her old home-life belonged to another and distant world. She could not tell how long she had been sitting, packed in buffalo skins, in this rough, queer sled, gliding noiselessly over the snow, with Dallas, silent, at her side, and the silent driver in front. The loneliness and unbroken monotony began to weigh upon her brain. This might be the entrance into Hades. Were they to go down for ever into these dead plains of snow, with the dead plains of sand beneath—into these unbroken, spectral forests of stunted and distorted trees, that even in daylight stretched out their black arms like the skeletons of mocking dwarfs, but in the cold moonlight grew almost human in their deformity and despairing motion? The very sky overhead was new to her—of thin, wet texture, kindling at sunset into shifting hues of such strange brilliancy that she fancied they curtained from her some untried world, into which she was about to enter.

Honora had traveled but little: she had borne lately great but repressed suffering; she grew superstitious, watchful of trifles. Her watch had stopped: when she wished to know the time the driver turned his back to the watery sun and measured his shadow on the snow. Every hour she saw they left the world of society and inventions farther behind, going down into this place where Nature lay with bared and awful face. She knew by instinct that some stupendous reality was hidden yonder. Its shadow fell everywhere. The driver, the few charcoal-burners whose lonely huts they passed, were stolid and ignorant, but men strangely grave and sincere.

She began to perceive a wonderful freshness and lightness in the air. The earth beneath her throbbed with a slow, dreadful pulse, and then she heard an inarticulate wail, the like of which had never chilled or dissatisfied her life before.

At last they crept down to the beach, and she saw the sea. Then she understood that the loneliness and monotony which had oppressed her was but the spell cast upon the land by this solitary creature, whose cry of pain began with the song which the morning stars sang together.

All day they skirted the coast: she said nothing to Dallas, but she could not remove her eyes from the inexplicable, sombre, perpetual motion, which seemed to her counter and alien to the order of the world. If she had ever secretly called God unjust, this thing made the thought audible for her. It was the outcry of the world's misery against the Hand that ruled it. There was in it something which the doctrine of fatalism that she had found in her Thirty-nine Articles could not answer.

Dallas, after the sun had passed noon, noticed how haggard and careworn she was, watching the sea; but he had no way to comfort her. He knew it was his ill-fortune that had brought ruin on her. He got out of the sled, and went before it, through the marshes and up into the towering pine forests. They were near Manasquan now.

He walked slowly, not to lose sight of Honora's face, looking out from the furs. It was beginning to have that galled yet obdurate look which he found on his own. It was very bitter to Dallas to see it. For himself, he had bent his broad back to the yoke long ago. The Power that drove him down, down continually, was stronger than he, but he was too strong to fret and jibe against it. Yet there was a malignant humor in this implacable Fate, which had set before him always the choice, and when he clung to the right had paid him with heavier strokes. Even this simple duty of coming to Lizzy was to bring on himself the bitterest pain of all.

For he knew now what this fishing village and its people were to him. There was not a headland, nor tree, nor osprey's nest which he did not remember. There were only a few miles yet to walk before they reached the village. In that time his bitterness wore away under the recognition of the old sights and sounds. There was no change in them to break the old boyish glamour with which he saw them. He came alongside of the sled now and then to speak a few words and then hurry on; and Honora saw a curious change in him: his step was elastic; he laughed at times nervously; he had forgotten, for the first time since she knew him, his grave control. She knew that great, live pain and the remembrance of singular happiness lay beneath his simple, abrupt talk.

"I have found my name on four trees," with a laugh. "I was fond of seeing it then in big, bold letters. There are places were it has been scraped away—*where it was cut with others.*"

She laid her hand on his, but did not speak.

Again, after a longer absence, he came back and walked beside her, silent for a long time, though she looked at him once or twice inquiringly.

"You can see the smoke of one or two of the village houses from here, off by the headland yonder. It is not a village, only scattered farm-houses and fishermen's huts."

She was not to be put aside by his assumed carelessness. Something in the woods yonder, she knew, had wrung the heart terribly of the simple, dogged fellow.

"What did you see, Dallas?" she said, under her breath.

He glanced down at her quickly: "A little hut I used to live in. I went to find it. I built it myself."

"Some one else has occupied it?"

"No. It is vacant. No one else would care to live in it. They are a superstitious people here." He stopped, but Honora was waiting.

"*What* was it, Dallas?"

"It is better that you should know it. I found the walls scrawled over with my name, and a word added. Always the same word. The boys of the village had done it. I know now of what crime I am held guilty here." She took his hand in both her own, holding it a long time before he spoke again. "The man in whose name Laddoun's cheque was drawn was old and lived alone. He was found robbed and dead soon after. Before Laddoun and I had left the city."

"And these people believe you guilty? They wrote murderer after your name on the walls? They will call it after you when you go among them?" She looked slowly over the distant houses as she spoke. If the look of the quiet, little gentlewoman could have swept Manasquan and its people into death, she would not have spared it.

"Perhaps they will do it. It would be but natural," in his moderate, just tone. "My story has passed into the legends of the village, and the boys have exaggerated it. It was they who wrote my name there. The boys!" He turned his head away with the word. She understood. It was here, in Manasquan, that he himself had been young.

All the healthy, happy associations of his life were with the boys here. They wrote him murderer on their walls: the little children were frightened to sleep with his name.

She held her shut hand tight across her breast: "Shall we go on, Dallas?"

"Yes. It is right to go. Even this will have an end."

She ventured after a while to touch the flap of his overcoat as he walked beside her, holding her hand up toward the rigid, pale face, shadowed by the planter's hat. "I am here, Dallas. You are not alone."

"I know," quickly, smiling down at her. But the smile was soon gone and she forgotten. The wife could not atone for the man's place and good name, lost for ever. He remained silent after that, keeping beside her, his hand on the edge of the sled. They passed some of his old haunts, but he did not even turn his head toward them.

It was a veiled, gray afternoon, a west wind edging the great violet flood of the sea with yellow foam. Dallas, with every step, felt the familiar scene press closer upon his pained senses. There was an unwonted silence: the very surf beat softly on the sand; the fishermen's boats, pulled above high-tide mark, were unridden by the usual red-shirted loungers; doors and windows were closed in the farm-houses that they passed. There was old Doctor Noanes' red cottage back in the pines—still the great place of the village; and there were Jim Van Zeldt's roomy porches about his lead-colored house, the pillars shaped like anchors. But they were all deserted and empty. When they reached Nixon's low, little tavern by the roadside, Dallas looked quickly to see the old group, Graah and Becker, and the rest, sitting nursing their knees and smoking as usual; but even the little bar within was vacant—the fire covered, and the cat asleep before it.

They were avoiding him purposely: they meant to let him come and go without seeing a single old familiar face. He thought that he had steeled himself thoroughly, but this wrenched him to the heart. He turned to the driver (who was a stranger to him, not a Manasquan man): "Did they know I was coming here to-day? My name is Galbraith."

The fellow nodded with a furtive glance, and turned his tobacco in his mouth: "Dallas Galbraith? They know you be coming. They got your letter. I was to meet you."

Dallas drew back. "There is the house to which I am going," he said. "You can see Elizabeth's place through the trees," to Honora, with an effort at his usual composed tone. She should not see how little of a man he was—that his old friends had yet power to wring his heart so sorely. But the driver, with sudden energy, drove past the opening to the Byrne place, and drew up his sled in front of a low pine house in the very midst of the woods.

"It was here I was bid to stop. You be expected, as I told you."

It was the house in which they had confined and tried him—he saw that at a glance: saw, too, that the room inside was filled, as then, with the villagers. There was a crowd of brawny fishermen upon the steps, who, the moment the sled stopped, closed around him. He knew them all—the young Graahs, the old man himself, Calcroft the clam-digger, all the others of the seining gang —at their head, Cradock the sheriff. Their red faces all wore a certain air of excitement and expectation, but they did not recognize him by a word or look. They began to lift the buffalo-robes from about Honora civilly enough.

"Be keerful of the lady, William," muttered old Graah.

Dallas looked keenly into the crowded little hall. There was not a silent, anxious face there which he did not know. Behind his wooden desk sat Squire Boles, as he had done on that old night long ago when Dallas had lost the chance among men which had never come to him again. Back of the old Squire stood Father Kimball, and on the other side the detective Bunsen.

A nameless, undefined fear came to Dallas at the sight of this man. He turned quickly: "Stay here, Honora. I will go in and know why I have been summoned here. These men," looking steadily into old Graah's face, "are not my friends, but they will care for my wife kindly."

Graah's heavy face began to work for a word, but before it came Honora had slipped down beside her husband: "I will go with you, Dallas."

They went up the wooden steps together, the men following close and silently. At the door Dallas stopped and turned to Honora, with a sudden perception of the truth. Bunsen had contrived to fasten the murder upon him, and had entrapped him here by means of these old fishermen. Even in that moment his first thought was for his wife. Before he could speak, Cradock stooped and whispered to her, and with a wild, terrified look at Dallas, she drew back from him into the crowd, and left him standing alone.

The instant her touch left his arm the man's combative instinct started up and fully armed him. He was no longer the boy to yield without a struggle. He went forward quietly to the very place by the window where he had stood before to be judged.

The old Squire stood up, his rusty wig pushed from his forehead, fumbling at the leaves of a yellow register. The crowd closed behind Dallas. There was a breathless silence.

"Dallas, Dallas Galbraith!" in the shrill voice of a crier in court.

"I am here."

"We have waited for you." He wiped his wrinkled lips as if they were dry, and began in a strained, formal tone: "It is six years since you were heard before me on a criminal charge, and, being found guilty, were committed to the charge of this officer. Six years! I think it is six"—beginning to turn over the leaves with trembling fingers.

The long pause of waiting was too much for Dallas' fortitude; he bent forward, his head on his breast, his hands clutched on the bench in front of him; he turned to look for Honora, but red blotches swam in the air before him. The crowd about him pressed closer; they brooked delay with less patience than he; there was a rising, indignant murmur—a woman's voice outside, in a smothered cry.

The old man's hands trembled still more—the book fell from them. "I—I cannot do this," he cried. "Father Kimball, it is your place to tell Dallas Galbraith why we have brought him among us again." The old preacher, whose shrewd gray eye had never wandered from Dallas' face, left his post hastily, and came toward him, Bunsen keeping step close behind him. He laid his hand on Galbraith's shoulder:

"My friends and neighbors," he said, in a low, husky voice, "you all know why we have come here to-day? It is to say to this boy, who once went in and out of our homes, and was very dear to us all, that we have proof now that he was innocent of the great crime laid to his charge; that we have done him a great and grievous wrong; that there is not one of us now who, when his own boy comes to manhood, would not be glad to find him as stern in his integrity and as loyal to his fellow-men as Dallas Galbraith." He choked and broke down here—wrung Dallas' hand. "Thank God I see you at home again, dear boy!" he muttered, and drew back to give way to the crowd who pressed behind.

But when they saw Dallas' face, they stood still, awed and silent. They had not guessed before how deep the hurt had been to the gruff, reserved boy, nor what these few words had brought to him. His wife came up before them all, and laid her head on his breast, and Lizzy caught his hand and sobbed over it. But Honora did not sob or cry.

"They have been talking to me of you, Dallas," she whispered, watching him anxiously. "There never were friends such as these of yours at Manasquan."

The simple words made it real to him. He looked about at them a moment in silence, and then the past miserable years seemed to fall from him at once like a worn-out garment. It was the old, simple face of the boy Dallas that looked up at Squire Boles, and his hearty voice that rung out like old times:

"Do you mean that my innocence is *proved?* Stand back, Jim Van Zeldt—you too, Tim Graah. I know you both. But I'll take no man's hand until I know I am proved to be honest." But he kept his hand on little Jim Van Zeldt's shoulder, and there was not one of them all that his blue eyes did not take note of and welcome as he waited for Boles' slow reply—the same eyes which the children used to love, sparkling and cordial.

"We have better testimony for your acquittal than we had of your guilt," he began, with a formal cough.

But Doctor Noanes pressed forward: "Let Bunsen speak, Boles, and set this matter right. He has the gift of the lawyers' lingo, and all we know is, that we are cursedly ashamed of ourselves, and want to welcome this old fellow to his place among us again."

"You are quite right, Mr. Galbraith," Bunsen began, quite fluently, being primed and ready. "A convict is not to be proved innocent, as he has been found guilty, by a show of circumstantial evidence. But in your case there is the fullest proof, I am glad to say. I have here"—taking out a large letter, the envelope of which bore a great blot of wax, sealed with a crest—"I have here the declaration of George Laddoun, made and sworn to in Panama, during his illness there some months ago, in the fear, I imagine, of immediate death. You can read it at your leisure. It is full and complete, even to the story of the letter you destroyed for Lizzy's sake, which contained the proof against him. He remarks," with a twitch in his fat, unexpressive face, "that he had always tried to instill into you true chivalric and gentlemanly ideas, and that your conduct about that letter showed that his efforts had not failed in effect." Bunsen handed the letter to Dallas, who folded it and held it in his hand.

"You'll not read it now, eh? Some people have that feeling about them as is lately dead. You'll find it characteristic. There's a lot of fine writing and swagger in it; but as for remorse, not a bit of it. He had made a lucky stroke this year in a silver mine, with a man named McGill. He says he leaves his whole property to you. He meant, also, to make his way North if he was strong enough, and let the closing act of his life—the grand finale—be one of reparation to you. 'Dall,' he says, 'is among well-bred people. They will appreciate a heroism of which few men beside George Laddoun would be capable.' But," with a graver tone, "the fellow was sincere at bottom; for, lest he should never live to reach you, he directed this paper to be forwarded, when he left Panama, to Mr. Kimball. That is the story. Except," with a bow, "that our friends here sent for me, anxious to wipe away every stain upon your name, and that, if you will entrust me with the declaration, I will lay it before the Governor of New York, and see that you are cleared from all dishonor and restored to your privileges as a citizen." Bunsen, having finished his speech, held out his hand to Dallas.

But what was he to do with all their hands? This outbreak of excitement had been pent up for weeks, and when the barrier of reserve was once broken down between these silent, grave people and the silent, grave lad who had secretly been their hero so long, who was going to control the fever?

Not Squire Boles, who, after trying to overlook the crowd with a judicially pleased demeanor, scrambled down from his high stool and made one in the tide that ebbed and swelled about Dallas, getting near enough now and then to exchange a hearty word with "the lad," and then finding himself drifted out to the outskirts again, seizing on Nixon or Cradock, adjusting his wig and assuring them that he never had known so memorable a day in Manasquan, and that the circumstances deserved to be chronicled in some permanent manner for the benefit of our children.

Not the New York detective, for, after he had smiled patronizingly on them once or twice, he strolled down to the deserted tavern and helped himself freely to apple-jack. They all breathed freer when he was gone.

After all, Dallas was more akin by nature to these fishermen than to anybody else in the world, and through all the tumult of jokes and tears and questions with which they welcomed him back, there was silently among them a deep and tender recognition of this. He and his wife quite belonged to themselves, in spite of Honora's delicate bearing and the renown which Dallas had won in the world; of which renown Lizzy had given them a picture, not lacking in high colors we may be very sure. They were proud of the one and of the other as things belonging to Manasquan, as much as Jim Van Zeldt's new schooner or the railroad which would soon be built, but which never will be.

There was no time for idleness. They had been waiting for weeks, ever since the letter came, for this great day, and now that it was here, not a man, woman or child of them all but was determined to express all the enjoyment out of it which they had planned. Every one of them must separately shake hands with Dallas, and make a prepared speech, which generally ended in a choke and clearing of the throat, and separately obtain some item about New Mexico and its wonders to talk over hereafter; and give him a sketch of their own family history since he went away, ending with, "But come over, lad, and bring your good lady, and see for yourself. There is not a house on the Point that isn't ready for a home for you both." Then, although they had all already been talking to Honora, every one must be solemnly presented to her in due form by Dallas himself.

She had won great respect from the first by her firm, reticent face and steady self-control. Father Kimball had been seen to nod approvingly after watching her; and old Graah took Dallas aside to tell him confidentially that his "little woman was one of them that would do to anchor to; and far from ill-lookin'—very far."

But when old Rachel Noanes and one or two of the Quaker women and fishers' wives took Nora to one corner and began telling her of all that Dallas had been in the village after he first came among them, a poor boy, bringing up Joe Noanes as one of the children he had saved from death in the year of the great sickness, their homely affection and praise was too much for Honora. She tried to speak, but only sobbed aloud, holding their hard hands tight, saying, when she could articulate, that "no one knew what Dallas was! And his life had been so hard—so hard!" The women silently petted her, and the men turned away affecting not to see; but the little womanly outbreak won all their hearts.

When she came among them again, smiling, they treated her with a tender, grave deference, glancing askance at her flushed, tear-marked face, telling each other that "Dallas' good lady was a first-class beauty. There could be no doubt of that, with them as were judges!"

When it grew near sunset there was a little stir among them. Doctor Noanes, as one might say, was called to the chair; that is to say, after straightening his brown coat, he stood with his back to the stove and with a preparatory hem, raised his voice and told Dallas that there had been considerable argument among them as to where he should make his home among them, "Each one of your old friends countin' his claim better than the others'. Graah, here, held on to his rights like the bull-dog he is, and I was toler'bly stiff-necked myself. But it was arranged at last that you should go home with Lizzy here to-night. She wants to have you to herself a bit. We thought that was only fair. But to-morrow all friends will meet at my house for a bite of dinner. Eh? And after that we'll hand you both around as we choose. You have to submit."

There was a sort of admiring murmur at this light way of mentioning the grand banquet which Mrs. Noanes had been engaged in preparing for days, and then the little assemblage broke up and went out into the pleasant winter evening, the rays of the setting sun streaming redly through the pines. When they were out in the great woods, Honora was surprised to see what a handful of them there were, all told.

They all escorted them to the winding path that led to Lizzy's place, and then stopped and bade them good-night, lingering to hear Father Kimball's parting words, as if he spoke for them all:

"We know, Dallas, that your work is in the West, but we hoped that you would give us part of every year. There is no one here who seems to belong to us so much as you. You must give your summers to us."

"I will do that. Manasquan is home to me."

He noticed a curious anxiety on their faces until he had spoken, and then a quick exchange of significant, approving glances, which made him fancy there was some hidden meaning in the question. But he forgot it when they were all gone, and he turned to follow Lizzy, who went before with Honora, leading the way to her solitary home. Even his slow eyes noticed how her native air had brought the color to her cheeks again and the waiting laugh to her eyes. She had put off her dingy chocolate dress, and wore a pretty, neat-fitting one of blue, and a bit of blue ribbon twisted in her beautiful hair, in honor of his coming. Honora, as they walked side by side quite silent, watched her with a keen, anxious scrutiny. She had guessed, as women will, Lizzy's secret. She knew that she had been a faithful friend to Dallas. But could his triumph have driven from her mind the lover she had lost years ago? Had she forgotten the musical voice and the moonlight and the ebbing tide? Could a woman forget? In Honora's creed, for a dead love there was no resurrection, and no flower that grows on the earth was fit to cover its perpetually yawning grave.

To reach the Byrne house they passed the outskirts of Jim Van Zeldt's great farm. It was a pleasant, comfortable homestead, even in winter—the best kept and fullest in the village. Jim himself, in his sailor clothes, was at the gate waiting for them to come up. A puny little fellow, Honora thought (who measured the world of men by Dallas' brawny build), but with a rare genuineness in his look and bearing—good sense and fidelity. Honora had not forgotten how long he had been true to Lizzy before he married. But poor Lizzy had the grave of her sacred old love to guard, of course! Though it *was* a pity—glancing from trusty, cheerful Jim to the snug house behind him. Lizzy quickened her pace nervously as they came near, as though she would have hurried by.

But that dull, tactless Dallas stopped short, taking Van Zeldt's outstretched hand. "Well, Jim, old fellow, you're grown into a staid citizen and householder, they tell me?"

"Yes, Galbraith."

"And your wife—Jenny Noanes? The prettiest and best girl in the county, eh?"

How pale Lizzy grew at that! Honora, angry at Dallas' stupidity (which was certainly growing upon him every day), tried to draw her away. But Jim stood in the road before them.

"My wife," he said, sturdily, regardless of either her paleness or trembling, "*is* the prettiest and best woman in the world—to me. But it is not Jenny Noanes." He put out his hand and took Lizzy's in his own. "I served for her as long as Jacob did for Rachel, madam," he said, smiling.

Honora stood aghast, but stupid Dallas had them both by the hands before Jim had done speaking, shaking them again and again, the words tumbling out headlong with delight: "I guessed it the minute I saw Lizzy! I remembered your cousin, Long Jim Van Zeldt, as we used to call him, and thought he was a good deal more likely than you to make a fool of himself with Jenny Noanes. And you're happy at last, dear girl? Honora, are you never going to understand?"

"I am beginning now," humbly, giving Jim a feeble, bewildered, congratulatory smile.

"And here is home," said Lizzy, opening the gate, the tears coming to her bright eyes as she saw Dallas enter it.

They thought they never had known the real Lizzy before. She was so cheerful and winning and pretty a wife, so full of odd, attractive little devices to make every moment different from and pleasanter than any that had gone before. The house was not a chilling model of neatness, as Honora would have feared. It was all in use—bright, warm, just dis-ordered enough to be cozy and comfortable. And Lizzy and Jim himself seemed to have reached their last wish in life when they had Dallas and his wife under their roof at last, to give them the best of their home and its welcome.

Honora went up to Lizzy as they sat by the supper-table waiting for Dallas and Van Zeldt to come in from their inspection of the stock. "It is so comfortable and good that you are married," she said heartily, and put her arms about her neck and kissed her. "It is a great deal better than—"

"Than what, Honora?" with wondering face.

"Than anything I had planned for you, dear." She really could not bring the idea of plump, smiling Lizzy at the head of her well-filled tea-table and that perpetually yawning grave of a dead love together at all.

"Yet it scarcely seems natural to see you here, Lizzy," said Dallas, as they lingered talking over the table. "The house in which you lived will always be my remembrance of a home in Manasquan." He was silent suddenly.

Lizzy and her husband exchanged a quick, significant glance: they remembered doubtless the chamber in it that had been made ready for Dallas, and in which he had never been suffered to sleep. A sad quiet fell on them all. They could not forget how many years of his life had been wasted. After they rose from supper, Lizzy went to Dallas, where he stood by the window, and touched him gently:

"The little room—you remember, Dallas?"

"Yes, I remember."

"When Jim and I knew that the time was coming that you could go into it again, we arranged it just as it was on that first night. It was Jim's plan then, you know," with a blush. "There is nothing missing—not the least of the gifts they gave you to show how true friends they were to you. The house is sold. I have this home now, and I parted with the other. But it is vacant, and we have the use of it for to-night. We arranged your room. We thought you would like, if it were but for once only, to see the old gifts, and to think that of all the friends who gave them there is not one lost to you."

"I would like it, Lizzy." But he kept his face turned from her.

"We will go now, then," quickly. In a few moments they were on their way. When they came to the Byrne place, Honora noticed that the out-buildings surrounding the house were in singularly good repair, the house itself covered with vines which would shelter it in summer: behind it were Dallas' old interminable pine woods, and in front the sea rolled in with slow, lapping murmur on the yellow beach. But Dallas saw nothing. He walked with his head down, silent—his breath coming heavily.

In all his prison-life he had thought of that homely room as of the one place from which he was barred. It had come to signify to him the manly honor, the trust, he had lost. Some day he might reach the door of heaven, but the door of that little chamber, with all its meaning, was shut for ever upon him.

Now it was open to him.

He did not even see that Lizzy had had the house brilliantly lighted, as for an illumination. It had been furnished for the owner, like the other houses of the neighborhood, with plain homespun carpets and such simple wooden furniture as the village workmen could make. Lizzy and Jim waited outside.

"There is no one there," they said. "You must go in alone."

He went in, taking Honora by the hand, as one child would another. The door of his old room was open: a fire burned, as on that night long ago, on the hearth. There were the old, homely gifts: nothing missing or decayed: the name of the giver on each. He went about the room slowly without a word, putting his fingers on one and then another, as though each dumb, tender touch brought back a friend again, long dead, to life.

But when he came to the little table in front of the fire, he stood still, and after a moment covered his eyes with his hand. For there, as on an altar, lay the Bible open, and beside it a deed of the house and farm, and on the fly-leaf was written:

"To Dallas Galbraith and Honora his wife, from the people of Manasquan, in token of the love they bear them."

There was an arrival at Nixon's tavern two or three days after that. There had been an arrival expected in Manasquan for some time. William and Aaron Platzek were looked for during this month or the next to harvest their winter crop of furs on this coast for the New York market. But the two men who stepped out of Joshua Sutphen's sled, in front of the little porch, were not the pelt-hucksters: that was plain to all of the group assembled smoking around the fire in the little bar-room. They had never been seen on this beach before. One was a stout, florid man, with eyebrows, whiskers and frogged overcoat alike fierce, black and assertant; the other a tall, spare, gray-headed old gentleman, with pale, delicate face and hands, a hook nose, keen, kindly eyes.

Nixon, after reconnoitering the arrival in perfect silence through the window for some minutes without rising, knocked the ashes from his pipe leisurely, laid it on the bricks of the chimney, and with a preparatory jerk of his suspenders went out and shut the door behind him. After a short colloquy, in which the stout man was violent, the old gentleman silent and anxious, and Nixon stolid as the log against which he leaned, the strangers turned off irresolutely, and Joe came back and relighted his pipe.

No one spoke, these fishermen who smoked the winter away there being as incurious and stoical as Indians. At last Nixon chuckled aloud: "They'll not make much of a run here. I becalmed their boats, *I* reckon."

"How so, Joseph?"

"They were inquiring for Dallas Galbraith. But I knowed nothin' of Dallas Galbraith. How could I tell what was their errand with the lad?" with a shrewd nod.

"Seems as if you be a little too keerful, Nixon," said Becker.

"How did I know," sententiously, "but the news of the property Laddoun's left him had got abroad? There be quite an extra lot of sharpers in New York this winter, I judge by the papers, and they'd think nothin' of runnin' down the lad even here, and fleecin' him. I thought of that, instant. You don't catch a weasel asleep when that weasel be Joe Nixon."

"That's so, Joseph. You were right there," knitting their brows solemnly.

They decided that "Dallas should be warned immediate," but went on smoking for the next two hours, chewing the cud of the matter.

The strangers stood undecided upon the road for a few moments.

"It is not possible that we can have missed them, after all," said the younger man. "Of all the dead, forgotten corners of the world, this is the queerest. I'll go to some of these houses and see if I can find Dallas."

"I think I will try the woods." His long, uncertain search and this last disappointment had told on the frail, old man more than even his companion knew. But the search was almost over, for before he had threaded the winding paths in the sand through the dark pines for more than half an hour, he saw a broad-shouldered fellow on his knees digging with a trowel, while a little woman in a water-proof cloak and hood held a basket ready to receive the treasure, whatever it was. He went up softly behind them and touched them.

"Children, it is time for you to come home," he said. His throat was dry and husky, and he could scarcely articulate. But they would have understood if he had not spoken at all.

Colonel Pervis met them coming through the woods soon after, the old man in the middle, holding them both as if afraid if he let them go they might vanish out of his sight; so unlike were the three to each other, so sharply lined the outer differences between them, each difference but holding them closer together: so gay and tender, yet so full of sorrowful remembrances, the integral bond between them, that even the Colonel dully recognized them as a rare and strangely united little company, whose fellowship of instincts together was a something which few men were born able to understand.

He broke in on them like a thunderstorm: "God bless you, Dallas! Thank the Lord, I see you again! And Honora has taken to digging, too? You've told them all about it?" anxiously, in an audible aside.

"No, I forgot to mention the particulars. I could think of nothing but the children. But Dallas knows that he is clear. That is the essential part."

"Oh! that is essential of course. But the property? Is it possible you did not mention the property? Laddoun's will, Dallas. He left it with Dick Potter at the gate, and it establishes your innocence, and—are you listening, Honora?—and leaves you I don't know how much money and his share in a silver mine. Now don't be excited, boy. It's not a great fortune, but it's enough to bring back the old times to the Stonepost farm. You'll live at your ease for the rest of your life. By George! We'll have a carouse that'll waken the county when we get home!"

The Colonel's outbreak found no echo. They walked in silence for a little while, when Dallas said, gravely turning to his grandfather: "I have considered this matter with Honora, sir, and our feeling is the same with regard to the money. I hope you will understand the decision we made about it."

"I think I understand it now, Dallas," with a smile, looking at him.

Dallas' face brightened and he nodded. "No," he said, soberly. "I have no ill-will to Laddoun, God knows. But I could not live in idleness and eat the bread and butter that were bought with his money. He gave it to me as an act of reparation. If I use it to save other boys from that hell where he thrust me, it will be such an act of reparation, I think. But it is not mine."

The Colonel's jaw fell: "You don't mean it, Dallas! It's one of your dry jokes, that's all! You've not caught Dour's mania about the development of the inner self through poverty? He talks of founding an inner-developing brotherhood, to wear sackcloth and live on split peas; but you're madder than he is."

Dallas laughed: "I can't join Dour. I'm always a better man after a good dinner and with a decent coat on my back, and I may try to be a rich man yet. But— No matter. We are at home now," pausing at the door of their own house. For Honora had insisted on making it their home at once. Much to the delight of the people, who took care that she should not want the material for housekeeping, though they would hardly suffer her to break bread under her own roof.

Their hospitality reached its climax when Mr. Galbraith and Colonel Pervis were formally made known to them and were installed at once as guests of the village. It was a week before they went back, taking Dallas and Honora with them; and in that time there was not a fisherman or wrecker in Ocean county with whom the Colonel was not on terms of intimacy and mutual confidence. He matched their seafaring exploits by his bear stories, swore that apple-jack was the best native drink in the States, took a demijohn of it home, and promised to come back every summer—a promise which he religiously kept.

The group about the bar-room fire chuckled over their pipes when he was mentioned. "Colonel's thorough-grit," they said. "But the old gentleman, he's got the real strain of blood. Same as Dallas."

CHAPTER XXXVIII.

THANKSGIVING-DAY. It came under Madam Galbraith's jurisdiction at irregular times, for it was her fancy to keep it, not by the governor's appointment, but along with Nature, when the barns were still empty, but the fields full of corn, when the purple plums yet dotted the rank grass of the orchard, and the ungathered crimson peaches grew mottled with black under the bee's sting. She had chosen in these last few years to give thanks, not when both summer and summer's work were done, and the air shivered with coming winter, but on one of those October days when, from very excess of warmth and life, the world and man are at rest and quiet.

"It is not for the use of the earth we should praise Him, Dallas," she would say, "but for the hint it gives us of His great glory."

He humored her in this whim as in every other. She was full of such fancies now, in all of which they detected a meaning unselfish and genuine.

This Thanksgiving-day was late in the month, for they had waited for Dallas to return, who had been gone for months, "digging," as Honora loosely stated, in the West. The wind from the north was cold, but the west was burning with a golden sunset, which mellowed the outline of the mountains and valley—a landscape which is one of the most masculine and articulate with meaning in the world. But this low afternoon light softened it: the mountains drew farther away in melancholy gray shadow, while, wherever a rough little water-course ran through the valley, a soft thread of mist hung over it, bright with the changeful hues of the opal, and, as though the ground tried to vie with the water, its dullness and brownness burst in this sunlight into a sweet madness of color and perfume, such as belong in the Western States only to the low-lying inland bottoms. Color unmatched in purity, Mr. Galbraith thought, from the brilliant dyes of the massed forests on the distant hill-sides to the browns and purples of the feathery moss and lichen that hung from the stone walls of the house.

Four years had passed since Dallas was married—the epoch from which history was dated in that house. Four years since Madam Galbraith's colony had failed. Nature, whose charity always covers before it cures, had hid the charred, unsightly signs of her folly under this moss and lichen before she absorbed them back into the earth. You could see the green heaps from the balcony of the old homestead of the Dours, set like a watch-tower on the side of the mountain. Madam Galbraith stood there now. She glanced at the mossy piles, but with only a passing frown: there were cheerfuller objects in the quiet landscape. For they had kept the day in the old royal fashion at the farm, and the groups of friends and neighbors were making their way home through the winding roads and shady lanes in the pleasant evening light. Colonel Pervis stood at the gate speeding them on their way, his hat off, the wind blowing back his hair from his face. There was a good deal of gray in the hair now, but his voice was as loud as ever, and his face as red and hearty. It would have been like putting out the fire in the hospitable house of the Galbraiths to miss the Colonel from its hearth.

She stooped to wave her hand to Peggy Beck and her husband in their snug carry-all, turning into the lonely road leading to the Queen. They have both grown stouter and jollier with time, and the heavy recklessness with which Beck talks of stocks, and the trim ribbons in Peggy's bonnet, hint that the store in the old tea-pot is not diminished. Matt, a manly, curly-headed lad, is left behind playing with a frank-faced little fellow on the lawn. Madam Galbraith turns from everything else to watch them.

One can see in this clear light as she stoops that the shining white mane of hair, rolled like a crown about her head, is dimmed in the last few years—that her uncouth, unwomanly frame is more rawboned and swarthy than before. Yet the imperious grace which gave magnetic power to her youth and beauty lingers in the ungainly body, like the music of a song of which the words are forgotten. Matt and the boy with whom he plays find a companion in her, who will make their remembrance of childhood enchanted ground for them when she and childhood belong only to remembrance. She likes best to talk to them. They find in her a childish love of laughter and fun which does not belong to younger, graver people: a store of odd, old superstitions, strange, pathetic fancies, which, it seems, she has always nourished, come to light as she grows older. They learn, day by day, from her, too, an awful reverence for God, outside of all the creeds of the churches.

The stony scales of the shell are worn away, it is so old; and the delicate tints are bared in which the living creature within has hid itself so long.

Four years have passed since she stood on the same place in her flash of triumph only to witness her defeat—to see her life's scheme swept away by the torrent of flame in a single night—to see, when the morning dawned, black ruin traced on every mountain side, every valley and field.

But now the mountain sides, valleys and fields are full of a noble stir and life, which make her old heart beat with a pride of which the Dour blood knew nothing. For in these years all traces of the ruin and waste have been blotted out, and from the shaded roads and fields there floats up the sound of voices, whose meaning makes the ancient dominion of the Dours shine fair in her eyes as the garden of the Lord.

For so she idealizes Dallas' great charity.

But to him and the workers in it, it is practical and difficult enough. She can see from where she stands the house where Mr. Rattlin lives with his troop of boys. It is almost a hamlet now in the woods, with school, workshops and farm out-buildings. There is no machine-management in it, even Mrs. Duffield acknowledges, adding that it is because neither Mr. Rattlin nor Dallas have any metallic force. They are imposed upon, and that often, but they go on steadily, studying each boy's capacity, educating him from that hint, furnishing him with tools, or land, or capital, and bidding him, in God's name, work his own way.

Dour is engaged in the work with the energy and foresight of a genuine New Englander. He shows a great deal of sound judgment and tact in his management: he is a spiritualist now, has suffered Emerson to grow dusty on his shelves, and talks no more of the discipline of poverty upon the inner life. On the contrary, he eats heartily, has grown fat, and is laying up a snug sum in railroad bonds.

Dallas has no railroad bonds: he has not yet begun to make himself a rich man. He travels and digs and analyzes as constantly as other men breathe; but such work as his is not well paid—in money.

It is probable that he will dig and analyze to the end.

He sits now on the grassy slope in front of the great entrance, in the gray, loose clothes in which he feels himself at home. A powerful man, with broad chest, white throat, grave, far-seeing eyes and a ready, tender smile. One can detect a curious likeness in his face to that of an older, weaker man who sits on the bench behind him. They are seldom apart, though they talk but little when together. Yet one is restless and uneasy when the other is away. Mr. Galbraith, even, has grown so infatuated with Dallas' pursuits that he goes with him on his shorter journeys.

Presently, when the sun was low and threw the long shadows of the walnut tree across the warm grass, Honora came through them and sat down beside her husband. Her uncle stroked the soft brown hair, and Dallas took her hand in his—a soft hand and a strong one. So the little company of the old times was complete. Yet there was a change in them, as though life, in som way, widened and sweetened for them all, turned into a new and broader current.

After a while, the boy who was Madam Galbraith's friend came running and stood among them, and then, looking in their faces, one could know the cause of their change—that in these years gone God had chosen for them from His treasure-house the best gift of all.

The sun was almost down. Through

the twilight they caught the echo of a quiet, cheery song, and looked at each other smiling. It was Dallas' mother singing to herself when she thought no one heard her. Her voice was broken: she never sang, even for the boy, dear as he was to her. Mr. Rattlin passed them, a little grayer, a little stouter— a change in his dress that showed the world had gone well with him. No happier face, for that Nature could not make. Then the evening grew quite still, the solemn shadows lengthening over the genial, ruddy light.

The little preacher paused at the gate, looking back at them. The holy meaning of the day was upon him still, and seemed to give to the eyes of the old man who walked so close to his Master, doing His work so quietly, a prophetic insight. God had taken thought for him and his unused strength, and late in the day had given to him a share in a great work. In the years to come he saw himself gathering to the land of the old, clean-blooded Dours, from prison, from city den and almshouse, the wronged and the outcast, learning through him a better, more gracious life than their youth had ever known—learning through him a certain way to that God which they had never known.

Yet though the simple follower of Christ had given his whole heart to his work, and would be very dear to the little outcasts, they will have another friend whom they will love far better—the strong, healthy man yonder, reticent to all others, but to them frank, cheerful and outspoken; a strange, pathetic tenderness in his care for them—coming closer to them than any other man could ever do, through some instinct or secret of his life to them unknown.

"So it will always be in these years to come. God has fitted him for this work," he said, lingering, as he looked back at Dallas. "He has been down like his Master in the depths from which he would save them, and has learned there some secret which I can never know."

The air is growing chilly and rustles the leaves of the great sycamores which darken the front of the house. But through them they see the ruddy light of the open windows, and the Colonel within, glancing over the supper-table, and stirring the fire to make all ready for the evening. Madam Galbraith on her balcony, and Mrs. Duffield from her window, are both looking for the boy before they go down. For over all the women in the house Master Dour Galbraith is king.

He waits for his grandfather, however, taking away the old man's cane and putting the delicate, withered hand upon his own curly head, walking very stiffly and slow, fancying that all the strength of the party lies in his own little body. He gives one hand to his mother also as they go, she being a woman and needing help. So they walk, very gravely, to the house, not daring to smile to each other lest the child should see them and be disheartened.

But Dallas lingers behind. The golden light of the evening, as it bathes the valley and far-off mountains, the old homestead set against the hills, and the retreating figures, falls upon him with a great calm. It seems to him a thanksgiving. The meaning of the day grows clearer to him here in the open air; and owing to his habits and odd bent of thought, all the solitary places in the world with which he is familiar become curiously present to him, and take part in this quiet glow—the vast flats of the West, trailed with black buffalo herds, the rank, strong-smelling Mississippi bayous, the drowsy Manasquan village, with the sea lashing its silent stretches of gray sand.

He knows but little of any book but that which these open to him. But year by year he spells more clearly the meaning which underlies its letters—the Eternal Order, in which no atom fails of its work in the sure justice and help which each renders to the other.

The inevitable Good at last.

He turns to go in. There is a grave yonder in that hill-gap which will not take its part in the great Thanksgiving day. And yet he looks at it with doubting eyes. Good as well as evil were shut out from the world in Laddoun's grave. There are dewy mosses and sweet flowers which have taken the place of the unwholesome body. Is it in the soul of man alone that the evil, useless and unalterable elements of God's universe lie? What slow processes are His in that well-veiled secresy of Death? Nature in her great charity covers before she cures.

And as he goes to his home in the quiet evening, his own life becomes present to Dallas Galbraith as never before, in all its full and completed meaning; and seeing in that home, in his wife and child, only another name for God's tenderness to him, feeling how his old wrong had softened his heart toward all hurt people, all those who had sinned and been oppressed with the burden of untoward fate, he knows the share his life has borne in the great scheme of order — knows that as the strange flower upon the peak of the Sierras was evidence of an unknown, immutable law, so in the story of the humblest man there is no such thing as luck or chance —that God is under the hardest circumstance, and that God is good.

Published by
J. B. LIPPINCOTT & CO.

Gold Elsie.
From the German of E. MARLITT, author of "The Old Mam'selle's Secret." By Mrs. A. L. WISTER. 12mo. Cloth. $1.75.

Dallas Galbraith.
By Mrs. R. HARDING DAVIS, author of "Margaret Howth," "Waiting for the Verdict," "Life in the Iron Mills," etc. 8vo. Cloth. $2.00.

Horace Wilde.
A Baptist Novel. By Mrs. M. JEANIE MALLARY. 12mo. Tinted paper. Fine cloth, beveled boards. $1.50.

Ante Bellum.
Southern Life as it Was. By MARY LENNOX. 12mo. Cloth. $2.00.

The Old Mam'selle's Secret.
After the German of E. MARLITT, author of "Gold Elsie." By Mrs. A. L. WISTER. 12mo. Cloth. $1.75.

John Ward's Governess.
By ANNIE L. MACGREGOR. 12mo. Fine cloth. $1.75.

The White Rose.
By G. J. WHYTE MELVILLE, author of "Cerise," "The Gladiators," etc. 12mo. Cloth. $1.50.

Tricotrin.
The Story of a Waif and Stray. By "OUIDA," author of "Idalia," "Under Two Flags," "Strathmore," etc. *Nearly Ready.*

Abraham Page, Esq.
Life and Opinions of Abraham Page, Esq. 12mo. Tinted paper. Fine cloth. $1.50.

For sale by all Booksellers, or will be sent by mail, postage free, on receipt of price by

J. B. LIPPINCOTT & CO.,
Publishers and Booksellers,
715 and 717 Market Street,
PHILADELPHIA

COMPLETION OF CHAMBERS'S ENCYCLOPÆDIA.

JUST COMPLETED!

CHAMBERS'S ENCYCLOPÆDIA,

A DICTIONARY OF

UNIVERSAL KNOWLEDGE FOR THE PEOPLE.

ILLUSTRATED WITH

MAPS AND NUMEROUS WOOD ENGRAVINGS.

IN TEN VOLUMES ROYAL OCTAVO.

Price per Volume, Cloth, $4.50; Sheep, $5.00; Half Turkey, $5.50.

The Publishers have the pleasure of announcing that they have just issued the concluding PART OF CHAMBERS'S ENCYCLOPÆDIA, and that the work is now complete in

TEN ROYAL OCTAVO VOLUMES, of over 800 pages each, illustrated with about 4000 engravings, and accompanied by

AN ATLAS OF NEARLY FORTY MAPS; the whole, it is believed, forming the most complete work of reference extant.

The design of this work, as explained in the Notice prefixed to the first volume, is that of a DICTIONARY OF UNIVERSAL KNOWLEDGE FOR THE PEOPLE—not a mere collection of elaborate treatises in alphabetical order, but a work to be readily consulted as a DICTIONARY on every subject on which people generally require some distinct information. Commenced in 1859, the work is now brought to a close in 1868, and the Editors confidently point to the Ten volumes of which it is composed as forming the most COMPREHENSIVE—as it certainly is the CHEAPEST—ENCYCLOPÆDIA ever issued in the English language.

TO TEACHERS, who are frequently called upon to give succinct explanations of topics in the various branches of education, often beyond the mere outline of information contained in the text-books, no other work will be found so useful; while the conciseness of the several articles has made it practicable to bring the whole work within the compass of a few volumes, and to afford it at a small cost compared to others of its class.

FOR SCHOOL LIBRARIES the work is peculiarly fitted, owing to its adaptation, as a "Dictionary of *Universal* Knowledge," to the wants of both teachers and pupils. Says the REV. DR. S. K. TALMAGE, President of Oglethorpe University, Ga.: "I have no hesitation in saying that the friends of education will do injustice to themselves, and to the cause of literature, science and general knowledge, if they fail to reward the enterprising publishers with a liberal patronage."

FOR THE FAMILY.—Says the REV. DR. FINNEY, late President of Oberlin College, Ohio: "Chambers's Encyclopædia should find a place in every family. Should families deny themselves in other things, and obtain and study such works, they would find themselves mentally much enriched."

FOR THE GENERAL READER.—"Upon its literary merits," says DR. R. SHELTON MACKENZIE, "its completeness and accuracy, and the extent and variety of its information, there can be only one opinion. The work is worthy of the high aim and established reputation of its projectors. Art and science, theology and jurisprudence, natural history and metaphysics, topography and geography, medicine and antiquities, biography and belles-lettres, are all discussed here, not in long treatises, but to an extent sufficient to give requisite information at a glance, as it were. Sometimes, when the subject justifies it, more minute details are given. . . . Its fullness upon American subjects ought to recommend it especially in this country; and its low price makes it one of the cheapest and most accessible works ever published."

Copies of the work will be sent to any address in the United States, free of postage, on receipt of the price by the Publishers. A liberal discount made to Agents, and to the Trade.

J. B. LIPPINCOTT & CO., Publishers,

715 & 717 MARKET ST., PHILADELPHIA.

The Standard Library Edition

OF

THACKERAY'S WORKS,

ELEGANTLY ILLUSTRATED.

To be completed in about Twenty Volumes, large Crown 8vo., printed in Large Type, on Superfine Tinted Paper, and handsomely bound in fine Cloth, Gilt, beveled boards. Price $3.50 per volume. Fine Cloth, Gilt Top, $3.75 per volume. Half Turkey Morocco, $5.50 per volume. Half Calf, Gilt, $5.50 per volume.

NOW READY.

EACH COMPLETE IN TWO VOLUMES.

1. *Vanity Fair.*
   With 40 Steel Engravings and 150 Wood-cuts.

2. *Pendennis.*
   With 46 Steel Engravings and 120 Wood-cuts.

3. *The Newcomes.*
   With 46 Steel Engravings, and 118 Wood-cuts by RICHARD DOYLE.

4. *Philip.*
   Prefixed by a Shabby Genteel Story. With numerous Illustrations.

5. *The Virginians.*
   With 47 Steel Plates and numerous Wood-cuts.

IN ONE VOLUME.

6. *Henry Esmond.*
   With numerous Illustrations.

THE REMAINING WORKS WILL BE ISSUED IN MONTHLY VOLUMES.

For Sale by Booksellers generally.

J. B. LIPPINCOTT & CO.,
PUBLISHERS, PHILADELPHIA.

I.
NOVELS.
PRICE $2.00 EACH

GRANVILLE DE VIGNE; OR, HELD IN BONDAGE.
A TALE OF THE DAY.

"This is one of the most powerful and spicy works of fiction which the present century, so prolific in light literature, has produced. The style is elegant, forcible, sparkling; the characters are powerfully drawn, and many of the scenes are passionate and thrilling, and the knowledge of the world displayed in the book is very great. The author seems at home in all spheres—alike in the drawing-room, the battle-field, the college and the club. It is one of the best novels which we have ever read."

STRATHMORE; OR, WROUGHT BY HIS OWN HAND.

"It is romance of the intense school, but it is written with more power, fluency and brilliancy than the works of Miss Braddon and Mrs. Wood, while its scenes and characters are taken from high life."—*Boston Transcript.*

CHANDOS.

"Those who have read these two last-named brilliant works of fiction (Granville de Vigne and Strathmore) will be sure to read *Chandos*. It is characterized by the same gorgeous coloring of style and somewhat exaggerated portraiture of scenes and characters, but it is a story of surpassing power and interest, and will take front rank in that department of fiction which is styled sensational."—*Pittsburg Evening Chronicle.*

IDALIA.

"It is a story of love and hatred, of affection and jealousy, of intrigue and devotion. . . . . . We think this novel will attain a wide popularity, especially among those whose refined taste enables them to appreciate and enjoy what is truly beautiful in literature."—*Albany Evening Journal.*

UNDER TWO FLAGS.
A STORY OF THE HOUSEHOLD AND THE DESERT.

"'Under Two Flags' is immeasurably superior to 'Idalia,' and while many readers will find fault with it as extravagant and sensational, no one will be able to resist its fascination who once begins its perusal."—*Philadelphia Evening Bulletin.*

II.
NOVELETTES.
Each of these volumes contains a selection of "Ouida's" popular Tales and Stories.
PRICE $1.75 EACH.

FIRST SERIES.
CECIL CASTLEMAINE'S GAGE.
SECOND SERIES.
RANDOLPH GORDON.
THIRD SERIES.
BEATRICE BOVILLE.

"'The many works already in print by this versatile authoress have established her reputation as a novelist, and these short stories contribute largely to the stock of pleasing narratives and adventures alive to the memory of all who are given to romance and fiction."—*New Haven Journal.*

The above are all handsomely and uniformly bound in cloth, and are for sale by booksellers generally, or will be sent by mail, postage free, on receipt of price.

J. B. LIPPINCOTT & CO., Publishers, Booksellers and Importers,
715 and 717 MARKET STREET, PHILADELPHIA.

"LEGIBLE, PORTABLE, HANDSOME AND CHEAP."

JUST COMPLETED.

THE GLOBE EDITION
OF
BULWER'S NOVELS.

THIS EDITION OF THE NOVELS OF
SIR EDWARD BULWER LYTTON, BART.,
(Lord Lytton),

IS NOW COMPLETE IN

TWENTY-TWO NEAT 16MO. VOLUMES.

Printed on Tinted Paper, with Engraved Frontispiece.

EACH OF THE VOLUMES AVERAGING OVER 700 PAGES.

HANDSOMELY BOUND IN GREEN MOROCCO CLOTH.

PRICE $1.50 PER VOL.

Price per Set.—Cloth, $33.00. Extra cloth, gilt top, $38.50. Half calf, neat, $44.00. Half calf extra, gilt top, $66.00. Half Turkey, gilt top, $66.00.

THE FOLLOWING ARE EACH COMPLETE IN ONE VOLUME:

THE CAXTONS.—PELHAM.—EUGENE ARAM.—THE LAST OF THE BARONS.—LUCRETIA.—DEVEREUX.—THE LAST DAYS OF POMPEII.—RIENZI.—GODOLPHIN.—A STRANGE STORY.—ZANONI.—HAROLD.—LEILA, PILGRIMS OF THE RHINE, AND CALDERON.—NIGHT AND MORNING.—ERNEST MALTRAVERS.—ALICE.—PAUL CLIFFORD.—THE DISOWNED.

EACH COMPLETE IN TWO VOLUMES:
"MY NOVEL."—WHAT WILL HE DO WITH IT?

THE PRESS SAYS OF THE "GLOBE BULWER."

"We have more than once commended the Globe as the best edition of Bulwer accessible to American readers."—*Cincinnati Gazette.*

.... "The convenient size, beautiful style and cheapness of this edition are worthy the attention of book-buyers."—*Pittsburg Gazette.*

"The beauty of this edition has frequently challenged our admiration, and it certainly deserves commendation."—*Chicago Evening Journal.*

.... "They are models well worthy the imitation of other American book-makers."—*Philadelphia Age.*

N. B.—Any of the above volumes will be mailed free to any party sending two subscriptions ($8) to *Lippincott's Magazine.*

EACH NOVEL SOLD SEPARATELY.

For sale by all Booksellers, or will be sent by mail, postage free, on receipt of price, by

J. B. LIPPINCOTT & CO., Publishers,
715 & 717 MARKET ST., PHILADELPHIA.

VALUABLE AND INSTRUCTIVE WORKS

Recently Published by

J. B. LIPPINCOTT & CO.

I.
THE FOUR GOSPELS.

The Unconscious Truth of the Four Gospels. By Rev. W. H. Furness, D.D. 12mo. Tinted paper. Fine cloth. $1.25.

II.
A SUMMER IN ICELAND.

By C. W. Paijkull. Translated by M. R. Barnard, B.A. With Map and numerous Illustrations. 8vo. Cloth. $5.00.

III.
FIVE YEARS WITHIN THE GOLDEN GATE.

By Isabella Saxon. Crown 8vo. Fine stamped cloth. $2.50.

IV.
AMONG THE ARABS.

A Narrative of Adventures in Algeria. By G. Naphegyi, M.D. 12mo. With Portrait of Author. Tinted paper. Fine cloth. $1.75.

V.
THE HERMITS.

By Rev. Charles Kingsley. Illustrated. 12mo. Fine cloth. $2.00. Making the second volume of the Sunday Library.

VI.
CURIOUS MYTHS.

Curious Myths of the Middle Ages. By S. Baring Gould. Second Series. 12mo. Illustrated. Tinted paper. Fine cloth. $2.50.

VII.
CAMEOS FROM ENGLISH HISTORY.

By the author of "The Heir of Redclyffe." 12mo. Tinted paper. Fine cloth. $1.75.

VIII.
LAS CASAS.

The Life of Las Casas, the "Apostle of the Indies." By Arthur Helps, author of "Friends in Council," etc. With Map. Crown 8vo. Tinted paper. Fine vellum cloth. $2.75.

For sale by all Booksellers, or will be sent by mail, postage free, on receipt of price by

J. B. LIPPINCOTT & CO.,
Publishers, Booksellers, and Importers,
PHILADELPHIA.

www.ingramcontent.com/pod-product-compliance
Lightning Source LLC
Chambersburg PA
CBHW020804230426
43666CB00007B/851